The VIVEKANANDA

Swami Vivekananda (12 January 1863–4 July 1902), born as Narendranath Datta, was an Indian Hindu monk and chief disciple of the nineteenth-century Indian mystic Ramakrishna Paramahansa. He was a key figure who introduced Indian philosophy, especially focusing on Vedanta and Yoga, to the Western world. Vivekananda is credited as the one who brought Hinduism to the status of a major world religion during the late nineteenth century. He represented Hinduism at the first World Parliament of Religions in Chicago in 1893 where he was an instant success. Subsequently, he was invited to speak all over America and Europe.

A major force in the revival of Hinduism in India, he founded the Ramakrishna Math and the Ramakrishna Mission—an order of monks who dedicate their lives to the upliftment of the poor and needy. A firm believer in action over and above ethical or spiritual discourse, Vivekananda exhorted the youth of India to rise and build a nation.

The Definitive
VIVEKANANDA

RUPA

Published by
Rupa Publications India Pvt. Ltd 2018
7/16, Ansari Road, Daryaganj
New Delhi 110002

Sales Centres:
Allahabad Bengaluru Chennai
Hyderabad Jaipur Kathmandu
Kolkata Mumbai

Copyright © Rupa Publications India Pvt. Ltd 2018

The views and opinions expressed in this book are the author's own and the facts
are as reported by him which have been verified to the extent possible, and the
publishers are not in any way liable for the same.

All rights reserved.
No part of this publication may be reproduced, transmitted, or stored in a retrieval
system, in any form or by any means, electronic, mechanical, photocopying,
recording or otherwise, without the prior permission of the publisher.

ISBN: 978-93-5304-140-3

Second impression 2019

10 9 8 7 6 5 4 3 2

Printed at Parksons Graphics Pvt. Ltd, Mumbai

This book is sold subject to the condition that it shall not, by way of
trade or otherwise, be lent, resold, hired out, or otherwise circulated,
without the publisher's prior consent, in any form of binding
or cover other than that in which it is published.

CONTENTS

Section 3: Lectures From Colombo to Almora

Section 4: From The Raja-Yoga

Section 5: Thoughts of Swami Vivekananda

LECTURES FROM CHICAGO VISIT

1

RESPONSE TO WELCOME

At the World's Parliament of Religions, Chicago

(11 September 1893)

Sisters and Brothers of America,

It fills my heart with joy unspeakable to rise in response to the warm and cordial welcome which you have given us. I thank you in the name of the most ancient order of monks in the world; I thank you in the name of the mother of religions; and I thank you in the name of millions and millions of Hindu people of all classes and sects.

My thanks, also, to some of the speakers on this platform who, referring to the delegates from the Orient, have told you that these men from far-off nations may well claim the honour of bearing to different lands the idea of toleration. I am proud to belong to a religion which has taught the world both tolerance and universal acceptance. We believe not only in universal toleration, but we accept all religions as true. I am proud to belong to a nation which has sheltered the persecuted and the refugees of all religions and all nations of the earth. I am proud to tell you that we have gathered in our bosom the purest remnant of the Israelites, who came to southern India and took refuge with us in the very year in which their holy temple was shattered to pieces by Roman tyranny. I am proud to belong to the religion which has sheltered and is still fostering the remnant Zoroastrian nation. I will quote to you, brethren, a few lines from a hymn, which I remember to have repeated from my earliest boyhood, which is every day repeated by millions of human beings: 'As the different streams having their sources in different places all mingle their water in the sea, so, O Lord, the different paths which men take through different tendencies, various though they appear, crooked or straight, all lead to Thee.'

The present convention, which is one of the most august assemblies ever held, is in itself a vindication, a declaration to the world of the wonderful doctrine preached in the Gita: 'Whosoever comes to Me, through whatsoever form, I reach him; all men are struggling through paths which in the end lead to me.' Sectarianism, bigotry, and its horrible descendant, fanaticism, have long possessed this beautiful earth. They have filled the earth with violence, drenched it often and often with human blood, destroyed civilization and sent whole nations to despair. Had it not been for these horrible demons, human society would be far more advanced than it is now. But their time has come; and I fervently hope that the bell that tolled this morning in honour of this convention may be the death-knell of all fanaticism, of all persecutions with the sword or with the pen, and of all uncharitable feelings between persons wending their way to the same goal.

2

WHY WE DISAGREE

(15 September 1893)

I will tell you a little story. You have heard the eloquent speaker who has just finished say, 'Let us cease from abusing each other,' and he was very sorry that there should be always so much variance.

But I think I should tell you a story which would illustrate the cause of this variance. A frog lived in a well. It had lived there for a long time. It was born there and brought up there, and yet was a little, small frog. Of course the evolutionists were not there then to tell us whether the frog lost its eyes or not, but, for our story's sake, we must take it for granted that it had its eyes, and that it every day cleansed the water of all the worms and bacilli that lived in it with an energy that would do credit to our modern bacteriologists. In this way, it went on and became a little sleek and fat. Well, one day another frog that lived in the sea came and fell into the well.

'Where are you from?'

'I am from the sea.'

'The sea! How big is that? Is it as big as my well?' and he took a leap from one side of the well to the other.

'My friend,' said the frog of the sea, 'how do you compare the sea with your little well?'

Then the frog took another leap and asked, 'Is your sea so big?'

'What nonsense you speak, to compare the sea with your well!'

'Well, then,' said the frog of the well, 'nothing can be bigger than my well; there can be nothing bigger than this; this fellow is a liar, so turn him out.'

That has been the difficulty all the while.

I am a Hindu. I am sitting in my own little well and thinking that the whole world is my little well. The Christian sits in his little well and thinks the whole world is his well. The Mohammedan sits in his little well and thinks that is the whole world. I have to thank you of America for the great attempt you are making to break down the barriers of this little world of ours, and hope that, in the future, the Lord will help you to accomplish your purpose.

3

PAPER ON HINDUISM
Read at the Parliament
(19 September 1893)

Three religions now stand in the world, which have come down to us from time prehistoric—Hinduism, Zoroastrianism and Judaism. They have all received tremendous shocks and all of them prove by their survival their internal strength. But while Judaism failed to absorb Christianity and was driven out of its place of birth by its all-conquering daughter, and a handful of Parsees is all that remains to tell the tale of their grand religion, sect after sect arose in India and seemed to shake the religion of the Vedas to its very foundations, but like the waters of the seashore in a tremendous earthquake it receded only for a while, only to return in an all-absorbing flood, a thousand times more vigorous, and when the tumult of the rush was over, these sects were all sucked in, absorbed, and assimilated into the immense body of the mother faith.

From the high spiritual flights of the Vedanta philosophy, of which the latest discoveries of science seem like echoes, to the low ideas of idolatry with its multifarious mythology, the agnosticism of the Buddhists, and the atheism of the Jains, each and all have a place in the Hindu's religion. Where then, the question arises, where is the common centre to which all these widely diverging radii converge? Where is the common basis upon which all these seemingly hopeless contradictions rest? And this is the question I shall attempt to answer.

The Hindus have received their religion through revelation, the Vedas. They hold that the Vedas are without beginning and without end. It may sound ludicrous to this audience, how a book can be without beginning or end. But by the Vedas no books are meant. They mean the accumulated treasury of spiritual laws discovered by different persons in different times. Just as the law of gravitation existed before its discovery, and would exist if all humanity forgot it, so is it with the laws that govern the spiritual world. The moral, ethical, and spiritual relations between soul and soul and between individual spirits and the Father of all spirits, were there before their discovery, and would remain even if we forgot them.

The discoverers of these laws are called rishis, and we honour them as perfected beings. I am glad to tell this audience that some of the very greatest of them were women. Here it may be said that these laws as laws may be without end, but they must have had a beginning. The Vedas teach us that creation is without beginning or end. Science is said to have proved that the sum total of cosmic energy is always the same. Then, if there was a time when nothing existed, where was all this manifested energy? Some say it was in a potential form in God. In that case God is sometimes potential and sometimes kinetic, which would make Him mutable. Everything mutable is a compound, and everything compound must undergo that change which is called destruction. So God would die, which is absurd. Therefore, there never was a time when there was no creation.

If I may be allowed to use a simile, creation and creator are two lines, without beginning and without end, running parallel to each other. God is the ever active providence, by whose power systems after systems are being evolved out of chaos, made to run for a time and again destroyed. This is what the Brahmin boy repeats every day: 'The sun and the moon, the Lord created like the suns and moons of previous cycles.' And this agrees with modern science.

Here I stand and if I shut my eyes, and try to conceive my existence, 'I', 'I', 'I', what is the idea before me? The idea of a body. Am I, then, nothing but a combination of material substances? The Vedas declare, 'No'. I am a spirit living in a body. I am not the body. The body will die, but I shall not die. Here am I in this body; it will fall, but I shall go on living. I had also a past. The soul was not created, for creation means a combination, which means a certain future dissolution. If then the soul was created, it must die. Some are born happy, enjoy perfect health, with beautiful body, mental vigour and all wants supplied. Others are born miserable, some are without hands or feet, others again are idiots and only drag on a wretched existence. Why, if they are all created, why does a just and merciful God create one happy and another unhappy, why is He so partial? Nor would it mend matters in the least to hold that those who are miserable in this life will be happy in a future one. Why should a man be miserable even here in the reign of a just and merciful God?

In the second place, the idea of a creator God does not explain the anomaly, but simply expresses the cruel fiat of an all-powerful being. There must have been causes, then, before his birth, to make a man miserable or happy and those were his past actions.

Are not all the tendencies of the mind and the body accounted for by inherited aptitude? Here are two parallel lines of existence—one of the mind, the other of matter. If matter and its transformations answer for all that we have, there is no necessity for supposing the existence of a soul. But it cannot be proved that thought has been evolved out of matter, and if a philosophical monism is inevitable, spiritual monism is certainly logical and no less desirable than a materialistic monism; but neither of these is necessary here.

We cannot deny that bodies acquire certain tendencies from heredity, but those tendencies only mean the physical configuration, through which a peculiar mind alone can act in a peculiar way. There are other tendencies peculiar to a soul caused by its past actions. And a soul with a certain tendency would by the laws of affinity take birth in a body which is the fittest instrument for the display of that tendency. This is in accord with science wants to explain everything by habit, and habit has got through repetitions. So repetitions are necessary to explain the natural habits of a new-born soul. And since they were not obtained in this present life, they must have come down from past lives.

There is another suggestion. Taking all these for granted, now is it that I do not remember anything of my past life? This can be easily explained I am now speaking English. It is not my mother tongue, in fact no words of my mother tongue are now present in my consciousness; but let me try to bring them up, and they rush in. That shows that consciousness is only the surface of the mental ocean, and within its depths are stored up all our experiences. Try and struggle, they would come up and you would by conscious even of your past life.

This is direct and demonstrative evidence. Verification is the perfect proof of a theory, and here is the challenge thrown to the world by the rishis. We have discovered the secret by which the very depths of the ocean of memory can be stirred up—try it and you would get a complete reminiscence of your past life.

So then, the Hindu believes that he is a spirit. Him the sword cannot pierce—him the fire cannot burn—him the water cannot melt—him the air cannot dry. The Hindu believes that every soul is a circle whose circumference is nowhere, but whose centre is located in the body, and that death means the change of this centre from body to body. Not is the soul bound by the conditions of matter. In its very essence, it is free, unbounded, holy, pure, and perfect. But somehow or other, it finds itself tied down to matter and thinks of itself as matter.

Why should the free, perfect, and pure being be thus under the thraldom of matter, is the next question. How can the perfect soul be deluded into the belief that it is imperfect? We have been told that the Hindus shirk the question and say that no such question can be there. Some thinkers want to answer it by positing one or more quasi-perfect beings, and use big scientific names to fill up the gap. But naming is not explaining. The question remains the same. How can the perfect become the quasi-perfect; how can the pure, the absolute, change even a microscopic particle of its nature? But the Hindu is sincere. He does not want to take shelter under sophistry. He is brave enough to face the question in a manly fashion; and his answer is: 'I do not know. I do not know how the perfect being, the soul, came to think of itself as imperfect, as joined to and conditioned by matter.' But the fact is a fact for all that. It is a fact in everybody's consciousness that one thinks of oneself as the body. The Hindu does not attempt to explain why one thinks one is the body. The answer that it is the will of God is no explanation. This is nothing more than what the Hindu says, 'I do not know.'

Well, then, the human soul is eternal and immortal, perfect and infinite, and death means only a change of centre from one body to another. The present is determined by our past actions, and the future by the present. The soul will go on evolving up or reverting from birth to birth and death to death. But here is another question: Is man a tiny boat in a tempest, raised one moment on the foamy crest of a billow and dashed down into a yawning chasm the next, rolling to and fro at the mercy of good and bad actions—a powerless, helpless wreck in an ever-raging, ever-rushing, uncompromising current of cause and effect; a little moth placed under the wheel of causation which rolls on crushing everything in its way and waits not for the widow's tears or the orphan's cry? The heart sinks at the idea, yet this is the law of Nature. Is there no hope? Is there no escape?—was the cry that went up from the bottom of the heart of despair. It reached the throne of mercy, and words of hope and consolation came down and inspired a Vedic sage, and he stood up before the world and in trumpet voice proclaimed the glad tidings: 'Hear, ye children of immortal bliss! even ye that reside in higher spheres! I have found the Ancient One who is beyond all darkness, all delusion: knowing Him alone you shall be saved from death over again.' 'Children of immortal bliss'—what a sweet, what a hopeful name! Allow me to call you, brethren, by that sweet name—heirs of immortal bliss—yea, the Hindu refuses to call you sinners. Ye are the Children of God, the sharers of immortal bliss, holy and perfect beings. Ye divinities on earth—sinners! It is a sin to call a man so; it is a standing libel on human nature. Come up, O lions, and shake off the delusion that you are sheep; you are souls immortal, spirits free, blest and eternal; ye are not matter, ye are not bodies; matter is your servant, not you the servant of matter. Thus, it is that the Vedas proclaim not a dreadful combination of unforgiving laws, not an endless prison of cause and effect, but that at the head of all these laws, in and through every particle of matter and force, stands One 'by whose command the wind blows, the fire burns, the clouds rain, and death stalks upon the earth.'

And what is His nature?

He is everywhere, the pure and formless One, the Almighty and the All-merciful. 'Thou art our father, Thou art our mother, Thou art our beloved friend, Thou art the source of all strength; give us strength. Thou art He that beareth the burdens of the universe; help me bear the little burden of this life.' Thus sang the rishis of the Vedas. And how to worship Him? Through love. 'He is to be worshipped as the one beloved, dearer than everything in this and the next life.'

This is the doctrine of love declared in the Vedas, and let us see how it is fully developed and taught by Krishna, whom the Hindus believe to have been God incarnate on earth.

He taught that a man ought to live in this world like a lotus leaf, which grows in water but is never moistened by water; so a man ought to live in the world—his heart to God and his hands to work.

It is good to love God for hope of reward in this or the next world, but it is better to love God for love's sake, and the prayer goes: 'Lord, I do not want wealth, nor children, nor learning. If it be Thy will, I shall go from birth to birth, but grant me this, that I may love Thee without the hope of reward—love unselfishly for love's sake.' One of the disciples of Krishna, the then Emperor of India, was driven from his kingdom by his enemies and had to take shelter with his queen in a forest in the Himalayas, and there one day the queen asked him how it was that he, the most virtuous of men, should suffer so much misery. Yudhishthira answered, 'Behold, my queen, the Himalayas, how grand and beautiful they are; I love them. They do not give me anything, but my nature is to love the grand, the beautiful, therefore I love them. Similarly, I love the Lord. He is the source of all beauty, of all sublimity. He is the only object to be loved; my nature is to love Him, and therefore I love. I do not pray for anything; I do not ask for anything. Let Him place me wherever He likes. I must love Him for love's sake. I cannot trade love.'

The Vedas teach that the soul is divine, only held in the bondage of matter; perfection will be reached when this bond will burst, and the word they use for it is therefore, Mukti—freedom, freedom from the bonds of imperfection, freedom from death and misery.

And this bondage can only fall off through the mercy of God, and this mercy comes on the pure. So purity is the condition of His mercy. How does that mercy act? He reveals Himself to the pure heart; the pure and the stainless see God, yea, even in this life; then and then only all the crookedness of the heart is made straight. Then all doubt ceases. He is no more the freak of a terrible law of causation. This is the very centre, the very vital conception of Hinduism. The Hindu does not want to live upon words and theories. If there are existences beyond the ordinary sensuous existence, he wants to come face to face with them. If there is a soul in him which is not matter, if there is an all-merciful universal Soul, he will go to Him direct. He must see Him, and that alone can destroy all doubts. So the best proof a Hindu sage gives about the soul, about God, is: 'I have seen the soul; I have seen God.' And that is the only condition of perfection. The Hindu religion does not consist in struggles and attempts to believe a certain doctrine or dogma, but in realising—not in believing, but in being and becoming.

Thus, the whole object of their system is by constant struggle to become perfect, to become divine, to reach God and see God, and this reaching God, seeing God, becoming perfect even as the Father in Heaven is perfect, constitutes the religion of the Hindus.

And what becomes of a man when he attains perfection? He lives a life of bliss infinite. He enjoys infinite and perfect bliss, having obtained the only thing in which man ought to have pleasure, namely God, and enjoys the bliss with God.

So far all the Hindus are agreed. This is the common religion of all the sects of India; but, then, perfection is absolute, and the absolute cannot be two or three. It cannot have any qualities. It cannot be an individual. And so when a soul becomes perfect and absolute, it must become one with Brahman, and it would only realize the Lord as the perfection, the reality, of its own nature and existence, the existence absolute, knowledge absolute, and bliss absolute. We have often and often read this called the losing of individuality and becoming a stock or a stone.

'He jests at scars that never felt a wound.'

I tell you it is nothing of the kind. If it is happiness to enjoy the consciousness of this small body, it must be greater happiness to enjoy the consciousness of two bodies, the measure of happiness increasing with the consciousness of an increasing number of bodies, the aim, the ultimate of happiness being reached when it would become a universal consciousness.

Therefore, to gain this infinite universal individuality, this miserable little prison-individuality must go. Then alone can death cease when

I am one with life, then alone can misery cease when I am one with happiness itself, then alone can all errors cease when I am one with knowledge itself; and this is the necessary scientific conclusion. Science has proved to me that physical individuality is a delusion, that really my body is one little continuously changing body in an unbroken ocean of matter; and Advaita (unity) is the necessary conclusion with my other counterpart, soul.

Science is nothing but the finding of unity. As soon as science would reach perfect unity, it would stop from further progress, because it would reach the goal. Thus, Chemistry could not progress farther when it would discover one element out of which all others could be made. Physics would stop when it would be able to fulfil its services in discovering one energy of which all the others are but manifestations, and the science of religion becomes perfect when it would discover Him who is the one life in a universe of death, Him who is the constant basis of an ever-changing world. One who is the only Soul of which all souls are but delusive manifestations. Thus is it, through multiplicity and duality, that the ultimate unity is reached. Religion can go no farther. This is the goal of all science.

All science is bound to come to this conclusion in the long run. Manifestation, and not creation, is the word of science today, and the Hindu is only glad that what he has been cherishing in his bosom for ages is going to be taught in more forcible language, and with further light from the latest conclusions of science.

Descend we now from the aspirations of philosophy to the religion of the ignorant. At the very outset, I may tell you that there is no polytheism in India. In every temple, if one stands by and listens, one will find the worshippers applying all the attributes of God, including omnipresence, to the images. It is not polytheism, nor would the name henotheism explain the situation. 'The rose called by any other name would smell as sweet.' Names are not explanations.

I remember, as a boy, hearing a Christian missionary preach to a crowd in India. Among other sweet things he was telling them was that if he gave a blow to their idol with his stick, what could it do? One of his hearers sharply answered, 'If I abuse your God, what can He do?' 'You would be punished,' said the preacher, 'when you die.'

'So my idol will punish you when you die,' retorted the Hindu.

The tree is known by its fruits. When I have seen amongst them that are called idolaters, men, the like of whom in morality and spirituality and love I have never seen anywhere, I stop and ask myself, 'Can sin beget holiness?'

Superstition is a great enemy of man, but bigotry is worse. Why does a Christian go to church? Why is the cross holy? Why is the face turned toward the sky in prayer? Why are there so many images in the Catholic Church? Why are there so many images in the minds of Protestants when they pray? My brethren, we can no more think about anything without a mental image than we can live without breathing. By the law of association, the material image calls up the mental idea and vice versa. This is why the Hindu uses an external symbol when he worships. He will tell you, it helps to keep his mind fixed on the Being to whom he prays. He knows as well as you do that the image is not God, is not omnipresent. After all, how much does omnipresence mean to almost the whole world? It stands merely as a word, a symbol. Has God superficial area? If not, when we repeat that word 'omnipresent', we think of the extended sky or of space, that is all.

As we find that somehow or other, by the laws of our mental constitution, we have to associate our ideas of infinity with the image of the blue sky, or of the sea, so we naturally connect our idea of holiness with the image of a church, a mosque, or a cross. The Hindus have associated the idea of holiness, purity, truth, omnipresence, and such other ideas with different images and forms. But with this difference that while some people devote their whole lives to their idol of a church and never rise higher, because with them religion means an intellectual assent to certain doctrines and doing good to their fellows, the whole religion of the Hindu is centred in realization. Man is to become divine by realising the divine. Idols or temples or churches or books are only the supports, the helps, of his spiritual childhood: but on and on he must progress.

He must not stop anywhere. 'External worship, material worship,' say the scriptures, 'is the lowest stage; struggling to rise high, mental prayer is the next stage, but the highest stage is when the Lord has been realized.' Mark, the same earnest man who is kneeling before the idol tells you, 'Him the sun cannot express, nor the moon, nor the stars, the lightning cannot express Him, nor what we speak of as fire; through Him they shine.' But he does not abuse any one's idol or call its worship sin. He recognizes in it a necessary stage of life. 'The child is father of the man.' Would it be right for an old man to say that childhood is a sin or youth a sin?

If a man can realize his divine nature with the help of an image, would it be right to call that a sin? Nor even when he has passed that stage, should he call it an error. To the Hindu, man is not travelling from error to truth, but from truth to truth, from lower to higher truth. To him all the religions, from the lowest fetishism to the highest absolutism, mean so many attempts of the human soul to grasp and realize the Infinite, each determined by the conditions of its birth and association, and each of these marks a stage of progress; and every soul is a young eagle soaring higher and higher, gathering more and more strength, till it reaches the Glorious Sun.

Unity in variety is the plan of nature, and the Hindu has recognized it. Every other religion lays down certain fixed dogmas, and tries to force society to adopt them. It places before society only one coat which must fit Jack and John and Henry, all alike. If it does not fit John or Henry, he must go without a coat to cover his body. The Hindus have discovered that the absolute can only be realized, or thought of, or stated, through the relative, and the images, crosses, and crescents are simply so many symbols—so many pegs to hang the spiritual ideas on. It is not that this help is necessary for every one, but those that do not need it have no right to say that it is wrong. Nor is it compulsory in Hinduism.

One thing I must tell you. Idolatry in India does not mean anything horrible. It is not the mother of harlots. On the other hand, it is the attempt of undeveloped minds to grasp high spiritual truths. The Hindus have their faults, they sometimes have their exceptions; but mark this, they are always for punishing their own bodies, and never for cutting the throats of their neighbours. If the Hindu fanatic burns himself on the pyre, he never lights the fire of Inquisition. And even this cannot be laid at the door of his religion any more than the burning of witches can be laid at the door of Christianity.

To the Hindu, then, the whole world of religions is only a travelling, a coming up, of different men and women, through various conditions and circumstances, to the same goal. Every religion is only evolving a God out of the material man, and the same God is the inspirer of all of them. Why, then, are there so many contradictions? They are only apparent, says the Hindu. The contradictions come from the same truth adapting itself to the varying circumstances of different natures.

It is the same light coming through glasses of different colours. And these little variations are necessary for purposes of adaptation. But in the heart of everything the same truth reigns. The Lord has declared to the Hindu in His incarnation as Krishna, 'I am in every religion as the thread through a string of pearls. Wherever thou seest extraordinary holiness and extraordinary power raising and purifying humanity, know thou that I am there.' And what has been the result? I challenge the world to find, throughout the whole system of Sanskrit philosophy, any such expression as that the Hindu alone will be saved and not others. Says Vyasa, 'We find perfect men even beyond the pale of our caste and creed. 'One thing more. How, then, can the Hindu, whose whole fabric of thought centres in God, believe in Buddhism which is agnostic, or in Jainism which is atheistic?

The Buddhists or the Jains do not depend upon God; but the whole force of their religion is directed to the great central truth in every religion, to evolve a God out of man. They have not seen the Father, but they have seen the Son. And he that hath seen the Son hath seen the Father also.

This, brethren, is a short sketch of the religious ideas of the Hindus. The Hindu may have failed to carry out all his plans, but if there is ever to be a universal religion, it must be one which will have no location in place or time; which will be infinite like the God it will preach, and whose sun will shine upon the followers of Krishna and of Christ, on saints and sinners alike; which will not be Brahminic or Buddhistic, Christian or Mohammedan, but the sum total of all these, and still have infinite space for development; which in its catholicity will embrace in its infinite arms, and find a place for, every human being, from the lowest grovelling savage not far removed from the brute, to the highest man towering by the virtues of his head and heart almost above humanity, making society stand in awe of him and doubt his human nature. It will be a religion which will have no place for persecution or intolerance in its polity, which will recognize divinity in every man and woman, and whose whole scope, whose whole force, will be created in aiding humanity to realize its own true, divine nature.

Offer such a religion, and all the nations will follow you. Asoka's council was a council of the Buddhist faith. Akbar's, though more to the purpose, was only a parlour-meeting. It was reserved for America to proclaim to all quarters of the globe that the Lord is in every religion.

May He who is the Brahman of the Hindus, the Ahura-Mazda of the Zoroastrians, the Buddha of the Buddhists, the Jehovah of the Jews, the Father in Heaven of the Christians, give strength to you to carry out your noble idea! The star arose in the East; it travelled steadily towards the West, sometimes dimmed and sometimes effulgent, till it made a circuit of the world; and now it is again rising on the very horizon of the East, the borders of the Sanpo, a thousandfold more effulgent than it ever was before.

Hail, Columbia, motherland of liberty! It has been given to thee, who never dipped her hand in her neighbour's blood, who never found out that the shortest way of becoming rich was by robbing one's neighbours, it has been given to thee to march at the vanguard of civilization with the flag of harmony.

4

RELIGION NOT THE CRYING
NEED OF INDIA

(20 September 1893)

Christians must always be ready for good criticism, and I hardly think that you will mind if I make a little criticism. You Christians, who are so fond of sending out missionaries to save the soul of the heathen—why do you not try to save their bodies from starvation? In India, during the terrible famines, thousands died from hunger, yet you Christians did nothing. You erect churches all through India, but the crying evil in the East is not religion—they have religion enough—but it is bread that the suffering millions of burning India cry out for with parched throats. They ask us for bread, but we give them stones. It is an insult to a starving people to offer them religion; it is an insult to a starving man to teach him metaphysics. In India a priest that preached for money would lose caste and be spat upon by the people. I came here to seek aid for my impoverished people, and I fully realized how difficult it was to get help for heathens from Christians in a Christian land.

5

BUDDHISM, THE FULFILMENT OF HINDUISM

(26 September 1893)

I am not a Buddhist, as you have heard, and yet I am. If China, or Japan, or Ceylon follow the teachings of the Great Master, India worships him as God incarnate on earth. You have just now heard that I am going to criticise Buddhism, but by that I wish you to understand only this. Far be it from me to criticise him whom I worship as God incarnate on earth. But our views about Buddha are that he was not understood properly by his disciples. The relation between Hinduism (by Hinduism, I mean the religion of the Vedas) and what is called Buddhism at the present day is nearly the same as between Judaism and Christianity. Jesus Christ was a Jew, and Shakya Muni was a Hindu. The Jews rejected Jesus Christ, nay, crucified him, and the Hindus have accepted Shakya Muni as God and worship him. But the real difference that we Hindus want to show between modern Buddhism and what we should understand as the teachings of Lord Buddha lies principally in this: Shakya Muni came to preach nothing new. He also, like Jesus, came to fulfil and not to destroy. Only, in the case of Jesus, it was the old people, the Jews, who did not understand him, while in the case of Buddha, it was his own followers who did not realize the import of this teachings. As the Jew did not understand the fulfilment of the Old Testament, so the Buddhist did not understand the fulfilment of the truths of the Hindu religion. Again, I repeat, Shakya Muni came not to destroy, but he was the fulfilment, the logical conclusion, the logical development of the religion of the Hindus.

The religion of the Hindus is divided into two parts: the ceremonial and the spiritual. The spiritual portion is specially studied by the monks.

In that there is no caste. A man from the highest caste and a man from the lowest may become a monk in India, and the two castes become equal. In religion, there is no caste; caste is simply a social institution. Shakya Muni himself was a monk, and it was his glory that he had the large-heartedness to bring out the truths from the hidden Vedas and throw them broadcast all over the world. He was the first being in the world who brought missionarizing into practise—nay, he was the first to conceive the idea of proselytising.

The great glory of the Master lay in his wonderful sympathy for everybody, especially for the ignorant and the poor. Some of his disciples were Brahmins. When Buddha was teaching, Sanskrit was no more the spoken language in India. It was then only in the books of the learned. Some of Buddha's Brahmin disciples wanted to translate his teachings into Sanskrit, but he distinctly told them, 'I am for the poor, for the people; let me speak in the tongue of the people.' And so to this day the great bulk of his teachings are in the vernacular of that day in India.

Whatever may be the position of philosophy, whatever may be the position of metaphysics, so long as there is such a thing as death in the world, so long as there is such a thing as weakness in the human heart, so long as there is a cry going out of the heart of man in his very weakness, there shall be a faith in God.

On the philosophic side the disciples of the Great Master dashed themselves against the eternal rocks of the Vedas and could not crush them, and on the other side they took away from the nation that eternal God to which every one, man or woman, clings so fondly. And the result was that Buddhism had to die a natural death in India. At the present day, there is not one who calls oneself a Buddhist in India, the land of its birth.

But at the same time, Brahminism lost something—that reforming zeal, that wonderful sympathy and charity for everybody, that wonderful heaven which Buddhism had brought to the masses and which had rendered Indian society so great that a Greek historian who wrote about India of that time was led to say that no Hindu was known to tell an untruth and no Hindu woman was known to be unchaste.

Hinduism cannot live without Buddhism, nor Buddhism without Hinduism. Then realize what the separation has shown to us, that the Buddhists cannot stand without the brain and philosophy of the Brahmins, nor the Brahmin without the heart of the Buddhist. This separation between the Buddhists and the Brahmins is the cause of the downfall of India. That is why India is populated by three hundred millions of beggars, and that is why India has been the slave of conquerors for the last thousand years. Let us then join the wonderful intellect of the Brahmins with the heart, the noble soul, the wonderful humanizing power of the Great Master.

6

ADDRESS AT THE FINAL SESSION

(27 September 1893)

The World's Parliament of Religions has become an accomplished fact, and the merciful Father has helped those who laboured to bring it into existence, and crowned with success their most unselfish labour.

My thanks to those noble souls whose large hearts and love of truth first dreamed this wonderful dream and then realized it. My thanks to the shower of liberal sentiments that has overflowed this platform. My thanks to this enlightened audience for their uniform kindness to me and for their appreciation of every thought that tends to smooth the friction of religions. A few jarring notes were heard from time to time in this harmony. My special thanks to them, for they have, by their striking contrast, made general harmony the sweeter.

Much has been said of the common ground of religious unity. I am not going just now to venture my own theory. But if any one here hopes that this unity will come by the triumph of any one of the religions and the destruction of the other, to him I say, 'Brother, yours is an impossible hope.' Do I wish that the Christian would become Hindu? God forbid. Do I wish that the Hindu or Buddhist would become Christian? God forbid.

The seed is put in the ground, and earth and air and water are placed around it. Does the seed become the earth, or the air, or the water? No. It becomes a plant, it develops after the law of its own growth, assimilates the air, the earth, and the water, converts them into plant substance, and grows into a plant.

Similar is the case with religion. The Christian is not to become a Hindu or a Buddhist, nor a Hindu or a Buddhist to become a Christian. But each must assimilate the spirit of the others and yet preserve his individuality and grow according to his own law of growth.

If the Parliament of Religions has shown anything to the world, it is this: It has proved to the world that holiness, purity, and charity are not the exclusive possessions of any church in the world, and that every system has produced men and women of the most exalted character. In the face of this evidence, if anybody dreams of the exclusive survival of his own religion and the destruction of the others, I pity him from the bottom of my heart, and point out to him that upon the banner of every religion will soon be written, in spite of resistance: 'Help and not Fight,' 'Assimilation and not Destruction,' 'Harmony and Peace and not Dissension.'

SECTION 2

FROM THE KARMA YOGA

7

KARMA IN ITS EFFECT ON CHARACTER
From The Karma Yoga: The Yoga of Action

The word Karma is derived from the Sanskrit *Kri*, to do; all action is Karma. Technically, this word also means the effects of actions. In connection with metaphysics, it sometimes means the effects, of which our past actions were the causes. But in Karma-Yoga we have simply to do with the word Karma as meaning work. The goal of mankind is knowledge. That is the one ideal placed before us by Eastern philosophy. Pleasure is not the goal of man, but knowledge. Pleasure and happiness come to an end. It is a mistake to suppose that pleasure is the goal. The cause of all the miseries we have in the world is that men foolishly think pleasure to be the ideal to strive for. After a time man finds that it is not happiness, but knowledge, towards which he is going, and that both pleasure and pain are great teachers, and that he learns as much from evil as from good. As pleasure and pain pass before his soul they have upon it different pictures, and the result of these combined impressions is what is called man's 'character'. If you take the character of any man, it really is but the aggregate of tendencies, the sum total of the bent of his mind; you will find that misery and happiness are equal factors in the formation of that character. Good and evil have an equal share in moulding character, and in some instances misery is a greater teacher than happiness. In studying the great characters the world has produced, I dare say, in the vast majority of cases, it would be found that it was misery that taught more than happiness, it was poverty that taught more than wealth, it was blows that brought out their inner fire more than praise.

Now this knowledge, again, is inherent in man. No knowledge comes from outside; it is all inside. What we say a man 'knows', should, in strict psychological language, be what he 'discovers' or 'unveils';

what a man 'learns' is really what he 'discovers', by taking the cover off his own soul, which is a mine of infinite knowledge.

We say Newton discovered gravitation. Was it sitting anywhere in a corner waiting for him? It was in his own mind; the time came and he found it out. All knowledge that the world has ever received comes from the mind; the infinite library of the universe is in your own mind. The external world is simply the suggestion, the occasion, which sets you to study your own mind, but the object of your study is always your own mind. The falling of an apple gave the suggestion to Newton, and he studied his own mind. He rearranged all the previous links of thought in his mind and discovered a new link among them, which we call the law of gravitation. It was not in the apple nor in anything in the centre of the earth.

All knowledge, therefore, secular or spiritual, is in the human mind. In many cases it is not discovered, but remains covered, and when the covering is being slowly taken off, we say, 'We are learning,' and the advance of knowledge is made by the advance of this process of uncovering. The man from whom this veil is being lifted is the more knowing man, the man upon whom it lies thick is ignorant, and the man from whom it has entirely gone is all-knowing, omniscient. There have been omniscient men, and, I believe, there will be yet; and that there will be myriads of them in the cycles to come. Like fire in a piece of flint, knowledge exists in the mind; suggestion is the friction which brings it out. So with all our feelings and actions—our tears and our smiles, our joys and our griefs, our weeping and our laughter, our curses and our blessings, our praises and our blames—every one of these we may find, if we calmly study our own selves, to have been brought out from within ourselves by so many blows. The result is what we are. All these blows taken together are called Karma—work, action. Every mental and physical blow that is given to the soul, by which, as it were, fire is struck from it, and by which its own power and knowledge are discovered, is Karma, this word being used in its widest sense. Thus, we are all doing Karma all the time. I am talking to you: that is Karma. You are listening: that is Karma. We breathe: that is Karma. We walk: Karma. Everything we do, physical or mental, is Karma, and it leaves its marks on us.

There are certain works which are, as it were, the aggregate, the sum total, of a large number of smaller works. If we stand near the seashore and hear the waves dashing against the shingle, we think it is such a great noise, and yet we know that one wave is really composed of millions and millions of minute waves. Each one of these is making a noise, and yet we do not catch it; it is only when they become the big aggregate that we hear. Similarly, every pulsation of the heart is work. Certain kinds of work we feel and they become tangible to us; they are, at the same time, the aggregate of a number of small works. If you really want to judge of the character of a man, look not at his great performances. Every fool may become a hero at one time or another. Watch a man do his most common actions; those are indeed the things which will tell you the real character of a great man. Great occasions rouse even the lowest of human beings to some kind of greatness, but he alone is the really great man whose character is great always, the same wherever he be.

Karma in its effect on character is the most tremendous power than man has to deal with. Man is, as it were, a centre, and is attracting all the powers of the universe towards himself, and in this centre is fusing them all and again sending them off in a big current. Such a centre is the real man—the almighty, the omniscient—and he draws the whole universe towards him. Good and bad, misery and happiness, all are running towards him and clinging round him; and out of them he fashions the mighty stream of tendency called character and throws it outwards. As he has the power of drawing in anything, so has he the power of throwing it out.

All the actions that we see in the world, all the movements in human society, all the works that we have around us, are simply the display of thought, the manifestation of the will of man. Machines or instruments, cities, ships, or men-of-war, all these are simply the manifestation of the will of man; and this will is caused by character, and character is manufactured by Karma. As is Karma, so is the manifestation of the will. The men of mighty will the world has produced have all been tremendous workers—gigantic souls, with wills powerful enough to overturn worlds, wills they got by persistent work, through ages, and ages. Such a gigantic will as that of a Buddha or a Jesus could not be obtained in one life, for we know who their fathers were. It is not known that their fathers ever spoke a word for the good of mankind. Millions and millions of carpenters like Joseph had gone; millions are still living. Millions and millions of petty kings like Buddha's father had been in the world. If it was only a case of hereditary transmission, how do you account for this petty prince, who was not, perhaps, obeyed by his own servants, producing this son, whom half a world worships? How do you explain the gulf between the carpenter and his son, whom millions of human beings worship as God? It cannot be solved by the theory of heredity. The gigantic will which Buddha and Jesus threw over the world, whence did it come? Whence came this accumulation of power? It must have been there through ages and ages, continually growing bigger and bigger, until it burst on society in a Buddha or a Jesus, even rolling down to the present day.

All this is determined by Karma, work. No one can get anything unless he earns it. This is an eternal law. We may sometimes think it is not so, but in the long run we become convinced of it. A man may struggle all his life for riches; he may cheat thousands, but he finds at last that he did not deserve to become rich, and his life becomes a trouble and a nuisance to him. We may go on accumulating things for our physical enjoyment, but only what we earn is really ours. A fool may buy all the books in the world, and they will be in his library; but he will be able to read only those that he deserves to; and this deserving is produced by Karma. Our Karma determines what we deserve and what we can assimilate. We are responsible for what we are; and whatever we wish ourselves to be, we have the power to make ourselves. If what we are now has been the result of our own past actions, it certainly follows that whatever we wish to be in future can be produced by our present actions; so we have to know how to act. You will say, 'What is the use of learning how to work? Everyone works in some way or other in this world.' But there is such a thing as frittering away our energies. With regard to Karma-Yoga, the Gita says that it is doing work with cleverness and as a science; by knowing how to work, one can obtain the greatest results. You must remember that all work is simply to bring out the power of the mind which is already there, to wake up the soul. The power is inside every man, so is knowing; the different works are like blows to bring them out, to cause these giants to wake up.

Man works with various motives. There cannot be work without motive. Some people want to get fame, and they work for fame. Others want money, and they work for money. Others want to have power, and they work for power. Others want to get to heaven, and they work for the same. Others want to leave a name when they die, as they do in China, where no man gets a title until he is dead; and that is a better way, after all, than with us. When a man does something very good there, they give a title of nobility to his father, who is dead, or to his grandfather. Some people work for that. Some of the followers of certain Mohammedan sects work all their lives to have a big tomb built for them when they die. I know sects among whom, as soon as a child is born, a tomb is prepared for it; that is among them the most important work a man has to do, and the bigger and the finer the tomb, the better off the man is supposed to be. Others work as a penance; do all sorts of wicked things, then erect a temple, or give something to the priests to buy them off and obtain from them a passport to heaven. They think that this kind of beneficence will clear them and they will go scot-free in spite of their sinfulness. Such are some of the various motives for work.

Work for work's sake. There are some who are really the salt of the earth in every country and who work for work's sake, who do not care for name, or fame, or even to go to heaven. They work just because good will come of it. There are others who do good to the poor and help mankind from still higher motives, because they believe in doing good and love good. The motive for name and fame seldom brings immediate results, as a rule; they come to us when we are old and have almost done with life. If a man works without any selfish motive in view, does he not gain anything? Yes, he gains the highest. Unselfishness is more paying, only people have not the patience to practise it. It is more paying from the point of view of health also. Love, truth and unselfishness are not merely moral figures of speech, but they form our highest ideal, because in them lies such a manifestation of power. In the first place, a man who can work for five days, or even for five minutes, without any selfish motive whatever, without thinking of future, of heaven, of punishment, or anything of the kind, has in him the capacity to become a powerful moral giant. It is hard to do it, but in the heart of our hearts we know its value, and the good it brings. It is the greatest manifestation of power—this tremendous restraint; self-restraint is a manifestation of greater power than all outgoing action. A carriage with four horses may rush down a hill unrestrained, or the coachman may curb the horses. Which is the greater manifestation of power, to let them go or to hold them? A cannon-ball flying through the air goes a long distance and falls. Another is cut short in its flight by striking against a wall, and the impact generates intense heat. All outgoing energy following a selfish motive is frittered away; it will not cause power to return to you; but if restrained, it will result in development of power. This self-control will tend to produce a mighty will, a character which makes a Christ or a Buddha. Foolish men do not know this secret; they nevertheless want to rule mankind. Even a fool may rule the whole world if he works and waits. Let him wait a few years, restrain that foolish idea of governing; and when that idea is wholly gone, he will be a power in the world. The majority of us cannot see beyond a few years, just as some animals cannot see beyond a few steps. Just a little narrow circle—that is our world. We have not the patience to look beyond, and thus become immoral and wicked. This is our weakness, our powerlessness.

Even the lowest forms of work are not to be despised. Let the man, who knows no better, work for selfish ends, for name and fame; but everyone should always try to get towards higher and higher motives and to understand them. 'To work we have the right, but not to the fruits thereof.' Leave the fruits alone. Why care for results? If you wish to help a man, never think what that man's attitude should be towards you. If you want to do a great or a good work, do not trouble to think what the result will be.

There arises a difficult question in this ideal of work. Intense activity is necessary; we must always work. We cannot live a minute without work. What then becomes of rest? Here is one side of the life-struggle—work, in which we are whirled rapidly round. And here is the other—that of calm, retiring renunciation: everything is peaceful around, there is very little of noise and show, only nature with her animals and flowers and mountains. Neither of them is a perfect picture. A man used to solitude, if brought in contact with the surging whirlpool of the world, will be crushed by it; just as the fish that lives in the deep sea water, as soon as it is brought to the surface, breaks into pieces, deprived of the weight of water on it that had kept it together. Can a man who has been used to the turmoil and the rush of life live at ease if he comes to a quiet place? He suffers and perchance may lose his mind. The ideal man is he who, in the midst of the greatest silence and solitude, finds the intensest activity, and in the midst of the intensest activity finds the silence and solitude of the desert. He has learnt the secret of restraint, he has controlled himself. He goes through the streets of a big city with all its traffic, and his mind is as calm as if he were in a cave, where not a sound could reach him; and he is intensely working all the time. That is the ideal of Karma-Yoga, and if you have attained to that you have really learnt the secret of work.

But we have to begin from the beginning, to take up the works as they come to us and slowly make ourselves more unselfish every day. We must do the work and find out the motive power that prompts us; and, almost without exception, in the first years, we shall find that our motives are always selfish; but gradually this selfishness will melt by persistence, till at last will come the time when we shall be able to do really unselfish work. We may all hope that some day or other, as we struggle through the paths of life, there will come a time when we shall become perfectly unselfish; and the moment we attain to that, all our powers will be concentrated, and the knowledge which is ours will be manifest.

8

EACH IS GREAT IN HIS OWN PLACE

According to the Sankhya philosophy, nature is composed of three forces called, in Sanskrit, Sattva, Rajas, and Tamas. These as manifested in the physical world are what we may call equilibrium, activity, and inertness. Tamas is typified as darkness or inactivity; Rajas is activity, expressed as attraction or repulsion; and Sattva is the equilibrium of the two. In every man there are these three forces. Sometimes Tamas prevails. We become lazy, we cannot move, we are inactive, bound down by certain ideas or by mere dullness. At other times activity prevails, and at still other times that calm balancing of both. Again, in different men, one of these forces is generally predominant. The characteristic of one man is inactivity, dullness and laziness; that of another, activity, power, manifestation of energy; and in still another we find the sweetness, calmness, and gentleness, which are due to the balancing of both action and inaction. So in all creation—in animals, plants, and men—we find the more or less typical manifestation of all these different forces.

Karma-Yoga has specially to deal with these three factors. By teaching what they are and how to employ them, it helps us to do our work better. Human society is a graded organization. We all know about morality, and we all know about duty, but at the same time we find that in different countries the significance of morality varies greatly. What is regarded as moral in one country may in another be considered perfectly immoral. For instance, in one country cousins may marry; in another, it is thought to be very immoral; in one, men may marry their sisters-in-law; in another, it is regarded as immoral; in one country people may marry only once; in another, many times; and so forth. Similarly, in all other departments of morality, we find the standard varies greatly-yet we have the idea that there must be a universal standard of morality.

So it is with duty. The idea of duty varies much among different nations. In one country, if a man does not do certain things, people will say he has acted wrongly; while if he does those very things in another country, people will say that he did not act rightly—and yet we know that there must be some universal idea of duty. In the same way, one class of society thinks that certain things are among its duty, while another class thinks quite the opposite and would be horrified if it had to do those things. Two ways are left open to us—the way of the ignorant, who think that there is only one way to truth and that all the rest are wrong, and the way of the wise, who admit that, according to our mental constitution or the different planes of existence in which we are, duty and morality may vary. The important thing is to know that there are gradations of duty and of morality—that the duty of one state of life, in one set of circumstances, will not and cannot be that of another.

To illustrate: All great teachers have taught, 'Resist not evil,' that non-resistance is the highest moral ideal. We all know that, if a certain number of us attempted to put that maxim fully into practise, the whole social fabric would fall to pieces, the wicked would take possession of our properties and our lives, and would do whatever they like with us. Even if only one day of such non-resistance were practised, it would lead to disaster. Yet, intuitively, in our heart of hearts we feel the truth of the teaching 'Resist not evil.' This seems to us to be the highest ideal; yet to teach this doctrine only would be equivalent to condemning a vast portion of mankind. Not only so, it would be making men feel that they were always doing wrong, and cause in them scruples of conscience in all their actions; it would weaken them, and that constant self-disapproval would breed more vice than any other weakness would. To the man who has begun to hate himself the gate to degeneration has already opened; and the same is true of a nation. Our first duty is not to hate ourselves, because to advance we must have faith in ourselves first and then in God. He who has no faith in himself can never have faith in God. Therefore, the only alternative remaining to us is to recognize that duty and morality vary under different circumstances; not that the man who resists evil is doing what is always and in itself wrong, but that in the different circumstances in which he is placed it may become even his duty to resist evil.

In reading the Bhagavad Gita, many of you in Western countries may have felt astonished at the second chapter, wherein Sri Krishna calls Arjuna a hypocrite and a coward because of his refusal to fight, or offer resistance, on account of his adversaries being his friends and relatives, making the plea that non-resistance was the highest ideal of love. This is a great lesson for us all to learn, that in all matters the two extremes are alike. The extreme positive and the extreme negative are always similar. When the vibrations of light are too slow, we do not see them, nor do we see them when they are too rapid. So with sound; when very low in pitch, we do not hear it; when very high, we do not hear it either. Of like nature is the difference between resistance and non-resistance. One man does not resist because he is weak, lazy, and cannot, not because he will not; the other man knows that he can strike an irresistible blow if he likes; yet he not only does not strike, but blesses his enemies. The one who from weakness resists not commits a sin, and as such cannot receive any benefit from the non-resistance; while the other would commit a sin by offering resistance. Buddha gave up his throne and renounced his position, that was true renunciation; but there cannot be any question of renunciation in the case of a beggar who has nothing to renounce. So we must always be careful about what we really mean when we speak of this non-resistance and ideal love. We must first take care to understand whether we have the power of resistance or not. Then, having the power, if we renounce it and do not resist, we are doing a grand act of love; but if we cannot resist, and yet, at the same time, try to deceive ourselves into the belief that we are actuated by motives of the highest love, we are doing the exact opposite. Arjuna became a coward at the sight of the mighty array against him; his 'love' make him forget his duty towards his country and king. That is why Sri Krishna told him that he was a hypocrite; Thou talkest like a wise man, but thy actions betray thee to be a coward; therefore stand up and fight!

Such is the central idea of Karma-Yoga. The Karma-Yogi is the man who understands that the highest ideal is non-resistance, and who also knows that this non-resistance is the highest manifestation of power in actual possession, and also what is called the resisting of evil is but a step on the way towards the manifestation of this highest power, namely, non-resistance. Before reaching this highest ideal, man's duty is to resist evil; let him work, let him fight, let him strike straight from the shoulder. Then only, when he has gained the power to resist, will non-resistance be a virtue.

I once met a man in my country whom I had known before as a very stupid, dull person, who knew nothing and had not the desire to know anything, and was living the life of a brute. He asked me what he should do to know God, how he was to get free. 'Can you tell a lie?' I asked him. 'No,' he replied. 'Then you must learn to do so. It is better to tell a lie than to be a brute, or a log of wood. You are inactive; you have not certainly reached the highest state, which is beyond all actions, calm and serene; you are too dull even to do something wicked.' That was an extreme case, of course, and I was joking with him; but what I meant was that a man must be active in order to pass through activity to perfect calmness.

Inactivity should be avoided by all means. Activity always means resistance. Resist all evils, mental and physical; and when you have succeeded in resisting, then will calmness come. It is very easy to say, 'Hate nobody, resist not evil,' but we know what that kind of thing generally means in practise. When the eyes of society are turned towards us, we may make a show of non-resistance, but in our hearts it is canker all the time. We feel the utter want of the calm of non-resistance; we feel that it would be better for us to resist. If you desire wealth, and know at the same time that the whole world regards him who aims at wealth as a very wicked man, you, perhaps, will not dare to plunge into the struggle for wealth, yet your mind will be running day and night after money. This is hypocrisy and will serve no purpose. Plunge into the world, and then, after a time, when you have suffered and enjoyed all that is in it, will renunciation come; then will calmness come. So fulfil your desire for power and everything else, and after you have fulfilled the desire, will come the time when you will know that they are all very little things; but until you have fulfilled this desire, until you have passed through that activity, it is impossible for you to come to the state of calmness, serenity, and self-surrender. These ideas of serenity and renunciation have been preached for thousands of years; everybody has heard of them from childhood, and yet we see very few in the world who have really reached that stage. I do not know if I have seen twenty persons in my life who are really calm and non-resisting, and I have travelled over half the world.

Every man should take up his own ideal and endeavour to accomplish it. That is a surer way of progress than taking up other men's ideals, which he can never hope to accomplish. For instance, we take a child and at once give him the task of walking twenty miles. Either the little one dies, or one in a thousand crawls the twenty miles, to reach the end exhausted and half-dead. That is like what we generally try to do with the world. All the men and women, in any society, are not of the same mind, capacity, or of the same power to do things; they must have different ideals, and we have no right to sneer at any ideal. Let every one do the best he can for realising his own ideal. Nor is it right that I should be judged by your standard or you by mine. The apple tree should not be judged by the standard of the oak, nor the oak by that of the apple. To judge the apple tree you must take the apple standard, and for the oak, its own standard.

Unity in variety is the plan of creation. However, men and women may vary individually, there is unity in the background. The different individual characters and classes of men and women are natural variations in creation. Hence, we ought not to judge them by the same standard or put the same ideal before them. Such a course creates only an unnatural struggle, and the result is that man begins to hate himself and is hindered from becoming religious and good. Our duty is to encourage every one in his struggle to live up to his own highest ideal, and strive at the same time to make the ideal as near as possible to the truth.

In the Hindu system of morality we find that this fact has been recognized from very ancient times; and in their scriptures and books on ethics different rules are laid down for the different classes of men—the householder, the Sannyasin (the man who has renounced the world), and the student.

The life of every individual, according to the Hindu scriptures, has its peculiar duties apart from what belongs in common to universal humanity. The Hindu begins life as a student; then he marries and becomes a householder; in old age he retires; and lastly he gives up the world and becomes a Sannyasin. To each of these stages of life certain duties are attached. No one of these stages is intrinsically superior to another. The life of the married man is quite as great as that of the celibate who has devoted himself to religious work. The scavenger in the street is quite as great and glorious as the king on his throne. Take him off his throne, make him do the work of the scavenger, and see how he fares. Take up the scavenger and see how he will rule. It is useless to say that the man who lives out of the world is a greater man than he who lives in the world; it is much more difficult to live in the world and worship God than to give it up and live a free and easy life. The four stages of life in India have in later times been reduced to two—that of the householder and of the monk. The householder marries and carries on his duties as a citizen, and the duty of the other is to devote his energies wholly to religion, to preach and to worship God. I shall read to you a few passages from the Maha-Nirvana-Tantra, which treats of this subject, and you will see that it is a very difficult task for a man to be a householder, and perform all his duties perfectly:

The householder should be devoted to God; the knowledge of God should be his goal of life. Yet he must work constantly, perform all his duties; he must give up the fruits of his actions to God. It is the most difficult thing in this world to work and not care for the result, to help a man and never think that he ought to be grateful, to do some good work and at the same time never look to see whether it brings you name or fame, or nothing at all. Even the most arrant coward becomes brave when the world praises him. A fool can do heroic deeds when the approbation of society is upon him, but for a man to constantly do good without caring for the approbation of his fellow men is indeed the highest sacrifice man can perform. The great duty of the householder is to earn a living, but he must take care that he does not do it by telling lies, or by cheating, or by robbing others; and he must remember that his life is for the service of God, and the poor.

Knowing that mother and father are the visible representatives of God, the householder, always and by all means, must please them. If the mother is pleased, and the father, God is pleased with the man. That child is really a good child who never speaks harsh words to his parents.

Before parents one must not utter jokes, must not show restlessness, must not show anger or temper. Before mother or father, a child must bow down low, and stand up in their presence, and must not take a seat until they order him to sit.

If the householder has food and drink and clothes without first seeing that his mother and his father, his children, his wife, and the poor, are supplied, he is committing a sin. The mother and the father are the causes of this body; so a man must undergo a thousand troubles in order to do good to them.

Even so is his duty to his wife. No man should scold his wife, and he must always maintain her as if she were his own mother. And even when he is in the greatest difficulties and troubles, he must not show anger to his wife.

He who thinks of another woman besides his wife, if he touches her even with his mind—that man goes to dark hell.

Before women he must not talk improper language, and never brag of his powers. He must not say, 'I have done this, and I have done that.'

The householder must always please his wife with money, clothes, love, faith, and words like nectar, and never do anything to disturb her. That man who has succeeded in getting the love of a chaste wife has succeeded in his religion and has all the virtues.

The following are duties towards children:

A son should be lovingly reared up to his fourth year; he should be educated till he is sixteen. When he is twenty years of age he should be employed in some work; he should then be treated affectionately by his father as his equal. Exactly in the same manner the daughter should be brought up, and should be educated with the greatest care. And when she marries, the father ought to give her jewels and wealth.

Then the duty of the man is towards his brothers and sisters, and towards the children of his brothers and sisters, if they are poor, and towards his other relatives, his friends and his servants. Then his duties are towards the people of the same village, and the poor, and any one that comes to him for help. Having sufficient means, if the householder does not take care to give to his relatives and to the poor, know him to be only a brute; his is not a human being.

Excessive attachment to food, clothes, and the tending of the body, and dressing of the hair should be avoided. The householder must be pure in heart and clean in body, always active and always ready for work.

To his enemies the householder must be a hero. Them he must resist. That is the duty of the householder. He must not sit down in a corner and weep, and talk nonsense about non-resistance. If he does not show himself a hero to his enemies he has not done his duty. And to his friends and relatives he must be as gentle as a lamb.

It is the duty of the householder not to pay reverence to the wicked; because, if he reverences the wicked people of the world, he patronizes wickedness; and it will be a great mistake if he disregards those who are worthy of respect, the good people. He must not be gushing in his friendship; he must not go out of the way making friends everywhere; he must watch the actions of the men he wants to make friends with, and their dealings with other men, reason upon them, and then make friends.

These three things he must not talk of. He must not talk in public of his own fame; he must not preach his own name or his own powers; he must not talk of his wealth, or of anything that has been told to him privately.

A man must not say he is poor, or that he is wealthy—he must not brag of his wealth. Let him keep his own counsel; this is his religious duty. This is not mere worldly wisdom; if a man does not do so, he may be held to be immoral.

The householder is the basis, the prop, of the whole society. He is the principal earner. The poor, the weak, the children and the women who do not work—all live upon the householder; so there must be certain duties that he has to perform, and these duties must make him feel strong to perform them, and not make him think that he is doing things beneath his ideal. Therefore, if he has done something weak, or has made some mistake, he must not say so in public; and if he is engaged in some enterprise and knows he is sure to fail in it, he must not speak of it. Such self-exposure is not only uncalled for, but also unnerves the man and makes him unfit for the performance of his legitimate duties in life. At the same time, he must struggle hard to acquire these things—firstly, knowledge, and secondly, wealth. It is his duty, and if he does not do his duty, he is nobody. A householder who does not struggle to get wealth is immoral. If he is lazy and content to lead an idle life, he is immoral, because upon him depend hundreds. If he gets riches, hundreds of others will be thereby supported.

If there were not in this city hundreds who had striven to become rich, and who had acquired wealth, where would all this civilization, and these alms-houses and great houses be?

Going after wealth in such a case is not bad, because that wealth is for distribution. The householder is the centre of life and society. It is a worship for him to acquire and spend wealth nobly, for the householder who struggles to become rich by good means and for good purposes is doing practically the same thing for the attainment of salvation as the anchorite does in his cell when he is praying; for in them we see only the different aspects of the same virtue of self-surrender and self-sacrifice prompted by the feeling of devotion to God and to all that is His.

He must struggle to acquire a good name by all means. He must not gamble, he must not move in the company of the wicked, he must not tell lies, and must not be the cause of trouble to others.

Often people enter into things they have not the means to accomplish, with the result that they cheat others to attain their own ends. Then there is in all things the time factor to be taken into consideration; what at one time might be a failure, would perhaps at another time be a very great success.

The householder must speak the truth, and speak gently, using words which people like, which will do good to others; nor should he talk of the business of other men.

The householder by digging tanks, by planting trees on the roadsides, by establishing rest-houses for men and animals, by making roads and building bridges, goes towards the same goal as the greatest Yogi. This is one part of the doctrine of Karma-Yoga—activity, the duty of the householder. There is a passage later on, where it says that 'if the householder dies in battle, fighting for his country or his religion, he comes to the same goal as the Yogi by meditation,' showing thereby that what is duty for one is not duty for another. At the same time, it does not say that this duty is lowering and the other elevating. Each duty has its own place, and according to the circumstances in which we are placed, must we perform our duties.

One idea comes out of all this—the condemnation of all weakness. This is a particular idea in all our teachings which I like, either in philosophy, or in religion, or in work. If you read the Vedas, you will find this word always repeated—fearlessness—fear nothing. Fear is a sign of weakness. A man must go about his duties without taking notice of the sneers and the ridicule of the world.

If a man retires from the world to worship God, he must not think that those who live in the world and work for the good of the world are not worshipping God: neither must those who live in the world, for wife and children, think that those who give up the world are low vagabonds. Each is great in his own place. This thought I will illustrate by a story.

A certain king used to inquire of all the Sannyasins that came to his country, 'Which is the greater man—he who gives up the world and becomes a Sannyasin, or he who lives in the world and performs his duties as a householder?' Many wise men sought to solve the problem. Some asserted that the Sannyasin was the greater, upon which the king demanded that they should prove their assertion. When they could not, he ordered them to marry and become householders. Then others came and said, 'The householder who performs his duties is the greater man.' Of them, too the king demanded proofs. When they could not give them, he made them also settle down as householders.

At last there came a young Sannyasin, and the king similarly inquired of him also. He answered, 'Each, O king, is equally great in his place.' 'Prove this to me,' asked the king. 'I will prove it to you,' said the Sannyasin, 'but you must first come and live as I do for a few days, that I may be able to prove to you what I say.' The king consented and followed the Sannyasin out of his own territory and passed through many other countries until they came to a great kingdom. In the capital of that kingdom a great ceremony was going on. The king and the Sannyasin heard the noise of drums and music, and heard also the criers; the people were assembled in the streets in gala dress, and a great proclamation was being made. The king and the Sannyasin stood there to see what was going on. The crier was proclaiming loudly that the princess, daughter of the king of that country, was about to choose a husband from among those assembled before her.

It was an old custom in India for princesses to choose husbands in this way. Each princess had certain ideas of the sort of man she wanted for a husband. Some would have the handsomest man, others would have only the most learned, others again the richest, and so on. All the princes of the neighbourhood put on their bravest attire and presented themselves before her. Sometimes they too had their own criers to enumerate their advantages and the reasons why they hoped the princess would choose them. The princess was taken round on a throne, in the most splendid array, and looked at and heard about them. If she was not pleased with what she saw and heard, she said to her bearers, 'Move on,' and no more notice was taken of the rejected suitors. If, however, the princess was pleased with any one of them, she threw a garland of flowers over him and he became her husband.

The princess of the country to which our king and the Sannyasin had come was having one of these interesting ceremonies. She was the most beautiful princess in the world, and the husband of the princess would be ruler of the kingdom after her father's death. The idea of this princess was to marry the handsomest man, but she could not find the right one to please her. Several times these meetings had taken place, but the princess could not select a husband. This meeting was the most splendid of all; more people than ever had come it it. The princess came in on a throne, and the bearers carried her from place to place. She did not seem to care for any one, and every one became disappointed that this meeting also was going to be a failure. Just then came a young man, a Sannyasin, handsome as if the sun had come down to the earth, and stood in one corner of the assembly, watching what was going on. The throne with the princess came near him, and as soon as she saw the beautiful Sannyasin, she stopped and threw the garland over him. The young Sannyasin seized the garland and threw it off, exclaiming, 'What nonsense is this? I am a Sannyasin. What is marriage to me?' The king of that country thought that perhaps this man was poor and so dared not marry the princess, and said to him, 'With my daughter goes half my kingdom now, and the whole kingdom after my death!' and put the garland again on the Sannyasin. The young man threw it off once more, saying, 'Nonsense! I do not want to marry,' and walked quickly away from the assembly.

Now the princess had fallen so much in love with this young man that she said, 'I must marry this man or I shall die'; and she went after him to bring him back. Then our other Sannyasin, who had brought the king there, said to him, 'King, let us follow this pair'; so they walked after them, but at a good distance behind. The young Sannyasin who had refused to marry the princess walked out into the country for several miles. When he came to a forest and entered into it, the princess followed him, and the other two followed them. Now this young Sannyasin was well acquainted with that forest and knew all the intricate paths in it. He suddenly passed into one of these and disappeared, and the princess could not discover him. After trying for a long time to find him she sat down under a tree and began to weep, for she did not know the way out. Then our king and the other Sannyasin came up to her and said, 'Do not weep; we will show you the way out of this forest, but it is too dark for us to find it now. Here is a big tree; let us rest under it, and in the morning we will go early and show you the road.'

Now a little bird and his wife and their three little ones lived on that tree, in a nest. This little bird looked down and saw the three people under the tree and said to his wife, 'My dear, what shall we do? Here are some guests in the house, and it is winter, and we have no fire.' So he flew away and got a bit of burning firewood in his beak and dropped it before the guests, to which they added fuel and made a blazing fire. But the little bird was not satisfied. He said again to his wife, 'My dear, what shall we do? There is nothing to give these people to eat, and they are hungry. We are householders; it is our duty to feed any one who comes to the house. I must do what I can, I will give them my body.' So he plunged into the midst of the fire and perished. The guests saw him falling and tried to save him, but he was too quick for them.

The little bird's wife saw what her husband did, and she said, 'Here are three persons and only one little bird for them to eat. It is not enough; it is my duty as a wife not to let my husband's effort go in vain; let them have my body also.' Then she fell into the fire and was burned to death.

Then the three baby-birds, when they saw what was done and that there was still not enough food for the three guests, said, 'Our parents have done what they could and still it is not enough. It is our duty to carry on the work of our parents; let our bodies go too.' And they all dashed down into the fire also.

Amazed at what they saw, the three people could not of course eat these birds. They passed the night without food, and in the morning the king and the Sannyasin showed the princess the way, and she went back to her father.

Then the Sannyasin said to the king, 'King, you have seen that each is great in his own place. If you want to live in the world, live like those birds, ready at any moment to sacrifice yourself for others. If you want to renounce the world, be like that young man to whom the most beautiful woman and a kingdom were as nothing. If you want to be a householder, hold your life a sacrifice for the welfare of others; and if you choose the life of renunciation, do not even look at beauty and money and power. Each is great in his own place, but the duty of the one is not the duty of the other.'

9

THE SECRET OF WORK

Helping others physically, by removing their physical needs, is indeed great, but the help is great according as the need is greater and according as the help is far reaching. If a man's wants can be removed for an hour, it is helping him indeed; if his wants can be removed for a year, it will be more help to him; but if his wants can be removed for ever, it is surely the greatest help that can be given him. Spiritual knowledge is the only thing that can destroy our miseries for ever; any other knowledge satisfies wants only for a time. It is only with the knowledge of the spirit that the faculty of want is annihilated for ever; so helping man spiritually is the highest help that can be given to him. He who gives man spiritual knowledge is the greatest benefactor of mankind and as such we always find that those were the most powerful of men who helped man in his spiritual needs, because spirituality is the true basis of all our activities in life. A spiritually strong and sound man will be strong in every other respect, if he so wishes. Until there is spiritual strength in man even physical needs cannot be well satisfied. Next to spiritual comes intellectual help. The gift of knowledge is a far higher gift than that of food and clothes; it is even higher than giving life to a man, because the real life of man consists of knowledge. Ignorance is death, knowledge is life. Life is of very little value, if it is a life in the dark, groping through ignorance and misery. Next in order comes, of course, helping a man physically. Therefore, in considering the question of helping others, we must always strive not to commit the mistake of thinking that physical help is the only help that can be given. It is not only the last but the least, because it cannot bring about permanent satisfaction. The misery that I feel when I am hungry is satisfied by eating, but hunger returns; my misery can cease only when I am satisfied beyond all want. Then hunger will not make me miserable; no distress, no sorrow will be able to move me. So, that help which tends to make us strong spiritually is the highest, next to it comes intellectual help, and after that physical help.

The miseries of the world cannot be cured by physical help only. Until man's nature changes, these physical needs will always arise, and miseries will always be felt, and no amount of physical help will cure them completely. The only solution of this problem is to make mankind pure. Ignorance is the mother of all the evil and all the misery we see. Let men have light, let them be pure and spiritually strong and educated, then alone will misery cease in the world, not before. We may convert every house in the country into a charity asylum, we may fill the land with hospitals, but the misery of man will still continue to exist until man's character changes.

We read in the Bhagavad Gita again and again that we must all work incessantly. All work is by nature composed of good and evil. We cannot do any work which will not do some good somewhere; there cannot be any work which will not cause some harm somewhere. Every work must necessarily be a mixture of good and evil; yet we are commanded to work incessantly. Good and evil will both have their results, will produce their Karma. Good action will entail upon us good effect; bad action, bad. But good and bad are both bondages of the soul. The solution reached in the Gita in regard to this bondage-producing nature of work is that, if we do not attach ourselves to the work we do, it will not have any binding effect on our soul. We shall try to understand what is meant by this 'non-attachment to' to work.

This is the one central idea in the Gita: work incessantly, but be not attached to it. Samskara can be translated very nearly by 'inherent tendency'. Using the simile of a lake for the mind, every ripple, every wave that rises in the mind, when it subsides, does not die out entirely, but leaves a mark and a future possibility of that wave coming out again. This mark, with the possibility of the wave reappearing, is what is called Samskara. Every work that we do, every movement of the body, every thought that we think, leaves such an impression on the mind-stuff, and even when such impressions are not obvious on the surface, they are sufficiently strong to work beneath the surface, subconsciously. What we are every moment is determined by the sum total of these impressions on the mind. What I am just at this moment is the effect of the sum total of all the impressions of my past life. This is really what is meant by character; each man's character is determined by the sum total of these impressions. If good impressions prevail, the character becomes good; if bad, it becomes bad. If a man continuously hears bad words, thinks bad thoughts, does bad actions, his mind will be full of bad impressions; and they will influence his thought and work without his being conscious of the fact. In fact, these bad impressions are always working, and their resultant must be evil, and that man will be a bad man; he cannot help it. The sum total of these impressions in him will create the strong motive power for doing bad actions. He will be like a machine in the hands of his impressions, and they will force him to do evil. Similarly, if a man thinks good thoughts and does good works, the sum total of these impressions will be good; and they, in a similar manner, will force him to do good even in spite of himself. When a man has done so much good work and thought so many good thoughts that there is an irresistible tendency in him to do good in spite of himself and even if he wishes to do evil, his mind, as the sum total of his tendencies, will not allow him to do so; the tendencies will turn him back; he is completely under the influence of the good tendencies. When such is the case, a man's good character is said to be established.

As the tortoise tucks its feet and head inside the shell, and you may kill it and break it in pieces, and yet it will not come out, even so the character of that man who has control over his motives and organs is unchangeably established. He controls his own inner forces, and nothing can draw them out against his will. By this continuous reflex of good thoughts, good impressions moving over the surface of the mind, the tendency for doing good becomes strong, and as the result we feel able to control the Indriyas (the sense-organs, the nerve-centres). Thus alone will character be established, then alone a man gets to truth. Such a man is safe for ever; he cannot do any evil. You may place him in any company, there will be no danger for him. There is a still higher state than having this good tendency, and that is the desire for liberation. You must remember that freedom of the soul is the goal of all Yogas, and each one equally leads to the same result. By work alone men may get to where Buddha got largely by meditation or Christ by prayer. Buddha was a working Jnani, Christ was a Bhakta, but the same goal was reached by both of them. The difficulty is here. Liberation means entire freedom—freedom from the bondage of good, as well as from the bondage of evil. A golden chain is as much a chain as an iron one. There is a thorn in my finger, and I use another to take the first one out; and when I have taken it out, I throw both of them aside; I have no necessity for keeping the second thorn, because both are thorns after all. So the bad tendencies are to be counteracted by the good ones, and the bad impressions on the mind should be removed by the fresh waves of good ones, until all that is evil almost disappears, or is subdued and held in control in a corner of the mind; but after that, the good tendencies have also to be conquered. Thus the 'attached' becomes the 'unattached'. Work, but let not the action or the thought produce a deep impression on the mind. Let the ripples come and go, let huge actions proceed from the muscles and the brain, but let them not make any deep impression on the soul.

How can this be done? We see that the impression of any action, to which we attach ourselves, remains. I may meet hundreds of persons during the day, and among them meet also one whom I love; and when I retire at night, I may try to think of all the faces I saw, but only that face comes before the mind—the face which I met perhaps only for one minute, and which I loved; all the others have vanished. My attachment to this particular person caused a deeper impression on my mind than all the other faces. Physiologically the impressions have all been the same; every one of the faces that I saw pictured itself on the retina, and the brain took the pictures in, and yet there was no similarity of effect upon the mind. Most of the faces, perhaps, were entirely new faces, about which I had never thought before, but that one face of which I got only a glimpse found associations inside. Perhaps I had pictured him in my mind for years, knew hundreds of things about him, and this one new vision of him awakened hundreds of sleeping memories in my mind; and this one impression having been repeated perhaps a hundred times more than those of the different faces together, will produce a great effect on the mind.

Therefore, be 'unattached'; let things work; let brain centres work; work incessantly, but let not a ripple conquer the mind. Work as if you were a stranger in this land, a sojourner; work incessantly, but do not bind yourselves; bondage is terrible. This world is not our habitation, it is only one of the many stages through which we are passing. Remember that great saying of the Sankhya, 'The whole of nature is for the soul, not the soul for nature.' The very reason of nature's existence is for the education of the soul; it has no other meaning; it is there because the soul must have knowledge, and through knowledge free itself. If we remember this always, we shall never be attached to nature; we shall know that nature is a book in which we are to read, and that when we have gained the required knowledge, the book is of no more value to us. Instead of that, however, we are identifying ourselves with nature; we are thinking that the soul is for nature, that the spirit is for the flesh, and, as the common saying has it, we think that man 'lives to eat' and not 'eats to live'. We are continually making this mistake; we are regarding nature as ourselves and are becoming attached to it; and as soon as this attachment comes, there is the deep impression on the soul, which binds us down and makes us work not from freedom but like slaves.

The whole gist of this teaching is that you should work like a master and not as a slave; work incessantly, but do not do slave's work. Do you not see how everybody works? Nobody can be altogether at rest; ninety-nine per cent of mankind work like slaves, and the result is misery; it is all selfish work. Work through freedom! Work through love! The word 'love' is very difficult to understand; love never comes until there is freedom. There is no true love possible in the slave. If you buy a slave and tie him down in chains and make him work for you, he will work like a drudge, but there will be no love in him. So when we ourselves work for the things of the world as slaves, there can be no love in us, and our work is not true work. This is true of work done for relatives and friends, and is true of work done for our own selves. Selfish work is slave's work; and here is a test. Every act of love brings happiness; there is no act of love which does not bring peace and blessedness as its reaction. Real existence, real knowledge, and real love are eternally connected with one another, the three in one: where one of them is, the others also must be; they are the three aspects of the One without a second—the Existence-Knowledge-Bliss. When that existence becomes relative, we see it as the world; that knowledge becomes in its turn modified into the knowledge of the things of the world; and that bliss forms the foundation of all true love known to the heart of man. Therefore, true love can never react so as to cause pain either to the lover or to the beloved. Suppose a man loves a woman; he wishes to have her all to himself and feels extremely jealous about her every movement; he wants her to sit near him, to stand near him, and to eat and move at his bidding. He is a slave to her and wishes to have her as his slave. That is not love; it is a kind of morbid affection of the slave, insinuating itself as love. It cannot be love, because it is painful; if she does not do what he wants, it brings him pain. With love there is no painful reaction; love only brings a reaction of bliss; if it does not, it is not love; it is mistaking something else for love. When you have succeeded in loving your husband, your wife, your children, the whole world, the universe, in such a manner that there is no reaction of pain or jealousy, no selfish feeling, then you are in a fit state to be unattached.

Krishna says, 'Look at Me, Arjuna! If I stop from work for one moment, the whole universe will die. I have nothing to gain from work; I am the one Lord, but why do I work? Because I love the world.' God is unattached because He loves; that real love makes us unattached. Wherever there is attachment, the clinging to the things of the world, you must know that it is all physical attraction between sets of particles of matter—something that attracts two bodies nearer and nearer all the time and, if they cannot get near enough, produces pain; but where there is real love, it does not rest on physical attachment at all. Such lovers may be a thousand miles away from one another, but their love will be all the same; it does not die, and will never produce any painful reaction.

To attain this unattachment is almost a life-work, but as soon as we have reached this point, we have attained the goal of love and become free; the bondage of nature falls from us, and we see nature as she is; she forges no more chains for us; we stand entirely free and take not the results of work into consideration; who then cares for what the results may be?

Do you ask anything from your children in return for what you have given them? It is your duty to work for them, and there the matter ends. In whatever you do for a particular person, a city, or a state, assume the same attitude towards it as you have towards your children—expect nothing in return. If you can invariably take the position of a giver, in which everything given by you is a free offering to the world, without any thought of return, then will your work bring you no attachment. Attachment comes only where we expect a return.

If working like slaves results in selfishness and attachment, working as master of our own mind gives rise to the bliss of non-attachment. We often talk of right and justice, but we find that in the world right and justice are mere baby's talk. There are two things which guide the conduct of men: might and mercy. The exercise of might is invariably the exercise of selfishness. All men and women try to make the most of whatever power or advantage they have. Mercy is heaven itself; to be good, we have all to be merciful. Even justice and right should stand on mercy. All thought of obtaining return for the work we do hinders our spiritual progress; nay, in the end it brings misery. There is another way in which this idea of mercy and selfless charity can be put into practise; that is, by looking upon work as 'worship' in case we believe in a Personal God. Here we give up all the fruits our work unto the Lord, and worshipping Him thus, we have no right to expect anything from man kind for the work we do. The Lord Himself works incessantly and is ever without attachment. Just as water cannot wet the lotus leaf, so work cannot bind the unselfish man by giving rise to attachment to results. The selfless and unattached man may live in the very heart of a crowded and sinful city; he will not be touched by sin.

This idea of complete self-sacrifice is illustrated in the following story: After the battle of Kurukshetra the five Pandava brothers performed a great sacrifice and made very large gifts to the poor. All people expressed amazement at the greatness and richness of the sacrifice, and said that such a sacrifice the world had never seen before. But, after the ceremony, there came a little mongoose, half of whose body was golden, and the other half brown; and he began to roll on the floor of the sacrificial hall. He said to those around, 'You are all liars; this is no sacrifice.' 'What!' they exclaimed, 'you say this is no sacrifice; do you not know how money and jewels were poured out to the poor and every one became rich and happy? This was the most wonderful sacrifice any man ever performed.' But the mongoose said, 'There was once a little village, and in it there dwelt a poor Brahmin with his wife, his son, and his son's wife. They were very poor and lived on small gifts made to them for preaching and teaching. There came in that land a three years' famine, and the poor Brahmin suffered more than ever. At last when the family had starved for days, the father brought home one morning a little barley flour, which he had been fortunate enough to obtain, and he divided it into four parts, one for each member of the family. They prepared it for their meal, and just as they were about to eat, there was a knock at the door. The father opened it, and there stood a guest. Now in India a guest is a sacred person; he is as a god for the time being, and must be treated as such. So the poor Brahmin said, 'Come in, sir; you are welcome,' He set before the guest his own portion of the food, which the guest quickly ate and said, 'Oh, sir, you have killed me; I have been starving for ten days, and this little bit has but increased my hunger.' Then the wife said to her husband, 'Give him my share,' but the husband said, 'Not so.' The wife however insisted, saying, 'Here is a poor man, and it is our duty as householders to see that he is fed, and it is my duty as a wife to give him my portion, seeing that you have no more to offer him.' Then she gave her share to the guest, which he ate, and said he was still burning with hunger. So the son said, 'Take my portion also; it is the duty of a son to help his father to fulfil his obligations.' The guest ate that, but remained still unsatisfied; so the son's wife gave him her portion also. That was sufficient, and the guest departed, blessing them. That night those four people died of starvation. A few granules of that flour had fallen on the floor; and when I rolled my body on them, half of it became golden, as you see. Since then I have been travelling all over the world, hoping to find another sacrifice like that, but nowhere have I found one; nowhere else has the other half of my body been turned into gold. That is why I say this is no sacrifice.'

This idea of charity is going out of India; great men are becoming fewer and fewer. When I was first learning English, I read an English story book in which there was a story about a dutiful boy who had gone out to work and had given some of his money to his old mother, and this was praised in three or four pages. What was that? No Hindu boy can ever understand the moral of that story. Now I understand it when I hear the Western idea—every man for himself. And some men take everything for themselves, and fathers and mothers and wives and children go to the wall. That should never and nowhere be the ideal of the householder.

Now you see what Karma-Yoga means; even at the point of death to help any one, without asking questions. Be cheated millions of times and never ask a question, and never think of what you are doing. Never vaunt of your gifts to the poor or expect their gratitude, but rather be grateful to them for giving you the occasion of practising charity to them. Thus, it is plain that to be an ideal householder is a much more difficult task than to be an ideal Sannyasin; the true life of work is indeed as hard as, if not harder than, the equally true life of renunciation.

10

WHAT IS DUTY?

It is necessary in the study of Karma-Yoga to know what duty is. If I have to do something I must first know that it is my duty, and then I can do it. The idea of duty again is different in different nations. The Mohammedan says what is written in his book, the Koran, is his duty; the Hindu says what is in the Vedas is his duty; and the Christian says what is in the Bible is his duty. We find that there are varied ideas of duty, differing according to different states in life, different historical periods and different nations. The term 'duty', like every other universal abstract term, is impossible clearly to define; we can only get an idea of it by knowing its practical operations and results. When certain things occur before us, we have all a natural or trained impulse to act in a certain manner towards them; when this impulse comes, the mind begins to think about the situation. Sometimes it thinks that it is good to act in a particular manner under the given conditions; at other times it thinks that it is wrong to act in the same manner even in the very same circumstances. The ordinary idea of duty everywhere is that every good man follows the dictates of his conscience. But what is it that makes an act a duty? If a Christian finds a piece of beef before him and does not eat it to save his own life, or will not give it to save the life of another man, he is sure to feel that he has not done his duty. But if a Hindu dares to eat that piece of beef or to give it to another Hindu, he is equally sure to feel that he too has not done his duty; the Hindu's training and education make him feel that way. In the last century there were notorious bands of robbers in India called thugs; they thought it their duty to kill any man they could and take away his money; the larger the number of men they killed, the better they thought they were. Ordinarily if a man goes out into the street and shoots down another man, he is apt to feel sorry for it, thinking that he has done wrong. But if the very same man, as a soldier in his regiment, kills not one but twenty, he is certain to feel glad and think that he has done his duty remarkably well. Therefore we see that it is not the thing done that defines a duty. To give an objective definition of duty is thus entirely impossible. Yet there is duty from the subjective side. Any action that makes us go Godward is a good action, and is our duty; any action that makes us go downward is evil, and is not our duty. From the subjective standpoint we may see that certain acts have a tendency to exalt and ennoble us, while certain other acts have a tendency to degrade and to brutalize us. But it is not possible to make out with certainty which acts have which kind of tendency in relation to all persons, of all sorts and conditions. There is, however, only one idea of duty which has been universally accepted by all mankind, of all ages and sects and countries, and that has been summed up in a Sanskrit aphorism thus: 'Do not injure any being; not injuring any being is virtue, injuring any being is sin.'

The Bhagavad Gita frequently alludes to duties dependent upon birth and position in life. Birth and position in life and in society largely determine the mental and moral attitude of individuals towards the various activities of life. It is therefore our duty to do that work which will exalt and ennoble us in accordance with the ideals and activities of the society in which we are born. But it must be particularly remembered that the same ideals and activities do not prevail in all societies and countries; our ignorance of this is the main cause of much of the hatred of one nation towards another. An American thinks that whatever an American does in accordance with the custom of his country is the best thing to do, and that whoever does not follow his custom must be a very wicked man. A Hindu thinks that his customs are the only right ones and are the best in the world, and that whosoever does not obey them must be the most wicked man living. This is quite a natural mistake which all of us are apt to make. But it is very harmful; it is the cause of half the uncharitableness found in the world. When I came to this country and was going through the Chicago Fair, a man from behind pulled at my turban. I looked back and saw that he was a very gentlemanly-looking man, neatly dressed. I spoke to him; and when he found that I knew English, he became very much abashed. On another occasion in the same Fair, another man gave me a push. When I asked him the reason, he also was ashamed and stammered out an apology saying, 'Why do you dress that way?' The sympathies of these men were limited within the range of their own language and their own fashion of dress. Much of the oppression of powerful nations on weaker ones is caused by this prejudice. It dries up their fellow feeling for fellow men. That very man who asked me why I did not dress as he did and wanted to ill-treat me because of my dress may have been a very good man, a good father, and a good citizen; but the kindliness of his nature died out as soon as he saw a man in a different dress. Strangers are exploited in all countries, because they do not know how to defend themselves; thus they carry home false impressions of the peoples they have seen. Sailors, soldiers, and traders behave in foreign lands in very queer ways, although they would not dream of doing so in their own country; perhaps this is why the Chinese call Europeans and Americans 'foreign devils'. They could not have done this if they had met the good, the kindly sides of Western life.

Therefore, the one point we ought to remember is that we should always try to see the duty of others through their own eyes, and never judge the customs of other peoples by our own standard. I am not the standard of the universe. I have to accommodate myself to the world, and not the world to me. So we see that environments change the nature of our duties, and doing the duty which is ours at any particular time is the best thing we can do in this world. Let us do that duty which is ours by birth; and when we have done that, let us do the duty which is ours by our position in life and in society. There is, however, one great danger in human nature, viz that man never examines himself. He thinks he is quite as fit to be on the throne as the king. Even if he is, he must first show that he has done the duty of his own position; and then higher duties will come to him. When we begin to work earnestly in the world, nature gives us blows right and left and soon enables us to find out our position. No man can long occupy satisfactorily a position for which he is not fit. There is no use in grumbling against nature's adjustment. He who does the lower work is not therefore a lower man. No man is to be judged by the mere nature of his duties, but all should be judged by the manner and the spirit in which they perform them.

Later on we shall find that even this idea of duty undergoes change, and that the greatest work is done only when there is no selfish motive to prompt it. Yet it is work through the sense of duty that leads us to work without any idea of duty; when work will become worship—nay, something higher—then will work be done for its own sake. We shall find that the philosophy of duty, whether it be in the form of ethics or of love, is the same as in every other Yoga—the object being the attenuating of the lower self, so that the real higher Self may shine forth—the lessening of the frittering away of energies on the lower plane of existence, so that the soul may manifest itself on the higher ones. This is accomplished by the continuous denial of low desires, which duty rigorously requires. The whole organization of society has thus been developed, consciously or unconsciously, in the realms of action and experience, where, by limiting selfishness, we open the way to an unlimited expansion of the real nature of man.

Duty is seldom sweet. It is only when love greases its wheels that it runs smoothly; it is a continuous friction otherwise. How else could parents do their duties to their children, husbands to their wives, and vice versa? Do we not meet with cases of friction every day in our lives? Duty is sweet only through love, and love shines in freedom alone. Yet is it freedom to be a slave to the senses, to anger, to jealousies and a hundred other petty things that must occur every day in human life? In all these little roughnesses that we meet with in life, the highest expression of freedom is to forbear. Women, slaves to their own irritable, jealous tempers, are apt to blame their husbands, and assert their own 'freedom', as they think, not knowing that thereby they only prove that they are slaves. So it is with husbands who eternally find fault with their wives.

Chastity is the first virtue in man or woman, and the man who, however he may have strayed away, cannot be brought to the right path by a gentle and loving and chaste wife is indeed very rare. The world is not yet as bad as that. We hear much about brutal husbands all over the world and about the impurity of men, but is it not true that there are quite as many brutal and impure women as men? If all women were as good and pure as their own constant assertions would lead one to believe, I am perfectly satisfied that there would not be one impure man in the world. What brutality is there which purity and chastity cannot conquer? A good, chaste wife, who thinks of every other man except her own husband as her child and has the attitude of a mother towards all men, will grow so great in the power of her purity that there cannot be a single man, however brutal, who will not breathe an atmosphere of holiness in her presence. Similarly, every husband must look upon all women, except his own wife, in the light of his own mother or daughter or sister. That man, again, who wants to be a teacher of religion must look upon every woman as his mother, and always behave towards her as such.

The position of the mother is the highest in the world, as it is the one place in which to learn and exercise the greatest unselfishness. The love of God is the only love that is higher than a mother's love; all others are lower. It is the duty of the mother to think of her children first and then of herself. But, instead of that, if the parents are always thinking of themselves first, the result is that the relation between parents and children becomes the same as that between birds and their offspring which, as soon as they are fledged, do not recognize any parents. Blessed, indeed, is the man who is able to look upon woman as the representative of the motherhood of God. Blessed, indeed, is the woman to whom man represents the fatherhood of God. Blessed are the children who look upon their parents as Divinity manifested on earth.

The only way to rise is by doing the duty next to us, and thus gathering strength, go on until we reach the highest state. A young Sannyasin went to a forest; there he meditated, worshipped, and practised Yoga for a long time. After years of hard work and practise, he was one day sitting under a tree, when some dry leaves fell upon his head. He looked up and saw a crow and a crane fighting on the top of the tree, which made him very angry. He said, 'What! Dare you throw these dry leaves upon my head!' As with these words he angrily glanced at them, a flash of fire went out of his head—such was the Yogi's power—and burnt the birds to ashes. He was very glad, almost overjoyed at this development of power—he could burn the crow and the crane by a look. After a time he had to go to the town to beg his bread. He went, stood at a door, and said, 'Mother, give me food.' A voice came from inside the house, 'Wait a little, my son.' The young man thought, 'You wretched woman, how dare you make me wait! You do not know my power yet.' While he was thinking thus the voice came again: 'Boy, don't be thinking too much of yourself. Here is neither crow nor crane.' He was astonished; still he had to wait. At last the woman came, and he fell at her feet and said, 'Mother, how did you know that?' She said, 'My boy, I do not know your Yoga or your practises. I am a common everyday woman. I made you wait because my husband is ill, and I was nursing him. All my life I have struggled to do my duty. When I was unmarried, I did my duty to my parents; now that I am married, I do my duty to my husband; that is all the Yoga I practise. But by doing my duty I have become illumined; thus I could read your thoughts and know what you had done in the forest. If you want to know something higher than this, go to the market of such and such a town where you will find a Vyadha (The lowest class of people in India who used to live as hunters and butchers.) who will tell you something that you will be very glad to learn.' The Sannyasin thought, 'Why should I go to that town and to a Vyadha?' But after what he had seen, his mind opened a little, so he went. When he came near the town, he found the market and there saw, at a distance, a big fat Vyadha cutting meat with big knives, talking and bargaining with different people. The young man said, 'Lord help me! Is this the man from whom I am going to learn? He is the incarnation of a demon, if he is anything.' In the meantime this man looked up and said, 'O Swami, did that lady send you here? Take a seat until I have done my business.' The Sannyasin thought, 'What comes to me here?' He took his seat; the man went on with his work, and after he had finished he took his money and said to the Sannyasin, 'Come sir, come to my home.' On reaching home the Vyadha gave him a seat, saying, 'Wait here,' and went into the house. He then washed his old father and mother, fed them, and did all he could to please them, after which he came to the Sannyasin and said, 'Now, sir, you have come here to see me; what can I do for you?' The Sannyasin asked him a few questions about soul and about

God, and the Vyadha gave him a lecture which forms a part of the Mahabharata, called the Vyadha-Gita. It contains one of the highest flights of the Vedanta. When the Vyadha finished his teaching, the Sannyasin felt astonished. He said, 'Why are you in that body? With such knowledge as yours why are you in a Vyadha's body, and doing such filthy, ugly work?' 'My son,' replied the Vyadha, 'no duty is ugly, no duty is impure. My birth placed me in these circumstances and environments. In my boyhood I learnt the trade; I am unattached, and I try to do my duty well. I try to do my duty as a householder, and I try to do all I can to make my father and mother happy. I neither know your Yoga, nor have I become a Sannyasin, nor did I go out of the world into a forest; nevertheless, all that you have heard and seen has come to me through the unattached doing of the duty which belongs to my position.'

There is a sage in India, a great Yogi, one of the most wonderful men I have ever seen in my life. He is a peculiar man, he will not teach any one; if you ask him a question he will not answer. It is too much for him to take up the position of a teacher, he will not do it. If you ask a question, and wait for some days, in the course of conversation he will bring up the subject, and wonderful light will he throw on it. He told me once the secret of work, 'Let the end and the means be joined into one.' When you are doing any work, do not think of anything beyond. Do it as worship, as the highest worship, and devote your whole life to it for the time being. Thus, in the story, the Vyadha and the woman did their duty with cheerfulness and whole-heartedness; and the result was that they became illuminated, clearly showing that the right performance of the duties of any station in life, without attachment to results, leads us to the highest realization of the perfection of the soul.

It is the worker who is attached to results that grumbles about the nature of the duty which has fallen to his lot; to the unattached worker all duties are equally good, and form efficient instruments with which selfishness and sensuality may be killed, and the freedom of the soul secured. We are all apt to think too highly of ourselves. Our duties are determined by our deserts to a much larger extent than we are willing to grant. Competition rouses envy, and it kills the kindliness of the heart. To the grumbler all duties are distasteful; nothing will ever satisfy him, and his whole life is doomed to prove a failure. Let us work on, doing as we go whatever happens to be our duty, and being ever ready to put our shoulders to the wheel. Then surely shall we see the Light!

11

WE HELP OURSELVES, NOT THE WORLD

Before considering further how devotion to duty helps us in our spiritual progress, let me place before you in a brief compass another aspect of what we in India mean by Karma. In every religion there are three parts: Philosophy, mythology, and ritual. Philosophy of course is the essence of every religion; mythology explains and illustrates it by means of the more or less legendary lives of great men, stories and fables of wonderful things, and so on; ritual gives to that philosophy a still more concrete form, so that every one may grasp it—ritual is in fact concretized philosophy. This ritual is Karma; it is necessary in every religion, because most of us cannot understand abstract spiritual things until we grow much spiritually. It is easy for men to think that they can understand anything; but when it comes to practical experience, they find that abstract ideas are often very hard to comprehend. Therefore, symbols are of great help, and we cannot dispense with the symbolical method of putting things before us. From time immemorial, symbols have been used by all kinds of religions. In one sense we cannot think but in symbols; words themselves are symbols of thought. In another sense everything in the universe may be looked upon as a symbol. The whole universe is a symbol, and God is the essence behind. This kind of symbology is not simply the creation of man; it is not that certain people belonging to a religion sit down together and think out certain symbols, and bring them into existence out of their own minds. The symbols of religion have a natural growth. Otherwise, why is it that certain symbols are associated with certain ideas in the mind of almost every one? Certain symbols are universally prevalent. Many of you may think that the cross first came into existence as a symbol in connection with the Christian religion, but as a matter of fact it existed before Christianity was, before Moses was born, before the Vedas were given out, before there was any human record of human things. The cross may be found to have been in existence among the Aztecs and the Phoenicians; every race seems to have had the cross. Again, the symbol of the crucified Saviour, of a man crucified upon a cross, appears to have been known to almost every nation. The circle has been a great symbol throughout the world. Then there is the most universal of all symbols, the Swastika.

At one time it was thought that the Buddhists carried it all over the world with them, but it has been found out that ages before Buddhism it was used among nations. In Old Babylon and in Egypt it was to be found. What does this show? All these symbols could not have been purely conventional. There must be some reason for them; some natural association between them and the human mind. Language is not the result of convention; it is not that people ever agreed to represent certain ideas by certain words; there never was an idea without a corresponding word or a word without a corresponding idea; ideas and words are in their nature inseparable. The symbols to represent ideas may be sound symbols or colour symbols. Deaf and dumb people have to think with other than sound symbols. Every thought in the mind has a form as its counterpart. This is called in Sanskrit philosophy Nama-Rupa—name and form. It is as impossible to create by convention a system of symbols as it is to create a language. In the world's ritualistic symbols we have an expression of the religious thought of humanity. It is easy to say that there is no use of rituals and temples and all such paraphernalia; every baby says that in modern times. But it must be easy for all to see that those who worship inside a temple are in many respects different from those who will not worship there. Therefore the association of particular temples, rituals, and other concrete forms with particular religions has a tendency to bring into the minds of the followers of those religions the thoughts for which those concrete things stand as symbols; and it is not wise to ignore rituals and symbology altogether. The study and practise of these things form naturally a part of Karma-Yoga.

There are many other aspects of this science of work. One among the relation between thought and word and what can the power of the word. In every religion the power recognized, so much so that in some of them creation itself is said to have come out of the word. The external aspect of the thought of God is the Word, and as God thought and willed before He created, creation came out of the Word. In this stress and hurry of our materialistic life, our nerves lose sensibility and become hardened. The older we grow, the longer we are knocked about in the world, the more callous we become; and we are apt to neglect things that even happen persistently and prominently around us. Human nature, however, asserts itself sometimes, and we are led to inquire into and wonder at some of these common occurrences; wondering thus is the first step in the acquisition of light. Apart from the higher philosophic and religious value of the Word, we may see that sound symbols play a prominent part in the drama of human life. I am talking to you. I am not touching you; the pulsations of the air caused by my speaking go into your ear, they touch your nerves and produce effects in your minds. You cannot resist this. What can be more wonderful than this? One man calls another a fool, and at this the other stands up and clenches his fist and lands a blow on his nose. Look at the power of the word! There is a woman weeping and miserable; another woman comes along and speaks to her a few gentle words, the doubled up frame of the weeping woman becomes straightened at once, her sorrow is gone and she already begins to smile. Think of the power of words! They are a great force in higher philosophy as well as in common life. Day and night we manipulate this force without thought and without inquiry. To know the nature of this force and to use it well is also a part of Karma-Yoga.

Our duty to others means helping others; doing good to the world. Why should we do good to the world? Apparently to help the world, but really to help ourselves. We should always try to help the world, that should be the highest motive in us; but if we consider well, we find that the world does not require our help at all. This world was not made that you or I should come and help it. I once read a sermon in which it was said, 'All this beautiful world is very good, because it gives us time and opportunity to help others.' Apparently, this is a very beautiful sentiment, but is it not a blasphemy to say that the world needs our help? We cannot deny that there is much misery in it; to go out and help others is, therefore, the best thing we can do, although in the long run, we shall find that helping others is only helping ourselves. As a boy I had some white mice. They were kept in a little box in which there were little wheels, and when the mice tried to cross the wheels, the wheels turned and turned, and the mice never got anywhere. So it is with the world and our helping it. The only help is that we get moral exercise. This world is neither good nor evil; each man manufactures a world for himself. If a blind man begins to think of the world, it is either as soft or hard, or as cold or hot. We are a mass of happiness or misery; we have seen that hundreds of times in our lives. As a rule, the young are optimistic and the old pessimistic. The young have life before them; the old complain their day is gone; hundreds of desires, which they cannot fulfil struggle in their hearts. Both are foolish nevertheless. Life is good or evil according to the state of mind in which we look at it, it is neither by itself. Fire, by itself, is neither good nor evil. When it keeps us warm we say, 'How beautiful is fire!' When it burns our fingers, we blame it. Still, in itself it is neither good nor bad. According as we use it, it produces in us the feeling of good or bad; so also is this world. It is perfect. By perfection is meant that it is perfectly fitted to meet its ends. We may all be perfectly sure that it will go on beautifully well without us, and we need not bother our heads wishing to help it.

Yet we must do good; the desire to do good is the highest motive power we have, if we know all the time that it is a privilege to help others. Do not stand on a high pedestal and take five cents in your hand and say, 'Here, my poor man,' but be grateful that the poor man is there, so that by making a gift to him you are able to help yourself. It is not the receiver that is blessed, but it is the giver. Be thankful that you are allowed to exercise your power of benevolence and mercy in the world, and thus become pure and perfect. All good acts tend to make us pure and perfect. What can we do at best? Build a hospital, make roads, or erect charity asylums. We may organize a charity and collect two or three millions of dollars, build a hospital with one million, with the second give balls and drink champagne, and of the third let the officers steal half, and leave the rest finally to reach the poor; but what are all these? One mighty wind in five minutes can break all your buildings up. What shall we do then? One volcanic eruption may sweep away all our roads and hospitals and cities and buildings. Let us give up all this foolish talk of doing good to the world. It is not waiting for your or my help; yet we must work and constantly do good, because it is a blessing to ourselves. That is the only way we can become perfect. No beggar whom we have helped has ever owed a single cent to us; we owe everything to him, because he has allowed us to exercise our charity on him. It is entirely wrong to think that we have done, or can do, good to the world, or to think that we have helped such and such people. It is a foolish thought, and all foolish thoughts bring misery. We think that we have helped some man and expect him to thank us, and because he does not, unhappiness comes to us. Why should we expect anything in return for what we do? Be grateful to the man you help, think of him as God. Is it not a great privilege to be allowed to worship God by helping our fellow men? If we were really unattached, we should escape all this pain of vain expectation, and could cheerfully do good work in the world. Never will unhappiness or misery come through work done without attachment. The world will go on with its happiness and misery through eternity.

There was a poor man who wanted some money; and somehow he had heard that if he could get hold of a ghost, he might command him to bring money or anything else he liked; so he was very anxious to get hold of a ghost. He went about searching for a man who would give him a ghost, and at last he found a sage with great powers, and besought his help. The sage asked him what he would do with a ghost. I want a ghost to work for me; teach me how to get hold of one, sir; I desire it very much,' replied the man. But the sage said, 'Don't disturb yourself, go home.' The next day the man went again to the sage and began to weep and pray, 'Give me a ghost; I must have a ghost, sir, to help me.' At last the sage was disgusted, and said, 'Take this charm, repeat this magic word, and a ghost will come, and whatever you say to him he will do. But beware; they are terrible beings, and must be kept continually busy. If you fail to give him work, he will take your life.' The man replied, 'That is easy; I can give him work for all his life.' Then he went to a forest, and after long repetition of the magic word, a huge ghost appeared before him, and said, 'I am a ghost. I have been conquered by your magic; but you must keep me constantly employed. The moment you fail to give me work I will kill you.' The man said, 'Build me a palace,' and the ghost said, 'It is done; the palace is built.' 'Bring me money,' said the man. 'Here is your money,' said the ghost. 'Cut this forest down, and build a city in its place.' 'That is done,' said the ghost, 'anything more?' Now the man began to be frightened and thought he could give him nothing more to do; he did everything in a trice. The ghost said, 'Give me something to do or I will eat you up.' The poor man could find no further occupation for him, and was frightened. So he ran and ran and at last reached the sage, and said, 'Oh, sir, protect my life!' The sage asked him what the matter was, and the man replied, 'I have nothing to give the ghost to do. Everything I tell him to do he does in a moment, and he threatens to eat me up if I do not give him work.' Just then the ghost arrived, saying, 'I'll eat you up,' and he would have swallowed the man. The man began to shake, and begged the sage to save his life. The sage said, 'I will find you a way out. Look at that dog with a curly tail. Draw your sword quickly and cut the tail off and give it to the ghost to straighten out.' The man cut off the dog's tail and gave it to the ghost, saying, 'Straighten that out for me.' The ghost took it and slowly and carefully straightened it out, but as soon as he let it go, it instantly curled up again. Once more he laboriously straightened it out, only to find it again curled up as soon as he attempted to let go of it. Again he patiently straightened it out, but as soon as he let it go, it curled up again. So he went on for days and days, until he was exhausted and said, 'I was never in such trouble before in my life. I am an old veteran ghost, but never before was I in such trouble.' 'I will make a compromise with you;' he said to the man, 'you let me off and I will let you keep all I have given you and will promise not to harm you.' The man was much pleased, and accepted the offer gladly.

This world is like a dog's curly tail, and people have been striving to straighten it out for hundreds of years; but when they let it go, it has curled up again. How could it be otherwise? One must first know how to work without attachment, then one will not be a fanatic. When we know that this world is like a dog's curly tail and will never get straightened, we shall not become fanatics. If there were no fanaticism in the world, it would make much more progress than it does now. It is a mistake to think that fanaticism can make for the progress of mankind. On the contrary, it is a retarding element creating hatred and anger, and causing people to fight each other, and making them unsympathetic. We think that whatever we do or possess is the best in the world, and what we do not do or possess is of no value. So, always remember the instance of the curly tail of the dog whenever you have a tendency to become a fanatic. You need not worry or make yourself sleepless about the world; it will go on without you. When you have avoided fanaticism, then alone will you work well. It is the level-headed man, the calm man, of good judgment and cool nerves, of great sympathy and love, who does good work and so does good to himself. The fanatic is foolish and has no sympathy; he can never straighten the world, nor himself become pure and perfect.

To recapitulate the chief points in today's lecture: First, we have to bear in mind that we are all debtors to the world and the world does not owe us anything. It is a great privilege for all of us to be allowed to do anything for the world. In helping the world we really help ourselves. The second point is that there is a God in this universe. It is not true that this universe is drifting and stands in need of help from you and me. God is ever present therein, He is undying and eternally active and infinitely watchful. When the whole universe sleeps, He sleeps not; He is working incessantly; all the changes and manifestations of the world are His. Thirdly, we ought not to hate anyone. This world will always continue to be a mixture of good and evil. Our duty is to sympathize with the weak and to love even the wrongdoer. The world is a grand moral gymnasium wherein we have all to take exercise so as to become stronger and stronger spiritually. Fourthly, we ought not to be fanatics of any kind, because fanaticism is opposed to love. You hear fanatics glibly saying, 'I do not hate the sinner. I hate the sin,' but I am prepared to go any distance to see the face of that man who can really make a distinction between the sin and the sinner. It is easy to say so. If we can distinguish well between quality and substance, we may become perfect men. It is not easy to do this. And further, the calmer we are and the less disturbed our nerves, the more shall we love and the better will our work be.

12

NON-ATTACHMENT IS
THE COMPLETE SELF-ABNEGATION

Just as every action that emanates from us comes back to us as reaction, even so our actions may act on other people and theirs on us. Perhaps all of you have observed it as a fact that when persons do evil actions, they become more and more evil, and when they begin to do good, they become stronger and stronger and learn to do good at all times. This intensification of the influence of action cannot be explained on any other ground than that we can act and react upon each other. To take an illustration from physical science, when I am doing a certain action, my mind may be said to be in a certain state of vibration; all minds which are in similar circumstances will have the tendency to be affected by my mind. If there are different musical instruments tuned alike in one room, all of you may have noticed that when one is struck, the others have the tendency to vibrate so as to give the same note. So all minds that have the same tension, so to say, will be equally affected by the same thought. Of course, this influence of thought on mind will vary according to distance and other causes, but the mind is always open to affection. Suppose I am doing an evil act, my mind is in a certain state of vibration, and all minds in the universe, which are in a similar state, have the possibility of being affected by the vibration of my mind. So, when I am doing a good action, my mind is in another state of vibration; and all minds similarly strung have the possibility of being affected by my mind; and this power of mind upon mind is more or less according as the force of the tension is greater or less.

Following this simile further, it is quite possible that, just as light waves may travel for millions of years before they reach any object, so thought waves may also travel hundreds of years before they meet an object with which they vibrate in unison. It is quite possible, therefore, that this atmosphere of ours is full of such thought pulsations, both good and evil. Every thought projected from every brain goes on pulsating, as it were, until it meets a fit object that will receive it. Any mind which is open to receive some of these impulses will take them immediately. So, when a man is doing evil actions, he has brought his mind to a certain state of tension and all the waves which correspond to that state of tension, and which may be said to be already in the atmosphere, will struggle to enter into his mind. That is why an evil-doer generally goes on doing more and more evil. His actions become intensified. Such, also will be the case with the doer of good; he will open himself to all the good waves that are in the atmosphere, and his good actions also will become intensified. We run, therefore, a twofold danger in doing evil: first, we open ourselves to all the evil influences surrounding us; secondly, we create evil which affects others, may be hundreds of years hence. In doing evil we injure ourselves and others also. In doing good we do good to ourselves and to others as well; and, like all other forces in man, these forces of good and evil also gather strength from outside.

According to Karma-Yoga, the action one has done cannot be destroyed until it has borne its fruit; no power in nature can stop it from yielding its results. If I do an evil action, I must suffer for it; there is no power in this universe to stop or stay it. Similarly, if I do a good action, there is no power in the universe which can stop its bearing good results. The cause must have its effect; nothing can prevent or restrain this. Now comes a very fine and serious question about Karma-Yoga—namely, that these actions of ours, both good and evil, are intimately connected with each other. We cannot put a line of demarcation and say, this action is entirely good and this entirely evil. There is no action which does not bear good and evil fruits at the same time. To take the nearest example: I am talking to you, and some of you, perhaps, think I am doing good; and at the same time I am, perhaps, killing thousands of microbes in the atmosphere; I am thus doing evil to something else. When it is very near to us and affects those we know, we say that it is very good action if it affects them in a good manner. For instance, you may call my speaking to you very good, but the microbes will not; the microbes you do not see, but yourselves you do see. The way in which my talk affects you is obvious to you, but how it affects the microbes is not so obvious. And so, if we analyse our evil actions also, we may find that some good possibly results from them somewhere. He who in good action sees that there is something evil in it, and in the midst of evil sees that there is something good in it somewhere, has known the secret of work.

But what follows from it? That, howsoever we may try, there cannot be any action which is perfectly pure, or any which is perfectly impure, taking purity and impurity in the sense of injury and non-injury. We cannot breathe or live without injuring others, and every bit of the food we eat is taken away from another's mouth. Our very lives are crowding out other lives. It may be men, or animals, or small microbes, but some one or other of these we have to crowd out. That being the case, it naturally follows that perfection can never be attained by work. We may work through all eternity, but there will be no way out of this intricate maze. You may work on, and on, and on; there will be no end to this inevitable association of good and evil in the results of work.

The second point to consider is, what is the end of work? We find the vast majority of people in every country believing that there will be a time when this world will become perfect, when there will be no disease, nor death, nor unhappiness, nor wickedness. That is a very good idea, a very good motive power to inspire and uplift the ignorant; but if we think for a moment, we shall find on the very face of it that it cannot be so. How can it be, seeing that good and evil are the obverse and reverse of the same coin? How can you have good without evil at the same time? What is meant by perfection? A perfect life is a contradiction in terms. Life itself is a state of continuous struggle between ourselves and everything outside. Every moment we are fighting actually with external nature, and if we are defeated, our life has to go. It is, for instance, a continuous struggle for food and air. If food or air fails, we die. Life is not a simple and smoothly flowing thing, but it is a compound effect. This complex struggle between something inside and the external world is what we call life. So it is clear that when this struggle ceases, there will be an end of life.

What is meant by ideal happiness is the cessation of this struggle. But then life will cease, for the struggle can only cease when life itself has ceased. We have seen already that in helping the world we help ourselves. The main effect of work done for others is to purify ourselves. By means of the constant effort to do good to others we are trying to forget ourselves; this forgetfulness of self is the one great lesson we have to learn in life. Man thinks foolishly that he can make himself happy, and after years of struggle finds out at last that true happiness consists in killing selfishness and that no one can make him happy except himself. Every act of charity, every thought of sympathy, every action of help, every good deed, is taking so much of self-importance away from our little selves and making us think of ourselves as the lowest and the least, and, therefore, it is all good. Here we find that Jnana, Bhakti, and Karma—all come to one point. The highest ideal is eternal and entire self-abnegation, where there is no 'I,' but all is 'Thou'; and whether he is conscious or unconscious of it, Karma-Yoga leads man to that end. A religious preacher may become horrified at the idea of an Impersonal God; he may insist on a Personal God and wish to keep up his own identity and individuality, whatever he may mean by that. But his ideas of ethics, if they are really good, cannot but be based on the highest self-abnegation. It is the basis of all morality; you may extend it to men, or animals, or angels, it is the one basic idea, the one fundamental principle running through all ethical systems.

You will find various classes of men in this world. First, there are the God-men, whose self-abnegation is complete, and who do only good to others even at the sacrifice of their own lives. These are the highest of men. If there are a hundred of such in any country, that country need never despair. But they are unfortunately too few. Then there are the good men who do good to others so long as it does not injure themselves. And there is a third class who, to do good to themselves, injure others. It is said by a Sanskrit poet that there is a fourth unnamable class of people who injure others merely for injury's sake. Just as there are at one pole of existence the highest good men, who do good for the sake of doing good, so, at the other pole, there are others who injure others just for the sake of the injury. They do not gain anything thereby, but it is their nature to do evil.

Here are two Sanskrit words. The one is *Pravritti*, which means revolving towards, and the other is *Nivritti*, which means revolving away. The 'revolving towards' is what we call the world, the 'I and mine'; it includes all those things which are always enriching that 'me' by wealth and money and power, and name and fame, and which are of a grasping nature, always tending to accumulate everything in one centre, that centre being 'myself'. That is the Pravritti, the natural tendency of every human being; taking everything from everywhere and heaping it around one centre, that centre being man's own sweet self. When this tendency begins to break, when it is Nivritti or 'going away from,' then begin morality and religion. Both Pravritti and Nivritti are of the nature of work: the former is evil work, and the latter is good work. This Nivritti is the fundamental basis of all morality and all religion, and the very perfection of it is entire self-abnegation, readiness to sacrifice mind and body and everything for another being. When a man has reached that state, he has attained to the perfection of Karma-Yoga. This is the highest result of good works. Although a man has not studied a single system of philosophy, although he does not believe in any God, and never has believed, although he has not prayed even once in his whole life, if the simple power of good actions has brought him to that state where he is ready to give up his life and all else for others, he has arrived at the same point to which the religious man will come through his prayers and the philosopher through his knowledge; and so you may find that the philosopher, the worker, and the devotee, all meet at one point, that one point being self-abnegation. However much their systems of philosophy and religion may differ, all mankind stand in reverence and awe before the man who is ready to sacrifice himself for others. Here, it is not at all any question of creed, or doctrine—even men who are very much opposed to all religious ideas, when they see one of these acts of complete self-sacrifice, feel that they must revere it. Have you not seen even a most bigoted Christian, when he reads Edwin Arnold's Light of Asia, stand in reverence of Buddha, who Preached no God, preached nothing but self-sacrifice? The only thing is that the bigot does not know that his own end and aim in life is exactly the same as that of those from whom he differs. The worshipper, by keeping constantly before him the idea of God and a surrounding of good, comes to the same point at last and says, 'Thy will be done,' and keeps nothing to himself. That is self-abnegation. The philosopher, with his knowledge, sees that the seeming self is a delusion and easily gives it up. It is self-abnegation. So Karma, Bhakti, and Jnana all meet here; and this is what was meant by all the great preachers of ancient times, when they taught that God is not the world. There is one thing which is the world and another which is God; and this distinction is very true. What they mean by world is selfishness. Unselfishness is God. One may live on a throne, in a golden palace, and be perfectly unselfish; and then he is in God. Another may live in a hut and wear rags, and have nothing in the world; yet, if he is selfish, he is intensely merged in the world.

To come back to one of our main points, we say that we cannot do good without at the same time doing some evil, or do evil without doing some good. Knowing this, how can we work? There have, therefore, been sects in this world who have in an astoundingly preposterous way preached slow suicide as the only means to get out of the world, because if a man lives, he has to kill poor little animals and plants or do injury to something or some one. So according to them the only way out of the world is to die. The Jains have preached this doctrine as their highest ideal. This teaching seems to be very logical. But the true solution is found in the Gita. It is the theory of non-attachment, to be attached to nothing while doing our work of life. Know that you are separated entirely from the world, though you are in the world, and that whatever you may be doing in it, you are not doing that for your own sake. Any action that you do for yourself will bring its effect to bear upon you. If it is a good action, you will have to take the good effect, and if bad, you will have to take the bad effect; but any action that is not done for your own sake, whatever it be, will have no effect on you. There is to be found a very expressive sentence in our scriptures embodying this idea: 'Even if he kill the whole universe (or be himself killed), he is neither the killer nor the killed, when he knows that he is not acting for himself at all.' Therefore, Karma-Yoga teaches, 'Do not give up the world; live in the world, imbibe its influences as much as you can; but if it be for your own enjoyment's sake, work not at all.' Enjoyment should not be the goal. First kill your self and then take the whole world as yourself; as the old Christians used to say, 'The old man must die.' This old man is the selfish idea that the whole world is made for our enjoyment. Foolish parents teach their children to pray, 'O Lord, Thou hast created this sun for me and this moon for me,' as if the Lord has had nothing else to do than to create everything for these babies. Do not teach your children such nonsense. Then again, there are people who are foolish in another way: they teach us that all these animals were created for us to kill and eat, and that this universe is for the enjoyment of men. That is all foolishness. A tiger may say, 'Man was created for me' and pray, 'O Lord, how wicked are these men who do not come and place themselves before me to be eaten; they are breaking Your law.' If the world is created for us, we are also created for the world. That this world is created for our enjoyment is the most wicked idea that holds us down. This world is not for our sake. Millions pass out of it every year; the world does not feel it; millions of others are supplied in their place. Just as much as the world is for us, so we also are for the world.

To work properly, therefore, you have first to give up the idea of attachment. Secondly, do not mix in the fray, hold yourself as a witness and go on working. My master used to say, 'Look upon your children as a nurse does.' The nurse will take your baby and fondle it and play with it and behave towards it as gently as if it were her own child; but as soon as you give her notice to quit, she is ready to start off bag and baggage from the house. Everything in the shape of attachment is forgotten; it will not give the ordinary nurse the least pang to leave your children and take up other children. Even so are you to be with all that you consider your own. You are the nurse, and if you believe in God, believe that all these things which you consider yours are really His. The greatest weakness often insinuates itself as the greatest good and strength. It is a weakness to think that any one is dependent on me, and that I can do good to another. This belief is the mother of all our attachment, and through this attachment comes all our pain. We must inform our minds that no one in this universe depends upon us; not one beggar depends on our charity; not one soul on our kindness; not one living thing on our help. All are helped on by nature, and will be so helped even though millions of us were not here. The course of nature will not stop for such as you and me; it is, as already pointed out, only a blessed privilege to you and to me that we are allowed, in the way of helping others, to educate ourselves. This is a great lesson to learn in life, and when we have learned it fully, we shall never be unhappy; we can go and mix without harm in society anywhere and everywhere. You may have wives and husbands, and regiments of servants, and kingdoms to govern; if only you act on the principle that the world is not for you and does not inevitably need you, they can do you no harm. This very year some of your friends may have died. Is the world waiting without going on, for them to come again? Is its current stopped? No, it goes on. So drive out of your mind the idea that you have to do something for the world; the world does not require any help from you. It is sheer nonsense on the part of any man to think that he is born to help the world; it is simply pride, it is selfishness insinuating itself in the form of virtue. When you have trained your mind and your nerves to realize this idea of the world's non-dependence on you or on anybody, there will then be no reaction in the form of pain resulting from work. When you give something to a man and expect nothing—do not even expect the man to be grateful—his ingratitude will not tell upon you, because you never expected anything, never thought you had any right to anything in the way of a return. You gave him what he deserved; his own Karma got it for him; your Karma made you the carrier thereof. Why should you be proud of having given away something? You are the porter that carried the money or other kind of gift, and the world deserved it by its own Karma. Where is then the reason for pride in you? There is nothing very great in what you give to the world. When you have acquired the feeling of non-attachment, there will then be neither good nor evil for you. It is only selfishness that causes the difference between good and evil. It is a very hard thing to understand, but you will come to learn in time that nothing in the universe has power over you until you allow it to exercise such a power. Nothing has power over the Self of man, until the Self becomes a fool and loses independence. So, by non-attachment, you overcome and deny the power of anything to act upon you. It is very easy to say that nothing has the right to act upon you until you allow it to do so; but what is the true sign of the man who really does not allow anything to work upon him, who is neither happy nor unhappy when acted upon by the external world? The sign is that good or ill fortune causes no change in his mind: in all conditions he continues to remain the same.

There was a great sage in India called Vyasa. This Vyasa is known as the author of the Vedanta aphorisms, and was a holy man. His father had tried to become a very perfect man and had failed. His grandfather had also tried and failed. His great-grandfather had similarly tried and failed. He himself did not succeed perfectly, but his son, Shuka, was born perfect. Vyasa taught his son wisdom; and after teaching him the knowledge of truth himself, he sent him to the court of King Janaka. He was a great king and was called Janaka Videha. Videha means 'without a body'. Although a king, he had entirely forgotten that he was a body; he felt that he was a spirit all the time. This boy Shuka was sent to be taught by him. The king knew that Vyasa's son was coming to him to learn wisdom: So he made certain arrangements beforehand. And when the boy presented himself at the gates of the palace, the guards took no notice of him whatsoever. They only gave him a seat, and he sat there for three days and nights, nobody speaking to him, nobody asking him who he was or whence he was. He was the son of a very great sage, his father was honoured by the whole country, and he himself was a most respectable person; yet the low, vulgar guards of the palace would take no notice of him. After that, suddenly, the ministers of the king and all the big officials came there and received him with the greatest honours. They conducted him in and showed him into splendid rooms, gave him the most fragrant baths and wonderful dresses, and for eight days they kept him there in all kinds of luxury. That solemnly serene face of Shuka did not change even to the smallest extent by the change in the treatment accorded to him; he was the same in the midst of this luxury as when waiting at the door. Then he was brought before the king. The king was on his throne, music was playing, and dancing and other amusements were going on. The king then gave him a cup of milk, full to the brim, and asked him to go seven times round the hall without spilling even a drop. The boy took the cup and proceeded in the midst of the music and the attraction of the beautiful faces. As desired by the king, seven times did he go round, and not a drop of the milk was spilt. The boy's mind could not be attracted by anything in the world, unless he allowed it to affect him. And when he brought the cup to the king, the king said to him, 'What your father has taught you, and what you have learned yourself, I can only repeat. You have known the Truth; go home.'

Thus, the man that has practised control over himself cannot be acted upon by anything outside; there is no more slavery for him. His mind has become free. Such a man alone is fit to live well in the world. We generally find men holding two opinions regarding the world. Some are pessimists and say, 'How horrible this world is, how wicked!' Some others are optimists and say, 'How beautiful this world is, how wonderful!' To those who have not controlled their own minds, the world is either full of evil or at best a mixture of good and evil. This very world will become to us an optimistic world when we become masters of our own minds. Nothing will then work upon us as good or evil; we shall find everything to be in its proper place, to be harmonious. Some men, who begin by saying that the world is a hell, often end by saying that it is a heaven when they succeed in the practise of self-control. If we are genuine Karma-Yogis and wish to train ourselves to that attainment of this state, wherever we may begin we are sure to end in perfect self-abnegation; and as soon as this seeming self has gone, the whole world, which at first appears to us to be filled with evil, will appear to be heaven itself and full of blessedness. Its very atmosphere will be blessed; every human face there will be god. Such is the end and aim of Karma-Yoga, and such is its perfection in practical life.

Our various Yogas do not conflict with each other; each of them leads us to the same goal and makes us perfect. Only each has to be strenuously practised. The whole secret is in practising. First you have to hear, then think, and then practise. This is true of every Yoga. You have first to hear about it and understand what it is; and many things which you do not understand will be made clear to you by constant hearing and thinking. It is hard to understand everything at once. The explanation of everything is after all in yourself. No one was ever really taught by another; each of us has to teach himself. The external teacher offers only the suggestion which rouses the internal teacher to work to understand things. Then things will be made clearer to us by our own power of perception and thought, and we shall realize them in our own souls; and that realization will grow into the intense power of will. First it is feeling, then it becomes willing, and out of that willing comes the tremendous force for work that will go through every vein and nerve and muscle, until the whole mass of your body is changed into an instrument of the unselfish Yoga of work, and the desired result of perfect self-abnegation and utter unselfishness is duly attained. This attainment does not depend on any dogma, or doctrine, or belief. Whether one is Christian, or Jew, or Gentile, it does not matter. Are you unselfish? That is the question. If you are, you will be perfect without reading a single religious book, without going into a single church or temple. Each one of our Yogas is fitted to make man perfect even without the help of the others, because they have all the same goal in view. The Yogas of work, of wisdom, and of devotion are all capable of serving as direct and independent means for the attainment of Moksha. 'Fools alone say that work and philosophy are different, not the learned.' The learned know that, though apparently different from each other, they at last lead to the same goal of human perfection.

13

FREEDOM

In addition to meaning work, we have stated that psychologically the word Karma also implies causation. Any work, any action, any thought that produces an effect is called a Karma. Thus the law of Karma means the law of causation, of inevitable cause and sequence. Wheresoever there is a cause, there an effect must be produced; this necessity cannot be resisted, and this law of Karma, according to our philosophy, is true throughout the whole universe. Whatever we see, or feel, or do, whatever action there is anywhere in the universe, while being the effect of past work on the one hand, becomes, on the other, a cause in its turn, and produces its own effect. It is necessary, together with this, to consider what is meant by the word 'law'. By law is meant the tendency of a series to repeat itself. When we see one event followed by another, or sometimes happening simultaneously with another, we expect this sequence or co-existence to recur. Our old logicians and philosophers of the Nyaya school call this law by the name of Vyapti. According to them, all our ideas of law are due to association. A series of phenomena becomes associated with things in our mind in a sort of invariable order, so that whatever we perceive at any time is immediately referred to other facts in the mind. Any one idea or, according to our psychology, any one wave that is produced in the mind-stuff, Chitta, must always give rise to many similar waves. This is the psychological idea of association, and causation is only an aspect of this grand pervasive principle of association. This pervasiveness of association is what is, in Sanskrit, called Vyapti. In the external world the idea of law is the same as in the internal—the expectation that a particular phenomenon will be followed by another, and that the series will repeat itself. Really speaking, therefore, law does not exist in nature. Practically, it is an error to say that gravitation exists in the earth, or that there is any law existing objectively anywhere in nature. Law is the method, the manner in which our mind grasps a series of phenomena; it is all in the mind. Certain phenomena, happening one after another or together, and followed by the conviction of the regularity of their recurrence—thus enabling our minds to grasp the method of the whole series—constitute what we call law.

The next question for consideration is what we mean by law being universal. Our universe is that portion of existence which is characterized by what the Sanskrit psychologists call Desha-kala-nimitta, or what is known to European psychology as space, time, and causation. This universe is only a part of infinite existence, thrown into a peculiar mould, composed of space, time, and causation. It necessarily follows that law is possible only within this conditioned universe; beyond it there cannot be any law. When we speak of the universe, we only mean that portion of existence which is limited by our mind—the universe of the senses, which we can see, feel, touch, hear, think of, imagine. This alone is under law; but beyond it existence cannot be subject to law, because causation does not extend beyond the world of our minds. Anything beyond the range of our mind and our senses is not bound by the law of causation, as there is no mental association of things in the region beyond the senses, and no causation without association of ideas. It is only when 'being' or existence gets moulded into name and form that it obeys the law of causation, and is said to be under law; because all law has its essence in causation. Therefore, we see at once that there cannot be any such thing as free will; the very words are a contradiction, because will is what we know, and everything that we know is within our universe, and everything within our universe is moulded by the conditions of space, time, and causation. Everything that we know, or can possibly know, must be subject to causation, and that which obeys the law of causation cannot be free. It is acted upon by other agents, and becomes a cause in its turn. But that which has become converted into the will, which was not the will before, but which, when it fell into this mould of space, time, and causation, became converted into the human will, is free; and when this will gets out of this mould of space, time, and causation, it will be free again. From freedom it comes, and becomes moulded into this bondage, and it gets out and goes back to freedom again.

The question has been raised as to from whom this universe comes, in whom it rests, and to whom it goes; and the answer has been given that from freedom it comes, in bondage it rests, and goes back into that freedom again. So, when we speak of man as no other than that infinite being which is manifesting itself, we mean that only one very small part thereof is man; this body and this mind which we see are only one part of the whole, only one spot of the infinite being. This whole universe is only one speck of the infinite being; and all our laws, our bondages, our joys and our sorrows, our happinesses and our expectations, are only within this small universe; all our progression and digression are within its small compass. So you see how childish it is to expect a continuation of this universe—the creation of our minds—and to expect to go to heaven, which after all must mean only a repetition of this world that we know. You see at once that it is an impossible and childish desire to make the whole of infinite existence conform to the limited and conditioned existence which we know. When a man says that he will have again and again this same thing which he is hating now, or, as I sometimes put it, when he asks for a *comfortable* religion, you may know that he has become so degenerate that he cannot think of anything higher than what he is now; he is just his little present surroundings and nothing more. He has forgotten his infinite nature, and his whole idea is confined to these little joys, and sorrows, and heart-jealousies of the moment. He thinks that this finite thing is the infinite; and not only so, he will not let this foolishness go. He clings on desperately unto Trishna, and the thirst after life, what the Buddhists call Tanha and Tissa. There may be millions of kinds of happiness, and beings, and laws, and progress, and causation, all acting outside the little universe that we know; and, after all, the whole of this comprises but one section of our infinite nature.

To acquire freedom we have to get beyond the limitations of this universe; it cannot be found here. Perfect equilibrium, or what the Christians call the peace that passeth all understanding, cannot be had in this universe, nor in heaven, nor in any place where our mind and thoughts can go, where the senses can feel, or which the imagination can conceive. No such place can give us that freedom, because all such places would be within our universe, and it is limited by space, time, and causation. There may be places that are more ethereal than this earth of ours, where enjoyments may be keener, but even those places must be in the universe and, therefore, in bondage to law; so we have to go beyond, and real religion begins where this little universe ends. These little joys, and sorrows, and knowledge of things end there, and the reality begins. Until we give up the thirst after life, the strong attachment to this our transient conditioned existence we have no hope of catching even a glimpse of that infinite freedom beyond. It stands to reason then that there is only one way to attain to that freedom which is the goal of all the noblest aspirations of mankind, and that is by giving up this little life, giving up this little universe, giving up this earth, giving up heaven, giving up the body, giving up the mind, giving up everything that is limited and conditioned. If we give up our attachment to this little universe of the senses or of the mind, we shall be free immediately. The only way to come out of bondage is to go beyond the limitations of law, to go beyond causation.

But it is a most difficult thing to give up the clinging to this universe; few ever attain to that. There are two ways to do that mentioned in our books. One is called the 'Neti, Neti' (not this, not this), the other is called 'Iti' (this); the former is the negative, and the latter is the positive way. The negative way is the most difficult. It is only possible to the men of the very highest, exceptional minds and gigantic wills who simply stand up and say, 'No, I will not have this,' and the mind and body obey their will, and they come out successful. But such people are very rare. The vast majority of mankind choose the positive way, the way through the world, making use of all the bondages themselves to break those very bondages. This is also a kind of giving up; only it is done slowly and gradually, by knowing things, enjoying things and thus obtaining experience, and knowing the nature of things until the mind lets them all go at last and becomes unattached. The former way of obtaining non-attachment is by reasoning, and the latter way is through work and experience. The first is the path of Jnana-Yoga, and is characterized by the refusal to do any work; the second is that of Karma-Yoga, in which there is no cessation from work. Every one must work in the universe. Only those who are perfectly satisfied with the Self, whose desires do not go beyond the Self, whose mind never strays out of the Self, to whom the Self is all in all, only those do not work. The rest must work. A current rushing down of its own nature falls into a hollow and makes a whirlpool, and, after running a little in that whirlpool, it emerges again in the form of the free current to go on unchecked. Each human life is like that current. It gets into the whirl, gets involved in this world of space, time, and causation, whirls round a little, crying out, 'my father, my brother, my name, my fame', and so on, and at last emerges out of it and regains its original freedom. The whole universe is doing that. Whether we know it or not, whether we are conscious or unconscious of it, we are all working to get out of the dream of the world. Man's experience in the world is to enable him to get out of its whirlpool.

What is Karma-Yoga? The knowledge of the secret of work. We see that the whole universe is working. For what? For salvation, for liberty; from the atom to the highest being, working for the one end, liberty for the mind, for the body, for the spirit. All things are always trying to get freedom, flying away from bondage. The sun, the moon, the earth, the planets, all are trying to fly away from bondage. The centrifugal and the centripetal forces of nature are indeed typical of our universe. Instead of being knocked about in this universe, and after long delay and thrashing, getting to know things as they are, we learn from Karma-Yoga the secret of work, the method of work, the organising power of work. A vast mass of energy may be spent in vain if we do not know how to utilize it. Karma-Yoga makes a science of work; you learn by it how best to utilize all the workings of this world. Work is inevitable, it must be so; but we should work to the highest purpose. Karma-Yoga makes us admit that this world is a world of five minutes, that it is a something we have to pass through; and that freedom is not here, but is only to be found beyond. To find the way out of the bondages of the world we have to go through it slowly and surely. There may be those exceptional persons about whom I just spoke, those who can stand aside and give up the world, as a snake casts off its skin and stands aside and looks at it. There are no doubt these exceptional beings; but the rest of mankind have to go slowly through the world of work. Karma-Yoga shows the process, the secret, and the method of doing it to the best advantage.

What does it say? 'Work incessantly, but give up all attachment to work.' Do not identify yourself with anything. Hold your mind free. All this that you see, the pains and the miseries, are but the necessary conditions of this world; poverty and wealth and happiness are but momentary; they do not belong to our real nature at all. Our nature is far beyond misery and happiness, beyond every object of the senses, beyond the imagination; and yet we must go on working all the time. 'Misery comes through attachment, not through work.' As soon as we identify ourselves with the work we do, we feel miserable; but if we do not identify ourselves with it, we do not feel that misery. If a beautiful picture belonging to another is burnt, a man does not generally become miserable; but when his own picture is burnt, how miserable he feels! Why? Both were beautiful pictures, perhaps copies of the same original; but in one case very much more misery is felt than in the other. It is because in one case he identifies himself with the picture, and not in the other. This 'I and mine' causes the whole misery. With the sense of possession comes selfishness, and selfishness brings on misery. Every act of selfishness or thought of selfishness makes us attached to something, and immediately we are made slaves. Each wave in the Chitta that says 'I and mine' immediately puts a chain round us and makes us slaves; and the more we say 'I and mine', the more slavery grows, the more misery increases. Therefore Karma-Yoga tells us to enjoy the beauty of all the pictures in the world, but not to identify ourselves with any of them. Never say 'mine'. Whenever we say a thing is 'mine', misery will immediately come. Do not even say 'my child' in your mind. Possess the child, but do not say 'mine'. If you do, then will come the misery. Do not say 'my house,' do not say 'my body'. The whole difficulty is there. The body is neither yours, nor mine, nor anybody's. These bodies are coming and going by the laws of nature, but we are free, standing as witness. This body is no more free than a picture or a wall. Why should we be attached so much to a body? If somebody paints a picture, he does it and passes on. Do not project that tentacle of selfishness, 'I must possess it'. As soon as that is projected, misery will begin.

So Karma-Yoga says, first destroy the tendency to project this tentacle of selfishness, and when you have the power of checking it, hold it in and do not allow the mind to get into the ways of selfishness. Then you may go out into the world and work as much as you can. Mix everywhere, go where you please; you will never be contaminated with evil. There is the lotus leaf in the water; the water cannot touch and adhere to it; so will you be in the world. This is called 'Vairagya', dispassion or non-attachment. I believe I have told you that without non-attachment there cannot be any kind of Yoga. Non-attachment is the basis of all the Yogas. The man who gives up living in houses, wearing fine clothes, and eating good food, and goes into the desert, may be a most attached person. His only possession, his own body, may become everything to him; and as he lives he will be simply struggling for the sake of his body. Non-attachment does not mean anything that we may do in relation to our external body, it is all in the mind. The binding link of 'I and mine' is in the mind. If we have not this link with the body and with the things of the senses, we are non-attached, wherever and whatever we may be. A man may be on a throne and perfectly non-attached; another man may be in rags and still very much attached. First, we have to attain this state of non-attachment and then to work incessantly. Karma-Yoga gives us the method that will help us in giving up all attachment, though it is indeed very hard.

Here are the two ways of giving up all attachment. The one is for those who do not believe in God, or in any outside help. They are left to their own devices; they have simply to work with their own will, with the powers of their mind and discrimination, saying, 'I must be non-attached'. For those who believe in God there is another way, which is much less difficult. They give up the fruits of work unto the Lord; they work and are never attached to the results. Whatever they see, feel, hear, or do, is for Him. For whatever good work we may do, let us not claim any praise or benefit. It is the Lord's; give up the fruits unto Him. Let us stand aside and think that we are only servants obeying the Lord, our Master, and that every impulse for action comes from Him every moment. Whatever thou worshippest, whatever thou perceivest, whatever thou doest, give up all unto Him and be at rest. Let us be at peace, perfect peace, with ourselves, and give up our whole body and mind and everything as an eternal sacrifice unto the Lord. Instead of the sacrifice of pouring oblations into the fire, perform this one great sacrifice day and night—the sacrifice of your little self. 'In search of wealth in this world, Thou art the only wealth I have found; I sacrifice myself unto Thee. In search of some one to be loved, Thou art the only one beloved I have found; I sacrifice myself unto Thee.' Let us repeat this day and night, and say, 'Nothing for me; no matter whether the thing is good, bad, or indifferent; I do not care for it; I sacrifice all unto Thee.' Day and night let us renounce our seeming self until it becomes a habit with us to do so, until it gets into the blood, the nerves, and the brain, and the whole body is every moment obedient to this idea of self-renunciation. Go then into the midst of the battlefield, with the roaring cannon and the din of war, and you will find yourself to be free and at peace.

Karma-Yoga teaches us that the ordinary idea of duty is on the lower plane; nevertheless, all of us have to do our duty. Yet we may see that this peculiar sense of duty is very often a great cause of misery. Duty becomes a disease with us; it drags us ever forward. It catches hold of us and makes our whole life miserable. It is the bane of human life. This duty, this idea of duty is the midday summer sun which scorches the innermost soul of mankind. Look at those poor slaves to duty! Duty leaves them no time to say prayers, no time to bathe. Duty is ever on them. They go out and work. Duty is on them! They come home and think of the work for the next day. Duty is on them! It is living a slave's life, at last dropping down in the street and dying in harness, like a horse. This is duty as it is understood. The only true duty is to be unattached and to work as free beings, to give up all work unto God. All our duties are His. Blessed are we that we are ordered out here. We serve our time; whether we do it ill or well, who knows? If we do it well, we do not get the fruits. If we do it ill, neither do we get the care. Be at rest, be free, and work. This kind of freedom is a very hard thing to attain. How easy it is to interpret slavery as duty—the morbid attachment of flesh for flesh as duty! Men go out into the world and struggle and fight for money or for any other thing to which they get attached. Ask them why they do it. They say, 'It is a duty'. It is the absurd greed for gold and gain, and they try to cover it with a few flowers.

What is duty after all? It is really the impulsion of the flesh, of our attachment; and when an attachment has become established, we call it duty. For instance, in countries where there is no marriage, there is no duty between husband and wife; when marriage comes, husband and wife live together on account of attachment; and that kind of living together becomes settled after generations; and when it becomes so settled, it becomes a duty. It is, so to say, a sort of chronic disease. When it is acute, we call it disease; when it is chronic, we call it nature. It is a disease. So when attachment becomes chronic, we baptize it with the high sounding name of duty. We strew flowers upon it, trumpets sound for it, sacred texts are said over it, and then the whole world fights, and men earnestly rob each other for this duty's sake. Duty is good to the extent that it checks brutality. To the lowest kinds of men, who cannot have any other ideal, it is of some good; but those who want to be Karma-Yogis must throw this idea of duty overboard. There is no duty for you and me. Whatever you have to give to the world, do give by all means, but not as a duty. Do not take any thought of that. Be not compelled. Why should you be compelled? *Everything that you do under compulsion goes to build up attachment.* Why should you have any duty? Resign everything unto God. In this tremendous fiery furnace where the fire of duty scorches everybody, drink this cup of nectar and be happy. We are all simply working out His will, and have nothing to do with rewards and punishments. If you want the reward, you must also have the punishment; the only way to get out of the punishment is to give up the reward. The only way of getting out of misery is by giving up the idea of happiness, because these two are linked to each other. On one side there is happiness, on the other there is misery. On one side there is life, on the other there is death. The only way to get beyond death is to give up the love of life. Life and death are the same thing, looked at from different points. So the idea of happiness without misery, or of life without death, is very good for school-boys and children; but the thinker sees that it is all a contradiction in terms and gives up both. Seek no praise, no reward, for anything you do. No sooner do we perform a good action than we begin to desire credit for it. No sooner do we give money to some charity than we want to see our names blazoned in the papers. Misery must come as the result of such desires. The greatest men in the world have passed away unknown. The Buddhas and the Christs that we know are but second-rate heroes in comparison with the greatest men of whom the world knows nothing. Hundreds of these unknown heroes have lived in every country working silently. Silently they live and silently they pass away; and in time their thoughts find expression in Buddhas or Christs, and it is these latter that become known to us. The highest men do not seek to get any name or fame from their knowledge. They leave their ideas to the world; they put forth no claims for themselves and establish no schools or systems in their name. Their whole nature shrinks from such a thing. They are the pure Sattvikas, who can never make any stir, but only melt down in love. I have seen one such Yogi who lives in a cave in India. He is one of the most wonderful men I have ever seen. He has so completely lost the sense of his own individuality that we may say that the man in him is completely gone, leaving behind only the all comprehending sense of the divine. If an animal bites one of his arms, he is ready to give it his other arm also, and say that it is the Lord's will. Everything that comes to him is from the Lord. He does not show himself to men, and yet he is a magazine of love and of true and sweet ideas.

Next in order come the men with more Rajas, or activity, combative natures, who take up the ideas of the perfect ones and preach them to the world. The highest kind of men silently collect true and noble ideas, and others—the Buddhas and Christs—go from place to place preaching them and working for them. In the life of Gautama Buddha we notice him constantly saying that he is the twenty-fifth Buddha. The twenty-four before him are unknown to history, although the Buddha known to history must have built upon foundations laid by them. The highest men are calm, silent, and unknown. They are the men who really know the power of thought; they are sure that, even if they go into a cave and close the door and simply think five true thoughts and then pass away, these five thoughts of theirs will live through eternity. Indeed such thoughts will penetrate through the mountains, cross the oceans, and travel through the world. They will enter deep into human hearts and brains and raise up men and women who will give them practical expression in the workings of human life. These Sattvika men are too near the Lord to be active and to fight, to be working, struggling, preaching and doing good, as they say, here on earth to humanity. The active workers, however good, have still a little remnant of ignorance left in them. When our nature has yet some impurities left in it, then alone can we work. It is in the nature of work to be impelled ordinarily by motive and by attachment. In the presence of an ever active Providence who notes even the sparrow's fall, how can man attach any importance to his own work? Will it not be a blasphemy to do so when we know that He is taking care of the minutest things in the world? We have only to stand in awe and reverence before Him saying, 'Thy will be done'. The highest men cannot work, for in them there is no attachment. Those whose whole soul is gone into the Self, those whose desires are confined in the Self, who have become ever associated with the Self, for them there is no work. Such are indeed the highest of mankind; but apart from them every one else has to work. In so working we should never think that we can help on even the least thing in this universe. We cannot. We only help ourselves in this gymnasium of the world. This is the proper attitude of work. If we work in this way, if we always remember that our present opportunity to work thus is a privilege which has been given to us, we shall never be attached to anything. Millions like you and me think that we are great people in the world; but we all die, and in five minutes the world forgets us. But the life of God is infinite. 'Who can live a moment, breathe a moment, if this all-powerful One does not will it?' He is the ever active Providence. All power is His and within His command. Through His command the winds blow, the sun shines, the earth lives, and death stalks upon the earth. He is the all in all; He is all and in all. We can only worship Him. Give up all fruits of work; do good for its own sake; then alone will come perfect non-attachment. The bonds of the heart will thus break, and we shall reap perfect freedom. This freedom is indeed the goal of Karma-Yoga.

14

THE IDEAL OF KARMA-YOGA

The grandest idea in the religion of the Vedanta is that we may reach the same goal by different paths; and these paths I have generalized into four, viz those of work, love, psychology, and knowledge. But you must, at the same time, remember that these divisions are not very marked and quite exclusive of each other. Each blends into the other. But according to the type which prevails, we name the divisions. It is not that you can find men who have no other faculty than that of work, nor that you can find men who are no more than devoted worshippers only, nor that there are men who have no more than mere knowledge. These divisions are made in accordance with the type or the tendency that may be seen to prevail in a man. We have found that, in the end, all these four paths converge and become one. All religions and all methods of work and worship lead us to one and the same goal.

I have already tried to point out that goal. It is freedom as I understand it. Everything that we perceive around us is struggling towards freedom, from the atom to the man, from the insentient, lifeless particle of matter to the highest existence on earth, the human soul. The whole universe is in fact the result of this struggle for freedom. In all combinations every particle is trying to go on its own way, to fly from the other particles; but the others are holding it in check. Our earth is trying to fly away from the sun, and the moon from the earth. Everything has a tendency to infinite dispersion. All that we see in the universe has for its basis this one struggle towards freedom; it is under the impulse of this tendency that the saint prays and the robber robs. When the line of action taken is not a proper one, we call it evil; and when the manifestation of it is proper and high, we call it good. But the impulse is the same, the struggle towards freedom. The saint is oppressed with the knowledge of his condition of bondage, and he wants to get rid of it; so he worships God. The thief is oppressed with the idea that he does not possess certain things, and he tries to get rid of that want, to obtain freedom from it; so he steals. Freedom is the one goal of all nature, sentient or insentient; and consciously or unconsciously, everything is struggling towards that goal. The freedom which the saint seeks is very different from that which the robber seeks; the freedom loved by the saint leads him to the enjoyment of infinite, unspeakable bliss, while that on which the robber has set his heart only forges other bonds for his soul.

There is to be found in every religion the manifestation of this struggle towards freedom. It is the groundwork of all morality, of unselfishness, which means getting rid of the idea that men are the same as their little body. When we see a man doing good work, helping others, it means that he cannot be confined within the limited circle of 'me and mine'. There is no limit to this getting out of selfishness. All the great systems of ethics preach absolute unselfishness as the goal. Supposing this absolute unselfishness can be reached by a man, what becomes of him? He is no more the little Mr So-and-so; he has acquired infinite expansion. The little personality which he had before is now lost to him for ever; he has become infinite, and the attainment of this infinite expansion is indeed the goal of all religions and of all moral and philosophical teachings. The personalist, when he hears this idea philosophically put, gets frightened. At the same time, if he preaches morality, he after all teaches the very same idea himself. He puts no limit to the unselfishness of man. Suppose a man becomes perfectly unselfish under the personalistic system, how are we to distinguish him from the perfected ones in other system? He has become one with the universe and to become that is the goal of all; only the poor personalist has not the courage to follow out his own reasoning to its right conclusion. Karma-Yoga is the attaining through unselfish work of that freedom which is the goal of all human nature. Every selfish action, therefore, retards our reaching the goal, and every unselfish action takes us towards the goal; that is why the only definition that can be given of morality is this: That which is selfish is immoral, and that which is unselfish is moral.

But, if you come to details, the matter will not be seen to be quite so simple. For instance, environment often makes the details different as I have already mentioned. The same action under one set of circumstances may be unselfish, and under another set quite selfish. So we can give only a general definition, and leave the details to be worked out by taking into consideration the differences in time, place, and circumstances. In one country one kind of conduct is considered moral, and in another the very same is immoral, because the circumstances differ. The goal of all nature is freedom, and freedom is to be attained only by perfect unselfishness; every thought, word, or deed that is unselfish takes us towards the goal, and, as such, is called moral. That definition, you will find, holds good in every religion and every system of ethics. In some systems of thought morality is derived from a Superior Being—God. If you ask why a man ought to do this and not that, their answer is: 'Because such is the command of God.' But whatever be the source from which it is derived, their code of ethics also has the same central idea—not to think of self but to give up self. And yet some persons, in spite of this high ethical idea, are frightened at the thought of having to give up their little personalities. We may ask the man who clings to the idea of little personalities to consider the case of a person who has become perfectly unselfish, who has no thought for himself, who does no deed for himself, who speaks no word for himself, and then say where his 'himself' is. That 'himself' is known to him only so long as he thinks, acts, or speaks for himself. If he is only conscious of others, of the universe, and of the all, where is his 'himself'? It is gone for ever.

Karma-Yoga, therefore, is a system of ethics and religion intended to attain freedom through unselfishness, and by good works. The Karma-Yogi need not believe in any doctrine whatever. He may not believe even in God, may not ask what his soul is, nor think of any metaphysical speculation. He has got his own special aim of realising selflessness; and he has to work it out himself. Every moment of his life must be realization, because he has to solve by mere work, without the help of doctrine or theory, the very same problem to which the Jnani applies his reason and inspiration and the Bhakta his love.

Now comes the next question: What is this work? What is this doing good to the world? Can we do good to the world? In an absolute sense, no; in a relative sense, yes. No permanent or everlasting good can be done to the world; if it could be done, the world would not be this world. We may satisfy the hunger of a man for five minutes, but he will be hungry again. Every pleasure with which we supply a man may be seen to be momentary. No one can permanently cure this ever-recurring fever of pleasure and pain. Can any permanent happiness be given to the world? In the ocean we cannot raise a wave without causing a hollow somewhere else. The sum total of the good things in the world has been the same throughout in its relation to man's need and greed. It cannot be increased or decreased. Take the history of the human race as we know it today. Do we not find the same miseries and the same happiness, the same pleasures and pains, the same differences in position? Are not some rich, some poor, some high, some low, some healthy, some unhealthy? All this was just the same with the Egyptians, the Greeks, and the Romans in ancient times as it is with the Americans today. So far as history is known, it has always been the same; yet at the same time we find that, running along with all these incurable differences of pleasure and pain, there has ever been the struggle to alleviate them. Every period of history has given birth to thousands of men and women who have worked hard to smooth the passage of life for others. And how far have they succeeded? We can only play at driving the ball from one place to another. We take away pain from the physical plane, and it goes to the mental one. It is like that picture in Dante's hell where the misers were given a mass of gold to roll up a hill. Every time they rolled it up a little, it again rolled down. All our talks about the millennium are very nice as school-boys' stories, but they are no better than that. All nations that dream of the millennium also think that, of all peoples in the world, they will have the best of it then for themselves. This is the wonderfully unselfish idea of the millennium!

We cannot add happiness to this world; similarly, we cannot add pain to it either. The sum total of the energies of pleasure and pain displayed here on earth will be the same throughout. We just push it from this side to the other side, and from that side to this, but it will remain the same, because to remain so is its very nature. This ebb and flow, this rising and falling, is in the world's very nature;

it would be as logical to hold otherwise as to say that we may have life without death. This is complete nonsense, because the very idea of life implies death and the very idea of pleasure implies pain. The lamp is constantly burning out, and that is its life. If you want to have life, you have to die every moment for it. Life and death are only different expressions of the same thing looked at from different standpoints; they are the falling and the rising of the same wave, and the two form one whole. One looks at the 'fall' side and becomes a pessimist another looks at the 'rise' side and becomes an optimist. When a boy is going to school and his father and mother are taking care of him, everything seems blessed to him; his wants are simple, he is a great optimist. But the old man, with his varied experience, becomes calmer and is sure to have his warmth considerably cooled down. So, old nations, with signs of decay all around them, are apt to be less hopeful than new nations. There is a proverb in India: 'A thousand years a city, and a thousand years a forest.' This change of city into forest and vice versa is going on everywhere, and it makes people optimists or pessimists according to the side they see of it.

The next idea we take up is the idea of equality. These millennium ideas have been great motive powers to work. Many religions preach this as an element in them—that God is coming to rule the universe, and that then there will be no difference at all in conditions. The people who preach this doctrine are mere fanatics, and fanatics are indeed the sincerest of mankind. Christianity was preached just on the basis of the fascination of this fanaticism, and that is what made it so attractive to the Greek and the Roman slaves. They believed that under the millennial religion there would be no more slavery, that there would be plenty to eat and drink; and, therefore, they flocked round the Christian standard. Those who preached the idea first were of course ignorant fanatics, but very sincere. In modern times, this millennial aspiration takes the form of equality—of liberty, equality, and fraternity. This is also fanaticism. True equality has never been and never can be on earth. How can we all be equal here? This impossible kind of equality implies total death. What makes this world what it is? Lost balance. In the primal state, which is called chaos, there is perfect balance. How do all the formative forces of the universe come then? By struggling, competition, conflict. Suppose that all the particles of matter were held in equilibrium, would there be then any process of creation? We know from science that it is impossible. Disturb a sheet of water, and there you find every particle of the water trying to become calm again, one rushing against the other; and in the same way all the phenomena which we call the universe—all things therein—are struggling to get back to the state of perfect balance. Again a disturbance comes, and again we have combination and creation. Inequality is the very basis of creation. At the same time the forces struggling to obtain equality are as much a necessity of creation as those which destroy it.

Absolute equality, that which means a perfect balance of all the struggling forces in all the planes, can never be in this world. Before you attain that state, the world will have become quite unfit for any kind of life, and no one will be there. We find, therefore, that all these ideas of the millennium and of absolute equality are not only impossible but also that, if we try to carry them out, they will lead us surely enough to the day of destruction. What makes the difference between man and man? It is largely the difference in the brain. Nowadays no one but a lunatic will say that we are all born with the same brain power. We come into the world with unequal endowments; we come as greater men or as lesser men, and there is no getting away from that pre-natally determined condition. The American Indians were in this country for thousands of years, and a few handfuls of your ancestors came to their land. What difference they have caused in the appearance of the country! Why did not the Indians make improvements and build cities, if all were equal? With your ancestors a different sort of brain power came into the land, different bundles of past impressions came, and they worked out and manifested themselves. Absolute non-differentiation is death. So long as this world lasts, differentiation there will and must be, and the millennium of perfect equality will come only when a cycle of creation comes to its end. Before that, equality cannot be. Yet this idea of realising the millennium is a great motive power. Just as inequality is necessary for creation itself, so the struggle to limit it is also necessary. If there were no struggle to become free and get back to God, there would be no creation either. It is the difference between these two forces that determines the nature of the motives of men. There will always be these motives to work, some tending towards bondage and others towards freedom.

This world's wheel within wheel is a terrible mechanism; if we put our hands in it, as soon as we are caught we are gone. We all think that when we have done a certain duty, we shall be at rest; but before we have done a part of that duty, another is already in waiting. We are all being dragged along by this mighty, complex world-machine. There are only two ways out of it; one is to give up all concerns with the machine, to let it go and stand aside, to give up our desires. That is very easy to say, but is almost impossible to do. I do not know whether in twenty millions of men one can do that. The other way is to plunge into the world and learn the secret of work, and that is the way of Karma-Yoga. Do not fly away from the wheels of the world-machine, but stand inside it and learn the secret of work. Through proper work done inside, it is also possible to come out. Through this machinery itself is the way out.

We have now seen what work is. It is a part of natures foundation, and goes on always. Those that believe in God understand this better, because they know that God is not such an incapable being as will need our help. Although this universe will go on always, our goal is freedom, our goal is unselfishness; and according to Karma-Yoga, that goal is to be reached through work. All ideas of making the world perfectly happy may be good as motive powers for fanatics; but we must know that fanaticism brings forth as much evil as good. The Karma-Yogi asks why you require any motive to work other than the inborn love of freedom. Be beyond the common worldly motives. 'To work you have the right, but not to the fruits thereof.' Man can train himself to know and to practise that, says the Karma-Yogi. When the idea of doing good becomes a part of his very being, then he will not seek for any motive outside. Let us do good because it is good to do good; he who does good work even in order to get to heaven binds himself down, says the Karma-Yogi. Any work that is done with any the least selfish motive, instead of making us free, forges one more chain for our feet.

So the only way is to give up all the fruits of work, to be unattached to them. Know that this world is not we, nor are we this world; that we are really not the body; that we really do not work. We are the Self, eternally at rest and at peace. Why should we be bound by anything? It is very good to say that we should be perfectly non-attached, but what is the way to do it? Every good work we do without any ulterior motive, instead of forging a new chain, will break one of the links in the existing chains. Every good thought that we send to the world without thinking of any return, will be stored up there and break one link in the chain, and make us purer and purer, until we become the purest of mortals. Yet all this may seem to be rather quixotic and too philosophical, more theoretical than practical. I have read many arguments against the Bhagavad Gita, and many have said that without motives you cannot work. They have never seen unselfish work except under the influence of fanaticism, and, therefore, they speak in that way.

Let me tell you in conclusion a few words about one man who actually carried this teaching of Karma-Yoga into practise. That man is Buddha. He is the one man who ever carried this into perfect practise. All the prophets of the world, except Buddha, had external motives to move them to unselfish action. The prophets of the world, with this single exception, may be divided into two sets, one set holding that they are incarnations of God come down on earth, and the other holding that they are only messengers from God; and both draw their impetus for work from outside, expect reward from outside, however highly spiritual may be the language they use. But Buddha is the only prophet who said, 'I do not care to know your various theories about God. What is the use of discussing all the subtle doctrines about the soul? Do good and be good. And this will take you to freedom and to whatever truth there is.' He was, in the conduct of his life, absolutely without personal motives; and what man worked more than he? Show me in history one character who has soared so high above all. The whole human race has produced but one such character, such high philosophy, such wide sympathy. This great philosopher, preaching the highest philosophy, yet had the deepest sympathy for the lowest of animals, and never put forth any claims for himself. He is the ideal Karma-Yogi, acting entirely without motive, and the history of humanity shows him to have been the greatest man ever born; beyond compare the greatest combination of heart and brain that ever existed, the greatest soul-power that has even been manifested. He is the first great reformer the world has seen. He was the first who dared to say, 'Believe not because some old manuscripts are produced, believe not because it is your national belief, because you have been made to believe it from your childhood; but reason it all out, and after you have analysed it, then, if you find that it will do good to one and all, believe it, live up to it, and help others to live up to it.' He works best who works without any motive, neither for money, nor for fame, nor for anything else; and when a man can do that, he will be a Buddha, and out of him will come the power to work in such a manner as will transform the world. This man represents the very highest ideal of Karma-Yoga.

15

WOMEN OF INDIA
At the Shakespeare Club House, Pasadena, California
(18 January 1900)

Swami Vivekananda: 'Some persons desire to ask questions about Hindu Philosophy before the lecture and to question in general about India after the lecture; but the chief difficulty is I do not know what I am to lecture on. I would be very glad to lecture on any subject, either on Hindu Philosophy or on anything concerning the race, its history, or its literature. If you, ladies and gentlemen, will suggest anything, I would be very glad.'

Questioner: 'I would like to ask, Swami, what special principle in Hindu Philosophy you would have us Americans, who are a very practical people, adopt, and what that would do for us beyond what Christianity can do.'

Swami Vivekananda: 'That is very difficult for me to decide; it rests upon you. If you find anything which you think you ought to adopt, and which will be helpful, you should take that. You see I am not a missionary, and I am not going about converting people to my idea. My principle is that all such ideas are good and great, so that some of your ideas may suit some people in India, and some of our ideas may suit some people here; so ideas must be cast abroad, all over the world.'

Questioner: 'We would like to know the result of your philosophy; has your philosophy and religion lifted your women above our women?'

Swami Vivekananda: 'You see, that is a very invidious question: I like our women and your women too.'

Questioner: 'Well, will you tell us about your women, their customs and education, and the position they hold in the family?'

Swami Vivekananda: 'Oh, yes, those things I would be very glad to tell you. So you want to know about Indian women tonight, and not philosophy and other things?'

The Lecture

I must begin by saying that you may have to bear with me a good deal, because I belong to an Order of people who never marry; so my knowledge of women in all their relations, as mother, as wife, as daughter and sister, must necessarily not be so complete as it may be with other men. And then, India, I must remember, is a vast continent, not merely a country, and is inhabited by many different races. The nations of Europe are nearer to each other, more similar to each other, than the races in India. You may get just a rough idea of it if I tell you that there are eight different languages in all India. Different languages—not dialects—each having a literature of its own. The Hindi language, alone, is spoken by 100,000,000 people; the Bengali by about 60,000,000, and so on. Then, again, the four northern Indian languages differ more from the southern Indian languages than any two European languages from each other. They are entirely different, as much different as your language differs from the Japanese, so that you will be astonished to know, when I go to southern India, unless I meet some people who can talk Sanskrit, I have to speak to them in English. Furthermore, these various races differ from each other in manners, customs, food, dress, and in their methods of thought.

Then, again, there is caste. Each caste has become, as it were, a separate racial element. If a man lives long enough in India, he will be able to tell from the features what caste a man belongs to. Then, between castes, the manners and customs are different. And all these castes are exclusive; that is to say, they would meet socially, but they would not eat or drink together, nor intermarry. In those things they remain separate. They would meet and be friends to each other, but there it would end.

Although I have more opportunity than many other men to know women in general, from my position and my occupation as a preacher, continuously travelling from one place to another and coming in contact with all grades of society (and women, even in northern India, where they do not appear before men, in many places would break this law for religion and would come to hear us preach and talk to us)—still it would be hazardous on my part to assert that I know everything about the women of India.

So I will try to place before you the ideal. In each nation, man or woman represents an ideal consciously or unconsciously being worked out. The individual is the external expression of an ideal to be embodied. The collection of such individuals is the nation, which also represents a great ideal; towards that it is moving. And, therefore, it is rightly assumed that to understand a nation you must first understand its ideal, for each nation refuses to be judged by any other standard than its own.

All growth, progress, well-being, or degradation is but relative. It refers to a certain standard, and each man to be understood has to be referred to that standard of his perfection. You see this more markedly in nations: What one nation thinks good might not be so regarded by another nation. Cousin-marriage is quite permissible in this country. Now, in India, it is illegal; not only so, it would be classed with the most horrible incest. Widow-marriage is perfectly legitimate in this country. Among the higher castes in India it would be the greatest degradation for a woman to marry twice. So, you see, we work through such different ideas that to judge one people by the other's standard would be neither just nor practicable. Therefore, we must know what the ideal is that a nation has raised before itself. When speaking of different nations, we start with a general idea that there is one code of ethics and the same kind of ideals for all races; practically, however, when we come to judge of others, we think what is good for us must be good for everybody; what we do is the right thing, what we do not do, of course in others would be outrageous. I do not mean to say this as a criticism, but just to bring the truth home. When I hear Western women denounce the confining of the feet of Chinese ladies, they never seem to think of the corsets which are doing far more injury to the race. This is just one example; for you must know that cramping the feet does not do one-millionth part of the injury to the human form that the corset has done and is doing—when every organ is displaced and the spine is curved like a serpent. When measurements are taken, you can note the curvatures.

I do not mean that as a criticism but just to point out to you the situation, that as you stand aghast at women of other races, thinking that you are supreme, the very reason that they do not adopt your manners and customs shows that they also stand aghast at you.

Therefore, there is some misunderstanding on both sides. There is a common platform, a common ground of understanding, a common humanity, which must be the basis of our work. We ought to find out that complete and perfect human nature which is working only in parts, here and there. It has not been given to one man to have everything in perfection. You have a part to play; I, in my humble way, another; here is one who plays a little part; there, another. The perfection is the combination of all these parts. Just as with individuals, so with races. Each race has a part to play; each race has one side of human nature to develop. And we have to take all these together; and, possibly in the distant future, some race will arise in which all these marvellous individual race perfections, attained by the different races, will come together and form a new race, the like of which the world has not yet dreamed. Beyond saying that, I have no criticism to offer about anybody. I have travelled not a little in my life; I have kept my eyes open; and the more I go about the more my mouth is closed. I have no criticism to offer.

Now, the ideal woman in India is the mother, the mother first, and the mother last. The word woman calls up to the mind of the Hindu, motherhood; and God is called Mother. As children, every day, when we are boys, we have to go early in the morning with a little cup of water and place it before the mother, and mother dips her toe into it and we drink it.

In the West, the woman is wife. The idea of womanhood is concentrated there—as the wife. To the ordinary man in India, the whole force of womanhood is concentrated in motherhood. In the Western home, the wife rules. In an Indian home, the mother rules. If a mother comes into a Western home, she has to be subordinate to the wife; to the wife belongs the home. A mother always lives in our homes: the wife must be subordinate to her. See all the difference of ideas.

Now, I only suggest comparisons; I would state facts so that we may compare the two sides. Make this comparison. If you ask, 'What is an Indian woman as wife?' the Indian asks, 'Where is the American woman as mother? What is she, the all-glorious, who gave me this body? What is she who kept me in her body for nine months? Where is she who would give me twenty times her life, if I had need? Where is she whose love never dies, however wicked, however vile I am? Where is she, in comparison with her, who goes to the divorce court the moment I treat her a little badly? O American woman! where is she?' I will not find her in your country. I have not found the son who thinks mother is first. When we die, even then, we do not want our wives and our children to take her place. Our mother! We want to die with our head on her lap once more, if we die before her. Where is she? Is woman a name to be coupled with the physical body only? Ay! the Hindu mind fears all those ideals which say that the flesh must cling unto the flesh. No, no! Woman! thou shalt not be coupled with anything connected with the flesh. The name has been called holy once and for ever, for what name is there which no lust can ever approach, no carnality ever come near, than the one word mother? That is the ideal in India.

I belong to an Order very much like what you have in the Mendicant Friars of the Catholic Church; that is to say, we have to go about without very much in the way of dress and beg from door to door, live thereby, preach to people when they want it, sleep where we can get a place—that way we have to follow. And the rule is that the members of this Order have to call every woman 'mother'; to every woman and little girl we have to say 'mother'; that is the custom. Coming to the West, that old habit remained and I would say to ladies, 'Yes, mother', and they are horrified. I could not understand why they should be horrified. Later on, I discovered the reason: because that would mean that they are old. The ideal of womanhood in India is motherhood—that marvellous, unselfish, all-suffering, ever-forgiving mother. The wife walks behind—the shadow. She must imitate the life of the mother; that is her duty. But the mother is the ideal of love; she rules the family, she possesses the family. It is the father in India who thrashes the child and spanks when there is something done by the child, and always the mother puts herself between the father and the child. You see it is just the opposite here. It has become the mother's business to spank the children in this country, and poor father comes in between. You see, ideals are different. I do not mean this as any criticism. It is all good—this what you do; but our way is what we have been taught for ages. You never hear of a mother cursing the child; she is forgiving, always forgiving. Instead of 'Our Father in Heaven', we say 'Mother' all the time; that idea and that word are ever associated in the Hindu mind with Infinite Love, the mother's love being the nearest approach to God's love in this mortal world of ours. 'Mother, O Mother, be merciful; I am wicked! Many children have been wicked, but there never was a wicked mother'—so says the great saint Ramprasad.

There she is—the Hindu mother. The son's wife comes in as her daughter; just as the mother's own daughter married and went out, so her son married and brought in another daughter, and she has to fall in line under the government of the queen of queens, of his mother. Even I, who never married, belonging to an Order that never marries, would be disgusted if my wife, supposing I had married, dared to displease my mother. I would be disgusted. Why? Do I not worship my mother? Why should not her daughter-in-law? Whom I worship, why not she? Who is she, then, that would try to ride over my head and govern my mother? She has to wait till her womanhood is fulfilled; and the one thing that fulfils womanhood, that is womanliness in woman, is motherhood. Wait till she becomes a mother; then she will have the same right. That, according to the Hindu mind, is the great mission of woman—to become a mother. But oh, how different! Oh, how different! My father and mother fasted and prayed, for years and years, so that I would be born. They pray for every child before it is born. Says our great law-giver, Manu, giving the definition of an Aryan, 'He is the Aryan, who is born through prayer'. Every child not born through prayer is illegitimate, according to the great law-giver. The child must be prayed for. Those children that come with curses, that slip into the world, just in a moment of inadvertence, because that could not be prevented—what can we expect of such progeny? Mothers of America, think of that! Think in the heart of your hearts, are you ready to be women? Not any question of race or country, or that false sentiment of national pride. Who dares to be proud in this mortal life of ours, in this world of woes and miseries? What are we before this infinite force of God? But I ask you the question tonight: Do you all pray for the children to come? Are you thankful to be mothers, or not? Do you think that you are sanctified by motherhood, or not? Ask that of your minds. If you do not, your marriage is a lie, your womanhood is false, your education is superstition, and your children, if they come without prayer, will prove a curse to humanity.

See the different ideals now coming before us. From motherhood comes tremendous responsibility. There is the basis, start from that. Well, why is mother to be worshipped so much? Because our books teach that it is the pre-natal influence that gives the impetus to the child for good or evil. Go to a hundred thousand colleges, read a million books, associate with all the learned men of the world—better off you are when born with the right stamp. You are born for good or evil. The child is a born god or a born demon; that is what the books say. Education and all these things come afterwards—are a mere bagatelle. You are what you are born. Born unhealthful, how many drug stores, swallowed wholesale, will keep you well all through your life? How many people of good, healthy lives were born of weak parents, were born of sickly, blood-poisoned parents? How many? None—none. We come with a tremendous impetus for good or evil: born demons or born gods. Education or other things are a bagatelle.

Thus say our books: direct the pre-natal influence. Why should mother be worshipped? Because she made herself pure. She underwent harsh penances sometimes to keep herself as pure as purity can be. For, mind you, no woman in India thinks of giving up her body to any man; it is her own. The English, as a reform, have introduced at present what they call 'Restitution of conjugal rights', but no Indian would take advantage of it. When a man comes in physical contact with his wife, the circumstances she controls through what prayers and through what vows! For that which brings forth the child is the holiest symbol of God himself. It is the greatest prayer between man and wife, the prayer that is going to bring into the world another soul fraught with a tremendous power for good or for evil. Is it a joke? Is it a simple nervous satisfaction? Is it a brute enjoyment of the body?

Says the Hindu: no, a thousand times, no!

But then, following that, there comes in another idea. The idea we started with was that the ideal is the love for the mother—herself all-suffering, all-forbearing. The worship that is accorded to the mother has its fountain-head there. She was a saint to bring me into the world; she kept her body pure, her mind pure, her food pure, her clothes pure, her imagination pure, for years, because I would be born. Because she did that, she deserves worship. And what follows? Linked with motherhood is wifehood.

You Western people are individualistic. I want to do this thing because I like it; I will elbow every one. Why? Because I like to. I want my own satisfaction, so I marry this woman. Why? Because I like her. This woman marries me. Why? Because she likes me. There it ends. She and I are the only two persons in the whole, infinite world; and I marry her and she marries me—nobody else is injured, nobody else responsible.

Your Johns and your Janes may go into the forest and there they may live their lives; but when they have to live in society, their marriage means a tremendous amount of good or evil to us. Their children may be veritable demons—burning, murdering, robbing, stealing, drinking, hideous, vile.

So what is the basis of the Indian's social order? It is the caste law. I am born for the caste, I live for the caste. I do not mean myself, because, having joined an Order, we are outside. I mean those that live in civil society. Born in the caste, the whole life must be lived according to caste regulation. In other words, in the present-day language of your country, the Western man is born individualistic, while the Hindu is socialistic—entirely socialistic. Now, then, the books say: If I allow you freedom to go about and marry any woman you like, and the woman to marry any man she likes, what happens? You fall in love; the father of the woman was, perchance, a lunatic or a consumptive. The girl falls in love with the face of a man whose father was a roaring drunkard. What says the law then? The law lays down that all these marriages would be illegal. The children of drunkards, consumptives, lunatics, etc., shall not be married. The deformed, humpbacked, crazy, idiotic—no marriage for them, absolutely none, says the law.

But the Mohammedan comes from Arabia, and he has his own Arabian law; so the Arabian desert law has been forced upon us. The Englishman comes with his law; he forces it upon us, so far as he can. We are conquered. He says, 'Tomorrow I will marry your sister'. What can we do? Our law says, those that are born of the same family, though a hundred degrees distant, must not marry, that is illegitimate, it would deteriorate or make the race sterile. That must not be, and there it stops. So, I have no voice in my marriage, nor my sister. It is the caste that determines all that.

We are married sometimes when children. Why? Because the caste says: If they have to be married anyway without their consent, it is better that they are married very early, before they have developed this love: if they are allowed to grow up apart, the boy may like some other girl, and the girl some other boy, and then something evil will happen; and so, says the caste, stop it there. I do not care whether my sister is deformed, or good-looking, or bad-looking: she is my sister, and that is enough; he is my brother, and that is all I need to know. So they will love each other. You may say, 'Oh! they lose a great deal of enjoyment—those exquisite emotions of a man falling in love with a woman and a woman falling in love with a man. This is a sort of tame thing, loving each other like brothers and sisters, as though they have to.' So be it; but the Hindu says, 'We are socialistic. For the sake of one man's or woman's exquisite pleasure we do not want to load misery on hundreds of others.'

There they are—married. The wife comes home with her husband; that is called the second marriage. Marriage at an early age is considered the first marriage, and they grow up separately with women and with their parents. When they are grown, there is a second ceremony performed, called a second marriage. And then they live together, but under the same roof with his mother and father. When she becomes a mother, she takes her place in turn as queen of the family group.

Now comes another peculiar Indian institution. I have just told you that in the first two or three castes the widows are not allowed to marry. They cannot, even if they would. Of course, it is a hardship on many. There is no denying that not all the widows like it very much, because non-marrying entails upon them the life of a student. That is to say, a student must not eat meat or fish, nor drink wine, nor dress except in white clothes, and so on; there are many regulations. We are a nation of monks—always making penance, and we like it. Now, you see, a woman never drinks wine or eats meat. It was a hardship on us when we were students, but not on the girls. Our women would feel degraded at the idea of eating meat. Men eat meat sometimes in some castes; women never. Still, not being allowed to marry must be a hardship to many; I am sure of that.

But we must go back to the idea; they are intensely socialistic. In the higher castes of every country you will find the statistics show that the number of women is always much larger than the number of men. Why? Because in the higher castes, for generation after generation, the women lead an easy life. They 'neither toil nor spin, yet Solomon in all his glory was not arrayed like one of them'. And the poor boys, they die like flies. The girl has a cat's nine lives, they say in India. You will read in the statistics that they outnumber the boys in a very short time, except now when they are taking to work quite as hard as the boys. The number of girls in the higher castes is much larger than in the lower. Conditions are quite opposite in the lower castes. There they all work hard; women a little harder, sometimes, because they have to do the domestic work. But, mind you, I never would have thought of that, but one of your American travellers, Mark Twain, writes this about India: 'In spite of all that Western critics have said of Hindu customs, I never saw a woman harnessed to a plough with a cow or to a cart with a dog, as is done in some European countries. I saw no woman or girl at work in the fields in India. On both sides and ahead (of the railway train) brown-bodied naked men and boys are ploughing in the fields. But not a woman. In these two hours I have not seen a woman or a girl working in the fields. In India, even the lowest caste never does any hard work. They generally have an easy lot compared to the same class in other nations; and as to ploughing, they never do it.'

Now, there you are. Among the lower classes the number of men is larger than the number of women; and what would you naturally expect? A woman gets more chances of marriage, the number of men being larger.

Relative to such questions as to widows not marrying: among the first two castes, the number of women is disproportionately large, and here is a dilemma. Either you have a non-marriageable widow problem and misery, or the non-husband-getting young lady problem. To face the widow problem, or the old maid problem? There you are; either of the two. Now, go back again to the idea that the Indian mind is socialistic. It says, 'Now look here! we take the widow problem as the lesser one.' Why? 'Because they have had their chance; they have been married. If they have lost their chance, at any rate they have had one. Sit down, be quiet, and consider these poor girls—they have not had one chance of marriage.' Lord bless you! I remember once in Oxford Street, it was after ten o'clock, and all those ladies coming there, hundreds and thousands of them shopping; and some man, an American, looks around, and he says, 'My Lord! how many of them will ever get husbands, I wonder!' So the Indian mind said to the widows, 'Well, you have had your chance, and now we are very, very sorry that such mishaps have come to you, but we cannot help it; others are waiting.'

Then religion comes into the question; the Hindu religion comes in as a comfort. For, mind you, our religion teaches that marriage is something bad, it is only for the weak. The very spiritual man or woman would not marry at all. So the religious woman says, 'Well, the Lord has given me a better chance. What is the use of marrying? Thank God, worship God, what is the use of my loving man?' Of course, all of them cannot put their mind on God. Some find it simply impossible. They have to suffer; but the other poor people, they should not suffer for them. Now I leave this to your judgment; but that is their idea in India.

Next we come to woman as daughter. The great difficulty in the Indian household is the daughter. The daughter and caste combined ruin the poor Hindu, because, you see, she must marry in the same caste, and even inside the caste exactly in the same order; and so the poor man sometimes has to make himself a beggar to get his daughter married. The father of the boy demands a very high price for his son, and this poor man sometimes has to sell everything just to get a husband for his daughter. The great difficulty of the Hindu's life is the daughter. And, curiously enough, the word daughter in Sanskrit is 'duhita'. The real derivation is that, in ancient times, the daughter of the family was accustomed to milk the cows, and so the word 'duhita' comes from 'duh', to milk; and the word 'daughter' really means a milkmaid. Later on, they found a new meaning to that word 'duhita', the milkmaid—she who milks away all the milk of the family. That is the second meaning.

These are the different relations held by our Indian women. As I have told you, the mother is the greatest in position, the wife is next, and the daughter comes after them. It is a most intricate and complicated series of gradation. No foreigner can understand it, even if he lives there for years. For instance, we have three forms of the personal pronoun; they are a sort of verbs in our language. One is very respectful, one is middling, and the lowest is just like thou and thee. To children and servants the last is addressed. The middling one is used with equals. You see, these are to be applied in all the intricate relations of life. For example, to my elder sister I always throughout my life use the pronoun apani, but she never does in speaking to me; she says tumi to me. She should not, even by mistake, say apani to me, because that would mean a curse. Love, the love toward those that are superior, should always be expressed in that form of language. That is the custom. Similarly I would never dare address my elder sister or elder brother, much less my mother or father, as tu or tum or tumi. As to calling our mother and father by name, why, we would never do that. Before I knew the customs of this country, I received such a shock when the son, in a very refined family, got up and called the mother by name! However, I got used to that. That is the custom of the country. But with us, we never pronounce the name of our parents when they are present. It is always in the third person plural, even before them.

Thus we see the most complicated mesh-work in the social life of our men and our women and in our degree of relationship. We do not speak to our wives before our elders; it is only when we are alone or when inferiors are present. If I were married, I would speak to my wife before my younger sister, my nephews or nieces; but not before my elder sister or parents. I cannot talk to my sisters about their husbands at all. The idea is, we are a monastic race. The whole social organization has that one idea before it. Marriage is thought of as something impure, something lower. Therefore the subject of love would never be talked of. I cannot read a novel before my sister, or my brothers, or my mother, or even before others. I close the book.

Then again, eating and drinking is all in the same category. We do not eat before superiors. Our women never eat before men, except they be the children or inferiors. The wife would die rather than, as she says, 'munch' before her husband. Sometimes, for instance, brothers and sisters may eat together; and if I and my sister are eating, and the husband comes to the door, my sister stops, and the poor husband flies out.

These are the customs peculiar to the country. A few of these I note in different countries also. As I never married myself, I am not perfect in all my knowledge about the wife. Mother, sisters—i know what they are; and other people's wives I saw; from that I gather what I have told you.

As to education and culture, it all depends upon the man. That is to say, where the men are highly cultured, there the women are; where the men are not, women are not. Now, from the oldest times, you know, the primary education, according to the old Hindu customs, belongs to the village system. All the land from time immemorial was nationalized, as you say—belonged to the Government. There never is any private right in land. The revenue in India comes from the land, because every man holds so much land from the Government. This land is held in common by a community, it may be five, ten, twenty, or a hundred families. They govern the whole of the land, pay a certain amount of revenue to the Government, maintain a physician, a village schoolmaster, and so on.

Those of you who have read Herbert Spencer remember what he calls the 'monastery system' of education that was tried in Europe and which in some parts proved a success; that is, there is one schoolmaster, whom the village keeps. These primary schools are very rudimentary, because our methods are so simple. Each boy brings a little mat; and his paper, to begin with, is palm leaves. Palm leaves first, paper is too costly. Each boy spreads his little mat and sits upon it, brings out his inkstand and his books and begins to write. A little arithmetic, some Sanskrit grammar, a little of language and accounts—these are taught in the primary school.

A little book on ethics, taught by an old man, we learnt by heart, and I remember one of the lessons: 'For the good of a village, a man ought to give up his family;

For the good of a country, he ought to give up his village;
For the good of humanity, he may give up his country;
For the good of the world, everything.'

Such verses are there in the books. We get them by heart, and they are explained by teacher and pupil. These things we learn, both boys and girls together. Later on, the education differs. The old Sanskrit universities are mainly composed of boys. The girls very rarely go up to those universities; but there are a few exceptions.

In these modern days there is a greater impetus towards higher education on the European lines, and the trend of opinion is strong towards women getting this higher education. Of course, there are some people in India who do not want it, but those who do want it carried the day. It is a strange fact that Oxford and Cambridge are closed to women today, so are Harvard and Yale; but Calcutta University opened its doors to women more than twenty years ago. I remember that the year I graduated, several girls came out and graduated—the same standard, the same course, the same in everything as the boys; and they did very well indeed. And our religion does not prevent a woman being educated at all. In this way the girl should be educated; even thus she should be trained; and in the old books we find that the universities were equally resorted to by both girls and boys, but later the education of the whole nation was neglected. What can you expect under foreign rule? The foreign conqueror is not there to do good to us; he wants his money. I studied hard for twelve years and became a graduate of Calcutta University; now I can scarcely make $5.00 a month in my country. Would you believe it? It is actually a fact. So these educational institutions of foreigners are simply to get a lot of useful, practical slaves for a little money—to turn out a host of clerks, postmasters, telegraph operators, and so on. There it is.

As a result, education for both boys and girls is neglected, entirely neglected. There are a great many things that should be done in that land; but you must always remember, if you will kindly excuse me and permit me to use one of your own proverbs, 'What is sauce for the goose is sauce for the gander.' Your foreign born ladies are always crying over the hardships of the Hindu woman, and never care for the hardships of the Hindu man. They are all weeping salt tears. But who are the little girls married to? Some one, when told that they are all married to old men, asked, 'And what do the young men do? What! are all the girls married to old men, only to old men?' We are born old—perhaps all the men there.

The ideal of the Indian race is freedom of the soul. This world is nothing. It is a vision, a dream. This life is one of many millions like it. The whole of this nature is Maya, is phantasm, a pest house of phantasms. That is the philosophy. Babies smile at life and think it so beautiful and good, but in a few years they will have to revert to where they began. They began life crying, and they will leave it crying. Nations in the vigour of their youth think that they can do anything and everything: 'We are the gods of the earth. We are the chosen people.' They think that God Almighty has given them a charter to rule over all the world, to advance His plans, to do anything they like, to turn the world upside down. They have a charter to rob, murder, kill; God has given them this, and they do that because they are only babes. So empire after empire has arisen—glorious, resplendent— now vanished away—gone, nobody knows where; it may have been stupendous in its ruin.

As a drop of water upon a lotus leaf tumbles about and falls in a moment, even so is this mortal life. Everywhere we turn are ruins. Where the forest stands today was once the mighty empire with huge cities. That is the dominant idea, the tone, the colour of the Indian mind. We know, you Western people have the youthful blood coursing through your veins. We know that nations, like men, have their day. Where is Greece? Where is Rome? Where that mighty Spaniard of the other day? Who knows through it all what becomes of India? Thus they are born, and thus they die; they rise and fall. The Hindu as a child knows of the Mogul invader whose cohorts no power on earth could stop, who has left in your language the terrible word 'Tartar'. The Hindu has learnt his lesson. He does not want to prattle, like the babes of today. Western people, say what you have to say. This is your day. Onward, go on, babes; have your prattle out. This is the day of the babies, to prattle. We have learnt our lesson and are quiet. You have a little wealth today, and you look down upon us. Well, this is your day. Prattle, babes, prattle—this is the Hindu's attitude.

The Lord of Lords is not to be attained by much frothy speech. The Lord of Lords is not to be attained even by the powers of the intellect. He is not gained by much power of conquest. That man who knows the secret source of things and that everything else is evanescent, unto him He, the Lord, comes; unto none else. India has learnt her lesson through ages and ages of experience. She has turned her face towards Him. She has made many mistakes; loads and loads of rubbish are heaped upon the race. Never mind; what of that? What is the clearing of rubbish, the cleaning of cities, and all that? Does that give life? Those that have fine institutions, they die. And what of institutions, those tinplate Western institutions, made in five days and broken on the sixth? One of these little handful nations cannot keep alive for two centuries together. And our institutions have stood the test of ages. Says the Hindu, 'Yes, we have buried all the old nations of the earth and stand here to bury all the new races also, because our ideal is not this world, but the other. Just as your ideal is, so shall you be. If your ideal is mortal, if your ideal is of this earth, so shalt thou be. If your ideal is matter, matter shalt thou be. Behold! Our ideal is the Spirit. That alone exists, nothing else exists; and like Him, we live for ever.'

16

SOUL, GOD AND RELIGION

Through the vistas of the past the voice of the centuries is coming down to us; the voice of the sages of the Himalayas and the recluses of the forest; the voice that came to the Semitic races; the voice that spoke through Buddha and other spiritual giants; the voice that comes from those who live in the light that accompanied man in the beginning of the earth—the light that shines wherever man goes and lives with him for ever—is coming to us even now. This voice is like the little rivulets; that come from the mountains. Now they disappear, and now they appear again in stronger flow till finally they unite in one mighty majestic flood. The messages that are coming down to us from the prophets and holy men and women of all sects and nations are joining their forces and speaking to us with the trumpet voice of the past. And the first message it brings us is: Peace be unto you and to all religions. It is not a message of antagonism, but of one united religion.

Let us study this message first. At the beginning of this century it was almost feared that religion was at an end. Under the tremendous sledge-hammer blows of scientific research, old superstitions were crumbling away like masses of porcelain. Those to whom religion meant only a bundle of creeds and meaningless ceremonials were in despair; they were at their wit's end. Everything was slipping between their fingers. For a time it seemed inevitable that the surging tide of agnosticism and materialism would sweep all before it. There were those who did not dare utter what they thought. Many thought the case hopeless and the cause of religion lost once and for ever. But the tide has turned and to the rescue has come—what? The study of comparative religions. By the study of different religions we find that in essence they are one. When I was a boy, this scepticism reached me, and it seemed for a time as if I must give up all hope of religion. But fortunately for me I studied the Christian religion, the Mohammedan, the Buddhistic, and others, and what was my surprise to find that the same foundation principles taught by my religion were also taught by all religions. It appealed to me this way. What is the truth? I asked. Is this world true? Yes. Why? Because I see it. Are the beautiful sounds we just heard (the vocal and instrumental music) true? Yes. Because we heard them. We know that man has a body, eyes, and ears, and he has a spiritual nature which we cannot see. And with his spiritual faculties he can study these different religions and find that whether a religion is taught in the forests and jungles of India or in a Christian land, in essentials all religions are one. This only shows us that religion is a constitutional necessity of the human mind. The proof of one religion depends on the proof of all the rest. For instance, if I have six fingers, and no one else has, you may well say that is abnormal. The same reasoning may be applied to the argument that only one religion is true and all others false. One religion only, like one set of six fingers in the world, would be unnatural. We see, therefore, that if one religion is true, all others must be true. There are differences in non-essentials, but in essentials they are all one. If my five fingers are true, they prove that your five fingers are true too. Wherever man is, he must develop a belief, he must develop his religious nature.

And another fact I find in the study of the various religions of the world is that there are three different stages of ideas with regard to the soul and God. In the first place, all religions admit that, apart from the body which perishes, there is a certain part or something which does not change like the body, a part that is immutable, eternal, that never dies; but some of the later religions teach that although there is a part of us that never dies, it had a beginning. But anything that has a beginning must necessarily have an end. We—the essential part of us—never had a beginning, and will never have an end. And above us all, above this eternal nature, there is another eternal Being, without end—God. People talk about the beginning of the world, the beginning of man. The word beginning simply means the beginning of the cycle. It nowhere means the beginning of the whole Cosmos. It is impossible that creation could have a beginning. No one of you can imagine a time of beginning. That which has a beginning must have an end. 'Never did I not exist, nor you, nor will any of us ever hereafter cease to be,' says the Bhagavad Gita. Wherever the beginning of creation is mentioned, it means the beginning of a cycle. Your body will meet with death, but your soul, never.

Along with this idea of the soul we find another group of ideas in regard to its perfection. The soul in itself is perfect. The Old Testament of the Hebrews admits man perfect at the beginning. Man made himself impure by his own actions. But he is to regain his old nature, his pure nature. Some speak of these things in allegories, fables, and symbols. But when we begin to analyse these statements, we find that they all teach that the human soul is in its very nature perfect, and that man is to regain that original purity. How? By knowing God. Just as the Bible says, 'No man can see God but through the Son.' What is meant by it? That seeing God is the aim and goal of all human life. The sonship must come before we become one with the Father. Remember that man lost his purity through his own actions. When we suffer, it is because of our own acts; God is not to be blamed for it.

Closely connected with these ideas is the doctrine—which was universal before the Europeans mutilated it—the doctrine of reincarnation. Some of you may have heard of and ignored it. This idea of reincarnation runs parallel with the other doctrine of the eternity of the human soul. Nothing which ends at one point can be without a beginning and nothing that begins at one point can be without an end. We cannot believe in such a monstrous impossibility as the beginning of the human soul. The doctrine of reincarnation asserts the freedom of the soul. Suppose there was an absolute beginning. Then the whole burden of this impurity in man falls upon God. The all-merciful Father responsible for the sins of the world! If sin comes in this way, why should one suffer more than another? Why such partiality, if it comes from an all-merciful God? Why are millions trampled underfoot? Why do people starve who never did anything to cause it? Who is responsible? If they had no hand in it, surely, God would be responsible. Therefore, the better explanation is that one is responsible for the miseries one suffers. If I set the wheel in motion, I am responsible for the result. And if I can bring misery, I can also stop it. It necessarily follows that we are free. There is no such thing as fate. There is nothing to compel us. What we have done, that we can undo.

To one argument in connection with this doctrine I will ask your patient attention, as it is a little intricate. We gain all our knowledge through experience; that is the only way. What we call experiences are on the plane of consciousness. For illustration: A man plays a tune on a piano, he places each finger on each key consciously. He repeats this process till the movement of the fingers becomes a habit. He then plays a tune without having to pay special attention to each particular key. Similarly, we find in regard to ourselves that our tendencies are the result of past conscious actions. A child is born with certain tendencies. Whence do they come? No child is born with a *tabula rasa*—with a clean, blank page—of a mind. The page has been written on previously. The old Greek and Egyptian philosophers taught that no child came with a vacant mind. Each child comes with a hundred tendencies generated by past conscious actions. It did not acquire these in this life, and we are bound to admit that it must have had them in past lives. The rankest materialist has to admit that these tendencies are the result of past actions, only they add that these tendencies come through heredity. Our parents, grandparents, and great-grandparents come down to us through this law of heredity. Now if heredity alone explains this, there is no necessity of believing in the soul at all, because body explains everything. We need not go into the different arguments and discussions on materialism and spiritualism. So far the way is clear for those who believe in an individual soul. We see that to come to a reasonable conclusion we must admit that we have had past lives. This is the belief of the great philosophers and sages of the past and of modern times. Such a doctrine was believed in among the Jews. Jesus Christ believed in it. He says in the Bible, 'Before Abraham was, I am.' And in another place it is said, 'This is Elias who is said to have come.'

All the different religions which grew among different nations under varying circumstances and conditions had their origin in Asia, and the Asiatics understand them well. When they came out from the motherland, they got mixed up with errors. The most profound and noble ideas of Christianity were never understood in Europe,

because the ideas and images used by the writers of the Bible were
foreign to it. Take for illustration the pictures of the Madonna. Every
artist paints his Madonna according to his own pre-conceived ideas.
I have been seeing hundreds of pictures of the Last Supper of Jesus
Christ, and he is made to sit at a table. Now, Christ never sat at a
table; he squatted with others, and they had a bowl in which they
dipped bread—not the kind of bread you eat today. It is hard for any
nation to understand the unfamiliar customs of other people. How
much more difficult was it for Europeans to understand the Jewish
customs after centuries of changes and accretions from Greek, Roman,
and other sources! Through all the myths and mythologies by which
it is surrounded it is no wonder that the people get very little of the
beautiful religion of Jesus, and no wonder that they have made of it
a modern shop-keeping religion.

To come to our point. We find that all religions teach the eternity
of the soul, as well as that its lustre has been dimmed, and that its
primitive purity is to be regained by the knowledge of God. What
is the idea of God in these different religions? The primary idea of
God was very vague. The most ancient nations had different Deities—
sun, earth, fire, water. Among the ancient Jews we find numbers of
these gods ferociously fighting with each other. Then we find Elohim
whom the Jews and the Babylonians worshipped. We next find one
God standing supreme. But the idea differed according to different
tribes. They each asserted that their God was the greatest. And they
tried to prove it by fighting. The one that could do the best fighting
proved thereby that its God was the greatest. Those races were more
or less savage. But gradually better and better ideas took the place of
the old ones. All those old ideas are gone or going into the lumber-
room. All those religions were the outgrowth of centuries; not one
fell from the skies. Each had to be worked out bit by bit. Next come
the monotheistic ideas: belief in one God, who is omnipotent and
omniscient, the one God of the universe. This one God is extra-cosmic;
he lies in the heavens. He is invested with the gross conceptions of
His originators. He has a right side and a left side, and a bird in His
hand, and so on and so forth. But one thing we find, that the tribal
gods have disappeared for ever, and the one God of the universe has

taken their place: the God of gods. Still He is only an extra-cosmic God. He is unapproachable; nothing can come near Him. But slowly this idea has changed also, and at the next stage we find a God immanent in nature.

In the New Testament it is taught, 'Our Father who art in heaven'— God living in the heavens separated from men. We are living on earth and He is living in heaven. Further on we find the teaching that He is a God immanent in nature; He is not only God in heaven, but on earth too. He is the God in us. In the Hindu philosophy we find a stage of the same proximity of God to us. But we do not stop there. There is the non-dualistic stage, in which man realizes that the God he has been worshipping is not only the Father in heaven, and on earth, but that 'I and my Father are one.' He realizes in his soul that he is God Himself, only a lower expression of Him. All that is real in me is He; all that is real in Him is I. The gulf between God and man is thus bridged. Thus we find how, by knowing God, we find the kingdom of heaven within us.

In the first or dualistic stage, man knows he is a little personal soul, John, James, or Tom; and he says, 'I will be John, James, or Tom to all eternity, and never anything else.' As well might the murderer come along and say, 'I will remain a murderer for ever.' But as time goes on, Tom vanishes and goes back to the original pure Adam.

'Blessed are the pure in heart, for they shall see God.' Can we see God? Of course not. Can we know God? Of course not. If God can be known, He will be God no longer. Knowledge is limitation. But I and my Father are one: I find the reality in my soul. These ideas are expressed in some religions, and in others only hinted. In some they were expatriated. Christ's teachings are now very little understood in this country. If you will excuse me, I will say that they have never been very well understood.

The different stages of growth are absolutely necessary to the attainment of purity and perfection. The varying systems of religion are at bottom founded on the same ideas. Jesus says the kingdom of heaven is within you. Again he says, 'Our father who art in Heaven.' How do you reconcile the two sayings? In this way: He was talking to the uneducated masses when he said the latter, the masses who were uneducated in religion. It was necessary to speak to them in their own language. The masses want concrete ideas, something the senses can grasp. A man may be the greatest philosopher in the world, but a child in religion. When a man has developed a high state of spirituality he can understand that the kingdom of heaven is within him. That is the real kingdom of the mind. Thus, we see that the apparent contradictions and perplexities in every religion mark but different stages of growth. And as such we have no right to blame anyone for his religion. There are stages of growth in which forms and symbols are necessary; they are the language that the souls in that stage can understand.

The next idea that I want to bring to you is that religion does not consist in doctrines or dogmas. It is not what you read, nor what dogmas you believe that is of importance, but what you realize. 'Blessed are the pure in heart, for they shall see God,' yea, in this life. And that is salvation. There are those who teach that this can be gained by the mumbling of words. But no great Master ever taught that external forms were necessary for salvation. The power of attaining it is within ourselves. We live and move in God. Creeds and sects have their parts to play, but they are for children, they last but temporarily. Books never make religions, but religions make books. We must not forget that. No book ever created God, but God inspired all the great books. And no book ever created a soul. We must never forget that. The end of all religions is the realising of God in the soul. That is the one universal religion. If there is one universal truth in all religions, I place it here—in realising God. Ideals and methods may differ, but that is the central point. There may be a thousand different radii, but they all converge to the one centre, and that is the realization of God: Something behind this world of sense, this world of eternal eating and drinking and talking nonsense, this world of false shadows and selfishness. There is that beyond all books, beyond all creeds, beyond the vanities of this world and it is the realization of God within yourself. A man may believe in all the churches in the world, he may carry in his head all the sacred books ever written, he may baptize himself in all the rivers of the earth, still, if he has no perception of God, I would class him with the rankest atheist. And a man may have never entered a church or a mosque, nor performed any ceremony, but if he feels God within himself and is thereby lifted above the vanities of the world, that man is a holy man, a saint, call him what you will. As soon as a man stands up and says he is right or his church is right, and all others are wrong, he is himself all wrong. He does not know that upon the proof of all the others depends the proof of his own. Love and charity for the whole human race, that is the test of true religiousness. I do not mean the sentimental statement that all men are brothers, but that one must feel the oneness of human life. So far as they are not exclusive, I see that the sects and creeds are all mine; they are all grand. They are all helping men towards the real religion. I will add, it is good to be born in a church, but it is bad to die there. It is good to be born a child, but bad to remain a child. Churches, ceremonies, and symbols are good for children, but when the child is grown, he must burst the church or himself. We must not remain children for ever. It is like trying to fit one coat to all sizes and growths. I do not deprecate the existence of sects in the world. Would to God there were twenty millions more, for the more there are, there will be a greater field for selection. What I do object to is trying to fit one religion to every case. Though all religions are essentially the same, they must have the varieties of form produced by dissimilar circumstances among different nations. We must each have our own individual religion, individual so far as the externals of it go.

Many years ago, I visited a great sage of our own country, a very holy man. We talked of our revealed book, the Vedas, of your Bible, of the Koran, and of revealed books in general. At the close of our talk, this good man asked me to go to the table and take up a book; it was a book which, among other things, contained a forecast of the rainfall during the year. The sage said, 'Read that.' And I read out the quantity of rain that was to fall. He said, 'Now take the book and squeeze it.' I did so and he said, 'Why, my boy, not a drop of water comes out. Until the water comes out, it is all book, book. So until your religion makes you realize God, it is useless. He who only studies books for religion reminds one of the fable of the ass which carried a heavy load of sugar on its back, but did not know the sweetness of it.'

Shall we advise men to kneel down and cry, 'O miserable sinners that we are!' No, rather let us remind them of their divine nature. I will tell you a story. A lioness in search of prey came upon a flock of sheep, and as she jumped at one of them, she gave birth to a cub and died on the spot. The young lion was brought up in the flock, ate grass, and bleated like a sheep, and it never knew that it was a lion. One day a lion came across the flock and was astonished to see in it a huge lion eating grass and bleating like a sheep. At his sight the flock fled and the lion-sheep with them. But the lion watched his opportunity and one day found the lion-sheep asleep. He woke him up and said, 'You are a lion.' The other said, 'No,' and began to bleat like a sheep. But the stranger lion took him to a lake and asked him to look in the water at his own image and see if it did not resemble him, the stranger lion. He looked and acknowledged that it did. Then the stranger lion began to roar and asked him to do the same. The lion-sheep tried his voice and was soon roaring as grandly as the other. And he was a sheep no longer.

My friends, I would like to tell you all that you are mighty as lions.

If the room is dark, do you go about beating your chest and crying, 'It is dark, dark, dark!' No, the only way to get the light is to strike a light, and then the darkness goes. The only way to realize the light above you is to strike the spiritual light within you, and the darkness of sin and impurity will flee away. Think of your higher self, not of your lower.

◆

Some questions and answers here followed.

Q. A man in the audience said, 'If ministers stop preaching hell-fire, they will have no control over their people.'
A. They had better lose it then. The man who is frightened into religion has no religion at all. Better teach him of his divine nature than of his animal.

Q. What did the Lord mean when he said, 'The kingdom of heaven is not of this world?'
A. That the kingdom of heaven is within us. The Jewish idea was a kingdom of heaven upon this earth. That was not the idea of Jesus.

Q. Do you believe we come up from the animals?
A. I believe that, by the law of evolution, the higher beings have come up from the lower kingdoms.

Q. Do you know of anyone who remembers his previous life ?
A. I have met some who told me they did remember their previous life. They had reached a point where they could remember their former incarnations.

Q. Do you believe in Christ's crucifixion?
A. Christ was God incarnate; they could not kill him. That which was crucified was only a semblance, a mirage.

Q. If he could have produced such a semblance as that, would not that have been the greatest miracle of all?
A. I look upon miracles as the greatest stumbling-blocks in the way of truth. When the disciples of Buddha told him of a man who had performed a so-called miracle—had taken a bowl from a great height without touching it—and showed him the bowl, he took it and crushed it under his feet and told them never to build their faith on miracles, but to look for truth in everlasting principles. He taught them the true inner light—the light of the spirit, which is the only safe light to go by. Miracles are only stumbling-blocks. Let us brush them aside.

Q. Do you believe Jesus preached the Sermon on the Mount?
A. I do believe he did. But in this matter I have to go by the books as others do, and I am aware that mere book testimony is rather shaky ground. But we are all safe in taking the teachings of the Sermon on the Mount as a guide. We have to take what appeals to our inner spirit. Buddha taught five hundred years before Christ, and his words were full of blessings: never a curse came from his lips, nor from his life; never one from Zoroaster, nor from Confucius.

17

THE HINDU RELIGION

My religion is to learn. I read my Bible better in the light of your Bible and the dark prophecies of my religion become brighter when compared with those of your prophets. Truth has always been universal. If I alone were to have six fingers on my hand while all of you had only five, you would not think that my hand was the true intent of nature, but rather that it was abnormal and diseased. Just so with religion. If one creed alone were to be true and all the others untrue, you would have a right to say that that religion was diseased; if one religion is true, all the others must be true. Thus, the Hindu religion is your property as well as mine. Of the two hundred and ninety millions of people inhabiting India, only two millions are Christians, sixty millions Mohammedans and all the rest are Hindus.

The Hindus found their creed upon the ancient Vedas, a word derived from Vid, 'to know'. These are a series of books which, to our minds, contain the essence of all religion; but we do not think they alone contain the truths. They teach us the immortality of the soul. In every country and every human breast there is a natural desire to find a stable equilibrium—something that does not change. We cannot find it in nature, for all the universe is nothing but an infinite mass of changes. But to infer from that that nothing unchanging exists is to fall into the error of the Southern school of Buddhists and the Charvakas, which latter believe that all is matter and nothing mind, that all religion is a cheat, and morality and goodness, useless superstitions. The Vedanta philosophy teaches that man is not bound by his five senses. They only know the present, and neither the future nor the past; but as the present signifies both past and future, and all three are only demarcations of time, the present also would be unknown if it were not for something above the senses, something independent of time, which unifies the past and the future in the present.

But what is independent? Not our body, for it depends upon outward conditions; nor our mind, because the thoughts of which it is composed are caused. It is our soul. The Vedas say the whole world is a mixture of independence and dependence, of freedom and slavery, but through it all shines the soul independent, immortal, pure, perfect, holy. For if it is independent, it cannot perish, as death is but a change, and depends upon conditions; if independent, it must be perfect, for imperfection is again but a condition, and therefore dependent. And this immortal and perfect soul must be the same in the highest God as well as in the humblest man, the difference between them being only in the degree in which this soul manifests itself.

But why should the soul take to itself a body? For the same reason that I take a looking-glass—to see myself. Thus, in the body, the soul is reflected. The soul is God, and every human being has a perfect divinity within himself, and each one must show his divinity sooner or later. If I am in a dark room, no amount of protestation will make it any brighter—I must light a match. Just so, no amount of grumbling and wailing will make our imperfect body more perfect. But the Vedanta teaches—call forth your soul, show your divinity. Teach your children that they are divine, that religion is a positive something and not a negative nonsense; that it is not subjection to groans when under oppression, but expansion and manifestation.

Every religion has it that man's present and future are modified by the past, and that the present is but the effect of the past. How is it, then, that every child is born with an experience that cannot be accounted for by hereditary transmission? How is it that one is born of good parents, receives a good education and becomes a good man, while another comes from besotted parents and ends on the gallows? How do you explain this inequality without implicating God? Why should a merciful Father set His child in such conditions which must bring forth misery? It is no explanation to say God will make amends; later on—God has no blood-money. Then, too, what becomes of my liberty, if this be my first birth? Coming into this world without the experience of a former life, my independence would be gone, for my path would be marked out by the experience of others. If I cannot be the maker of my own fortune, then I am not free. I take upon myself the blame for the misery of this existence, and say I will unmake the evil I have done in another existence. This, then, is our philosophy of the migration of the soul. We come into this life with the experience of another, and the fortune or misfortune of this existence is the result of our acts in a former existence, always becoming better, till at last perfection is reached.

We believe in a God, the Father of the universe, infinite and omnipotent. But if our soul at last becomes perfect, it also must become infinite. But there is no room for two infinite unconditional beings, and hence we believe in a Personal God, and we ourselves are He. These are the three stages which every religion has taken. First we see God in the far beyond, then we come nearer to Him and give Him omnipresence so that we live in Him; and at last we recognize that we are He. The idea of an Objective God is not untrue—in fact, every idea of God, and hence every religion, is true, as each is but a different stage in the journey, the aim of which is the perfect conception of the Vedas. Hence, too, we not only tolerate, but we Hindus accept every religion, praying in the mosque of the Mohammedans, worshipping before the fire of the Zoroastrians, and kneeling before the cross of the Christians, knowing that all the religions, from the lowest fetishism to the highest absolutism, mean so many attempts of the human soul to grasp and realize the infinite, each determined by the conditions of its birth and association, and each of them marking a stage of progress. We gather all these flowers and bind them with the twine of love, making a wonderful bouquet of worship.

If I am God, then my soul is a temple of the Highest, and my every motion should be a worship—love for love's sake, duty for duty's sake, without hope of reward or fear of punishment. Thus, my religion means expansion, and expansion means realization and perception in the highest sense—no mumbling words or genuflections. Man is to become divine, realising the divine more and more from day to day in an endless progress.

18

WHAT IS RELIGION

A huge locomotive has rushed on over the line and a small worm that was creeping upon one of the rails saved its life by crawling out of the path of the locomotive. Yet this little worm, so insignificant that it can be crushed in a moment, is a living something, while this locomotive, so huge, so immense, is only an engine, a machine. You say the one has life and the other is only dead matter and all its powers and strength and speed are only those of a dead machine, a mechanical contrivance. Yet the poor little worm which moved upon the rail and which the least touch of the engine would have deprived of its life is a majestic being compared to that huge locomotive. It is a small part of the Infinite and, therefore, it is greater than this powerful engine. Why should that be so? How do we know the living from the dead? The machine mechanically performs all the movements its maker made it to perform, its movements are not those of life. How can we make the distinction between the living and the dead, then? In the living there is freedom, there is intelligence; in the dead all is bound and no freedom is possible, because there is no intelligence. This freedom that distinguishes us from mere machines is what we are all striving for. To be more free is the goal of all our efforts, for only in perfect freedom can there be perfection. This effort to attain freedom underlies all forms of worship, whether we know it or not.

If we were to examine the various sorts of worship all over the world, we would see that the rudest of mankind are worshipping ghosts, demons, and the spirits of their forefathers—serpent worship, worship of tribal gods, and worship of the departed ones. Why do they do this? Because they feel that in some unknown way these beings are greater, more powerful than themselves, and limit their freedom. They, therefore, seek to propitiate these beings in order to prevent them from molesting them, in other words, to get more freedom. They also seek to win favour from these superior beings, to get by gift of the gods what ought to be earned by personal effort.

On the whole, this shows that the world is expecting a miracle. This expectation never leaves us, and however we may try, we are all running after the miraculous and extraordinary. What is mind but that ceaseless inquiry into the meaning and mystery of life? We may say that only uncultivated people are going after all these things, but the question still is there: Why should it be so? The Jews were asking for a miracle. The whole world has been asking for the same these thousands of years. There is, again, the universal dissatisfaction. We make an ideal but we have rushed only half the way after it when we make a newer one. We struggle hard to attain to some goal and then discover we do not want it. This dissatisfaction we are having time after time, and what is there in the mind if there is to be only dissatisfaction? What is the meaning of this universal dissatisfaction? It is because freedom is every man's goal. He seeks it ever, his whole life is a struggle after it. The child rebels against law as soon as it is born. Its first utterance is a cry, a protest against the bondage in which it finds itself. This longing for freedom produces the idea of a Being who is absolutely free. The concept of God is a fundamental element in the human constitution. In the Vedanta, Sat-chit-ananda (Existence-Knowledge-Bliss) is the highest concept of God possible to the mind. It is the essence of knowledge and is by its nature the essence of bliss. We have been stifling that inner voice long enough, seeking to follow law and quiet the human nature, but there is that human instinct to rebel against nature's laws. We may not understand what the meaning is, but there is that unconscious struggle of the human with the spiritual, of the lower with the higher mind, and the struggle attempts to preserve one's separate life, what we call our 'individuality'.

Even hells stand out with this miraculous fact that we are born rebels; and the first fact of life—the inrushing of life itself—against this we rebel and cry out, 'No law for us.' As long as we obey the laws we are like machines, and on goes the universe, and we cannot break it. Laws as laws become man's nature. The first inkling of life on its higher level is in seeing this struggle within us to break the bond of nature and to be free. 'Freedom, O Freedom! Freedom, O Freedom!' is the song of the soul. Bondage, alas, to be bound in nature, seems its fate.

Why should there be serpent, or ghost, or demon worship and all these various creeds and forms for having miracles? Why do we say that there is life, there is being in anything? There must be a meaning in all this search, this endeavour to understand life, to explain being. It is not meaningless and vain. It is man's ceaseless endeavour to become free. The knowledge which we now call science has been struggling for thousands of years in its attempt to gain freedom, and people ask for freedom. Yet there is no freedom in nature. It is all law. Still the struggle goes on. Nay, the whole of nature from the very sun to the atoms is under law, and even for man there is no freedom. But we cannot believe it. We have been studying laws from the beginning and yet cannot—nay, will not—believe that man is under law. The soul cries ever, 'Freedom, O Freedom!' With the conception of God as a perfectly free Being, man cannot rest eternally in this bondage. Higher he must go, and unless the struggle were for himself, he would think it too severe. Man says to himself, 'I am a born slave, I am bound; nevertheless, there is a Being who is not bound by nature. He is free and Master of nature.'

The conception of God, therefore, is as essential and as fundamental a part of mind as is the idea of bondage. Both are the outcome of the idea of freedom. There cannot be life, even in the plant, without the idea of freedom. In the plant or in the worm, life has to rise to the individual concept. It is there, unconsciously working, the plant living its life to preserve the variety, principle, or form, not nature. The idea of nature controlling every step onward overrules the idea of freedom. Onward goes the idea of the material world, onward moves the idea of freedom. Still the fight goes on. We are hearing about all the quarrels of creeds and sects, yet creeds and sects are just and proper, they must be there. The chain is lengthening and naturally the struggle increases, but there need be no quarrels if we only knew that we are all striving to reach the same goal.

The embodiment of freedom, the Master of nature, is what we call God. You cannot deny Him. No, because you cannot move or live without the idea of freedom. Would you come here if you did not believe you were free? It is quite possible that the biologist can and will give some explanation of this perpetual effort to be free. Take all that for granted, still the idea of freedom is there. It is a fact, as much so as the other fact that you cannot apparently get over, the fact of being under nature.

Bondage and liberty, light and shadow, good and evil must be there, but the very fact of the bondage shows also this freedom hidden there. If one is a fact, the other is equally a fact. There must be this idea of freedom. While now we cannot see that this idea of bondage, in uncultivated man, is his struggle for freedom, yet the idea of freedom is there. The bondage of sin and impurity in the uncultivated savage is to his consciousness very small, for his nature is only a little higher than the animal's. What he struggles against is the bondage of physical nature, the lack of physical gratification, but out of this lower consciousness grows and broadens the higher conception of a mental or moral bondage and a longing for spiritual freedom. Here, we see the divine dimly shining through the veil of ignorance. The veil is very dense at first and the light may be almost obscured, but it is there, ever pure and undimmed—the radiant fire of freedom and perfection. Man personifies this as the Ruler of the Universe, the One Free Being. He does not yet know that the universe is all one, that the difference is only in degree, in the concept.

The whole of nature is worship of God. Wherever there is life, there is this search for freedom and that freedom is the same as God. Necessarily this freedom gives us mastery over all nature and is impossible without knowledge. The more we are knowing, the more we are becoming masters of nature. Mastery alone is making us strong and if there be some being entirely free and master of nature, that being must have a perfect knowledge of nature, must be omnipresent and omniscient. Freedom must go hand in hand with these, and that being alone who has acquired these will be beyond nature.

Blessedness, eternal peace, arising from perfect freedom, is the highest concept of religion underlying all the ideas of God in Vedanta—absolutely free Existence, not bound by anything, no change, no nature, nothing that can produce a change in Him. This same freedom is in you and in me and is the only real freedom.

God is still, established upon His own majestic changeless Self. You and I try to be one with Him, but plant ourselves upon nature, upon the trifles of daily life, on money, on fame, on human love, and all these changing forms in nature which make for bondage. When nature shines, upon what depends the shining? Upon God and not upon the sun, nor the moon, nor the stars. Wherever anything shines, whether it is the light in the sun or in our own consciousness, it is He. He shining, all shines after Him.

Now we have seen that this God is self-evident, impersonal, omniscient, the Knower and Master of nature, the Lord of all. He is behind all worship and it is being done according to Him, whether we know it or not. I go one step further. That at which all marvel, that which we call evil, is His worship too. This too is a part of freedom. Nay, I will be terrible even and tell you that, when you are doing evil, the impulse behind is also that freedom. It may have been misguided and misled, but it was there; and there cannot be any life or any impulse unless that freedom be behind it. Freedom breathes in the throb of the universe. Unless there is unity at the universal heart, we cannot understand variety. Such is the conception of the Lord in the Upanishads. Sometimes it rises even higher, presenting to us an ideal before which at first we stand aghast—that we are in essence one with God. He who is the colouring in the wings of the butterfly, and the blossoming of the rose-bud, is the power that is in the plant and in the butterfly. He who gives us life is the power within us. Out of His fire comes life, and the direst death is also His power. He whose shadow is death, His shadow is immortality also. Take a still higher conception. See how we are flying like hunted hares from all that is terrible, and like them, hiding our heads and thinking we are safe. See how the whole world is flying from everything terrible. Once when I was in Varanasi, I was passing through a place where there was a large tank of water on one side and a high wall on the other. It was in the grounds where there were many monkeys. The monkeys of Varanasi are huge brutes and are sometimes surly. They now took it into their heads not to allow me to pass through their street, so they howled and shrieked and clutched at my feet as I passed. As they pressed closer, I began to run, but the faster I ran, the faster came the monkeys and they began to bite at me. It seemed impossible to escape, but just then I met a stranger who called out to me, 'Face the brutes.' I turned and faced the monkeys, and they fell back and finally fled. That is a lesson for all life—face the terrible, face it boldly. Like the monkeys, the hardships of life fall back when we cease to flee before them. If we are ever to gain freedom, it must be by conquering nature, never by running away. Cowards never win victories. We have to fight fear and troubles and ignorance if we expect them to flee before us.

What is death? What are terrors? Do you not see the Lord's face in them? Fly from evil and terror and misery, and they will follow you. Face them, and they will flee. The whole world worships ease and pleasure, and very few dare to worship that which is painful. To rise above both is the idea of freedom. Unless man passes through this gate he cannot be free. We all have to face these. We strive to worship the Lord, but the body rises between, nature rises between Him and us and blinds our vision. We must learn how to worship and love Him in the thunderbolt, in shame, in sorrow, in sin. All the world has ever been preaching the God of virtue. I preach a God of virtue and a God of sin in one. Take Him if you dare—that is the one way to salvation; then alone will come to us the Truth Ultimate which comes from the idea of oneness. Then will be lost the idea that one is greater than another. The nearer we approach the law of freedom, the more we shall come under the Lord, and troubles will vanish. Then we shall not differentiate the door of hell from the gate of heaven, nor differentiate between men and say, 'I am greater than any being in the universe.' Until we see nothing in the world but the Lord Himself, all these evils will beset us and we shall make all these distinctions; because it is only in the Lord, in the Spirit, that we are all one; and until we see God everywhere, this unity will not exist for us.

Two birds of beautiful plumage, inseparable companions, sat upon the same tree, one on the top and one below. The beautiful bird below was eating the fruits of the tree, sweet and bitter, one moment a sweet one and another a bitter. The moment he ate a bitter fruit, he was sorry, but after a while he ate another and when it too was bitter, he looked up and saw the other bird who ate neither the sweet nor the bitter, but was calm and majestic, immersed in his own glory. And then the poor lower bird forgot and went on eating the sweet and bitter fruits again, until at last he ate one that was extremely bitter; and then he stopped again and once more looked up at the glorious bird above. Then he came nearer and nearer to the other bird; and when he had come near enough, rays of light shone upon him and enveloped him, and he saw he was transformed into the higher bird. He became calm, majestic, free, and found that there had been but one bird all the time on the tree. The lower bird was but the reflection of the one above. So we are in reality one with the Lord, but the reflection makes us seem many, as when the one sun reflects in a million dew-drops and seems a million tiny suns. The reflection must vanish if we are to identify ourselves with our real nature which is divine. The universe itself can never be the limit of our satisfaction. That is why the miser gathers more and more money, that is why the robber robs, the sinner sins, that is why you are learning philosophy. All have one purpose. There is no other purpose in life, save to reach this freedom. Consciously or unconsciously, we are all striving for perfection. Every being must attain to it.

The man who is groping through sin, through misery, the man who is choosing the path through hells, will reach it, but it will take time. We cannot save him. Some hard knocks on his head will help him to turn to the Lord. The path of virtue, purity, unselfishness, spirituality, becomes known at last and what all are doing unconsciously, we are trying to do consciously. The idea is expressed by St. Paul, 'The God that ye ignorantly worship, Him declare I unto you.' This is the lesson for the whole world to learn. What have these philosophies and theories of nature to do, if not to help us to attain to this one goal in life? Let us come to that consciousness of the identity of everything and let man see himself in everything. Let us be no more the worshippers of creeds or sects with small limited notions of God, but see Him in everything in the universe. If you are knowers of God, you will everywhere find the same worship as in your own heart.

Get rid, in the first place, of all these limited ideas and see God in every person—working through all hands, walking through all feet, and eating through every mouth. In every being He lives, through all minds He thinks. He is self-evident, nearer unto us than ourselves. To know this is religion, is faith, and may it please the Lord to give us this faith! When we shall feel that oneness, we shall be immortal. We are physically immortal even, one with the universe. So long as there is one that breathes throughout the universe, I live in that one. I am not this limited little being, I am the universal. I am the life of all the sons of the past. I am the soul of Buddha, of Jesus, of Mohammed. I am the soul of the teachers, and I am all the robbers that robbed, and all the murderers that were hanged, I am the universal. Stand up then; this is the highest worship. You are one with the universe. That only is humility—not crawling upon all fours and calling yourself a sinner. That is the highest evolution when this veil of differentiation is torn off. The highest creed is Oneness. I am so-and-so is a limited idea, not true of the real 'I'. I am the universal; stand upon that and ever worship the Highest through the highest form, for God is Spirit and should be worshipped in spirit and in truth. Through lower forms of worship, man's material thoughts rise to spiritual worship and the Universal Infinite One is at last worshipped in and through the spirit. That which is limited is material. The Spirit alone is infinite. God is Spirit, is infinite; man is Spirit and, therefore, infinite, and the Infinite alone can worship the Infinite. We will worship the Infinite; that is the highest spiritual worship. The grandeur of realising these ideas, how difficult it is! I theorize, talk, philosophize; and the next moment something comes against me, and I unconsciously become angry, I forget there is anything in the universe but this little limited self, I forget to say, 'I am the Spirit, what is this trifle to me? I am the Spirit.' I forget it is all myself playing, I forget God, I forget freedom.

Sharp as the blade of a razor, long and difficult and hard to cross, is the way to freedom. The sages have declared this again and again. Yet do not let these weaknesses and failures bind you. The Upanishads have declared, 'Arise! Awake! and stop not until the goal is reached.' We will then certainly cross the path, sharp as it is like the razor, and long and distant and difficult though it be. Man becomes the master of gods and demons. No one is to blame for our miseries but ourselves. Do you think there is only a dark cup of poison if man goes to look for nectar? The nectar is there and is for every man who strives to reach it. The Lord Himself tells us, 'Give up all these paths and struggles. Do thou take refuge in Me. I will take thee to the other shore, be not afraid.' We hear that from all the scriptures of the world that come to us. The same voice teaches us to say, 'Thy will be done upon earth, as it is in heaven,' for 'Thine is the kingdom and the power and the glory.' It is difficult, all very difficult. I say to myself, 'This moment I will take refuge in Thee, O Lord. Unto Thy love I will sacrifice all, and on Thine altar I will place all that is good and virtuous. My sins, my sorrows, my actions, good and evil, I will offer unto Thee; do Thou take them and I will never forget.' One moment I say, 'Thy will be done,' and the next moment something comes to try me and I spring up in a rage. The goal of all religions is the same, but the language of the teachers differs. The attempt is to kill the false 'I', so that the real 'I', the Lord, will reign. 'I the Lord thy God am a jealous God. Thou shalt have no other gods before me,' say the Hebrew scriptures. God must be there all alone. We must say, 'Not I, but Thou,' and then we should give up everything but the Lord. He, and He alone, should reign. Perhaps we struggle hard, and yet the next moment our feet slip, and then we try to stretch out our hands to Mother. We find we cannot stand alone. Life is infinite, one chapter of which is, 'Thy will be done,' and unless we realize all the chapters we cannot realize the whole. 'Thy will be done'—every moment the traitor mind rebels against it, yet it must be said, again and again, if we are to conquer the lower self. We cannot serve a traitor and yet be saved. There is salvation for all except the traitor and we stand condemned as traitors, traitors against our own selves, against the majesty of Mother, when we refuse to obey the voice of our higher Self. Come what will, we must give our bodies and minds up to the Supreme Will. Well has it been said by the Hindu philosopher, 'If man says twice, "Thy will be done," he commits sin.' 'Thy will be done,' what more is needed, why say it twice? What is good is good. No more shall we take it back. 'Thy will be done on earth as it is in heaven, for Thine is the kingdom and the power and the glory for evermore.'

19

VEDIC RELIGIOUS IDEALS

What concerns us most is the religious thought—on soul and God and all that appertains to religion. We will take the Samhitas. These are collections of hymns forming, as it were, the oldest Aryan literature, properly speaking, the oldest literature in the world. There may have been some scraps of literature of older date here and there, older than that even, but not books, or literature properly so called. As a collected book, this is the oldest the world has, and herein is portrayed the earliest feeling of the Aryans, their aspirations, the questions that arose about their manners and methods, and so on. At the very outset we find a very curious idea. These hymns are sung in praise of different gods, Devas as they are called, the bright ones. There is quite a number of them. One is called Indra, another Varuna, another Mitra, Parjanya, and so on. Various mythological and allegorical figures come before us one after the other—for instance, Indra the thunderer, striking the serpent who has withheld the rains from mankind. Then he lets fly his thunderbolt, the serpent is killed, and rain comes down in showers. The people are pleased, and they worship Indra with oblations. They make a sacrificial pyre, kill some animals, roast their flesh upon spits, and offer that meat to Indra. And they had a popular plant called Soma. What plant it was nobody knows now; it has entirely disappeared, but from the books we gather that, when crushed, it produced a sort of milky juice, and that was fermented; and it can also be gathered that this fermented Soma juice was intoxicating. This also they offered to Indra and the other gods, and they also drank it themselves. Sometimes they drank a little too much, and so did the gods. Indra on occasions got drunk. There are passages to show that Indra at one time drank so much of this Soma juice that he talked irrelevant words. So with Varuna. He is another god, very powerful, and is in the same way protecting his votaries, and they are praising him with their libations of Soma. So is the god of war, and so on. But the popular idea that strikes one as making the mythologies of the Samhitas entirely different from the other mythologies is, that along with every one of these gods is the idea of an infinity. This infinite is abstracted, and sometimes described as Aditya. At other times it is affixed, as it were, to all the other gods. Take, for example, Indra. In some of the books you will find that Indra has a body, is very strong, sometimes is wearing golden armour, and comes down, lives and eats with his votaries, fights the demons, fights the snakes, and so on. Again, in one hymn we find that Indra has been given a very high position; he is omnipresent and omnipotent, and Indra sees the heart of every being. So with Varuna. This Varuna is god of the air and is in charge of the water, just as Indra was previously; and then, all of a sudden, we find him raised up and said to be omnipresent, omnipotent, and so on. I will read one passage about this Varuna in his highest form, and you will understand what I mean. It has been translated into English poetry, so it is better that I read it in that form.

The mighty Lord on high our deeds, as if at hand, espies; The gods know all men do, though men would fain their acts disguise; Whoever stands, whoever moves, or steals from place to place, Or hides him in his secret cell—the gods his movements trace. Wherever two together plot, and deem they are alone, King Varuna is there, a third, and all their schemes are known. This earth is his, to him belong those vast and boundless skies; Both seas within him rest, and yet in that small pool he lies, Whoever far beyond the sky should think his way to wing. He could not there elude the grasp of Varuna the King. His spies, descending from the skies, glide all this world around; Their thousand eyes all-scanning sweep to earth's remotest bound.

So we can multiply examples about the other gods; they all come, one after the other, to share the same fate—they first begin as gods, and then they are raised to this conception as the Being in whom the whole universe exists, who sees every heart, who is the ruler of the universe. And in the case of Varuna, there is another idea, just the germ of one idea which came, but was immediately suppressed by the Aryan mind, and that was the idea of fear. In another place we read they are afraid they have sinned and ask Varuna for pardon. These ideas were never allowed, for reasons you will come to understand later on, to grow on Indian soil, but the germs were there sprouting, the idea of fear, and the idea of sin. This is the idea, as you all know, of what is called monotheism. This monotheism, we see, came to India at a very early period. Throughout the Samhitas, in the first and oldest part, this monotheistic idea prevails, but we shall find that it did not prove sufficient for the Aryans; they threw it aside, as it were, as a very primitive sort of idea and went further on, as we Hindus think. Of course in reading books and criticisms on the Vedas written by Europeans, the Hindu cannot help smiling when he reads, that the writings of our authors are saturated with this previous education alone. Persons who have sucked in as their mother's milk the idea that the highest ideal of God is the idea of a Personal God, naturally dare not think on the lines of these ancient thinkers of India, when they find that just after the Samhitas, the monotheistic idea with which the Samhita portion is replete was thought by the Aryans to be useless and not worthy of philosophers and thinkers, and that they struggled hard for a more philosophical and transcendental idea. The monotheistic idea was much too human for them, although they gave it such descriptions as 'The whole universe rests in Him,' and 'Thou art the keeper of all hearts.' The Hindus were bold, to their great credit be it said, bold thinkers in all their ideas, so bold that one spark of their thought frightens the so-called bold thinkers of the West. Well has it been said by Professor Max Müller about these thinkers that they climbed up to heights where their lungs only could breathe, and where those of other beings would have burst. These brave people followed reason wherever it led them, no matter at what cost, never caring if all their best superstitions were smashed to pieces, never caring what society would think about them, or talk about them; but what they thought was right and true, they preached and they talked.

Before going into all these speculations of the ancient Vedic sages, we will first refer to one or two very curious instances in the Vedas. The peculiar fact—that these gods are taken up, as it were, one after the other, raised and sublimated, till each has assumed the proportions of the infinite Personal God of the Universe—calls for an explanation. Professor Max Müller creates for it a new name, as he thinks it peculiar to the Hindus: he calls it 'Henotheism'. We need not go far for the explanation. It is within the book. A few steps from the very place where we find those gods being raised and sublimated, we find the explanation also. The question arises how the Hindu mythologies should be so unique, so different from all others. In Babylonian or Greek mythologies, we find one god struggling upwards, and he assumes a position and remains there, while the other gods die out. Of all the Molochs, Jehovah becomes supreme, and the other Molochs are forgotten, lost for ever; he is the God of gods. So, too, of all the Greek gods, Zeus comes to the front and assumes big proportions, becomes the God of the Universe, and all the other gods become degraded into minor angels. This fact was repeated in later times. The Buddhists and the Jains raised one of their prophets to the Godhead, and all the other gods they made subservient to Buddha, or to Jina. This is the world-wide process, but there we find an exception, as it were. One god is praised, and for the time being it is said that all the other gods obey his commands, and the very one who is said to be raised up by Varuna, is himself raised up, in the next book, to the highest position. They occupy the position of the Personal God in turns. But the explanation is there in the book, and it is a grand explanation, one that has given the theme to all subsequent thought in India, and one that will be the theme of the whole world of religions: 'Ekam Sat Vipra Bahudha Vadanti—That which exists is One; sages call It by various names.' In all these cases where hymns were written about all these gods, the Being perceived was one and the same; it was the perceiver who made the difference. It was the hymnist, the sage, the poet, who sang in different languages and different words, the praise of one and the same Being. 'That which exists is One; sages call It by various names.' Tremendous results have followed from that one verse. Some of you, perhaps, are surprised to think that India is the only country where there never has been a religious persecution, where never was any man disturbed for his religious faith. Theists or atheists, monists, dualists, monotheists are there and always live unmolested. Materialists were allowed to preach from the steps of Brahminical temples, against the gods, and against God Himself; they went preaching all over the land that the idea of God was a mere superstition, and that gods, and

Vedas, and religion were simply superstitions invented by the priests for their own benefit, and they were allowed to do this unmolested. And so, wherever he went, Buddha tried to pull down every old thing sacred to the Hindus to the dust, and Buddha died of ripe old age. So did the Jains, who laughed at the idea of God. 'How can it be that there is a God?' they asked; 'it must be a mere superstition.' So on, endless examples there are. Before the Mohammedan wave came into India, it was never known what religious persecution was; the Hindus had only experienced it as made by foreigners on themselves. And even now it is a patent fact how much Hindus have helped to build Christian churches, and how much readiness there is to help them. There never has been bloodshed. Even heterodox religions that have come out of India have been likewise affected; for instance, Buddhism. Buddhism is a great religion in some respects, but to confuse Buddhism with Vedanta is without meaning; anyone may mark just the difference that exists between Christianity and the Salvation Army. There are great and good points in Buddhism, but these great points fell into hands which were not able to keep them safe. The jewels which came from philosophers fell into the hands of mobs, and the mobs took up their ideas. They had a great deal of enthusiasm, some marvellous ideas, great and humanitarian ideas, but, after all, there is something else that is necessary—thought and intellect—to keep everything safe. Wherever you see the most humanitarian ideas fall into the hands of the multitude, the first result, you may notice, is degradation. It is learning and intellect that keep things sure. Now this Buddhism went as the first missionary religion to the world, penetrated the whole of the civilized world as it existed at that time, and never was a drop of blood shed for that religion. We read how in China the Buddhist missionaries were persecuted, and thousands were massacred by two or three successive emperors, but after that, fortune favoured the Buddhists, and one of the emperors offered to take vengeance on the persecutors, but the missionaries refused. All that we owe to this one verse. That is why I want you to remember it: 'Whom they call Indra, Mitra, Varuna—That which exists is One; sages call It by various names.'

It was written, nobody knows at what date, it may be 8,000 years ago, in spite of all modern scholars may say, it may be 9,000 years ago. Not one of these religious speculations is of modern date, but they are as fresh today as they were when they were written, or rather, fresher, for at that distant date man was not so civilized as we know him now. He had not learnt to cut his brother's throat because he differed a little in thought from himself; he had not deluged the world in blood, he did not become demon to his own brother. In the name of humanity he did not massacre whole lots of mankind then. Therefore these words come to us today very fresh, as great stimulating, life-giving words, much fresher than they were when they were written: 'That which exists is One; sages call It by various names.' We have to learn yet that all religions, under whatever name they may be called, either Hindu, Buddhist, Mohammedan, or Christian, have the same God, and he who derides any one of these derides his own God.

That was the solution they arrived at. But, as I have said, this ancient monotheistic idea did not satisfy the Hindu mind. It did not go far enough, it did not explain the visible world: a ruler of the world does not explain the world—certainly not. A ruler of the universe does not explain the universe, and much less an external ruler, one outside of it. He may be a moral guide, the greatest power in the universe, but that is no explanation of the universe; and the first question that we find now arising, assuming proportions, is the question about the universe: 'Whence did it come?' 'How did it come?' 'How does it exist?' Various hymns are to be found on this question struggling forward to assume form, and nowhere do we find it so poetically, so wonderfully expressed as in the following hymn:

'Then there was neither aught nor naught, nor air, nor sky, nor anything. What covered all? Where rested all? Then death was not, nor deathlessness, nor change to night and day.' The translation loses a good deal of the poetical beauty. 'Then death was not, nor deathlessness, nor change to night and day;' the very sound of the Sanskrit is musical. '*That* existed, that breath, covering as it were, that God's existence; but it did not begin to move.' It is good to remember this one idea that it existed motionless, because we shall find how this idea sprouts up afterwards in the cosmology, how according to the Hindu metaphysics and philosophy, this whole universe is a mass of vibrations, as it were, motions; and there are periods when this whole mass of motions subsides and becomes finer and finer, remaining in that state for some time. That is the state described in this hymn. It existed unmoved, without vibration, and when this creation began, this began to vibrate and all this creation came out of it, that one breath, calm, self-sustained, naught else beyond it.

'Gloom existed first.' Those of you who have ever been in India or any tropical country, and have seen the bursting of the monsoon, will understand the majesty of these words. I remember three poets' attempts to picture this. Milton says, 'No light, but rather darkness visible.' Kalidasa says, 'Darkness which can be penetrated with a needle,' but none comes near this Vedic description, 'Gloom hidden in gloom.' Everything is parching and sizzling, the whole creation seems to be burning away, and for days it has been so, when one afternoon there is in one corner of the horizon a speck of cloud, and in less than half an hour it has extended unto the whole earth, until, as it were, it is covered with cloud, cloud over cloud, and then it bursts into a tremendous deluge of rain. The cause of creation was described as will. That which existed at first became changed into will, and this will began to manifest itself as desire. This also we ought to remember, because we find that this idea of desire is said to be the cause of all we have. This idea of will has been the corner-stone of both the Buddhist and the Vedantic system, and later on, has penetrated into German philosophy and forms the basis of Schopenhauer's system of philosophy. It is here we first hear of it.

'Now first arose desire, the primal seed of mind. Sages, searching in their hearts by wisdom, found the bond, Between existence and non-existence.'

It is a very peculiar expression; the poet ends by saying that 'perhaps He even does not know.' We find in this hymn, apart from its poetical merits, that this questioning about the universe has assumed quite definite proportions, and that the minds of these sages must have advanced to such a state, when all sorts of common answers would not satisfy them. We find that they were not even satisfied with this Governor above. There are various other hymns where the same idea, comes in, about how this all came, and just as we have seen, when they were trying to find a Governor of the universe, a Personal God, they were taking up one Deva after another, raising him up to that position, so now we shall find that in various hymns one or other idea is taken up, and expanded infinitely and made responsible for everything in the universe. One particular idea is taken as the support, in which everything rests and exists, and that support has become all this. So on with various ideas. They tried this method with Prana, the life principle. They expanded the idea of the life principle until it became universal and infinite. It is the life principle that is supporting everything; not only the human body, but it is the light of the sun and the moon, it is the power moving everything, the universal motive energy. Some of these attempts are very beautiful, very poetical. Some of them as, 'He ushers the beautiful morning,' are marvellously lyrical in the way they picture things. Then this very desire, which, as we have just read, arose as the first primal germ of creation, began to be stretched out, until it became the universal God. But none of these ideas satisfied.

Here the idea is sublimated and finally abstracted into a personality. 'He alone existed in the beginning; He is the one Lord of all that exists; He supports this universe; He who is the author of souls, He who is the author of strength, whom all the gods worship, whose shadow is life, whose shadow is death; whom else shall we worship? Whose glory the snow-tops of the Himalayas declare, whose glory the oceans with all their waters proclaim.' So on it goes, but, as I told you just now, this idea did not satisfy them.

At last we find a very peculiar position. The Aryan mind had so long been seeking an answer to the question from outside. They questioned everything they could find, the sun, the moon, and stars, and they found all they could in this way. The whole of nature at best could teach them only of a personal Being who is the Ruler of the universe; it could teach nothing further. In short, out of the external world we can only get the idea of an architect, that which is called the Design Theory. It is not a very logical argument, as we all know; there is something childish about it, yet it is the only little bit of anything we can know about God from the external world, that this world required a builder. But this is no explanation of the universe. The materials of this world were before Him, and this God wanted all these materials, and the worst objection is that He must be limited by the materials. The builder could not have made a house without the materials of which it is composed. Therefore he was limited by the materials; he could only do what the materials enabled him to. Therefore the God that the Design Theory gives is at best only an architect, and a limited architect of the universe; He is bound and restricted by the materials; He is not independent at all. That much they had found out already, and many other minds would have rested at that. In other countries the same thing happened; the human mind could not rest there; the thinking, grasping minds wanted to go further, but those that were backward got hold of them and did not allow them to grow. But fortunately these Hindu sages were not the people to be knocked on the head; they wanted to get a solution, and now we find that they were leaving the external for the internal. The first thing that struck them was, that it is not with the eyes and the senses that we perceive that external world, and know anything about religion; the first idea, therefore, was to find the deficiency, and that deficiency was both physical and moral, as we shall see. You do not know, says one of these sages, the cause of this universe; there has arisen a tremendous difference between you and me—why? Because you have been talking sense things and are satisfied with sense-objects and with the mere ceremonials of religion, while I have known the Purusha beyond.

Along with this progress of spiritual ideas that I am trying to trace for you, I can only hint to you a little about the other factor in the growth, for that has nothing to do with our subject, therefore I need not enlarge upon it—the growth of rituals. As those spiritual ideas progressed in arithmetical progression, so the ritualistic ideas progressed in geometrical progression. The old superstitions had by this time developed into a tremendous mass of rituals, which grew and grew till it almost killed the Hindu life And it is still there, it has got hold of and permeated every portion of our life and made us born slaves. Yet, at the same time, we find a fight against this advance of ritual from the very earliest days. The one objection raised there is this, that love for ceremonials, dressing at certain times, eating in a certain way, and shows and mummeries of religion like these are only external religion, because you are satisfied with the senses and do not want to go beyond them. This is a tremendous difficulty with us, with every human being. At best when we want to hear of spiritual things our standard is the senses; or a man hears things about philosophy, and God, and transcendental things, and after hearing about them for days, he asks: After all, how much money will they bring, how much sense-enjoyment will they bring? For his enjoyment is only in the senses, quite naturally. But that satisfaction in the senses, says our sage, is one of the causes which have spread the veil between truth and ourselves. Devotion to ceremonials, satisfaction in the senses, and forming various theories, have drawn a veil between ourselves and truth. This is another great landmark, and we shall have to trace this ideal to the end, and see how it developed later on into that wonderful theory of Maya of the Vedanta, how this veil will be the real explanation of the Vedanta, how the truth was there all the time, it was only this veil that had covered it.

Thus, we find that the minds of these ancient Aryan thinkers had begun a new theme. They found out that in the external world no search would give an answer to their question. They might seek in the external world for ages, but there would be no answer to their questions. So they fell back upon this other method; and according to this, they were taught that these desires of the senses, desires for ceremonials and externalities have caused a veil to come between themselves and the truth, and that this cannot be removed by any ceremonial. They had to fall back on their own minds, and analyse the mind to find the truth in themselves. The outside world failed and they turned back upon the inside world, and then it became the real philosophy of the Vedanta; from here the Vedanta philosophy begins. It is the foundation-stone of Vedanta philosophy. As we go on, we find that all its inquiries are inside. From the very outset they seemed to declare—look not for the truth in any religion; it is here in the human soul, the miracle of all miracles in the human soul, the emporium of all knowledge, the mine of all existence—seek here. What is not here cannot be there. And they found out step by step that that which is external is but a dull reflection at best of that which is inside. We shall see how they took, as it were, this old idea of God, the Governor of the universe, who is external to the universe, and first put Him inside the universe. He is not a God outside, but He is inside; and they took Him from there into their own hearts. Here, He is in the heart of man, the Soul of our souls, the Reality in us.

Several great ideas have to be understood, in order to grasp properly the workings of the Vedanta philosophy. In the first place it is not philosophy in the sense we speak of the philosophy of Kant and Hegel. It is not one book, or the work of one man. Vedanta is the name of a series of books written at different times. Sometimes in one of these productions there will be fifty different things. Neither are they properly arranged; the thoughts, as it were, have been jotted down. Sometimes in the midst of other extraneous things, we find some wonderful idea. But one fact is remarkable, that these ideas in the Upanishads would be always progressing. In that crude old language, the working of the mind of every one of the sages has been, as it were, painted just as it went; how the ideas are at first very crude, and they become finer and finer till they reach the goal of the Vedanta, and this goal assumes a philosophical name. Just at first it was a search after the Devas, the bright ones, and then it was the origin of the universe, and the very same search is getting another name, more philosophical, clearer—the unity of all things—'Knowing which everything else becomes known.'

20

REASON AND RELIGION
Delivered in England

A sage called Narada went to another sage named Sanatkumara to learn about truth, and Sanatkumara inquired what he had studied already. Narada answered that he had studied the Vedas, Astronomy, and various other things, yet he had got no satisfaction. Then there was a conversation between the two, in the course of which Sanatkumara remarked that all this knowledge of the Vedas, of Astronomy, and of Philosophy, was but secondary; sciences were but secondary. That which made us realize the Brahman was the supreme, the highest knowledge. This idea we find in every religion, and that is why religion always claimed to be supreme knowledge. Knowledge of the sciences covers, as it were, only part of our lives, but the knowledge which religion brings to us is eternal, as infinite as the truth it preaches. Claiming this superiority, religions have many times looked down, unfortunately, on all secular knowledge, and not only so, but many times have refused to be justified by the aid of secular knowledge. In consequence, all the world over there have been fights between secular knowledge and religious knowledge, the one claiming infallible authority as its guide, refusing to listen to anything that secular knowledge has to say on the point, the other, with its shining instrument of reason, wanting to cut to pieces everything religion could bring forward. This fight has been and is still waged in every country. Religions have been again and again defeated, and almost exterminated. The worship of the goddess of Reason during the French Revolution was not the first manifestation of that phenomenon in the history of humanity, it was a re-enactment of what had happened in ancient times, but in modern times it has assumed greater proportions. The physical sciences are better equipped now than formerly, and religions have become less and less equipped.

The foundations have been all undermined, and the modern man, whatever he may say in public, knows in the privacy of his heart that he can no more 'believe'. Believing certain things because an organized body of priests tells him to believe, believing because it is written in certain books, believing because his people like him to believe, the modern man knows to be impossible for him. There are, of course, a number of people who seem to acquiesce in the so-called popular faith, but we also know for certain that they do not think. Their idea of belief may be better translated as 'not-thinking-carelessness'. This fight cannot last much longer without breaking to pieces all the buildings of religion.

The question is: Is there a way out? To put it in a more concrete form: Is religion to justify itself by the discoveries of reason, through which every other science justifies itself? Are the same methods of investigation, which we apply to sciences and knowledge outside, to be applied to the science of Religion? In my opinion this must be so, and I am also of opinion that the sooner it is done the better. If a religion is destroyed by such investigations, it was then all the time useless, unworthy superstition; and the sooner it goes the better. I am thoroughly convinced that its destruction would be the best thing that could happen. All that is dross will be taken off, no doubt, but the essential parts of religion will emerge triumphant out of this investigation. Not only will it be made scientific—as scientific, at least, as any of the conclusions of physics or chemistry—but will have greater strength, because physics or chemistry has no internal mandate to vouch for its truth, which religion has.

People who deny the efficacy of any rationalistic investigation into religion seem to me somewhat to be contradicting themselves. For instance, the Christian claims that his religion is the only true one, because it was revealed to so-and-so. The Mohammedan makes the same claim for his religion; his is the only true one, because it was revealed to so-and-so. But the Christian says to the Mohammedan, 'Certain parts of your ethics do not seem to be right. For instance, your books say, my Mohammedan friend, that an infidel may be converted to the religion of Mohammed by force, and if he will not accept the Mohammedan religion he may be killed; and any Mohammedan who kills such an infidel will get a sure entry into heaven, whatever may have been his sins or misdeeds.' The Mohammedan will retort by saying, 'It is right for me to do so, because my book enjoins it. It will be wrong on my part not to do so.' The Christian says, 'But my book does not say so.' The Mohammedan replies, 'I do not know; I am not bound by the authority of your book; my book says, 'Kill all the infidels'. How do you know which is right and which is wrong? Surely what is written in my book is right and what your book says, 'Do not kill,' is wrong. You also say the same thing, my Christian friend; you say that what Jehovah declared to the Jews is right to do, and what he forbade them to do is wrong. So say I, Allah declared in my book that certain things should be done, and that certain things should not be done, and that is all the test of right and wrong.' In spite of that the Christian is not satisfied; he insists on a comparison of the morality of the Sermon on the Mount with the morality of the Koran. How is this to be decided? Certainly not by the books, because the books, fighting between themselves, cannot be the judges. Decidedly then we have to admit that there is something more universal than these books, something higher than all the ethical codes that are in the world, something which can judge between the strength of inspirations of different nations. Whether we declare it boldly, clearly, or not—it is evident that here we appeal to reason.

Now, the question arises if this light of reason is able to judge between inspiration and inspiration, and if this light can uphold its standard when the quarrel is between prophet and prophet, if it has the power of understanding anything whatsoever of religion. If it has not, nothing can determine the hopeless fight of books and prophets which has been going on through ages; for it means that all religions are mere lies, hopelessly contradictory, without any constant idea of ethics. The proof of religion depends on the truth of the constitution of man, and not on any books. These books are the outgoings, the effects of man's constitution; man made these books. We are yet to see the books that made man. Reason is equally an effect of that common cause, the constitution of man, where our appeal must be. And yet, as reason alone is directly connected with this constitution, it should be resorted to, as long as it follows faithfully the same.

What do I mean by reason? I mean what every educated man or woman is wanting to do at the present time, to apply the discoveries of secular knowledge to religion. The first principle of reasoning is that the particular is explained by the general, the general by the more general, until we come to the universal. For instance, we have the idea of law. If something happens and we believe that it is the effect of such and such a law, we are satisfied; that is an explanation for us. What we mean by that explanation is that it is proved that this one effect, which had dissatisfied us, is only one particular of a general mass of occurrences which we designate by the word 'law'. When one apple fell, Newton was disturbed; but when he found that all apples fell, it was gravitation, and he was satisfied. This is one principle of human knowledge. I see a particular being, a human being, in the street. I refer him to the bigger conception of man, and I am satisfied; I know he is a man by referring him to the more general. So the particulars are to be referred to the general, the general to the more general, and everything at last to the universal, the last concept that we have, the most universal—that of existence. Existence is the most universal concept.

We are all human beings; that is to say, each one of us, as it were, a particular part of the general concept, humanity. A man, and a cat, and a dog, are all animals. These particular examples, as man, or dog, or cat, are parts of a bigger and more general concept, animal. The man, and the cat, and the dog, and the plant, and the tree, all come under the still more general concept, life. Again, all these, all beings and all materials, come under the one concept of existence, for we all are in it. This explanation merely means referring the particular to a higher concept, finding more of its kind. The mind, as it were, has stored up numerous classes of such generalizations. It is, as it were, full of pigeon-holes where all these ideas are grouped together, and whenever we find a new thing the mind immediately tries to find out its type in one of these pigeon-holes. If we find it, we put the new thing in there and are satisfied, and we are said to have known the thing. This is what is meant by knowledge, and no more. And if we do not find that there is something like it, we are dissatisfied, and have to wait until we find a further classification for it, already existing in the mind. Therefore, as I have already pointed out, knowledge is more or less classification. There is something more. A second explanation of knowledge is that the explanation of a thing must come from inside and not from outside. There had been the belief that, when a man threw up a stone and it fell, some demon dragged it down. Many occurrences which are really natural phenomena are attributed by people to unnatural beings. That a ghost dragged down the stone was an explanation that was not in the thing itself, it was an explanation from outside; but the second explanation of gravitation is something in the nature of the stone; the explanation is coming from inside. This tendency you will find throughout modern thought; in one word, what is meant by science is that the explanations of things are in their own nature, and that no external beings or existences are required to explain what is going on in the universe. The chemist never requires demons, or ghosts, or anything of that sort, to explain his phenomena. The physicist never requires any one of these to explain the things he knows, nor does any other scientist. And this is one of the features of science which I mean to apply to religion. In this religions are found wanting and that is why they are crumbling into pieces. Every science wants its explanations from inside, from the very nature of things; and the religions are not able to supply this. There is an ancient theory of a personal deity entirely separate from the universe, which has been held from the very earliest time. The arguments in favour of this have been repeated again and again, how it is necessary to have a God entirely separate from the universe, an extra-cosmic deity, who has created the universe out of his will, and is conceived by religion to be its ruler. We find, apart from all these arguments, the Almighty God painted as the All-merciful, and at the same time, inequalities remain in the world. These things do not concern the philosopher at all, but he says the heart of the thing was wrong; it was an explanation from outside, and not inside. What is the cause of the universe? Something outside of it, some being who is moving this universe! And just as it was found insufficient to explain the phenomenon of the falling stone, so this was found insufficient to explain religion. And religions are falling to pieces, because they cannot give a better explanation than that.

Another idea connected with this, the manifestation of the same principle, that the explanation of everything comes from inside it, is the modern law of evolution. The whole meaning of evolution is simply that the nature of a thing is reproduced, that the effect is nothing but the cause in another form, that all the potentialities of the effect were present in the cause, that the whole of creation is but an evolution and not a creation. That is to say, every effect is a reproduction of a preceding cause, changed only by the circumstances, and thus it is going on throughout the universe, and we need not go outside the universe to seek the causes of these changes; they are within. It is unnecessary to seek for any cause outside. This also is breaking down religion. What I mean by breaking down religion is that religions that have held on to the idea of an extra-cosmic deity, that he is a very big man and nothing else, can no more stand on their feet; they have been pulled down, as it were.

Can there be a religion satisfying these two principles? I think there can be. In the first place we have seen that we have to satisfy the principle of generalization. The generalization principle ought to be satisfied along with the principle of evolution. We have to come to an ultimate generalization, which not only will be the most universal of all generalizations, but out of which everything else must come. It will be of the same nature as the lowest effect; the cause, the highest, the ultimate, the primal cause, must be the same as the lowest and most distant of its effects, a series of evolutions. The Brahman of the Vedanta fulfils that condition, because Brahman is the last generalization to which we can come. It has no attributes but is Existence, Knowledge, and Bliss—Absolute. Existence, we have seen, is the very ultimate generalization which the human mind can come to. Knowledge does not mean the knowledge we have, but the essence of that, that which is expressing itself in the course of evolution in human beings or in other animals as knowledge. The essence of that knowledge is meant, the ultimate fact beyond, if I may be allowed to say so, even consciousness. That is what is meant by knowledge and what we see in the universe as the essential unity of things. To my mind, if modern science is proving anything again and again, it is this, that we are one—mentally, spiritually, and physically. It is wrong to say we are even physically different. Supposing we are materialists, for argument's sake, we shall have to come to this, that the whole universe is simply an ocean of matter, of which you and I are like little whirlpools. Masses of matter are coming into each whirlpool, taking the whirlpool form, and coming out as matter again. The matter that is in my body may have been in yours a few years ago, or in the sun, or may have been the matter in a plant, and so on, in a continuous state of flux. What is meant by your body and my body? It is the oneness of the body. So with thought. It is an ocean of thought, one infinite mass, in which your mind and my mind are like whirlpools. Are you not seeing the effect now, how my thoughts are entering into yours, and yours into mine? The whole of our lives is one; we are one, even in thought. Coming to a still further generalization, the essence of matter and thought is their potentiality of spirit; this is the unity from which all have come, and that must essentially be one. We are absolutely one; we are physically one, we are mentally one, and as spirit, it goes without saying, that we are one, if we believe in spirit at all. This oneness is the one fact that is being proved every day by modern science. To proud man it is told: You are the same as that little worm there; think not that you are something enormously different from it; you are the same. You have been that in a previous incarnation, and the worm has crawled up to this man state, of which you are so proud. This grand preaching, the oneness of things, making us one with everything that exists, is the great lesson to learn, for most of us are very glad to be made one with higher beings, but nobody wants to be made one with lower beings. Such is human ignorance, that if anyone's ancestors were men whom society honoured, even if they were brutish, if they were robbers, even robber barons, everyone of us would try to trace our ancestry to them; but if among our ancestors we had poor, honest gentlemen, none of us wants to trace our ancestry to them. But the scales are falling from our eyes, truth is beginning to manifest itself more and more, and that is a great gain to religion. That is exactly the teaching of the Advaita, about which I am lecturing to you. The Self is the essence of this universe, the essence of all souls; He is the essence of your own life, nay, 'Thou art That'. You are one with this universe. He who says he is different from others, even by a hair's breadth, immediately becomes miserable. Happiness belongs to him who knows this oneness, who knows he is one with this universe.

Thus we see that the religion of the Vedanta can satisfy the demands of the scientific world, by referring it to the highest generalization and to the law of evolution. That the explanation of a thing comes from within itself is still more completely satisfied by Vedanta. The Brahman, the God of the Vedanta, has nothing outside of Himself; nothing at all. All this indeed is He: He is in the universe: He is the universe Himself. 'Thou art the man, Thou art the woman, Thou art the young man walking in the pride of youth, Thou art the old man tottering in his step.' He is here. Him we see and feel: in Him we live, and move, and have our being. You have that conception in the New Testament. It is that idea, God immanent in the universe, the very essence, the heart, the soul of things. He manifests Himself, as it were, in this universe. You and I are little bits, little points, little channels, little expressions, all living inside of that infinite ocean of Existence, Knowledge, and Bliss. The difference between man and man, between angels and man, between man and animals, between animals and plants, between plants and stones is not in kind, because everyone from the highest angel to the lowest particle of matter is but an expression of that one infinite ocean, and the difference is only in degree. I am a low manifestation, you may be a higher, but in both the materials are the same. You and I are both outlets of the same channel, and that is God; as such, your nature is God, and so is mine. You are of the nature of God by your birthright; so am I. You may be an angel of purity, and I may be the blackest of demons. Nevertheless, my birthright is that infinite ocean of Existence, Knowledge, and Bliss. So is yours. You have manifested yourself more today. Wait; I will manifest myself more yet, for I have it all within me. No extraneous explanation is sought; none is asked for. The sum total of this whole universe is God Himself. Is God then matter? No, certainly not, for matter is that God perceived by the five senses; that God as perceived through the intellect is mind; and when the spirit sees, He is seen as spirit. He is not matter, but whatever is real in matter is He. Whatever is real in this chair is He, for the chair requires two things to make it. Something was outside which my senses brought to me, and to which my mind contributed something else, and the combination of these two is the chair. That which existed eternally, independent of the senses and of the intellect, was the Lord Himself. Upon Him the senses are painting chairs, and tables, and rooms, houses, and worlds, and moons, and suns, and stars, and everything else. How is it, then, that we all see this same chair, that we are all alike painting these various things on the Lord, on this Existence, Knowledge, and Bliss? It need not be that all paint the same way, but those who paint the same way are on the same plane of existence and therefore they see one another's paintings as well as one another. There may be millions of beings between you and me who do not paint the Lord in the same way, and them and their paintings we do not see.

On the other hand, as you all know, the modern physical researches are tending more and more to demonstrate that what is real is but the finer; the gross is simply appearance. However that may be, we have seen that if any theory of religion can stand the test of modern reasoning, it is the Advaita, because it fulfils its two requirements. It is the highest generalization, beyond even personality, generalization which is common to every being. A generalization ending in the Personal God can never be universal, for, first of all, to conceive of a Personal God we must say, He is all-merciful, all-good. But this world is a mixed thing, some good and some bad. We cut off what we like, and generalize that into a Personal God! Just as you say a Personal God is this and that, so you have also to say that He is not this and not that. And you will always find that the idea of a Personal God has to carry with it a personal devil. That is how we clearly see that the idea of a Personal God is not a true generalization, we have to go beyond, to the Impersonal. In that the universe exists, with all its joys and miseries, for whatever exists in it has all come from the Impersonal. What sort of a God can He be to whom we attribute evil and other things? The idea is that both good and evil are different aspects, or manifestations of the same thing. The idea that they were two was a very wrong idea from the first, and it has been the cause of a good deal of the misery in this world of ours—the idea that right and wrong are two separate things, cut and dried, independent of each other, that good and evil are two eternally separable and separate things. I should be very glad to see a man who could show me something which is good all the time, and something which is bad all the time. As if one could stand and gravely define some occurrences in this life of ours as good and good alone, and some which are bad and bad alone. That which is good today may be evil tomorrow. That which is bad today may be good tomorrow. What is good for me may be bad for you. The conclusion is, that like every other thing, there is an evolution in good and evil too. There is something which in its evolution, we call, in one degree, good, and in another, evil. The storm that kills my friend I call evil, but that may have saved the lives of hundreds of thousands of people by killing the bacilli in the air. They call it good, but I call it evil. So both good and evil belong to the relative world, to phenomena. The Impersonal God we propose is not a relative God; therefore it cannot be said that It is either good or bad, but that It is something beyond, because It is neither good nor evil. Good, however, is a nearer manifestation of It than evil.

What is the effect of accepting such an Impersonal Being, an Impersonal Deity? What shall we gain? Will religion stand as a factor in human life, our consoler, our helper? What becomes of the desire of the human heart to pray for help to some being? That will all remain. The Personal God will remain, but on a better basis. He has been strengthened by the Impersonal. We have seen that without the Impersonal, the Personal cannot remain. If you mean to say there is a Being entirely separate from this universe, who has created this universe just by His will, out of nothing, that cannot be proved. Such a state of things cannot be. But if we understand the idea of the Impersonal, then the idea of the Personal can remain there also. This universe, in its various forms, is but the various readings of the same Impersonal. When we read it with the five senses, we call it the material world. If there be a being with more senses than five, he will read it as something else. If one of us gets the electrical sense, he will see the universe as something else again. There are various forms of that same Oneness, of which all these various ideas of worlds are but various readings, and the Personal God is the highest reading that can be attained to, of that Impersonal, by the human intellect. So that the Personal God is true as much as this chair is true, as much as this world is true, but no more. It is not absolute truth. That is to say, the Personal God is that very Impersonal God and, therefore, it is true, just as I, as a human being, am true and not true at the same time. It is not true that I am what you see I am; you can satisfy yourself on that point. I am not the being that you take me to be. You can satisfy your reason as to that, because light, and various vibrations, or conditions of the atmosphere, and all sorts of motions inside me have contributed to my being looked upon as what I am, by you. If any one of these conditions change, I am different again. You may satisfy yourself by taking a photograph of the same man under different conditions of light. So I am what I appear in relation to your senses, and yet, in spite of all these facts, there is an unchangeable something of which all these are different states of existence, the impersonal me, of which thousands of me's are different persons. I was a child, I was young, I am getting older. Every day of my life, my body and thoughts are changing, but in spite of all these changes, the sum-total of them constitutes a mass which is a constant quantity. That is the impersonal me, of which all these manifestations form, as it were, parts.

Similarly, the sum-total of this universe is immovable, we know, but everything pertaining to this universe consists of motion, everything is in a constant state of flux, everything changing and moving. At the same time, we see that the universe as a whole is immovable, because motion is a relative term. I move with regard to the chair, which does not move. There must be at least two to make motion. If this whole universe is taken as a unit there is no motion; with regard to what should it move? Thus the Absolute is unchangeable and immovable, and all the movements and changes are only in the phenomenal world, the limited. That whole is Impersonal, and within this Impersonal are all these various persons beginning with the lowest atom, up to God, the Personal God, the Creator, the Ruler of the Universe, to whom we pray, before whom we kneel, and so on. Such a Personal God can be established with a great deal of reason. Such a Personal God is explicable as the highest manifestation of the Impersonal. You and I are very low manifestations, and the Personal God is the highest of which we can conceive. Nor can you or I become that Personal God. When the Vedanta says you and I are God, it does not mean the Personal God. To take an example. Out of a mass of clay a huge elephant of clay is manufactured, and out of the same clay, a little clay mouse is made. Would the clay mouse ever be able to become the clay elephant? But put them both in water and they are both clay; as clay they are both one, but as mouse and elephant there will be an eternal difference between them. The Infinite, the Impersonal, is like the clay in the example. We and the Ruler of the Universe are one, but as manifested beings, men, we are His eternal slaves, His worshippers. Thus we see that the Personal God remains. Everything else in this relative world remains, and religion is made to stand on a better foundation. Therefore it is necessary, that we first know the Impersonal in order to know the Personal.

As we have seen, the law of reason says, the particular is only known through the general. So all these particulars, from man to God, are only known through the Impersonal, the highest generalization. Prayers will remain, only they will get a better meaning. All those senseless ideas of prayer, the low stages of prayer, which are simply giving words to all sorts of silly desire in our minds, perhaps, will have to go. In all sensible religions, they never allow prayers to God; they allow prayers to gods. That is quite natural. The Roman Catholics pray to the saints; that is quite good. But to pray to God is senseless. To ask God to give you a breath of air, to send down a shower of rain, to make fruits grow in your garden, and so on, is quite unnatural. The saints, however, who were little beings like ourselves, may help us. But to pray to the Ruler of the Universe, prating every little need of ours, and from our childhood saying, 'O Lord, I have a headache; let it go,' is ridiculous. There have been millions of souls that have died in this world, and they are all here; they have become gods and angels; let them come to your help. But God! It cannot be. Unto Him we must go for higher things. A fool indeed is he who, resting on the banks of the Ganga, digs a little well for water; a fool indeed is he who, living near a mine of diamonds, digs for bits of crystal.

And indeed we shall be fools if we go to the Father of all mercy, Father of all love, for trivial earthly things. Unto Him, therefore, we shall go for light, for strength, for love. But so long as there is weakness and a craving for servile dependence in us, there will be these little prayers and ideas of the worship of the Personal God. But those who are highly advanced do not care for such little helps, they have wellnigh forgotten all about this seeking things for themselves, wanting things for themselves. The predominant idea in them is—not I, but thou, my brother. Those are the fit persons to worship the Impersonal God. And what is the worship of the Impersonal God? No slavery there—'O Lord, I am nothing, have mercy on me.' You know the old Persian poem, translated into English: 'I came to see my beloved. The doors were closed. I knocked and a voice came from inside. 'Who art thou?' 'I am so-and-so' The door was not opened. A second time I came and knocked; I was asked the same question, and gave the same answer. The door opened not. I came a third time, and the same question came. I answered, 'I am thee, my love,' and the door opened.' Worship of the Impersonal God is through truth. And what is truth? That I am He. When I say that I am not Thou, it is untrue. When I say I am separate from you it is a lie, a terrible lie. I am one with this universe, born one. It is self evident to my senses that I am one with the universe. I am one with the air that surrounds me, one with heat, one with light, eternally one with the whole Universal Being, who is called this universe, who is mistaken for the universe, for it is He and nothing else, the eternal subject in the heart who says, 'I am,' in every heart—the deathless one, the sleepless one, ever awake, the immortal, whose glory never dies, whose powers never fail. I am one with That.

This is all the worship of the Impersonal, and what is the result? The whole life of man will be changed. Strength, strength it is that we want so much in this life, for what we call sin and sorrow have all one cause, and that is our weakness. With weakness comes ignorance, and with ignorance comes misery. It will make us strong. Then miseries will be laughed at, then the violence of the vile will be smiled at, and the ferocious tiger will reveal, behind its tiger's nature, my own Self. That will be the result. That soul is strong that has become one with the Lord; none else is strong. In your own Bible, what do you think was the cause of that strength of Jesus of Nazareth, that immense, infinite strength which laughed at traitors, and blessed those that were willing to murder him? It was that, 'I and my Father are one'; it was that prayer, 'Father, just as I am one with you, so make them all one with me.' That is the worship of the Impersonal God. Be one with the universe, be one with Him. And this Impersonal God requires no demonstrations, no proofs. He is nearer to us than even our senses, nearer to us than our own thoughts; it is in and through Him that we see and think. To see anything, I must first see Him. To see this wall I first see Him, and then the wall, for He is the eternal subject. Who is seeing whom? He is here in the heart of our hearts. Bodies and minds change; misery, happiness, good and evil come and go; days and years roll on; life comes and goes; but He dies not. The same voice, 'I am, I am,' is eternal, unchangeable. In Him and through Him we know everything. In Him and through Him we see everything. In Him and through Him we sense, we think, we live, and we are. And that 'I,' which we mistake to be a little 'I,' limited, is not only my 'I,' but yours, the 'I' of everyone, of the animals, of the angels, of the lowest of the low. That 'I am' is the same in the murderer as in the saint, the same in the rich as in the poor, the same in man as in woman, the same in man as in animals. From the lowest amoeba to the highest angel, He resides in every soul, and eternally declares, 'I am He, I am He.' When we have understood that voice eternally present there, when we have learnt this lesson, the whole universe will have expressed its secret. Nature will have given up her secret to us. Nothing more remains to be known. Thus we find the truth for which all religions search, that all this knowledge of material sciences is but secondary. That is the only true knowledge which makes us one with this Universal God of the Universe.

21

THE FREE SOUL

Delivered in New York, 1896

The analysis of the Sankhyas stops with the duality of existence—Nature and souls. There are an infinite number of souls, which, being simple, cannot die, and must therefore be separate from Nature. Nature in itself changes and manifests all these phenomena; and the soul, according to the Sankhyas, is inactive. It is a simple by itself, and Nature works out all these phenomena for the liberation of the soul; and liberation consists in the soul discriminating that it is not Nature. At the same time we have seen that the Sankhyas were bound to admit that every soul was omnipresent. Being a simple, the soul cannot be limited, because all limitation comes either through time, space, or causation. The soul being entirely beyond these cannot have any limitation. To have limitation one must be in space, which means the body; and that which is body must be in Nature. If the soul had form, it would be identified with Nature; therefore the soul is formless, and that which is formless cannot be said to exist here, there, or anywhere. It must be omnipresent. Beyond this the Sankhya philosophy does not go.

The first argument of the Vedantists against this is that this analysis is not a perfect one. If their Nature be absolute and the soul be also absolute, there will be two absolutes, and all the arguments that apply in the case of the soul to show that it is omnipresent will apply in the case of Nature, and Nature too will be beyond all time, space, and causation, and as the result there will be no change or manifestation. Then will come the difficulty of having two absolutes, which is impossible. What is the solution of the Vedantist? His solution is that, just as the Sankhyas say, it requires some sentient Being as the motive power behind, which makes the mind think and Nature work, because Nature in all its modifications, from gross matter up to Mahat (Intelligence), is simply insentient. Now, says the Vedantist, this sentient Being which is behind the whole universe is what we call *God*, and consequently this universe is not different from Him. It is He Himself who has become this universe. He not only is the instrumental cause of this universe, but also the material cause. Cause is never different from effect, the effect is but the cause reproduced in another form. We see that every day. So this Being is the cause of Nature. All the forms and phases of Vedanta, either dualistic, or qualified-monistic, or monistic, first take this position that God is not only the instrumental, but also the material cause of this universe, that everything which exists is He. The second step in Vedanta is that these souls are also a part of God, one spark of that Infinite Fire. 'As from a mass of fire millions of small particles fly, even so from this Ancient One have come all these souls.' So far so good, but it does not yet satisfy. What is meant by a part of the Infinite? The Infinite is indivisible; there cannot be parts of the Infinite. The Absolute cannot be divided. What is meant, therefore, by saying that all these sparks are from Him? The Advaitist, the non-dualistic Vedantist, solves the problem by maintaining that there is really no part; that each soul is really not a part of the Infinite, but actually is the Infinite Brahman. Then how can there be so many? The sun reflected from millions of globules of water appears to be millions of suns, and in each globule is a miniature picture of the sun-form; so all these souls are but reflections and not real. They are not the real 'I' which is the God of this universe, the one undivided Being of the universe. And all these little different beings, men and animals etc. are but reflections, and not real. They are simply illusory reflections upon Nature. There is but one Infinite Being in the universe, and that Being appears as you and as I; but this appearance of divisions is after all a delusion. He has not been divided, but only appears to be divided. This apparent division is caused by looking at Him through the network of time, space, and causation. When I look at God through the network of time, space, and causation, I see Him as the material world. When I look at Him from a little higher plane, yet through the same network, I see Him as an animal, a little higher as a man, a little higher as a god, but yet He is the One Infinite Being of the universe, and that

Being we are. I am That, and you are That. Not parts of It, but the whole of It. 'It is the Eternal Knower standing behind the whole phenomena; He Himself is the phenomena.' He is both the subject and the object, He is the 'I' and the 'You'. How is this? 'How to know the Knower? The Knower cannot know Himself; I see everything but cannot see myself. The Self, the Knower, the Lord of all, the Real Being, is the cause of all the vision that is in the universe, but it is impossible for Him to see Himself or know Himself, excepting through reflection. You cannot see your own face except in a mirror, and so the Self cannot see Its own nature until It is reflected, and this whole universe therefore is the Self trying to realize Itself. This reflection is thrown back first from the protoplasm, then from plants and animals, and so on and on from better and better reflectors, until the best reflector, the perfect man, is reached—just as a man who, wanting to see his face, looks first in a little pool of muddy water, and sees just an outline; then he comes to clear water, and sees a better image; then to a piece of shining metal, and sees a still better image; and at last to a looking-glass, and sees himself reflected as he is. Therefore, the perfect man is the highest reflection of that Being who is both subject and object. You now find why man instinctively worships everything, and how perfect men are instinctively worshipped as God in every country. You may talk as you like, but it is they who are bound to be worshipped. That is why men worship Incarnations, such as Christ or Buddha. They are the most perfect manifestations of the eternal Self. They are much higher than all the conceptions of God that you or I can make. A perfect man is much higher than such conceptions. In him the circle becomes complete; the subject and the object become one. In him all delusions go away and in their place comes the realization that he has always been that perfect Being. How came this bondage then? How was it possible for this perfect Being to degenerate into the imperfect? How was it possible that the free became bound? The Advaitist says, he was never bound, but was always free. Various clouds of various colours come before the sky. They remain there a minute and then pass away. It is the same eternal blue sky stretching there for ever. The sky never changes: it is the cloud that is changing. So you are always perfect, eternally perfect.

Nothing ever changes your nature, or ever will. All these ideas that I am imperfect, I am a man, or a woman, or a sinner, or I am the mind, I have thought, I will think—all are hallucinations; you never think, you never had a body; you never were imperfect. You are the blessed Lord of this universe, the one Almighty ruler of everything that is and ever will be, the one mighty ruler of these suns and stars and moons and earths and planets and all the little bits of our universe. It is through you that the sun shines and the stars shed their lustre, and the earth becomes beautiful. It is through your blessedness that they all love and are attracted to each other. You are in all, and you are all. Whom to avoid, and whom to take? You are the all in all. When this knowledge comes delusion immediately vanishes.

I was once travelling in the desert in India. I travelled for over a month and always found the most beautiful landscapes before me, beautiful lakes and all that. One day I was very thirsty and I wanted to have a drink at one of these lakes; but when I approached that lake it vanished. Immediately with a blow came into my brain the idea that this was a mirage about which I had read all my life; and then I remembered and smiled at my folly, that for the last month all the beautiful landscapes and lakes I had been seeing were this mirage, but I could not distinguish them then. The next morning I again began my march; there was the lake and the landscape, but with it immediately came the idea, 'This is a mirage.' Once known it had lost its power of illusion. So this illusion of the universe will break one day. The whole of this will vanish, melt away. This is realization. Philosophy is no joke or talk. It has to be realized; this body will vanish, this earth and everything will vanish, this idea that I am the body or the mind will for some time vanish, or if the Karma is ended it will disappear, never to come back; but if one part of the Karma remains, then as a potter's wheel, after the potter has finished the pot, will sometimes go on from the past momentum, so this body, when the delusion has vanished altogether, will go on for some time. Again this world will come, men and women and animals will come, just as the mirage came the next day, but not with the same force; along with it will come the idea that I know its nature now, and it will cause no bondage, no more pain, nor grief, nor misery. Whenever anything miserable will come, the mind will be able to say, 'I know you as hallucination.' When a man has reached that state, he is called Jivanmukta, living-free', free even while living. The aim and end in this life for the Jnana-Yogi is to become this Jivanmukta, 'living-free'. He is Jivanmukta who can live in this world without being attached. He is like the lotus leaves in water, which are never wetted by the water. He is the highest of human beings, nay, the highest of all beings, for he has realized his identity with the Absolute, he has realized that he is one with God. So long as you think you have the least difference from God, fear will seize you, but when you have known that you are He, that there is no difference, entirely no difference, that you are He, all of Him, and the whole of Him, all fear ceases. 'There, who sees whom? Who worships whom? Who talks to whom? Who hears whom? Where one sees another, where one talks to another, where one hears another, that is little. Where none sees none, where none speaks to none, that is the highest, that is the great, that is the Brahman.' Being That, you are always That. What will become of the world then? What good shall we do to the world? Such questions do not arise 'What becomes of my gingerbread if I become old?' says the baby! 'What becomes of my marbles if I grow? So I will not grow,' says the boy! 'What will become of my dolls if I grow old?' says the little child! It is the same question in connection with this world, it has no existence in the past, present, or future. If we have known the Atman as It is, if we have known that there is nothing else but this Atman, that everything else is but a dream, with no existence in reality, then this world with its poverties, its miseries, its wickedness, and its goodness will cease to disturb us. If they do not exist, for whom and for what shall we take trouble? This is what the Jnana-Yogis teach. Therefore, dare to be free, dare to go as far as your thought leads, and dare to carry that out in your life. It is very hard to come to Jnana. It is for the bravest and most daring, who dare to smash all idols, not only intellectual, but in the senses. This body is not I; it must go. All sorts of curious things may come out of this. A man stands up and says, 'I am not the body, therefore my headache must be cured'; but where is the headache if not in his body? Let a thousand headaches and a thousand bodies come and go. What is that to me? I have neither birth nor death; father or mother I never had; friends and foes I have none, because they are all I. I am my own friend, and I am my own enemy. I am Existence-Knowledge-Bliss Absolute. I am He, I am He. If in a thousand bodies I am suffering from fever and other ills, in millions of bodies I am healthy. If in a thousand bodies I am starving, in other thousand bodies I am feasting. If in thousands of bodies I am suffering misery, in thousands of bodies I am happy. Who shall blame whom, who praise whom? Whom to seek, whom to avoid? I seek none, nor avoid any, for I am all the universe. I praise myself, I blame myself, I suffer for myself, I am happy at my own will, I am free. This is the Jnani, the brave and daring. Let the whole universe tumble down; he smiles and says it never existed, it was all a hallucination. He sees the universe tumble down. Where was it! Where has it gone!

Before going into the practical part, we will take up one more intellectual question. So far the logic is tremendously rigorous. If man reasons, there is no place for him to stand until he comes to this, that there is but One Existence, that everything else is nothing. There is no other way left for rational mankind but to take this view. But how is it that what is infinite, ever perfect, ever blessed, Existence-Knowledge-Bliss Absolute, has come under these delusions? It is the same question that has been asked all the world over. In the vulgar form the question becomes, 'How did sin come into this world?' This is the most vulgar and sensuous form of the question, and the other is the most philosophic form, but the answer is the same. The same question has been asked in various grades and fashions, but in its lower forms it finds no solution, because the stories of apples and serpents and women do not give the explanation. In that state, the question is childish, and so is the answer. But the question has assumed very high proportions now: 'How did this illusion come?' And the answer is as fine. The answer is that we cannot expect any answer to an impossible question. The very question is impossible in terms. You have no right to ask that question. Why? What is perfection? That which is beyond time, space, and causation—that is perfect. Then you ask how the perfect became imperfect. In logical language the question may be put in this form: 'How did that which is beyond causation become caused?' You contradict yourself. You first admit it is beyond causation, and then ask what causes it. This question can only be asked within the limits of causation. As far as time and space and causation extend, so far can this question be asked. But beyond that it will be nonsense to ask it, because the question is illogical. Within time, space, and causation it can never be answered, and what answer may lie beyond these limits can only be known when we have transcended them; therefore the wise will let this question rest. When a man is ill, he devotes himself to curing his disease without insisting that he must first learn how he came to have it.

There is another form of this question, a little lower, but more practical and illustrative: What produced this delusion? Can any reality produce delusion? Certainly not. We see that one delusion produces another, and so on. It is delusion always that produces delusion. It is disease that produces disease, and not health that produces disease. The wave is the same thing as the water, the effect is the cause in another form. The effect is delusion, and therefore the cause must be delusion. What produced this delusion? Another delusion. And so on without beginning. The only question that remains for you to ask is: Does not this break your monism, because you get two existences in the universe, one yourself and the other the delusion? The answer is: Delusion cannot be called an existence. Thousands of dreams come into your life, but do not form any part of your life. Dreams come and go; they have no existence. To call delusion existence will be sophistry. Therefore there is only one individual existence in the universe, ever free, and ever blessed; and that is what you are. This is the last conclusion reached by the Advaitists.

It may then be asked: What becomes of all these various forms of worship? They will remain; they are simply groping in the dark for light, and through this groping light will come. We have just seen that the Self cannot see Itself. Our knowledge is within the network of Maya (unreality), and beyond that is freedom. Within the network there is slavery, it is all under law; beyond that there is no law. So far as the universe is concerned, existence is ruled by law, and beyond that is freedom. As long as you are in the network of time, space, and causation, to say you are free is nonsense, because in that network all is under rigorous law, sequence, and consequence. Every thought that you think is caused, every feeling has been caused; to say that the will is free is sheer nonsense. It is only when the infinite existence comes, as it were, into this network of Maya that it takes the form of will. Will is a portion of that being, caught in the network of Maya, and therefore 'free will' is a misnomer. It means nothing—sheer nonsense. So is all this talk about freedom. There is no freedom in Maya.

Every one is as much bound in thought, word, deed, and mind, as a piece of stone or this table. That I talk to you now is as rigorous in causation as that you listen to me. There is no freedom until you go beyond Maya. That is the real freedom of the soul. Men, however sharp and intellectual, however clearly they see the force of the logic that nothing here can be free, are all compelled to think they are free; they cannot help it. No work can go on until we begin to say we are free. It means that the freedom we talk about is the glimpse of the blue sky through the clouds and that the real freedom—the blue sky itself—is behind. True freedom cannot exist in the midst of this delusion, this hallucination, this nonsense of the world, this universe of the senses, body, and mind. All these dreams, without beginning or end, uncontrolled and uncontrollable, ill-adjusted, broken, inharmonious, form our idea of this universe. In a dream, when you see a giant with twenty heads chasing you, and you are flying from him, you do not think it is inharmonious; you think it is proper and right. So is this law. All that you call law is simply chance without meaning. In this dream state you call it law. Within Maya, so far as this law of time, space and causation exists, there is no freedom; and all these various forms of worship are within this Maya. The idea of God and the ideas of brute and of man are within this Maya, and as such are equally hallucinations; all of them are dreams. But you must take care not to argue like some extraordinary men of whom we hear at the present time. They say the idea of God is a delusion, but the idea of this world is true. Both ideas stand or fall by the same logic. He alone has the right to be an atheist who denies this world, as well as the other. The same argument is for both. The same mass of delusion extends from God to the lowest animal, from a blade of grass to the Creator. They stand or fall by the same logic. The same person who sees falsity in the idea of God ought also to see it in the idea of his own body or his own mind. When God vanishes, then also vanish the body and mind; and when both vanish, that which is the Real Existence remains for ever. 'There the eyes cannot go, nor the speech, nor the mind. We cannot see it, neither know it.' And we now understand that so far as speech and thought and knowledge and intellect go, it is all within this Maya within bondage. Beyond that is Reality. There neither thought, nor mind, nor speech, can reach.

So far it is intellectually all right, but then comes the practise. The real work is in the practise. Are any practises necessary to realize this Oneness? Most decidedly. It is not that you become this Brahman. You are already that. It is not that you are going to become God or perfect; you are already perfect; and whenever you think you are not, it is a delusion. This delusion which says that you are Mr So-and-so or Mrs So-and-so can be got rid of by another delusion, and that is practise. Fire will eat fire, and you can use one delusion to conquer another delusion. One cloud will come and brush away another cloud, and then both will go away. What are these practises then? We must always bear in mind that we are not going to be free, but are free already. Every idea that we are bound is a delusion. Every idea that we are happy or unhappy is a tremendous delusion; and another delusion will come—that we have got to work and worship and struggle to be free—and this will chase out the first delusion, and then both will stop.

The fox is considered very unholy by the Mohammedans and by the Hindus. Also, if a dog touches any bit of food, it has to be thrown out, it cannot be eaten by any man. In a certain Mohammedan house a fox entered and took a little bit of food from the table, ate it up, and fled. The man was a poor man, and had prepared a very nice feast for himself, and that feast was made unholy, and he could not eat it. So he went to a Mulla, a priest, and said, 'This has happened to me; a fox came and took a mouthful out of my meal. What can be done? I had prepared a feast and wanted so much to eat it, and now comes this fox and destroys the whole affair.' The Mulla thought for a minute and then found only one solution and said, 'The only way for you is to get a dog and make him eat a bit out of the same plate, because dogs and foxes are eternally quarrelling. The food that was left by the fox will go into your stomach, and that left by the dog will go there too, and both will be purified.' We are very much in the same predicament. This is a hallucination that we are imperfect; and we take up another, that we have to practise to become perfect. Then one will chase the other, as we can use one thorn to extract another and then throw both away. There are people for whom it is sufficient knowledge to hear, 'Thou art That'. With a flash this universe goes away and the real nature shines, but others have to struggle hard to get rid of this idea of bondage.

The first question is: Who are fit to become Jnana-Yogis? Those who are equipped with these requisites: First, renunciation of all fruits of work and of all enjoyments in this life or another life. If you are the creator of this universe, whatever you desire you will have, because you will create it for yourself. It is only a question of time. Some get it immediately; with others the past Samskaras (impressions) stand in the way of getting their desires. We give the first place to desires for enjoyment, either in this or another life. Deny that there is any life at all; because life is only another name for death. Deny that you are a living being. Who cares for life? Life is one of these hallucinations, and death is its counterpart. Joy is one part of these hallucinations, and misery the other part, and so on. What have you to do with life or death ? These are all creations of the mind. This is called giving up desires of enjoyment either in this life or another.

Then comes controlling the mind, calming it so that it will not break into waves and have all sorts of desires, holding the mind steady, not allowing it to get into waves from external or internal causes, controlling the mind perfectly, just by the power of will. The Jnana-Yogi does not take any one of these physical helps or mental helps: simply philosophic reasoning, knowledge, and his own will, these are the instrumentalities he believes in. Next comes Titiksha, forbearance, bearing all miseries without murmuring, without complaining. When an injury comes, do not mind it. If a tiger comes, stand there. Who flies? There are men who practise Titiksha, and succeed in it. There are men who sleep on the banks of the Ganga in the midsummer sun of India, and in winter float in the waters of the Ganga for a whole day; they do not care. Men sit in the snow of the Himalayas, and do not care to wear any garment. What is heat? What is cold? Let things come and go, what is that to me, I am not the body. It is hard to believe this in these Western countries, but it is better to know that it is done. Just as your people are brave to jump at the mouth of a cannon, or into the midst of the battlefield, so our people are brave to think and act out their philosophy. They give up their lives for it. 'I am Existence-Knowledge-Bliss Absolute; I am He, I am He.' Just as the Western ideal is to keep up luxury in practical life, so ours is to keep up the highest form of spirituality, to demonstrate that religion is riot merely frothy words, but can be carried out, every bit of it, in this life. This is Titiksha, to bear everything, not to complain of anything. I myself have seen men who say, 'I am the soul; what is the universe to me? Neither pleasure nor pain, nor virtue nor vice, nor heat nor cold is anything to me.' That is Titiksha; not running after the enjoyments of the body. What is religion? To pray, 'Give me this and that'? Foolish ideas of religion! Those who believe them have no true idea of God and soul. My Master used to say, 'The vulture rise, higher and higher until he becomes a speck, but his eye is always on the piece of rotten carrion on the earth.' After all, what is the result of your ideas of religion? To cleanse the streets and have more bread and clothes? Who cares for bread and clothes? Millions come and go every minute. Who cares? Why care for the joys and vicissitudes of this little world? Go beyond that if you dare; go beyond law, let the whole universe vanish, and stand alone. 'I am Existence-Absolute, Knowledge-Absolute, Bliss-Absolute; I am He, I am He.'

22

UNITY, THE GOAL OF RELIGION
Delivered in New York, 1896

This universe of ours, the universe of the senses, the rational, the intellectual, is bounded on both sides by the illimitable, the unknowable, the ever unknown. Herein is the search, herein are the inquiries, here are the facts; from this comes the light which is known to the world as religion. Essentially, however, religion belongs to the supersensuous and not to the sense plane. It is beyond all reasoning and is not on the plane of intellect. It is a vision, an inspiration, a plunge into the unknown and unknowable, making the unknowable more than known for it can never be 'known'. This search has been in the human mind, as I believe, from the very beginning of humanity. There cannot have been human reasoning and intellect in any period of the world's history without this struggle, this search beyond. In our little universe, this human mind, we see a thought arise. Whence it arises we do not know; and when it disappears, where it goes, we know not either. The macrocosm and the microcosm are, as it were, in the same groove, passing through the same stages, vibrating in the same key.

I shall try to bring before you the Hindu theory that religions do not come from without, but from within. It is my belief that religious thought is in man's very constitution, so much so that it is impossible for him to give up religion until he can give up his mind and body, until he can give up thought and life. As long as a man thinks, this struggle must go on, and so long man must have some form of religion. Thus, we see various forms of religion in the world. It is a bewildering study; but it is not, as many of us think, a vain speculation. Amidst this chaos there is harmony, throughout these discordant sounds there is a note of concord; and he who is prepared to listen to it will catch the tone.

The great question of all questions at the present time is this: Taking for granted that the known and the knowable are bounded on both sides by the unknowable and the infinitely unknown, why struggle for that infinite unknown? Why shall we not be content with the known? Why shall we not rest satisfied with eating, drinking, and doing a little good to society? This idea is in the air. From the most learned professor to the prattling baby, we are told that to do good to the world is all of religion, and that it is useless to trouble ourselves about questions of the beyond. So much is this the case that it has become a truism.

But fortunately we *must* inquire into the beyond. This present, this expressed, is only one part of that unexpressed. The sense universe is, as it were, only one portion, one bit of that infinite spiritual universe projected into the plane of sense consciousness. How can this little bit of projection be explained, be understood, without. Knowing that which is beyond? It is said of Socrates that one day while lecturing at Athens, he met a Brahmin who had travelled into Greece, and Socrates told the Brahmin that the greatest study for mankind is man. The Brahmin sharply retorted: 'How can you know man until you know Gods' This God, this eternally Unknowable, or Absolute, or Infinite, or without name—you may call Him by what name you like—is the rationale, the only explanation, the *raison d'être* of that which is known and knowable, this present life. Take anything before you, the most material thing—take one of the most material sciences, as chemistry or physics, astronomy or biology—study it, push the study forward and forward, and the gross forms will begin to melt and become finer and finer, until they come to a point where you are bound to make a tremendous leap from these material things into the immaterial. The gross melts into the fine, physics into metaphysics, in every department of knowledge.

Thus man finds himself driven to a study of the beyond. Life will be a desert, human life will be vain, if we cannot know the beyond. It is very well to say: Be contented with the things of the present. The cows and the dogs are, and so are all animals; and that is what makes them animals. So if man rests content with the present and gives up all search into the beyond, mankind will have to go back to the animal plane again. It is religion, the inquiry into the beyond, that makes the difference between man and an animal. Well has it been said that man is the only animal that naturally looks upwards; every other animal naturally looks down. That looking upward and going upward and seeking perfection are what is called salvation; and the sooner a man begins to go higher, the sooner he raises himself towards this idea of truth as salvation. It does not consist in the amount of money in your pocket, or the dress you wear, or the house you live in, but in the wealth of spiritual thought in your brain. That is what makes for human progress, that is the source of all material and intellectual progress, the motive power behind, the enthusiasm that pushes mankind forward.

Religion does not live on bread, does not dwell in a house. Again and again you hear this objection advanced: 'What good can religion do? Can it take away the poverty of the poor?' Supposing it cannot, would that prove the untruth of religion? Suppose a baby stands up among you when you are trying to demonstrate an astronomical theorem, and says, 'Does it bring gingerbread?' 'No, it does not', you answer. 'Then,' says the baby, 'it is useless.' Babies judge the whole universe from their own standpoint, that of producing gingerbread, and so do the babies of the world. We must not judge of higher things from a low standpoint. Everything must be judged by its own standard and the infinite must be judged by the standard of infinity. Religion permeates the whole of man's life, not only the present, but the past, present, and future. It is, therefore, the eternal relation between the eternal soul and the eternal God. Is it logical to measure its value by its action upon five minutes of human life? Certainly not. These are all negative arguments.

Now comes the question: Can religion really accomplish anything? It can. It brings to man eternal life. It has made man what he is, and will make of this human animal a god. That is what religion can do. Take religion from human society and what will remain? Nothing but a forest of brutes. Sense-happiness is not the goal of humanity. Wisdom (Jnana) is the goal of all life. We find that man enjoys his intellect more than an animal enjoys its senses; and we see that man enjoys his spiritual nature even more than his rational nature.

So the highest wisdom must be this spiritual knowledge. With this knowledge will come bliss. All these things of this world are but the shadows, the manifestations in the third or fourth degree of the real Knowledge and Bliss.

One question more: What is the goal? Nowadays it is asserted that man is infinitely progressing, forward and forward, and there is no goal of perfection to attain to. Ever approaching, never attaining, whatever that may mean and however wonderful it may be, it is absurd on the face of it. Is there any motion in a straight line? A straight line infinitely projected becomes a circle, it returns to the starting point. You must end where you begin; and as you began in God, you must go back to God. What remains? Detail work. Through eternity you have to do the detail work.

Yet another question: Are we to discover new truths of religion as we go on? Yea and nay. In the first place, we cannot know anything more of religion, it has all been known. In all religions of the world you will find it claimed that there is a unity within us. Being one with divinity, there cannot be any further progress in that sense. Knowledge means finding this unity. I see you as men and women, and this is variety. It becomes scientific knowledge when I group you together and call you human beings. Take the science of chemistry, for instance. Chemists are seeking to resolve all known substances into their original elements, and if possible, to find the one element from which all these are derived. The time may come when they will find one element that is the source of all other elements. Reaching that, they can go no further; the science of chemistry will have become perfect. So it is with the science of religion. If we can discover this perfect unity, there cannot be any further progress.

The next question is: Can such a unity be found? In India the attempt has been made from the earliest times to reach a science of religion and philosophy, for the Hindus do not separate these as is customary in Western countries. We regard religion and philosophy as but two aspects of one thing which must equally be grounded in reason and scientific truth.

The system of the Sankhya philosophy is one of the most ancient in India, or in fact in the world. Its great exponent Kapila is the father of all Hindu psychology; and the ancient system that he taught is still the foundation of all accepted systems of philosophy in India today which are known as the Darshanas. They all adopt his psychology, however widely they differ in other respects.

The Vedanta, as the logical outcome of the Sankhya, pushes its conclusions yet further. While its cosmology agrees with that taught by Kapila, the Vedanta is not satisfied to end in dualism, but continues its search for the final unity which is alike the goal of science and religion.

23

ONE EXISTENCE APPEARING AS MANY
Delivered in New York, 1896

Vairagya or renunciation is the turning point in all the various Yogas. The Karmi (worker) renounces the fruits of his work. The Bhakta (devotee) renounces all little loves for the almighty and omnipresent love. The Yogi renounces his experiences, because his philosophy is that the whole Nature, although it is for the experience of the soul, at last brings him to know that he is not in Nature, but eternally separate from Nature. The Jnani (philosopher) renounces everything, because his philosophy is that Nature never existed, neither in the past, nor present, nor will It in the future. The question of utility cannot be asked in these higher themes. It is very absurd to ask it; and even if it be asked, after a proper analysis, what do we find in this question of utility? The ideal of happiness, that which brings man more happiness, is of greater utility to him than these higher things which do not improve his material conditions or bring him such great happiness. All the sciences are for this one end, to bring happiness to humanity; and that which brings the larger amount of happiness, man takes and gives up that which brings a lesser amount of happiness. We have seen how happiness is either in the body, or in the mind, or in the Atman. With animals, and in the lowest human beings who are very much like animals, happiness is all in the body. No man can eat with the same pleasure as a famished dog or a wolf; so in the dog and the wolf the happiness is entirely in the body. In men we find a higher plane of happiness, that of thought; and in the Jnani there is the highest plane of happiness in the Self, the Atman. So to the philosopher this knowledge of the Self is of the highest utility, because it gives him the highest happiness possible. Sense-gratifications or physical things cannot be of the highest utility to him, because he does not find in them the same pleasure that he finds in knowledge itself; and after all, knowledge is the one goal and is really the highest happiness that we know. All who work in ignorance are, as it were, the draught animals of the Devas. The word Deva is here used in the sense of a wise man. All the people that work and toil and labour like machines do not really enjoy life, but it is the wise man who enjoys. A rich man buys a picture at a cost of a hundred thousand dollars perhaps, but it is the man who understands art that enjoys it; and if the rich man is without knowledge of art, it is useless to him, he is only the owner. All over the world, it is the wise man who enjoys the happiness of the world. The ignorant man never enjoys; he has to work for others unconsciously.

Thus far we have seen the theories of these Advaitist philosophers, how there is but one Atman; there cannot be two. We have seen how in the whole of this universe there is but One Existence; and that One Existence when seen through the senses is called the world, the world of matter. When It is seen through the mind, It is called the world of thoughts and ideas; and when It is seen as it is, then It is the One Infinite Being. You must bear this in mind; it is not that there is a soul in man, although I had to take that for granted in order to explain it at first, but that there is only One Existence, and that one the Atman, the Self; and when this is perceived through the senses, through sense-imageries, It is called the body. When It is perceived through thought, It is called the mind. When It is perceived in Its own nature, It is the Atman, the One Only Existence. So it is not that there are three things in one, the body and the mind and the Self, although that was a convenient way of putting it in the course of explanation; but all is that Atman, and that one Being is sometimes called the body, sometimes the mind, and sometimes the Self, according to different vision. There is but one Being which the ignorant call the world. When a man goes higher in knowledge, he calls the very same Being the world of thought. Again, when knowledge itself comes, all illusions vanish, and man finds it is all nothing but Atman. I am that One Existence. This is the last conclusion. There are neither three nor two in the universe; it is all One. That One, under the illusion of Maya, is seen as many, just as a rope is seen as a snake. It is the very rope that is seen as a snake. There are not two things there, a rope separate and a snake separate. No man sees these two things there at the same time. Dualism and non-dualism are very good philosophic terms, but in perfect perception we never perceive the real and the false at the same time. We are all born monists, we cannot help it. We always perceive the one. When we perceive the rope, we do not perceive the snake at all; and when we see the snake, we do not see the rope at all—it has vanished. When you see illusion, you do not see reality. Suppose you see one of your friends coming at a distance in the street; you know him very well, but through the haze and mist that is before you, you think it is another man. When you see your friend as another man, you do not see your friend at all, he has vanished. You are perceiving only one. Suppose your friend is Mr A; but when you perceive Mr A as Mr B, you do not see Mr A at all. In each case you perceive only one. When you see yourself as a body, you are body and nothing else; and that is the perception of the vast majority of mankind. They may talk of soul and mind, and all these things, but what they perceive is the physical form, the touch, taste, vision, and so on. Again, with certain men in certain states of consciousness, they perceive themselves as thought. You know, of course, the story told of Sir Humphrey Davy, who has making experiments before his class with laughing-gas, and suddenly one of the tubes broke, and the gas escaping, he breathed it in. For some moments he remained like a statue. Afterwards he told his class that when he was in that state, he actually perceived that the whole world is made up of ideas. The gas, for a time, made him forget the consciousness of the body, and that very thing which he was seeing as the body, he began to perceive as ideas. When the consciousness rises still higher, when this little puny consciousness is gone for ever, that which is the Reality behind shines, and we see it as the One Existence-Knowledge-Bliss, the one Atman, the Universal. 'One that is only Knowledge itself, One that is Bliss itself, beyond all compare, beyond all limit, ever free, never bound, infinite as the sky, unchangeable as the sky. Such a One will manifest Himself in your heart in meditation.'

How does the Advaitist theory explain these various phases of heaven and hells and these various ideas we find in all religions? When a man dies, it is said that he goes to heaven or hell, goes here or there, or that when a man dies he is born again in another body either in heaven or in another world or somewhere. These are all hallucinations. Really speaking nobody is ever born or dies. There is neither heaven nor hell nor this world; all three never really existed. Tell a child a lot of ghost stories, add let him go out into the street in the evening. There is a little stump of a tree. What does the child see? A ghost, with hands stretched out, ready to grab him. Suppose a man comes from the corner of the street, wanting to meet his sweetheart; he sees that stump of the tree as the girl. A policeman coming from the street corner sees the stump as a thief. The thief sees it as a policeman. It is the same stump of a tree that was seen in various ways. The stump is the reality, and the visions of the stump are the projections of the various minds. There is one Being, this Self; It neither comes nor goes. When a man is ignorant, he wants to go to heaven or some place, and all his life he has been thinking and thinking of this; and when this earth dream vanishes, he sees this world as a heaven with Devas and angels flying about, and all such things. If a man all his life desires to meet his forefathers, he gets them all from Adam downwards, because he creates them. If a man is still more ignorant and has always been frightened by fanatics with ideas of hell, with all sorts of punishments, when he dies, he will see this very world as hell. All that is meant by dying or being born is simply changes in the plane of vision. Neither do you move, nor does that move upon which you project your vision. You are the permanent, the unchangeable. How can you come and go? It is impossible; you are omnipresent. The sky never moves, but the clouds move over the surface of the sky, and we may think that the sky itself moves, just as when you are in a railway train, you think the land is moving. It is not so, but it is the train which is moving. You are where you are; these dreams, these various clouds move. One dream follows another without connection. There is no such thing as law or connection in this world, but we are thinking that there is a great deal of connection. All of you have probably read *Alice in Wonderland*. It is the most wonderful book for children that has been written in this century. When I read it, I was delighted; it was always in my head to write that sort of a book for children. What pleased me most in it was what you think most incongruous, that there is no connection there. One idea comes and jumps into another, without any connection. When you were children, you thought that the most wonderful connection. So this man brought back his thoughts of childhood, which were perfectly connected to him as a child, and composed this book for children. And all these books which men write, trying to make children swallow their own ideas as men, are nonsense. We too are grown-up children, that is all. The world is the same unconnected thing—*Alice in Wonderland*—with no connection whatever. When we see things happen a number of times in a certain sequence, we call it cause and effect, and say that the thing will happen again. When this dream changes, another dream will seem quite as connected as this. When we dream, the things we see all seem to be connected; during the dream we never think they are incongruous; it is only when we wake that we see the want of connection. When we wake from this dream of the world and compare it with the Reality, it will be found all incongruous nonsense, a mass of incongruity passing before us, we do not know whence or whither, but we know it will end; and this is called Maya, and is like masses of fleeting fleecy clouds. They represent all this changing existence, and the sun itself, the unchanging, is you. When you look at that unchanging Existence from the outside, you call it God; and when you look at it from the inside, you call it yourself. It is but one. There is no God separate from you, no God higher than you, the real 'you'. All the gods are little beings to you, all the ideas of God and Father in heaven are but your own reflection. God Himself is your image. 'God created man after His own image.' That is wrong. Man creates God after his own image. That is right. Throughout the universe we are creating gods after our own image. We create the God and fall down at His feet and worship Him; and when this dream comes, we love it!

This is a good point to understand—that the sum and substance of this lecture is that there is but One Existence, and that One Existence seen through different constitutions appears either as the earth, or heaven, or hell, or gods, or ghosts, or men, or demons, or world, or all these things. But among these many, 'He who sees that One in this ocean of death, he who sees that One Life in this floating universe, who realizes that One who never changes, unto him belongs eternal peace; unto none else, unto none else.' This One existence has to be realized. How, is the next question. How is it to be realized? How is this dream to be broken, how shall we wake up from this dream that we are little men and women, and all such things? We are the Infinite Being of the universe and have become materialized into these little beings, men and women, depending upon the sweet word of one man, or the angry word of another, and so forth. What a terrible dependence, what a terrible slavery! I who am beyond all pleasure and pain, whose reflection is the whole universe, little bits of whose life are the suns and moons and stars—I am held down as a terrible slave! If you pinch my body, I feel pain. If one says a kind word, I begin to rejoice. See my condition—slave of the body, slave of the mind, slave of the world, slave of a good word, slave of a bad word, slave of passion, slave of happiness, slave of life, slave of death, slave of everything! This slavery has to be broken. How? 'This Atman has first to be heard, then reasoned upon, and then meditated upon.' This is the method of the Advaita Jnani. The truth has to be heard, then reflected upon, and then to be constantly asserted. Think always, 'I am Brahman'. Every other thought must be cast aside as weakening. Cast aside every thought that says that you are men or women. Let body go, and mind go, and gods go, and ghosts go. Let everything go but that One Existence. 'Where one hears another, where one sees another, that is small; where one does not hear another, where one does not see another, that is Infinite.' That is the highest when the subject and the object become one. When I am the listener and I am the speaker, when I am the teacher and I am the taught, when I am the creator and I am the created—then alone fear ceases; there is not another to make us afraid. There is nothing but myself, what can frighten me? This is to be heard day after day. Get rid of all other thoughts. Everything else must be thrown aside, and this is to be repeated continually, poured through the ears until it reaches the heart, until every nerve and muscle, every drop of blood tingles with the idea that I am He, I am He. Even at the gate of death say, 'I am He'. There was a man in India, a Sannyasin, who used to repeat 'Shivoham'—'I am Bliss Eternal'; and a tiger jumped on him one day and dragged him away and killed him; but so long as he was living, the sound came, 'Shivoham, Shivoham'. Even at the gate of death, in the greatest danger, in the thick of the battlefield, at the bottom of the ocean, on the tops of the highest mountains, in the thickest of the forest, tell yourself, 'I am He, I am He'. Day and night say, 'I am He'. It is the greatest strength; it is religion. 'The weak will never reach the Atman.' Never say, 'O Lord, I am a miserable sinner.' Who will help you? You are the help of the universe. What in this universe can help you? Where is the man, or the god, or the demon to help you? What can prevail over you? You are the God of the universe; where can you seek for help? Never help came from anywhere but from yourself. In your ignorance, every prayer that you made and that was answered, you thought was answered by some Being, but you answered the prayer yourself unknowingly. The help came from yourself, and you fondly imagined that some one was sending help to you. There is no help for you outside of yourself; you are the creator of the universe. Like the silkworm you have built a cocoon around yourself. Who will save you? Burst your own cocoon and come out as the beautiful butterfly, as the free soul. Then alone you will see Truth. Ever tell yourself, 'I am He.' These are words that will burn up the dross that is in the mind, words that will bring out the tremendous energy which is within you already, the infinite power which is sleeping in your heart. This is to be brought out by constantly hearing the truth and nothing else. Wherever there is thought of weakness, approach not the place. Avoid all weakness if you want to be a Jnani.

Before you begin to practise, clear your mind of all doubts. Fight and reason and argue; and when you have established it in your mind that this and this alone can be the truth and nothing else, do not argue any more; close your mouth. Hear not argumentation, neither argue yourself. What is the use of any more arguments? You have satisfied yourself, you have decided the question. What remains? The truth has now to be realized, therefore why waste valuable time in vain arguments? The truth has now to be meditated upon, and every idea that strengthens you must be taken up and every thought that weakens you must be rejected. The Bhakta meditates upon forms and images and all such things and upon God. This is the natural process, but a slower one. The Yogi meditates upon various centres in his body and manipulates powers in his mind. The Jnani says, the mind does not exist, neither the body. This idea of the body and of the mind must go, must be driven off; therefore it is foolish to think of them. It would be like trying to cure one ailment by bringing in another. His meditation therefore is the most difficult one, the negative; he denies everything, and what is left is the Self. This is the most analytical way. The Jnani wants to tear away the universe from the Self by the sheer force of analysis. It is very easy to say, 'I am a Jnani', but very hard to be really one. 'The way is long', it is, as it were, walking on the sharp edge of a razor; yet despair not. 'Awake, arise, and stop not until the goal is reached', say the Vedas.

So what is the meditation of the Jnani? He wants to rise above every idea of body or mind, to drive away the idea that he is the body. For instance, when I say, 'I Swami', immediately the idea of the body comes. What must I do then? I must give the mind a hard blow and say, 'No, I am not the body, I am the Self.' Who cares if disease comes or death in the most horrible form? I am not the body. Why make the body nice? To enjoy the illusion once more? To continue the slavery? Let it go, I am not the body. That is the way of the Jnani. The Bhakta says, 'The Lord has given me this body that I may safely cross the ocean of life, and I must cherish it until the journey is accomplished.' The Yogi says, 'I must be careful of the body, so that I may go on steadily and finally attain liberation.' The Jnani feels that he cannot wait, he must reach the goal this very moment. He says, 'I am free through eternity, I am never bound; I am the God of the universe through all eternity. Who shall make me perfect? I am perfect already.' When a man is perfect, he sees perfection in others. When he sees imperfection, it is his own mind projecting itself. How can he see imperfection if he has not got it in himself? So the Jnani does not care for perfection or imperfection. None exists for him. As soon as he is free, he does not see good and evil. Who sees evil and good? He who has it in himself. Who sees the body? He who thinks he is the body. The moment you get rid of the idea that you are the body, you do not see the world at all; it vanishes for ever. The Jnani seeks to tear himself away from this bondage of matter by the force of intellectual conviction. This is the negative way—the 'Neti, Neti'—'Not this, not this.'

24

CHRIST, THE MESSENGER

Delivered at Los Angeles, California, 1900

The wave rises on the ocean, and there is a hollow. Again another wave rises, perhaps bigger than the former, to fall down again, similarly, again to rise—driving onward. In the march of events, we notice the rise and fall, and we generally look towards the rise, forgetting the fall. But both are necessary, and both are great. This is the nature of the universe. Whether in the world of our thoughts, the world of our relations in society, or in our spiritual affairs, the same movement of succession, of rises and falls, is going on. Hence, great predominances in the march of events, the liberal ideals, are marshalled ahead, to sink down, to digest, as it were, to ruminate over the past—to adjust, to conserve, to gather strength once more for a rise and a bigger rise.

The history of nations also has ever been like that. The great soul, the Messenger we are to study this afternoon, came at a period of the history of his race which we may well designate as a great fall. We catch only little glimpses here and there of the stray records that have been kept of his sayings and doings; for verily it has been well said, that the doings and sayings of that great soul would fill the world if they had all been written down. And the three years of his ministry were like one compressed, concentrated age, which it has taken nineteen hundred years to unfold, and who knows how much longer it will yet take! Little men like you and me are simply the recipients of just a little energy. A few minutes, a few hours, a few years at best, are enough to spend it all, to stretch it out, as it were, to its fullest strength, and then we are gone for ever. But mark this giant that came; centuries and ages pass, yet the energy that he left upon the world is not yet stretched, nor yet expended to its full. It goes on adding new vigour as the ages roll on.

Now what you see in the life of Christ is the life of all the past. The life of every man is, in a manner, the life of the past. It comes to him through heredity, through surroundings, through education, through his own reincarnation—the past of the race. In a manner, the past of the earth, the past of the whole world is there, upon every soul. What are we, in the present, but a result, an effect, in the hands of that infinite past? What are we but floating waveless in the eternal current of events, irresistibly moved forward and onward and incapable of rest? But you and I are only little things, bubbles. There are always some giant waves in the ocean of affairs, and in you and me the life of the past race has been embodied only a little; but there are giants who embody, as it were, almost the whole of the past and who stretch out their hands for the future. These are the sign-posts here and there which point to the march of humanity; these are verily gigantic, their shadows covering the earth—they stand undying, eternal! As it has been said by the same Messenger, 'No man hath seen God at any time, but through the Son.' And that is true. And where shall we see God but in the Son? It is true that you and I, and the poorest of us, the meanest even, embody that God, even reflect that God. The vibration of light is everywhere, omnipresent; but we have to strike the light of the lamp before we can see the light. The Omnipresent God of the universe cannot be seen until He is reflected by these giant lamps of the earth—The Prophets, the man-Gods, the Incarnations, the embodiments of God.

We all know that God exists, and yet we do not see Him, we do not understand Him. Take one of these great Messengers of light, compare his character with the highest ideal of God that you ever formed, and you will find that your God falls short of the ideal, and that the character of the Prophet exceeds your conceptions. You cannot even form a higher ideal of God than what the actually embodied have practically realized and set before us as an example. Is it wrong, therefore, to worship these as God? Is it a sin to fall at the feet of these man-Gods and worship them as the only divine beings in the world? If they are really, actually, higher than all our conceptions of God, what harm is there in worshipping them? Not only is there no harm, but it is the only possible and positive way of worship. However much you may try by struggle, by abstraction, by whatsoever method you like, still so long as you are a man in the world of men, your world is human, your religion is human, and your God is human. And that must be so. Who is not practical enough to take up an actually existing thing and give up an idea which is only an abstraction, which he cannot grasp, and is difficult of approach except through a concrete medium? Therefore, these Incarnations of God have been worshipped in all ages and in all countries.

We are now going to study a little of the life of Christ, the Incarnation of the Jews. When Christ was born, the Jews were in that state which I call a state of fall between two waves; a state of conservatism; a state where the human mind is, as it were, tired for the time being of moving forward and is taking care only of what it has already; a state when the attention is more bent upon particulars, upon details, than upon the great, general, and bigger problems of life; a state of stagnation, rather than a towing ahead; a state of suffering more than of doing. Mark you, I do not blame this state of things. We have no right to criticize it—because had it not been for this fall, the next rise, which was embodied in Jesus of Nazareth would have been impossible. The Pharisees and Sadducees might have been insincere, they might have been doing things which they ought not to have done; they might have been even hypocrites; but whatever they were, these factors were the very cause, of which the Messenger was the effect. The Pharisees and Sadducees at one end were the very impetus which came out at the other end as the gigantic brain of Jesus of Nazareth.

The attention to forms, to formulas, to the everyday details of religion, and to rituals, may sometimes be laughed at; but nevertheless, within them is strength. Many times in the rushing forward we lose much strength. As a fact, the fanatic is stronger than the liberal man. Even the fanatic, therefore, has one great virtue, he conserves energy, a tremendous amount of it. As with the individual so with the race, energy is gathered to be conserved. Hemmed in all around by external enemies, driven to focus in a centre by the Romans, by the Hellenic tendencies in the world of intellect, by waves from Persia, India, and Alexandria—hemmed in physically, mentally, and morally—there stood the race with an inherent, conservative, tremendous strength, which their descendants have not lost even today. And the race was forced to concentrate and focus all its energies upon Jerusalem and Judaism. But all power when once gathered cannot remain collected; it must expend and expand itself. There is no power on earth which can be kept long confined within a narrow limit. It cannot be kept compressed too long to allow of expansion at a subsequent period.

This concentrated energy amongst the Jewish race found its expression at the next period in the rise of Christianity. The gathered streams collected into a body. Gradually, all the little streams joined together, and became a surging wave on the top of which we find standing out the character of Jesus of Nazareth. Thus, every Prophet is a creation of his own times, the creation of the past of his race; he himself is the creator of the future. The cause of today is the effect of the past and the cause for the future. In this position stands the Messenger. In him is embodied all that is the best and greatest in his own race, the meaning, the life, for which that race has struggled for ages; and he himself is the impetus for the future, not only to his own race but to unnumbered other races of the world.

We must bear another fact in mind: That my view of the great Prophet of Nazareth would be from the standpoint of the Orient. Many times you forget, also, that the Nazarene himself was an Oriental of Orientals. With all your attempts to paint him with blue eyes and yellow hair, the Nazarene was still an Oriental. All the similes, the imageries, in which the Bible is written—the scenes, the locations, the attitudes, the groups, the poetry, and symbol,—speak to you of the Orient: of the bright sky, of the heat, of the sun, of the desert, of the thirsty men and animals; of men and women coming with pitchers on their heads to fill them at the wells; of the flocks, of the ploughmen, of the cultivation that is going on around; of the water-mill and wheel, of the mill-pond, of the millstones. All these are to be seen today in Asia.

The voice of Asia has been the voice of religion. The voice of Europe is the voice of politics. Each is great in its own sphere. The voice of Europe is the voice of ancient Greece. To the Greek mind, his immediate society was all in all: beyond that, it is Barbarian.

None but the Greek has the right to live. Whatever the Greeks do is right and correct; whatever else there exists in the world is neither right nor correct, nor should be allowed to live. It is intensely human in its sympathies, intensely natural, intensely artistic, therefore. The Greek lives entirely in this world. He does not care to dream. Even his poetry is practical. His gods and goddesses are not only human beings, but intensely human, with all human passions and feelings almost the same as with any of us. He loves what is beautiful, but mind you, it is always external nature: the beauty of the hills, of the snows, of the flowers, the beauty of forms and of figures, the beauty in the human face, and, more often, in the human form—that is what the Greeks liked. And the Greeks being the teachers of all subsequent Europeanism, the voice of Europe is Greek.

There is another type in Asia. Think of that vast, huge continent, whose mountain-tops go beyond the clouds, almost touching the canopy of heaven's blue; a rolling desert of miles upon miles where a drop of water cannot be found, neither will a blade of grass grow; interminable forests and gigantic rivers rushing down into the sea. In the midst of all these surroundings, the oriental love of the beautiful and of the sublime developed itself in another direction. It looked inside, and not outside. There is also the thirst for nature, and there is also the same thirst for power; there is also the same thirst for excellence, the same idea of the Greek and Barbarian, but it has extended over a larger circle. In Asia, even today, birth or colour or language never makes a race. That which makes a race is its religion. We are all Christians; we are all Mohammedans; we are all Hindus, or all Buddhists. No matter if a Buddhist is a Chinaman, or is a man from Persia, they think that they are brothers, because of their professing the same religion. Religion is the tie, unity of humanity. And then again, the Oriental, for the same reason, is a visionary, is a born dreamer. The ripples of the waterfalls, the songs of the birds, the beauties of the sun and moon and the stars and the whole earth are pleasant enough; but they are not sufficient for the oriental mind; He wants to dream a dream beyond. He wants to go beyond the present. The present, as it were, is nothing to him. The Orient has been the cradle of the human race for ages, and all the vicissitudes of fortune are there—

kingdoms succeeding kingdoms, empires succeeding empires, human power, glory, and wealth, all rolling down there: a Golgotha of power and learning. That is the Orient: a Golgotha of power, of kingdoms, of learning. No wonder, the oriental mind looks with contempt upon the things of this world and naturally wants to see something that changeth not, something which dieth not, something which in the midst of this world of misery and death is eternal, blissful, undying. An oriental Prophet never tires of insisting upon these ideals; and, as for Prophets, you may also remember that without one exception, all the Messengers were Orientals.

We see, therefore, in the life of this area: Messenger of life, the first watchword: 'Not this life, but something higher'; and, like the true son of the Orient, he is practical in that. You people of the West are practical in your own department, in military affairs, and in managing political circles and other things. Perhaps the Oriental is not practical in those ways, but he is practical in his own field; he is practical in religion. If one preaches a philosophy, tomorrow there are hundreds who will struggle their best to make it practical in their lives. If a man preaches that standing on one foot would lead one to salvation, he will immediately get five hundred to stand on one foot. You may call it ludicrous; but, mark you, beneath that is their philosophy—that intense practicality. In the West, plans of salvation mean intellectual gymnastics—plans which are never worked out, never brought into practical life. In the West, the preacher who talks the best is the greatest preacher.

So, we find Jesus of Nazareth, in the first place, the true son of the Orient, intensely practical. He has no faith in this evanescent world and all its belongings. No need of text-torturing, as is the fashion in the West in modern times, no need of stretching out texts until the, will not stretch any more. Texts are not India rubber, and even that has its limits. Now, no making of religion to pander to the sense vanity of the present day! Mark you, let us all be honest. If we cannot follow the ideal, let us confess our weakness, but not degrade it; let not any try to pull it down. One gets sick at heart at the different accounts of the life of the Christ that Western people give. I do not know what he was or what he was not! One would make him a great politician; another, perhaps, would make of him a great military general; another, a great patriotic Jew; and so on. Is there any warrant in the books for all such assumptions? The best commentary on the life of a great teacher is his own life. 'The foxes have holes, the birds of the air have nests, but the Son of man hath not where to lay his head.' That is what Christ says as they only way to salvation; he lays down no other way. Let us confess in sackcloth and ashes that we cannot do that. We still have fondness for 'me and mine'. We want property, money, wealth. Woe unto us! Let us confess and not put to shame that great Teacher of Humanity! He had no family ties. But do you think that, that Man had any physical ideas in him? Do you think that, this mass of light, this God and not-man, came down to earth, to be the brother of animals? And yet, people make him preach all sorts of things. He had no sex ideas! He was a soul! Nothing but a soul—just working a body for the good of humanity; and that was all his relation to the body. In the soul there is no sex. The disembodied soul has no relationship to the animal, no relationship to the body. The ideal may be far away beyond us. But never mind, keep to the ideal. Let us confess that it is our ideal, but we cannot approach it yet.

He had no other occupation in life, no other thought except that one, that he was a spirit. He was a disembodied, unfettered, unbound spirit. And not only so, but he, with his marvellous vision, had found that every man and woman, whether Jew or Gentile, whether rich or poor, whether saint or sinner, was the embodiment of the same undying spirit as himself. Therefore, the one work his whole life showed was to call upon them to realize their own spiritual nature. Give up, he says, these superstitious dreams that you are low and that you are poor. Think not that you are trampled upon and tyrannized over as if you were slaves, for within you is something that can never be tyrannized over, never be trampled upon, never be troubled, never be killed. You are all Sons of God, immortal spirit. 'Know', he declared, 'the Kingdom of Heaven is within you.' 'I and my Father are one.' Dare you stand up and say, not only that 'I am the Son of God', but I shall also find in my heart of hearts that 'I and my Father are one'? That was what Jesus of Nazareth said. He never talks of this world and of this life. He has nothing to do with it, except that he wants to get hold of the world as it is, give it a push and drive it forward and onward until the whole world has reached to the effulgent Light of God, until everyone has realized his spiritual nature, until death is vanished and misery banished.

We have read the different stories that have been written about him; we know the scholars and their writings, and the higher criticism; and we know all that has been done by study. We are not here to discuss how much of the New Testament is true, we are not here to discuss how much of that life is historical. It does not matter at all whether the New Testament was written within five hundred years of his birth, nor does it matter even, how much of that life is true. But there is something behind it, something we want to imitate. To tell a lie, you have to imitate a truth, and that truth is a fact. You cannot imitate that which never existed. You cannot imitate that which you never perceived. But there must have been a nucleus, a tremendous power that came down, a marvellous manifestation of spiritual power—and of that we are speaking. It stands there. Therefore, we are not afraid of all the criticisms of the scholars. If I, as an Oriental, have to worship Jesus of Nazareth, there is only one way left to me, that is, to worship him as God and nothing else. Have we no right to worship him in that way, do you mean to say? If we bring him down to our own level and simply pay him a little respect as a great man, why should we worship at all? Our scriptures say, 'These great children of Light, who manifest the Light themselves, who are Light themselves, they, being worshipped, become, as it were, one with us and we become one with them.'

For, you see, in three ways man perceives God. At first the undeveloped intellect of the uneducated man sees God as far away, up in the heavens somewhere, sitting on a throne as a great Judge. He looks upon Him as a fire, as a terror. Now, that is good, for there is nothing bad in it. You must remember that humanity travels not from error to truth, but from truth to truth; it may be, if you like it better, from lower truth to higher truth, but never from error to truth. Suppose you start from here and travel towards the sun in a straight line. From here the sun looks only small in size. Suppose you go forward a million miles, the sun will be much bigger. At every stage the sun will become bigger and bigger. Suppose twenty thousand photographs had been taken of the same sun, from different standpoints; these twenty thousand photographs will all certainly differ from one another. But can you deny that each is a photograph of the same sun? So all forms of religion, high or low, are just different stages toward that eternal state of Light, which is God Himself. Some embody a lower view, some a higher, and that is all the difference. Therefore, the religions of the unthinking masses all over the world must be, and have always been, of a God who is outside of the universe, who lives in heaven, who governs from that place, who is a punisher of the bad and a rewarder of the good, and so on. As man advanced spiritually, he began to feel that God was omnipresent, that He must be in him, that He must be everywhere, that He was not a distant God, but dearly the Soul of all souls. As my soul moves my body, even so is God the mover of my soul. Soul within soul. And a few individuals who had developed enough and were pure enough, went still further, and at last found God. As the New Testament says, 'Blessed are the pure in heart, for they shall see God.' And they found at last that they and the Father were one.

You find that all these three stages are taught by the Great Teacher in the New Testament. Note the Common Prayer he taught: 'Our Father which art in Heaven, hallowed be Thy name,' and so on—a simple prayer, a child's prayer. Mark you, it is the 'Common Prayer' because it is intended for the uneducated masses. To a higher circle, to those who had advanced a little more, he gave a more elevated teaching: 'I am in my Father, and ye in me, and I in you.' Do you remember that? And then, when the Jews asked him who he was, he declared that he and his Father were one, and the Jews thought that that was blasphemy. What did he mean by that? This has been also told by your old Prophets, 'Ye are gods and all of you are children of the Most High.' Mark the same three stages. You will find that it is easier for you to begin with the first and end with the last.

The Messenger came to show the path: that the spirit is not in forms, that it is not through all sorts of vexations and knotty problems of philosophy that you know the spirit. Better that you had no learning, better that you never read a book in your life. These are not at all necessary for salvation—neither wealth, nor position nor power, not even learning; but what is necessary is that one thing, purity. 'Blessed are the pure in heart,' for the spirit in its own nature is pure. How can it be otherwise? It is of God, it has come from God. In the language of the Bible, 'It is the breath of God.' In the language of the Koran, 'It is the soul of God.' Do you mean to say that the Spirit of God can ever be impure? But, alas, it has been, as it were, covered over with the dust and dirt of ages, through our own actions, good and evil. Various works which were not correct, which were not true, have covered the same spirit with the dust and dirt of the ignorance of ages. It is only necessary to clear away the dust and dirt, and then the spirit shines immediately. 'Blessed are the pure in heart, for they shall see God.' 'The Kingdom of Heaven is within you.' Where goest thou to seek for the Kingdom of God, asks Jesus of Nazareth, when it is there, within you? Cleanse the spirit, and it is there. It is already yours. How can you get what is not yours? It is yours by right. You are the heirs of immortality, sons of the Eternal Father.

This is the great lesson of the Messenger, and another which is the basis of all religions, is renunciation. How can you make the spirit pure? By renunciation. A rich young man asked Jesus, 'Good Master, what shall I do that I may inherit eternal life?' And Jesus said unto him, 'One thing thou lackest; go thy way, sell whatsoever thou hast, and give to the poor, and thou shalt have treasures in heaven: and come, take up thy cross, and follow Me.' And he was sad at that saying and went away grieved; for he had great possessions. We are all more or less like that. The voice is ringing in our ears day and night. In the midst of our pleasures and joys, in the midst of worldly things, we think that we have forgotten everything else. Then comes a moment's pause and the voice rings in our ears 'Give up all that thou hast and follow Me.' 'Whosoever will save his life shall lose it; and whosoever shall lose his life for My sake shall find it.' For whoever gives up this life for His sake, finds the life immortal. In the midst of all our weakness there is a moment of pause and the voice rings: 'Give up all that thou hast; give it to the poor and follow me.' This is the one ideal he preaches, and this has been the ideal preached by all the great Prophets of the world: renunciation. What is meant by renunciation? That there is only one ideal in morality: unselfishness. Be selfless. The ideal is perfect unselfishness. When a man is struck on the right cheek, he turns the left also. When a man's coat is carried off, he gives away his cloak also.

We should work in the best way we can, without dragging the ideal down. Here is the ideal. When a man has no more self in him, no possession, nothing to call 'me' or 'mine', has given himself up entirely, destroyed himself as it were—in that man is God Himself; for in him self-will is gone, crushed out, annihilated. That is the ideal man. We cannot reach that state yet; yet, let us worship the ideal, and slowly struggle to reach the ideal, though, maybe, with faltering steps. It may be tomorrow, or it may be a thousand years hence; but that ideal has to be reached. For it is not only the end, but also the means. To be unselfish, perfectly selfless, is salvation itself; for the man within dies, and God alone remains.

One more point. All the teachers of humanity are unselfish. Suppose Jesus of Nazareth was teaching; and a man came and told him, 'What you teach is beautiful. I believe that it is the way to perfection, and I am ready to follow it; but I do not care to worship you as the only begotten Son of God.' What would be the answer of Jesus of Nazareth? 'Very well, brother, follow the ideal and advance in your own way. I do not care whether you give me the credit for the teaching or not. I am not a shopkeeper. I do not trade in religion. I only teach truth, and truth is nobody's property. Nobody can patent truth. Truth is God Himself. Go forward.' But what the disciples say nowadays is: 'No matter whether you practise the teachings or not, do you give credit to the Man? If you credit the Master, you will be saved; if not, there is no salvation for you.' And thus the whole teaching of the Master is degenerated, and all the struggle and fight is for the personality of the Man. They do not know that in imposing that difference, they are, in a manner, bringing shame to the very Man they want to honour—the very Man that would have shrunk with shame from such an idea. What did he care if there was one man in the world that remembered him or not? He had to deliver his message, and he gave it. And if he had twenty thousand lives, he would give them all up for the poorest man in the world. If he had to be tortured millions of times for a million despised Samaritans, and if for each one of them the sacrifice of his own life would be the only condition of salvation, he would have given his life. And all this without wishing to have his name known even to a single person. Quiet, unknown, silent, would he world, just as the Lord works. Now, what would the disciple say? He will tell you that you may be a perfect man, perfectly unselfish; but unless you give the credit to our teacher, to our saint, it is of no avail. Why? What is the origin of this superstition, this ignorance? The disciple thinks that the Lord can manifest Himself only once. There lies the whole mistake. God manifests Himself to you in man. But throughout nature, what happens once must have happened before, and must happen in future. There is nothing in nature which is not bound by law; and that means that whatever happens once must go on and must have been going on.

In India they have the same idea of the Incarnations of God. One of their great Incarnations, Krishna, whose grand sermon, the Bhagavad Gita, some of you might have read, says, 'Though I am unborn, of changeless nature, and Lord of beings, yet subjugating My Prakriti, I come into being by My own Maya. Whenever virtue subsides and immorality prevails, then I body Myself forth. For the protection of the good, for the destruction of the wicked, and for the establishment of Dharma, I come into being, in every age.' Whenever the world goes down, the Lord comes to help it forward; and so He does from time to time and place to place. In another passage He speaks to this effect: Wherever thou findest a great soul of immense power and purity struggling to raise humanity, know that he is born of My splendour, that I am there working through him.

Let us, therefore, find God not only in Jesus of Nazareth, but in all the great Ones that have preceded him, in all that came after him, and all that are yet to come. Our worship is unbounded and free. They are all manifestations of the same Infinite God. They are all pure and unselfish; they struggled and gave up their lives for us, poor human beings. They each and all suffer vicarious atonement for every one of us, and also for all that are to come hereafter.

In a sense you are all Prophets; every one of you is a Prophet, bearing the burden of the world on your own shoulders. Have you ever seen a man, have you ever seen a woman, who is not quietly, patiently, bearing his or her little burden of life? The great Prophets were giants—they bore a gigantic world on their shoulders. Compared with them we are pigmies, no doubt, yet we are doing the same task; in our little circles, in our little homes, we are bearing our little crosses. There is no one so evil, no one so worthless, but he has to bear his own cross. But with all our mistakes, with all our evil thoughts and evil deeds, there is a bright spot somewhere, there is still somewhere the golden thread through which we are always in touch with the divine. For, know for certain, that the moment the touch of the divine is lost there would be annihilation. And because none can be annihilated, there is always somewhere in our heart of hearts, however low and degraded we may be, a little circle of light which is in constant touch with the divine.

Our salutations go to all the past Prophets whose teachings and lives we have inherited, whatever might have been their race, clime, or creed! Our salutations go to all those Godlike men and women who are working to help humanity, whatever be their birth, colour, or race! Our salutations to those who are coming in the future—living Gods—to work unselfishly for our descendants.

25

INDIAN RELIGIOUS THOUGHT

Delivered under the auspices of the Brooklyn Ethical Society,
in the Art Gallery of tile Pouch Mansion,
Clinton Avenue, Brooklyn

India, although only half the size of the United States, contains a population of over two hundred and ninety millions, and there are three religions which hold sway over them—the Mohammedan, the Buddhist, and the Hindu. The adherents of the first mentioned number about sixty millions, of the second about nine millions, while the last embrace nearly two hundred and six millions. The cardinal features of the Hindu religion are founded on the meditative and speculative philosophy and on the ethical teachings contained in the various books of the Vedas, which assert that the universe is infinite in space and eternal in duration. It never had a beginning, and it never will have an end. Innumerable have been the manifestations of the power of the spirit in the realm of matter, of the force of the Infinite in the domain of the finite; but the Infinite Spirit Itself is self-existent, eternal, and unchangeable. The passage of time makes no mark whatever on the dial of eternity. In its supersensuous region which cannot be comprehended at all by the human understanding, there is no past, and there is no future. The Vedas teach that the soul of man is immortal. The body is subject to the law of growth and decay, what grows must of necessity decay. But the in dwelling spirit is related to the infinite and eternal life; it never had a beginning and it never will have an end, One of the chief distinctions between the Hindu and the (Christian religions is that the Christian religion teaches that each human soul had its beginning at its birth into this world, whereas the Hindu religion asserts that the spirit of man is an emanation of the Eternal Being, and had no more a beginning than God Himself. Innumerable have been and will be its manifestations in its passage from one personality to another, subject to the great law of spiritual evolution, until it reaches perfection, when there is no more change.

It has been often asked: If this be so, why is it we do not remember anything of our past lives? This is our explanation: Consciousness is the name of the surface only of the mental ocean, but within its depths are stored up all our experiences, both pleasant and painful. The desire of the human soul is to find out something that is stable. The mind and the body, in fact all the various phenomena of nature, are in a condition of incessant change. But the highest aspiration of our spirit is to find out something that does not change, that has reached a state of permanent perfection. And this is the aspiration of the human soul after the Infinite! The finer our moral and intellectual development, the stronger will become this aspiration after the Eternal that changes not.

The modern Buddhists teach that everything that cannot be known by the five senses is non-existent, and that it is a delusion to suppose that man is an independent entity. The idealists, on the contrary, claim that each individual is an independent entity, and the external world does not exist outside of his mental conception. But the sure solution of this problem is that nature is a mixture of independence and dependence, of reality and idealism. Our mind and bodies are dependent on the external world, and this dependence varies according to the nature of their relation to it; but the indwelling spirit is free, as God is free, and is able to direct in a greater or lesser degree, according to the state of their development, the movements of our minds and bodies.

Death is but a change of condition. We remain in the same universe, and are subject to the same laws as before. Those who have passed beyond and have attained high planes of development in beauty and wisdom are but the advance-guard of a universal army who are following after them. The spirit of the highest is related to the spirit of the lowest, and the germ of infinite perfection exists in all. We should cultivate the optimistic temperament, and endeavour to see the good that dwells in everything. If we sit down and lament over the imperfection of our bodies and minds, we profit nothing; it is the heroic endeavour to subdue adverse circumstances that carries our spirit upwards. The object of life is to learn the laws of spiritual progress. Christians can learn from Hindus, and Hindus can learn from Christians. Each has made a contribution of value to the wisdom of the world.

Impress upon your children that true religion is positive and not negative, that it does not consist in merely refraining from evil, but in a persistent performance of noble decals. True religion comes not front the teaching of men or the reading of books; it is the awakening of the spirit within us, consequent upon pure and heroic action. Every child born into the world brings with it a certain accumulated experience from previous incarnations; and the impress of this experience is seen in the structure of its mind and body. But the feeling of independence which possesses us all shows there is something in us besides mind and body. The soul that reigns within is independent stud creates the desire for freedom. If we are not free, how can we hope to make the world better? We hold that human progress is the result of the action of the human spirit. What the world is, and what we ourselves are, are the fruits of the freedom of the spirit.

We believe in one God, the Father of us all, who is omnipresent and omnipotent, and who guides and preserves His children with infinite love. We believe in a Personal God as the Christians do, but we go further: we below that we are He! That His personality is manifested in us, that God is in us, and that we are in God We believe there is a germ of truth in all religions, and the Hindu bows down to them all; for in this world, truth is to be found not in subtraction but in addition. We would offer God a bouquet of the most beautiful flowers of all the diverse faiths. We must love God for love's sake, not for the hope of reward. We must do our duty for duty's sake not for the hope of reward. We must worship the beautiful for beauty's sake, not for the hope of reward. Thus in the purity of our hearts shall we see God. Sacrifices genuflexions, mumblings, and mutterings are not religion. They are only good if they stimulate us to the brave performance of beautiful and heroic deeds and lift our thoughts to the apprehension of the divine perfection

What good is it, if we acknowledge in our prayers that God is the Father of us all, and in our daily lives do not treat every man as our brother? Books are only made so that they may point the way to a higher life; but no good results unless the path is trodden with unflinching steps! Every human personality may be compared to a glass globe. There is the same pure white light—an emission of the divine Being—in the centre of each, but the glass being of different colours and thickness, the rays assume diverse aspects in the transmission. The equality and beauty of each central flame is the same, and the apparent inequality is only in the imperfection of the temporal instrument of its expression. As we rise higher and higher in the scale of being, the medium becomes more and more translucent.

26

THE METHODS AND PURPOSE OF RELIGION

In studying the religions of the world we generally find two methods of procedure. The one is from God to man. That is to say, we have the Semitic group of religions in which the idea of God comes almost from the very first, and, strangely enough, without any idea of soul. It was very remarkable amongst the ancient Hebrews that, until very recent periods in their history, they never evolved any idea of a human soul. Man was composed of certain mind and material particles, and that was all. With death everything ended. But, on the other hand, there was a most wonderful idea of God evolved by the same race. This is one of the methods of procedure. The other is through man to God. The second is peculiarly Aryan, and the first is peculiarly Semitic.

The Aryan first began with the soul. His ideas of God were hazy, indistinguishable, not very clear; but, as his idea of the human soul began to be clearer, his idea of God began to be clearer in the same proportion. So the inquiry in the Vedas was always through the soul. All the knowledge the Aryans got of God was through the human soul; and, as such, the peculiar stamp that has been left upon their whole cycle of philosophy is that introspective search after divinity. The Aryan man was always seeking divinity inside his own self. It became, in course of time, natural, characteristic. It is remarkable in their art and in their commonest dealings. Even at the present time, if we take a European picture of a man in a religious attitude, the painter always makes his subject point his eyes upwards, looking outside of nature for God, looking up into the skies. In India, on the other hand, the religious attitude is always presented by making the subject close his eyes. He is, as it were, looking inward.

These are the two subjects of study for man, external and internal nature; and though at first these seem to be contradictory, yet external nature must, to the ordinary man, be entirely composed of internal nature, the world of thought. The majority of philosophies in every country, especially in the West, have started with the assumption that these two, matter and mind, are contradictory existences; but in the long run we shall find that they converge towards each other and in the end unite and form an infinite whole. So it is not that by this analysis I mean a higher or lower standpoint with regard to the subject. I do not mean that those who want to search after truth through external nature are wrong, nor that those who want to search after truth through internal nature are higher. These are the two modes of procedure. Both of them must live; both of them must be studied; and in the end we shall find that they meet. We shall see that neither is the body antagonistic to the mind, nor the mind to the body, although we find, many persons who think that this body is nothing. In old times, every country was full of people who thought this body was only a disease, a sin, or something of that kind. Later on, however, we see how, as it was taught in the Vedas, this body melts into the mind, and the mind into the body.

You must remember the one theme that runs through all the Vedas: 'Just as by the knowledge of one lump of clay we know all the clay that is in the universe, so what is that, knowing which we know everything else?' This, expressed more or less clearly, is the theme of all human knowledge. It is the finding of a unity towards which we are all going. Every action of our lives—the most material, the grossest as well as the finest, the highest, the most spiritual—is alike tending towards this one ideal, the finding of unity. A man is single. He marries. Apparently it may be a selfish act, but at the same time, the impulsion, the motive power, is to find that unity. He has children, he has friends, he loves his country, he loves the world, and ends by loving the whole universe. Irresistibly, we are impelled towards that perfection which consists in finding the unity, killing this little self and making ourselves broader and broader. This is the goal, the end towards which the universe is rushing. Every atom is trying to go and join itself to the next atom. Atoms after atoms combine, making huge balls, the earths, the suns, the moons, the stars, the planets. They in their turn, are trying to rush towards each other, and at last, we know that the whole universe, mental and material, will be fused into one.

The process that is going on in the cosmos on a large scale, is the same as that going on in the microcosm on a smaller scale. Just as this universe has its existence in separation, in distinction, and all the while is rushing towards unity, non-separation, so in our little worlds each soul is born, as it were, cut off from the rest of the world. The more ignorant, the more unenlightened the soul, the more it thinks that it is separate from the rest of the universe. The more ignorant the person, the more he thinks, he will die or will be born, and so forth—ideas that are an expression of this separateness. But we find that, as knowledge comes, man grows, morality is evolved and the idea of non-separateness begins. Whether men understand it or not, they are impelled by that power behind to become unselfish. That is the foundation of all morality. It is the quintessence of all ethics, preached in any language, or in any religion, or by any prophet in the world. 'Be thou unselfish', 'Not 'I', but 'thou'—that is the background of all ethical codes. And what is meant by this is the recognition of non-individuality—that you are a part of me, and I of you; the recognition that in hurting you I hurt myself, and in helping you I help myself; the recognition that there cannot possibly be death for me when you live. When one worm lives in this universe, how can I die? For my life is in the life of that worm. At the same time it will teach us that we cannot leave one of our fellow-beings without helping him, that in his good consists my good.

This is the theme that runs through the whole of Vedanta, and which runs through every other religion. For, you must remember, religions divide themselves generally into three parts. There is the first part, consisting of the philosophy, the essence, the principles of every religion. These principles find expression in mythology—lives of saints or heroes, demi-gods, or gods, or divine beings; and the whole idea of this mythology is that of power. And in the lower class of mythologies—the primitive—the expression of this power is in the muscles; their heroes are strong, gigantic. One hero conquers the whole world. As man advances, he must find expression for his energy higher than in the muscles; so his heroes also find expression in something higher. The higher mythologies have heroes who are gigantic moral men. Their strength is manifested in becoming moral and pure. They can stand alone, they can beat back the surging tide of selfishness and immorality. The third portion of all religions is symbolism, which you call ceremonials and forms. Even the expression through mythology, the lives of heroes, is not sufficient for all. There are minds still lower. Like children they must have their kindergarten of religion, and these symbologies are evolved—concrete examples which they can handle and grasp and understand, which they can see and feel as material somethings.

So in every religion you find there are the three stages: philosophy, mythology, and ceremonial. There is one advantage which can be pleaded for the Vedanta, that in India, fortunately, these three stages have been sharply defined. In other religions the principles are so interwoven with the mythology that it is very hard to distinguish one from the other. The mythology stands supreme, swallowing up the principles; and in course of centuries the principles are lost sight of. The explanation, the illustration of the principle, swallows up the principle, and the people see only the explanation, the prophet, the preacher, while the principles have gone out of existence almost—so much so that even today, if a man dares to preach the principles of Christianity apart from Christ, they will try to attack him and think he is wrong and dealing blows at Christianity. In the same way, if a man wants to preach the principles of Mohammedanism, Mohammedans will think the same; because concrete ideas, the lives of great men and prophets, have entirely overshadowed the principles.

In Vedanta the chief advantage is that it was not the work of one single man; and therefore, naturally, unlike Buddhism, or Christianity, or Mohammedanism, the prophet or teacher did not entirely swallow up or overshadow the principles. The principles live, and the prophets, as it were, form a secondary group, unknown to Vedanta. The Upanishads speak of no particular prophet, but they speak of various prophets and prophetesses. The old Hebrews had something of that idea; yet we find Moses occupying most of the space of the Hebrew literature. Of course I do not mean that it is bad that these prophets should take religious hold of a nation; but it certainly is very injurious if the whole field of principles is lost sight of. We can very much agree as to principles, but not very much as to persons. The persons appeal to our emotions; and the principles, to something higher, to our calm judgement. Principles must conquer in the long run, for that is the manhood of man. Emotions many times drag us down to the level of animals. Emotions have more connection with the senses than with the faculty of reason; and, therefore, when principles are entirely lost sight of and emotions prevail, religions degenerate into fanaticism and sectarianism. They are no better than party politics and such things. The most horribly ignorant notions will be taken up, and for these ideas thousands will be ready to cut the throats of their brethren. This is the reason that, though these great personalities and prophets are tremendous motive powers for good, at the same time their lives are altogether dangerous when they lead to the disregard of the principles they represent. That has always led to fanaticism, and has deluged the world in blood. Vedanta can avoid this difficulty, because it has not one special prophet. It has many Seers, who are called Rishis or sages. Seers—that is the literal translation—those who see these truths, the Mantras.

The word Mantra means 'thought out', cogitated by the mind; and the Rishi is the seer of these thoughts. They are neither the property of particular persons, nor the exclusive property of any man or woman, however great he or she may be; nor even the exclusive property of the greatest spirits—the Buddhas or Christs—whom the world has produced. They are as much the property of the lowest of the low, as they are the property of a Buddha, and as much the property of the smallest worm that crawls as of the Christ, because they are universal principles. They were never created. These principles have existed throughout time; and they will exist. They are non-create—uncreated by any laws which science teaches us today. They remain covered and become discovered, but are existing through all eternity in nature. If Newton had not been born, the law of gravitation would have remained all the same and would have worked all the same. It was Newton's genius which formulated it, discovered it, brought it into consciousness, made it a conscious thing to the human race. So are these religious laws, the grand truths of spirituality. They are working all the time. If all the Vedas and the Bibles and the Korans did not exist at all, if seers and prophets had never been born, yet these laws would exist. They are only held in abeyance, and slowly but surely would work to raise the human race, to raise human nature. But they are the prophets who see them, discover them, and such prophets are discoverers in the field of spirituality. As Newton and Galileo were prophets of physical science, so are they prophets of spirituality. They can claim no exclusive right to any one of these laws; they are the common property of all nature.

The Vedas, as the Hindus say, are eternal. We now understand what they mean by their being eternal, i.e. that the laws have neither beginning nor end, just as nature has neither beginning nor end. Earth after earth, system after system, will evolve, run for a certain time, and then dissolve back again into chaos; but the universe remains the same. Millions and millions of systems are being born, while millions are being destroyed. The universe remains the same. The beginning and the end of time can be told as regards a certain planet; but as regards the universe, time has no meaning at all. So are the laws of nature, the physical laws, the mental laws, the spiritual laws. Without beginning and without end are they; and it is within a few years, comparatively speaking, a few thousand years at best, that man has tried to reveal them. The infinite mass remains before us. Therefore the one great lesson that we learn from the Vedas, at the start, is that religion has just begun. The infinite ocean of spiritual truth lies before us to be worked on, to be discovered, to be brought into our lives. The world has seen thousands of prophets, and the world has yet to see millions.

There were times in olden days when prophets were many in every society. The time is to come when prophets will walk through every street in every city in the world. In olden times, particular, peculiar persons were, so to speak, selected by the operations of the laws of society to become prophets. The time is coming when we shall understand that to become religious means to become a prophet, that none can become religious until he or she becomes a prophet. We shall come to understand that the secret of religion is not being able to think and say all these thoughts; but, as the Vedas teach, to realize them, to realize newer and higher one than have ever been realized, to discover them, bring them to society; and the study of religion should be the training to make prophets. The schools and colleges should be training grounds for prophets. The whole universe must become prophets; and until a man becomes a prophet, religion is a mockery and a byword unto him. We must see religion, feel it, realize it in a thousand times more intense a sense than that in which we see the wall.

But there is one principle which underlies all these various manifestations of religion and which has been already mapped out for us. Every science must end where it finds a unity, because we cannot go any further. When a perfect unity is reached, that science has nothing more of principles to tell us. All the work that religions have to do is to work out the details. Take any science, chemistry, for example. Suppose we can find one element out of which we can manufacture all the other elements. Then chemistry, as a science, will have become perfect. What will remain for us is to discover every day new combinations of that one material and the application of those combinations for all the purposes of life. So with religion. The gigantic principles, the scope, the plan of religion were already discovered ages ago when man found the last words, as they are called, of the Vedas—'I am He'—that there is that One in whom this whole universe of matter and mind finds its unity, whom they call God, or Brahman, or Allah, or Jehovah, or any other name. We cannot go beyond that. The grand principle has been already mapped out for us. Our work lies in filling it in, working it out, applying it to every part of our lives. We have to work now so that every one will become a prophet. There is a great work before us.

In old times, many did not understand what a prophet meant. They thought it was something by chance, that just by a fiat of will or some superior intelligence, a man gained superior knowledge. In modern times, we are prepared to demonstrate that this knowledge is the birthright of every living being, whosoever and wheresoever he be, and that there is no chance in this universe. Every man who, we think, gets something by chance, has been working for it slowly and surely through ages. And the whole question devolves upon us: 'Do we want to be prophets?' If we want, we shall be.

This, the training of prophets, is the great work that lies before us; and, consciously or unconsciously, all the great systems of religion are working toward this one great goal, only with this difference, that in many religions you will find they declare that this direct perception of spirituality is not to be had in this life, that man must die, and after his death there will come a time in another world, when he will have visions of spirituality, when he will realize things which now he must believe. But Vedanta will ask all people who make such assertions, 'Then how do you know that spirituality exists?' And they will have to answer that there must have been always certain particular people who, even in this life, have got a glimpse of things which are unknown and unknowable.

Even this makes a difficulty. If they were peculiar people, having this power simply by chance, we have no right to believe in them. It would be a sin to believe in anything that is by chance, because we cannot know it. What is meant by knowledge? Destruction of peculiarity. Suppose a boy goes into a street or a menagerie, and sees a peculiarly shaped animal. He does not know what it is. Then he goes to a country where there are hundreds like that one, and he is satisfied, he knows what the species is. Our knowledge is knowing the principle. Our non-knowledge is finding the particular without reference to principle. When we find one case or a few cases separate from the principle, without any reference to the principle, we are in darkness and do not know. Now, if these prophets, as they say, were peculiar persons who alone had the right to catch a glimpse of that which is beyond and no one else has the right, we should not believe in these prophets, because they are peculiar cases without any reference to a principle. We can only believe in them if we ourselves become prophets.

You, all of you, hear about the various jokes that get into the newspapers about the sea-serpent; and why should it be so? Because a few persons, at long intervals, came and told their stories about the sea-serpent, and others never see it. They have no particular principle to which to refer, and therefore the world does not believe. If a man comes to me and says a prophet disappeared into the air and went through it, I have the right to see that. I ask him, 'Did your father or grandfather see it?' 'Oh, no,' he replies, 'but five thousand years ago such a thing happened.' And if I do not believe it, I have to be barbecued through eternity!

What a mass of superstition this is! And its effect is to degrade man from his divine nature to that of brutes. Why was reason given us if we have to believe? Is it not tremendously blasphemous to believe against reason? What right have we not to use the greatest gift that God has given to us? I am sure God will pardon a man who will use his reason and cannot believe, rather than a man who believes blindly instead of using the faculties He has given him. He simply degrades his nature and goes down to the level of the beasts—degrades his senses and dies. We must reason; and when reason proves to us the truth of these prophets and great men about whom the ancient books speak in every country, we shall believe in them. We shall believe in them when we see such prophets among ourselves. We shall then find that they were not peculiar men, but only illustrations of certain principles. They worked, and that principle expressed itself naturally, and we shall have to work to express that principle in us. They were prophets, we shall believe, when we become prophets. They were seers of things divine. They could go beyond the bounds of senses and catch a glimpse of that which is beyond. We shall believe that when we are able to do it ourselves and not before.

That is the one principle of Vedanta. Vedanta declares that religion is here and now, because the question of this life and that life, of life and death, this world and that world, is merely one of superstition and prejudice. There is no break in time beyond what we make. What difference is there between ten and twelve o'clock, except what we make by certain changes in nature? Time flows on the same. So what is meant by this life or that life? It is only a question of time, and what is lost in time may be made up by speed in work. So, says Vedanta, religion is to be realized now. And for you to become religious means that you will start without any religion work your way up and realize things, see things for yourself; and when you have done that, then, and then alone, you have religion. Before that you are no better than atheists, or worse, because the atheist is sincere—he stands up and says, 'I do not know about these things—while those others do not know but go about the world, saying, 'We arc very religious people.' What religion they have no one knows, because they have swallowed some grandmother's story, and priests have asked them to believe these things; if they do not, then let them take care. That is how it is going.

Realization of religion is the only way. Each one of us will have to discover. Of what use are these books, then, these Bibles of the world? They are of great use, just as maps are of a country. I have seen maps of England all my life before I came here, and they were great helps to me informing some sort of conception of England. Yet, when I arrived in this country, what a difference between the maps and the country itself! So is the difference between realization and the scriptures. These books are only the maps, the experiences of past men, as a motive power to us to dare to make the same experiences and discover in the same way, if not better.

This is the first principle of Vedanta, that realization is religion, and he who realizes is the religious man; and he who does not is no better than he who says, 'I do not know', if not worse, because the other says, 'I do not know', and is sincere. In this realization, again, we shall be helped very much by these books, not only as guides, but as giving instructions and exercises; for every science has its own particular method of investigation. You will find many persons in this world who will say. 'I wanted to become religious, I wanted to realize these things, but I have not been able, so I do not believe anything.' Even among the educated you will find these. Large numbers of people will tell you, 'I have tried to be religious all my life, but there is nothing in it.' At the same time you will find this phenomenon: Suppose a man is a chemist, a great scientific man. He comes and tells you this. If you say to him, 'I do not believe anything about chemistry, because I have all my life tried to become a chemist and do not find anything in it', he will ask, 'When did you try?' 'When I went to bed, I repeated, 'O chemistry, come to me', and it never came.' That is the very same thing. The chemist laughs at you and says, 'Oh, that is not the way. Why did you not go to the laboratory and get all the acids and alkalis and burn your hands from time to time? That alone would have taught you.' Do you take the same trouble with religion? Every science has its own method of learning, and religion is to be learnt the same way. It has its own methods, and here is something we can learn, and must learn, from all the ancient prophets of the world, every one who has found something, who has realized religion. They will give us the methods, the particular methods, through which alone we shall be able to realize the truths of religion. They struggled all their lives, discovered particular methods of mental culture, bringing the mind to a certain state, the finest perception, and through that they perceived the truths of religion. To become religious, to perceive religion, feel it, to become a prophet, we have to take these methods and practise them; and then if we find nothing, we shall have the right to say, 'There is nothing in religion, for I have tried and failed.'

This is the practical side of all religions. You will find it in every Bible in the world. Not only do they teach principles and doctrines, but in the lives of the saints you find practises; and when it is not expressly laid down as a rule of conduct, you will always find in the lives of these prophets that even they regulated their eating and drinking sometimes. Their whole living, their practise, their method, everything was different from the masses who surrounded them; and these were the causes that gave them the higher light, the vision of the Divine. And we, if we want to have this vision, must be ready to take up these methods. It is practise, work, that will bring us up to that. The plan of Vedanta, therefore, is: first, to lay down the principles, map out for us the goal, and then to teach us the method by which to arrive at the goal, to understand and realize religion.

Again, these methods must be various. Seeing that we are so various in our natures, the same method can scarcely be applied to any two of us in the same manner. We have idiosyncrasies in our minds, each one of us; so the method ought to be varied. Some, you will find, are very emotional in their nature; some very philosophical, rational; others cling to all sorts of ritualistic forms—want things which are concrete. You will find that one man does not care for any ceremony or form or anything of the sort; they are like death to him. And another man carries a load of amulets all over his body; he is so fond of these symbols! Another man who is emotional in his nature wants to show acts of charity to everyone; he weeps, he laughs, and so on. And all of these certainly cannot have the same method. If there were only one method to arrive at truth, it would be death for everyone else who is not similarly constituted. Therefore the methods should be various.

Vedanta understands that and wants to lay before the world different methods through which we can work. Take up any one you like; and if one does not suit you, another may. From this standpoint we see how glorious it is that there are so many religions in the world, how good it is that there are so many teachers and prophets, instead of there being only one, as many persons would like to have it. The Mohammedans want to have the whole world Mohammedan; the Christians, Christian; and the Buddhists, Buddhist; but Vedanta says, 'Let each person in the world be separate, if you will; the one principle, the units will be behind. The more prophets there are, the more books, the more seers, the more methods, so much the better for the world.' Just as in social life the greater the number of occupations in every society, the better for that society, the more chance is there for everyone of that society to make a living; so in the world of thought and of religion. How much better it is today when we have so many divisions of science—how much more is it possible for everyone to have great mental culture, with this great variety before us! How much better it is, even on the physical plane, to have the opportunity of so many various things spread before us, so that we may choose any one we like, the one which suits us best! So it is with the world of religions. It is a most glorious dispensation of the Lord that there are so many religions in the world; and would to God that these would increase every day, until every man had a religion unto himself!

Vedanta understands that and therefore preaches the one principle and admits various methods. It has nothing to say against anyone—whether you are a Christian, or a Buddhist, or a Jew, or a Hindu, whatever mythology you believe, whether you owe allegiance to the prophet of Nazareth, or of Mecca, or of India, or of anywhere else, whether you yourself are a prophet—it has nothing to say. It only preaches the principle which is the background of every religion and of which all the prophets and saints and seers are but illustrations and manifestations. Multiply your prophets if you like; it has no objection. It only preaches the principle, and the method it leaves to you. Take any path you like; follow any prophet you like; but have only that method which suits your own nature, so that you will be sure to progress.

27

THE NATURE OF THE SOUL AND ITS GOAL

The earliest idea is that a man, when he dies, is not annihilated. Something lives and goes on living even after the man is dead. Perhaps it would be better to compare the three most ancient nations—the Egyptians, the Babylonians, and the ancient Hindus—and take this idea from all of them. With the Egyptians and the Babylonians, we find a sort of soul idea—that of a double. Inside this body, according to them, there is another body which is moving and working here; and when the outer body dies, the double gets out and lives on for a certain length of time; but the life of the double is limited by the preservation of the outer body. If the body which the double has left is injured in any part, the double is sure to be injured in that part. That is why we find among the ancient Egyptians such solicitude to preserve the dead body of a person by embalming, building pyramids, etc. We find both with the Babylonians and the ancient Egyptians that this double cannot live on through eternity; it can, at best, live on for a certain time only, that is, just so long as the body it has left can be preserved.

The next peculiarity is that there is an element of fear connected with this double. It is always unhappy and miserable; its state of existence is one of extreme pain. It is again and again coming back to those that are living, asking for food and drink and enjoyments that it can no more have. It is wanting to drink of the waters of the Nile, the fresh waters which it can no more drink. It wants to get back those foods it used to enjoy while in this life; and when it finds it cannot get them, the double becomes fierce, sometimes threatening the living with death and disaster if it is not supplied with such food.

Coming to Aryan thought, we at once find a very wide departure. There is still the double idea there, but it has become a sort of spiritual body; and one great difference is that the life of this spiritual body, the soul, or whatever you may call it, is not limited by the body it has left. On the contrary, it has obtained freedom from this body, and hence the peculiar Aryan custom of burning the dead. They want to get rid of the body which the person has left, while the Egyptian wants to preserve it by burying, embalming, and building pyramids. Apart from the most primitive system of doing away with the dead, amongst nations advanced to a certain extent, the method of doing away with the bodies of the dead is a great indication of their idea of the soul. Wherever we find the idea of a departed soul closely connected with the idea of the dead body, we always find the tendency to preserve the body, and we also find burying in some form or other. On the other hand, with those in whom the idea has developed that the soul is a separate entity from the body and will not be hurt if the dead body is even destroyed, burning is always the process resorted to. Thus, we find among all ancient Aryan races burning of the dead, although the Parsees changed it to exposing the body on a tower. But the very name of the tower (Dakhma) means a burning-place, showing that in ancient times they also used to burn their bodies. The other peculiarity is that among the Aryans there was no element of fear with these doubles. They are not coming down to ask for food or help; and when denied that help, they do not become ferocious or try to destroy those that are living. They rather are joyful, are glad at getting free. The fire of the funeral pyre is the symbol of disintegration. The symbol is asked to take the departed soul gently up and to carry it to the place where the fathers live, where there is no sorrow, where there is joy for ever, and so on.

Of these two ideas we see at once that they are of a similar nature, the one optimistic, and the other pessimistic—being the elementary. The one is the evolution of the other. It is quite possible that the Aryans themselves had, or may have had, in very ancient times exactly the same idea as the Egyptians. In studying their most ancient records, we find the possibility of this very idea. But it is quite a bright thing, something bright. When a man dies, this soul goes to live with the fathers and lives there enjoying their happiness. These fathers receive it with great kindness; this is the most ancient idea in India of a soul. Later on, this idea becomes higher and higher. Then it was found out that what they called the soul before was not really the soul. This bright body, fine body, however fine it might be, was a body after all; and all bodies must be made up of materials, either gross or fine. Whatever had form or shape must be limited, and could not be eternal. Change is inherent in every form. How could that which is changeful be eternal? So, behind this bright body, as it were, they found something which was the soul of man. It was called the Atman, the Self. This Self idea then began. It had also to undergo various changes. By some it was thought that this Self was eternal; that it was very minute, almost as minute as an atom; that it lived in a certain part of the body, and when a man died, his Self went away, taking along with it the bright body. There were other people who denied the atomic nature of the soul on the same ground on which they had denied that this bright body was the soul.

Out of all these various opinions rose Sankhya philosophy, where at once we find immense differences. The idea there is that man has first this gross body; behind the gross body is the fine body, which is the vehicle of the mind, as it were; and behind even that is the Self, the Perceiver, as the Sankhyas call it, of the mind; and this is omnipresent. That is, your soul, my soul, everyone's soul is everywhere at the same time. If it is formless, how can it be said to occupy space? Everything that occupies space has form. The formless can only be infinite. So each soul is everywhere. The second theory put forward is still more startling. They all saw in ancient times that human beings are progressive, at least many of them. They grew in purity and power and knowledge; and the question was asked: Whence was this knowledge, this purity, this strength which men manifested? Here is a baby without any knowledge. This baby grows and becomes a strong, powerful, and wise man. Whence did that baby get its wealth of knowledge and power? The answer was that it was in the soul; the soul of the baby had this knowledge and power from the very beginning. This power, this purity, this strength were in that soul, but they were unmanifested; they have become manifested. What is meant by this manifestation or unmanifestation? That each soul is pure and perfect, omnipotent and omniscient, as they say in the Sankhya; but it can manifest itself externally only according to the mind it has got.

The mind is, as it were, the reflecting mirror of the soul. My mind reflects to a certain extent the powers of my soul; so your soul, and so everyone's. That mirror which is clearer reflects the soul better. So the manifestation varies according to the mind one possesses; but the souls in themselves are pure and perfect.

There was another school who thought that this could not be. Though souls are pure and perfect by their nature, this purity and perfection become, as they say, contracted at times, and expanded at other times. There are certain actions and certain thoughts which, as it were, contract the nature of the soul; and then also other thoughts and acts, which bring its nature out, manifest it. This again is explained. All thoughts and actions that make the power and purity of the soul get contracted are evil actions, evil thoughts; and all those thoughts and actions which make the soul manifest itself—make the powers come out, as it were—are good and moral actions. The difference between the two theories is very slight; it is more of less a play on the words expansion and contraction. The one that holds that the variation only depends on the mind the soul has got is the better explanation, no doubt, but the contracting and expanding theory wants to take refuge behind the two words; and they should be asked what is meant by contraction of soul, or expansion. Soul is a spirit. You can question what is meant by contraction or expansion with regard to material, whether gross which we call matter, or fine, the mind; but beyond that, if it is not matter, that which is not bound by space or by time, how to explain the words contraction and expansion with regard to that? So it seems that this theory which holds that the soul is pure and perfect all the time, only its nature is more reflected in some minds than in others, is the better. As the mind changes, its character grows, as it were, more and more clear and gives a better reflection of the soul. Thus it goes on, until the mind has become so purified that it reflects fully the quality of the soul; then the soul becomes liberated.

This is the nature of the soul. What is the goal? The goal of the soul among all the different sects in India seems to be the same. There is one idea with all, and that is liberation. Man is infinite; and this limitation in which he exists now is not his nature. But through these limitations he is struggling upward and forward until he reaches the infinite, the unlimited, his birthright, his nature. All these combinations and recombinations and manifestations that we see round us are not the aim or the goal, but merely by the way and in passing. These combinations as earths and suns, and moons and stars, right and wrong, good and bad, our laughter and our tears, our joys and sorrows, are to enable us to gain experience through which the soul manifests its perfect nature and throws off limitation. No more, then, is it bound by laws either of internal or external nature. It has gone beyond all law, beyond all limitation, beyond all nature. Nature has come under the control of the soul, not the soul under the control of nature, as it thinks it is now. That is the one goal that the soul has; and all the succeeding steps through which it is manifesting, all the successive experiences through which it is passing in order to attain to that goal—freedom—are represented as its births. The soul is, as it were, taking up a lower body and trying to express itself through that. It finds that to be insufficient, throws it aside, and a higher one is taken up. Through that it struggles to express itself. That also is found to be insufficient, is rejected, and a higher one comes; so on and on until a body is found through which the soul manifests its highest aspirations. Then the soul becomes free.

Now the question is: If the soul is infinite and exists everywhere, as it must do, if it is a spirit, what is meant by its taking up bodies and passing through body after body? The idea is that the soul neither comes nor goes, neither is born nor dies. How can the omnipresent be born? It is meaningless nonsense to say that the soul lives in a body. How can the unlimited live in a limited space? But as a man having a book in his hands reads one page and turns it over, goes to the next page, reads that, turns it over, and so on, yet it is the book that is being turned over, the pages that are revolving, and not he—he is where he is always—even so with regard to the soul. The whole of nature is that book which the soul is reading. Each life, as it were, is one page of that book; and that read, it is turned over, and so on and on, until the whole of the book is finished, and that soul becomes perfect, having got all the experiences of nature. Yet at the same time it never moved, nor came, nor went; it was only gathering experiences. But it appears to us that we are moving. The earth is moving, yet we think that the sun is moving instead of the earth, which we know to be a mistake, a delusion of the senses. So is also this, delusion that we are born and that we die, that we come or that we go. We neither come nor go, nor have we been born. For where is the soul to go? There is no place for it to go. Where is it not already?

Thus the theory comes of the evolution of nature and the manifestation of the soul. The processes of evolution, higher and higher combinations, are not in the soul; it is already what it is. They are in nature. But as nature is evolving forward into higher and higher combinations, more and more of the majesty of the soul is manifesting itself. Suppose here is a screen, and behind the screen is wonderful scenery. There is one small hole in the screen through which we can catch only a little bit of that scenery behind. Suppose that hole becomes increased in size. As the hole increases in size, more and more of the scenery behind comes within the range of vision; and when the whole screen has disappeared, there is nothing between the scenery and you; you see the whole of it. This screen is the mind of man. Behind it is the majesty, the purity, the infinite power of the soul, and as the mind becomes clearer and clearer, purer and purer, more of the majesty of the soul manifests itself. Not that the soul is changing, but the change is in the screen. The soul is the unchangeable One, the immortal, the pure, the ever-blessed One.

So, at last, the theory comes to this. From the highest to the lowest and most wicked man, in the greatest of; human beings and the lowest of crawling worms under our feet, is the soul, pure and perfect, infinite and ever-blessed. In the worm that soul is manifesting only an infinitesimal part of its power and purity, and in the greatest man it is manifesting most of it. The difference consists in the degree of manifestation, but not in the essence. Through all beings exists the same pure and perfect soul.

There are also the ideas of heavens and other places, but these are thought to be second-rate. The idea of heaven is thought to be a low idea. It arises from the desire for a place of enjoyment. We foolishly want to limit the whole universe with our present experience. Children think that the whole universe is full of children. Madmen think the whole universe a lunatic asylum, and so on. So those to whom this world is but sense-enjoyment, whose whole life is in eating and feasting, with very little difference between them and brute beasts— such are naturally found to conceive of places where they will have more enjoyments, because this life is short. Their desire for enjoyment is infinite, so they are bound to think of places where they will have unobstructed enjoyment of the senses; and we see, as we go on, that those who want to go to such places will have to go; they will dream, and when this dream is over, they will be in another dream where there is plenty of sense-enjoyment; and when that dream breaks, they will have to think of something else. Thus they will be driving about from dream to dream.

Then comes the last theory, one more idea about the soul. If the soul is pure and perfect in its essence and nature, and if every soul is infinite and omnipresent, how is it that there can be many souls? There cannot be many infinites. There cannot be two even, not to speak of many. If there were two infinites, one would limit the other, and both become finite. The infinite can only be one, and boldly the last conclusion is approached—that it is but one and not two.

Two birds are sitting on the same tree, one on the top, the other below, both of most beautiful plumage. The one eats the fruits, while the other remains, calm and majestic, concentrated in its own glory. The lower bird is eating fruits, good and evil, going after sense-enjoyments; and when it eats occasionally a bitter fruit, it gets higher and looks up and sees the other bird sitting there calm and majestic, neither caring for good fruit nor for bad, sufficient unto itself, seeking no enjoyment beyond itself. It itself is enjoyment; what to seek beyond itself? The lower bird looks at the upper bird and wants to get near. It goes a little higher; but its old impressions are upon it, and still it goes about eating the same fruit. Again an exceptionally bitter fruit comes; it gets a shock, looks up. There the same calm and majestic one! It comes near but again is dragged down by past actions, and continues to eat the sweet and bitter fruits. Again the exceptionally bitter fruit comes, the bird looks up, gets nearer; and as it begins to get nearer and nearer, the light from the plumage of the other bird is reflected upon it. Its own plumage is melting away, and when it has come sufficiently near, the whole vision changes. The lower bird never existed, it was always the upper bird, and what it took for the lower bird was only a little bit of a reflection.

Such is the nature of the soul. This human soul goes after sense-enjoyments, vanities of the world; like animals it lives only in the senses, lives only in momentary titillations of the nerves. When there comes a blow, for a moment the head reels, and everything begins to vanish, and it finds that the world was not what it thought it to be, that life was not so smooth. It looks upward and sees the infinite Lord a moment, catches a glimpse of the majestic One, comes a little nearer, but is dragged away by its past actions. Another blow comes, and sends it back again. It catches another glimpse of the infinite Presence, comes nearer, and as it approaches nearer and nearer, it begins to find out that its individuality—its low, vulgar, intensely selfish individuality—is melting away; the desire to sacrifice the whole world to make that little thing happy is melting away; and as it gets gradually nearer and nearer, nature begins to melt away. When it has come sufficiently near, the whole vision changes, and it finds that it was the other bird, that this infinity which it had viewed as from a distance was its own Self, this wonderful glimpse that it had got of the glory and majesty was its own Self, and it indeed was that reality. The soul then finds That which is true in everything. That which is in every atom, everywhere present, the essence of all things, the God of this universe—know that thou art He, know that thou art free.

28

MY MASTER

Two lectures delivered in New York and England in 1896 were combined subsequently under the present heading.

'Whenever virtue subsides and vice prevails, I come down to help mankind,' declares Krishna, in the Bhagavad Gita. Whenever this world of ours, on account of growth, on account of added circumstances, requires a new adjustment, a wave of power comes; and as a man is acting on two planes, the spiritual and the material, waves of adjustment come on both planes. On the one side, of the adjustment on the material plane, Europe has mainly been the basis during modern times; and of the adjustment on the other, the spiritual plane, Asia has been the basis throughout the history of the world. Today, man requires one more adjustment on the spiritual plane; today when material ideas are at the height of their glory and power, today when man is likely to forget his divine nature, through his growing dependence on matter, and is likely to be reduced to a mere money-making machine, an adjustment is necessary; the voice has spoken, and the power is coming to drive away the clouds of gathering materialism. The power has been set in motion which, at no distant date, will bring unto mankind once more the memory of its real nature; and again the place from which this power will start will be Asia.

This world of ours is on the plan of the division of labour. It is vain to say that one man shall possess everything. Yet how childish we are! The baby in its ignorance thinks that its doll is the only possession that is to be coveted in this whole universe. So a nation which is great in the possession of material power thinks that that is all that is to be coveted, that that is all that is meant by progress, that that is all that is meant by civilization, and if there are other nations which do not care for possession and do not possess that power, they are not fit to live, their whole existence is useless! On the other hand, another nation may think that mere material civilization is utterly useless. From the Orient came the voice which once told the world that if a man possesses everything that is under the sun and does not possess spirituality, what avails it? This is the oriental type; the other is the occidental type.

Each of these types has its grandeur, each has its glory. The present adjustment will be the harmonising, the mingling of these two ideals. To the Oriental, the world of spirit is as real as to the Occidental is the world of senses. In the spiritual, the Oriental finds everything he wants or hopes for; in it he finds all that makes life real to him. To the Occidental he is a dreamer; to the Oriental the Occidental is a dreamer playing with ephemeral toys, and he laughs to think that grown-up men and women should make so much of a handful of matter which they will have to leave sooner or later. Each calls the other a dreamer. But the oriental ideal is as necessary for the progress of the human race as is the occidental, and I think it is more necessary. Machines never made mankind happy and never will make. He who is trying to make us believe this will claim that happiness is in the machine; but it is always in the mind. That man alone who is the lord of his mind can become happy, and none else. And what, after all, is this power of machinery? Why should a man who can send a current of electricity through a wire be called a very great man and a very intelligent man? Does not nature do a million times more than that every moment? Why not then fall down and worship nature? What avails it if you have power over the whole of the world, if you have mastered every atom in the universe? That will not make you happy unless you have the power of happiness in yourself, until you have conquered yourself. Man is born to conquer nature, it is true, but the Occidental means by 'nature' only physical or external nature. It is true that external nature is majestic, with its mountains, and oceans, and rivers, and with its infinite powers and varieties. Yet, there is a more majestic internal nature of man, higher than the sun, moon, and stars, higher than this earth of ours, higher than the physical universe, transcending these little lives of ours; and it affords another field of study. There the Orientals excel, just as the Occidentals excel in the other. Therefore, it is fitting that, whenever there is a spiritual adjustment, it should come from the Orient. It is also fitting that when the Oriental wants to learn about machine-making, he should sit at the feet of the Occidental and learn from him. When the Occident wants to learn about the spirit, about God, about the soul, about the meaning and the mystery of this universe, he must sit at the feet of the Orient to learn.

I am going to present before you the life of one man who has put in motion such a wave in India. But before going into the life of this man, I will try to present before you the secret of India, what India means. If those whose eyes have been blinded by the glamour of material things, whose whole dedication of life is to eating and drinking and enjoying, whose ideal of possession is lands and gold, whose ideal of pleasure is that of the senses, whose God is money, and whose goal is a life of ease and comfort in this world and death after that, whose minds never look forward, and who rarely think of anything higher than the sense-objects in the midst of which they live—if such as these go to India, what do they see? Poverty, squalor, superstition, darkness, hideousness everywhere. Why? Because in their minds enlightenment means dress, education, social politeness. Whereas occidental nations have used every effort to improve their material position, India has done differently. There live the only men in the world who, in the whole history of humanity, never went beyond their frontiers to conquer anyone, who never coveted that which belonged to anyone else, whose only fault was that their lands were so fertile, and they accumulated wealth by the hard labour of their hands, and so tempted other nations to come and despoil them. They are contented to be despoiled, and to be called barbarians; and in return they want to send to this world visions of the Supreme, to lay bare for the world the secrets of human nature, to rend the veil that conceals the real man, because they know the dream, because they know that behind this materialism lives the real, divine nature of man which no sin can tarnish, no crime can spoil, no lust can taint, which fire cannot burn, nor water wet, which heat cannot dry nor death kill. And to them this true nature of man is as real as is any material object to the senses of an Occidental.

Just as you are brave to jump at the mouth of a cannon with a hurrah, just as you are brave in the name of patriotism to stand up and give up your lives for your country, so are they brave in the name of God. There it is that when a man declares that this is a world of ideas, that it is all a dream, he casts off clothes and property to demonstrate that what he believes and thinks is true. There it is that a man sits on the bank of a river, when he has known that life is eternal, and wants to give up his body just as nothing, just as you can give up a bit of straw. Therein lies their heroism, that they are ready to face death as a brother, because they are convinced that there is no death for them. Therein lies the strength that has made them invincible through hundreds of years of oppression and foreign invasion and tyranny. The nation lives today, and in that nation even in the days of the direst disaster, spiritual giants have, never failed to arise. Asia produces giants in spirituality, just as the Occident produces giants in politics, giants in science. In the beginning of the present century, when Western influence began to pour into India, when Western conquerors, sword in hand, came to demonstrate to the children of the sages that they were mere barbarians, a race of dreamers, that their religion was but mythology, and god and soul and everything they had been struggling for were mere words without meaning, that the thousands of years of struggle, the thousands of years of endless renunciation, had all been in vain, the question began to be agitated among young men at the universities whether the whole national existence up to then had been a failure, whether they must begin anew on the occidental plan, tear up their old books, burn their philosophies, drive away their preachers, and break down their temples. Did not the occidental conqueror, the man who demonstrated his religion with sword and gun, say that all the old ways were mere superstition and idolatry? Children brought up and educated in the new schools started on the occidental plan, drank in these ideas, from their childhood; and it is not to be wondered at that doubts arose. But instead of throwing away superstition and making a real search after truth, the test of truth became, 'What does the West say?' The priests must go, the Vedas must be burned, because the West has said so. Out of the feeling of unrest thus produced, there arose a wave of so-called reform in India.

If you wish to be a true reformer, three things are necessary. The first is to feel. Do you really feel for your brothers? Do you really feel that there is so much misery in the world, so much ignorance and superstition? Do you really feel that men are your brothers? Does this idea come into your whole being? Does it run with your blood? Does it tingle in your veins? Does it course through every nerve and filament of your body? Are you full of that idea of sympathy? If you are, that is only the first step. You must think next if you have found any remedy. The old ideas may be all superstition, but in and round these masses of superstition are nuggets of gold and truth. Have you discovered means by which to keep that gold alone, without any of the dross? If you have done that, that is only the second step; one more thing is necessary. What is your motive? Are you sure that you are not actuated by greed of gold, by thirst for fame or power? Are you really sure that you can stand to your ideals and work on, even if the whole world wants to crush you down? Are you sure you know what you want and will perform your duty, and that alone, even if your life is at stake? Are you sure that you will persevere so long as life endures, so long as there is one pulsation left in the heart? Then you are a real reformer, you are a teacher, a Master, a blessing to mankind. But man is so impatient, so short-sighted! He has not the patience to wait, he has not the power to see. He wants to rule, he wants results immediately. Why? He wants to reap the fruits himself, and does not really care for others. Duty for duty's sake is not what he wants. 'To work you have the right, but not to the fruits thereof,' says Krishna. Why cling to results? Ours are the duties. Let the fruits take care of themselves. But man has no patience. He takes up any scheme. The larger number of would-be reformers all over the world can be classed under this heading.

As I have said, the idea of reform came to India when it seemed as if the wave of materialism that had invaded her shores would sweep away the teachings of the sages. But the nation had borne the shocks of a thousand such waves of change. This one was mild in comparison. Wave after wave had flooded the land, breaking and crushing everything for hundreds of years. The sword had flashed, and 'Victory unto Allah' had rent the skies of India; but these floods subsided, leaving the national ideals unchanged.

The Indian nation cannot be killed. Deathless it stands, and it will stand so long as that spirit shall remain as the background, so long as her people do not give up their spirituality. Beggars they may remain, poor and poverty-stricken, dirt and squalor may surround them perhaps throughout all time, but let them not give up their God, let them not forget that they are the children of the sages. Just as in the West, even the man in the street wants to trace his descent from some robber-baron of the Middle Ages, so in India, even an Emperor on the throne wants to trace his descent from some beggar-sage in the forest, from a man who wore the bark of a tree, lived upon the fruits of the forest and communed with God. That is the type of descent we want; and so long as holiness is thus supremely venerated, India cannot die.

Many of you perhaps have read the article by Professor Max Müller in a recent issue of the *Nineteenth Century*, headed 'A Real Mahatman'. The life of Shri Ramakrishna is interesting, as it was a living illustration of the ideas that he preached. Perhaps it will be a little romantic for you who live in the West in an atmosphere entirely different from that of India. For the methods and manners in the busy rush of life in the West vary entirely from those of India. Yet perhaps it will be of all the more interest for that, because it will bring into a newer light, things about which many have already heard.

It was while reforms of various kinds were being inaugurated in India that a child was born of poor Brahmin parents on the eighteenth of February, 1836, in one of the remote villages of Bengal. The father and mother were very orthodox people. The life of a really orthodox Brahmin is one of continuous renunciation. Very few things can he do; and over and beyond them the orthodox Brahmin must not occupy himself with any secular business. At the same time he must not receive gifts from everybody. You may imagine how rigorous that life becomes. You have heard of the Brahmins and their priestcraft many times, but very few of you have ever stopped to ask what makes this wonderful band of men the rulers of their fellows. They are the poorest of all the classes in the country; and the secret of their power lies in their renunciation. They never covet wealth. Theirs is the poorest priesthood in the world, and therefore the most powerful. Even in this poverty, a Brahmin's wife will never allow a poor man to pass through the village without giving him something to eat. That is considered the highest duty of the mother in India; and because she is the mother it is her duty to be served last; she must see that everyone is served before her turn comes. That is why the mother is regarded as God in India. This particular woman, the mother of our subject, was the very type of a Hindu mother. The higher the caste, the greater the restrictions. The lowest caste people can eat and drink anything they like. But as men rise in the social scale, more and more restrictions come; and when they reach the highest caste, the Brahmin, the hereditary priesthood of India, their lives, as I have said, are very much circumscribed. Compared to Western manners, their lives are of continuous asceticism. The Hindus are perhaps the most exclusive nation in the world. They have the same great steadiness as the English, but much more amplified. When they get hold of an idea they carry it out to its very conclusion, and they, keep hold of it generation after generation until they make something out of it. Once give them an idea, and it is not easy to take it back; but it is hard to make them grasp a new idea.

The orthodox Hindus, therefore, are very exclusive, living entirely within their own horizon of thought and feeling. Their lives are laid down in our old books in every little detail, and the least detail is grasped with almost adamantine firmness by them. They would starve rather than eat a meal cooked by the hands of a man not belonging to their own small section of caste. But withal, they have intensity and tremendous earnestness. That force of intense faith and religious life occurs often among the orthodox Hindus, because their very orthodoxy comes from a tremendous conviction that it is right. We may not all think that what they hold on to with such perseverance is right; but to them it is. Now, it is written in our books that a man should always be charitable even to the extreme. If a man starves himself to death to help another man, to save that man's life, it is all right; it is even held that a man ought to do that. And it is expected of a Brahmin to carry this idea out to the very extreme. Those who are acquainted with the literature of India will remember a beautiful old story about this extreme charity, how a whole family, as related in the Mahabharata, starved themselves to death and gave their last meal to a beggar. This is not an exaggeration, for such things still happen. The character of the father and the mother of my Master was very much like that. Very poor they were, and yet many a time the mother would starve herself a whole day to help a poor man. Of them this child was born; and he was a peculiar child from very boyhood. He remembered his past from his birth and was conscious for what purpose he came into the world, and every power was devoted to the fulfilment of that purpose.

While he was quite young, his father died; and the boy was sent to school. A Brahmin's boy must go to school; the caste restricts him to a learned profession only. The old system of education in India, still prevalent in many parts of the country, especially in connection with Sannyasins, is very different from the modern system. The students had not to pay. It was thought that knowledge is so sacred that no man ought to sell it. Knowledge must be given freely and without any price. The teachers used to take students without charge, and not only so, most of them gave their students food and clothes. To support these teachers the wealthy families on certain occasions, such as a marriage festival, or at the ceremonies for the dead, made gifts to them. They were considered the first and foremost claimants to certain gifts; and they in their turn had to maintain their students. So whenever there is a marriage, especially in a rich family, these professors are invited, and they attend and discuss various subjects. This boy went to one of these gatherings of professors, and the professors were discussing various topics, such as logic or astronomy, subjects much beyond his age. The boy was peculiar, as I have said, and he gathered this moral out of it: 'This is the outcome of all their knowledge. Why are they fighting so hard? It is simply for money; the man who can show the highest learning here will get the best pair of cloth, and that is all these people are struggling for. I will not go to school any more.' And he did not; that was the end of his going to school. But this boy had an elder brother, a learned professor, who took him to Calcutta, however, to study with him. After a short time the boy became fully convinced that the aim of all secular learning was mere material advancement, and nothing more, and he resolved to give up study and devote himself solely to the pursuit of spiritual knowledge. The father being dead, the family was very poor; and this boy had to make his own living. He went to a place near Calcutta and became a temple priest. To become a temple priest is thought very degrading to a Brahmin. Our temples are not churches in your sense of the word, they are not places for public worship; for, properly speaking, there is no such thing as public worship in India. Temples are erected mostly by rich persons as a meritorious religious act.

If a man has much property, he wants to build a temple. In that he puts a symbol or an image of an Incarnation of God, and dedicates it to worship in the name of God. The worship is akin to that which is conducted in Roman Catholic churches, very much like the mass, reading certain sentences from the sacred books, waving a light before the image, and treating the image in every respect as we treat a great man. This is all that is done in the temple. The man who goes to a temple is not considered thereby a better man than he who never goes. More properly, the latter is considered the more religious man, for religion in India is to each man his own private affair. In the house of every man there is either a little chapel, or a room set apart, and there he goes morning and evening, sits down in a corner, and there does his worship. And this worship is entirely mental, for another man does not hear or know what he is doing. He sees him only sitting there, and perhaps moving his fingers in a peculiar fashion, or closing his nostrils and breathing in a peculiar manner. Beyond that, he does not know what his brother is doing; even his wife, perhaps, will not know. Thus, all worship is conducted in the privacy of his own home. Those who cannot afford to have a chapel go to the banks of a river, or a lake, or the sea if they live at the seaside, but people sometimes go to worship in a temple by making salutation to the image. There their duty to the temple ends. Therefore, you see, it has been held from the most ancient times in our country, legislated upon by Manu, that it is a degenerating occupation to become a temple priest. Some of the books say it is so degrading as to make a Brahmin worthy of reproach. Just as with education, but in a far more intense sense with religion, there is the other idea behind it that the temple priests who take fees for their work are making merchandise of sacred things. So you may imagine the feelings of that boy when he was forced through poverty to take up the only occupation open to him, that of a temple priest.

There have been various poets in Bengal whose songs have passed down to the people; they are sung in the streets of Calcutta and in every village. Most of these are religious songs, and their one central idea, which is perhaps peculiar to the religions of India, is the idea of realization. There is not a book in India on religion which does not breathe this idea. Man must realize God, feel God, see God, talk to God. That is religion. The Indian atmosphere is full of stories of saintly persons having visions of God. Such doctrines form the basis of their religion; and all these ancient books and scriptures are the writings of persons who came into direct contact with spiritual facts. These books were not written for the intellect, nor can any reasoning understand them, because they were written by men who saw the things of which they wrote, and they can be understood only by men who have raized themselves to the same height. They say there is such a thing as realization even in this life, and it is open to everyone, and religion begins with the opening of this faculty, if I may call it so. This is the central idea in all religions, and this is why we may find one man with the most finished oratorical powers, or the most convincing logic, preaching the highest doctrines and yet unable to get people to listen to him, while we may find another, a poor man, who scarcely can speak the language of his own motherland, yet half the nation worships him in his own lifetime as God. When in India the idea somehow or other gets abroad that a man has raized himself to that state of realization, that religion is no more a matter of conjecture to him, that he is no more groping in the dark in such momentous questions as religion, the immortality of the soul, and God, people come from all quarters to see him and gradually they begin to worship him.

In the temple was an image of the 'Blissful Mother'. This boy had to conduct the worship morning and evening, and by degrees this one idea filled his mind: 'Is there anything behind this images? Is it true that there is a Mother of Bliss in the universe? Is it true that She lives and guides the universe, or is it all a dream? Is there any reality in religion?'

This scepticism comes to the Hindu child. It is the scepticism of our country: Is this that we are doing real? And theories will not

satisfy us, although there are ready at hand almost all the theories that
have ever been made with regard to God and soul. Neither books nor
theories can satisfy us, the one idea that gets hold of thousands of
our people is this idea of realization. Is it true that there is a God?
If it be true, can I see Him? Can I realize the truth? The Western
mind may think all this very impracticable, but to us it is intensely
practical. For this their lives. You have just heard how from the earliest
times there have been persons who have given up all comforts and
luxuries to live in caves, and hundreds have given up their homes to
weep bitter tears of misery, on the banks of sacred rivers, in order to
realize this idea—not to know in the ordinary sense of the word, not
intellectual understanding, not a mere rationalistic comprehension of
the real thing, not mere groping in the dark, but intense realization,
much more real than this world is to our senses. That is the idea. I
do not advance any proposition as to that just now, but that is the
one fact that is impressed upon them. Thousands will be killed, other
thousands will be ready. So upon this one idea the whole nation for
thousands of years have been denying and sacrificing themselves. For
this idea thousands of Hindus every year give up their homes, and
many of them die through the hardships they have to undergo. To
the Western mind this must seem most visionary, and I can see the
reason for this point of view. But though I have resided in the West,
I still think this idea the most practical thing in life.

Every moment I think of anything else is so much loss to me—
even the marvels of earthly sciences; everything is vain if it takes me
away from that thought. Life is but momentary, whether you have
the knowledge of an angel or the ignorance of an animal. Life is but
momentary, whether you have the poverty of the poorest man in rags
or the wealth of the richest living person. Life is but momentary,
whether you are a downtrodden man living in one of the big streets of
the big cities of the West or a crowned Emperor ruling over millions.
Life is but momentary, whether you have the best of health or the
worst. Life is but momentary, whether you have the most poetical
temperament or the most cruel. There is but one solution of life, says
the Hindu, and that solution is what they call God and religion. If
these be true, life becomes explained, life becomes bearable, becomes

enjoyable. Otherwise, life is but a useless burden. That is our idea, but no amount of reasoning can demonstrate it; it can only make it probable, and there it rests. The highest demonstration of reasoning that we have in any branch of knowledge can only make a fact probable, and nothing further. The most demonstrable facts of physical science are only probabilities, not facts yet. Facts are only in the senses. Facts have to be perceived, and we have to perceive religion to demonstrate it to ourselves. We have to sense God to be convinced that there is a God. We must sense the facts of religion to know that they are facts. Nothing else, and no amount of reasoning, but our own perception can make these things real to us, can make my belief firm as a rock. That is my idea, and that is the Indian idea.

This idea took possession of the boy and his whole life became concentrated upon that. Day after day he would weep and say, 'Mother, is it true that Thou existest, or is it all poetry? Is the Blissful Mother an imagination of poets and misguided people, or is there such a Reality?' We have seen that of books, of education in our sense of the word, he had none, and so much the more natural, so much the more healthy, was his mind, so much the purer his thoughts, undiluted by drinking in the thoughts of others. Because he did not go to the university, therefore he thought for himself. Because we have spent half our lives in the university we are filled with a collection of other people's thoughts. Well has Professor Max Müller said in the article I have just referred to that this was a clean, original man; and the secret of that originality was that he was not brought up within the precincts of a university. However, this thought—whether God can be seen—which was uppermost in his mind gained in strength every day until he could think of nothing else. He could no more conduct the worship properly, could no more attend to the various details in all their minuteness. Often he would forget to place the food-offering before the image, sometimes he would forget to wave the light; at other times he would wave it for hours, and forget everything else.

And that one idea was in his mind every day: 'Is it true that Thou existest, O Mother? Why cost Thou not speak? Art Thou dead?' Perhaps some of us here will remember that there are moments in our lives when, tired of all these ratiocinations of dull and dead logic, tired of plodding through books—which after all teach us nothing, become nothing but a sort of intellectual opium-eating—we must have it at stated times or we die—tired with all this, the heart of our hearts sends out a wail: 'Is there no one in this universe who can show me the light? If Thou art, show the light unto me. Why dost Thou not speak? Why dost Thou make Thyself so scarce, why send so many Messengers and not Thyself come to me? In this world of fights and factions whom am I to follow and believe? If Thou art the God of every man and woman alike, why comest Thou not to speak to Thy child and see if he is not ready?' Well, to us all come such thoughts in moments of great depression; but such are the temptations surrounding us, that the next moment we forget. For the moment it seemed that the doors of the heavens were going to be opened, for the moment it seemed as if we were going to plunge into the light effulgent; but the animal man again shakes off all these angelic visions. Down we go, animal man once more eating and drinking and dying, and dying and drinking and eating again and again. But there are exceptional minds which are not turned away so easily, which once attracted can never be turned back, whatever may be the temptation in the way, which want to see the Truth knowing that life must go. They say, let it go in a noble conquest, and what conquest is nobler than the conquest of the lower man, than this solution of the problem of life and death, of good and evil?

At last it became impossible for him to serve in the temple. He left it and entered into a little wood that was near and lived there. About this part of his life, he told me many times that he could not tell when the sun rose or set, or how he lived. He lost all thought of himself and forgot to eat. During this period he was lovingly watched over by a relative who put into his mouth food which he mechanically swallowed.

Days and nights thus passed with the boy. When a whole day would pass, towards the evening when the peal of bells in the temples, and the voices singing, would reach the wood, it would make the boy very sad, and he would cry, 'Another day is gone in vain, Mother, and Thou hast not come. Another day of this short life has gone, and I have not known the Truth.' In the agony of his soul, sometimes he would rub his face against the ground and weep, and this one prayer burst forth: 'Do Thou manifest Thyself in me, Thou Mother of the universe! See that I need Thee and nothing else!' Verily, he wanted to be true to his own ideal. He had heard that the Mother never came until everything had been given up for Her. He had heard that the Mother wanted to come to everyone, but they Could not have Her, that people wanted all sorts of foolish little idols to pray to, that they wanted their own enjoyments, and not the Mother, and that the moment they really wanted Her with their whole soul, and nothing else, that moment She would come. So he began to break himself into that idea; he wanted to be exact, even on the plane of matter. He threw away all the little property he had, and took a vow that he would never touch money, and this one idea, 'I will not touch money', became a part of him. It may appear to be something occult, but even in after-life when he was sleeping, if I touched him with a piece of money his hand would become bent, and his whole body would become, as it were, paralysed. The other idea that came into his mind was that lust was the other enemy. Man is a soul, and soul is sexless, neither man nor woman. The idea of sex and the idea of money were the two things, he thought, that prevented him from seeing the Mother. This whole universe is the manifestation of the Mother, and She lives in every woman's body. 'Every woman represents the Mother; how can I think of woman in mere sex relation?' That was the idea: Every woman was his Mother, he must bring himself to the state when he would see nothing but Mother in every woman. And he carried it out in his life.

This is the tremendous thirst that seizes the human heart. Later on, this very man said to me, 'My child, suppose there is a bag of gold in one room, and a robber in the next room; do you think that the robber can sleep? He cannot. His mind will be always thinking how to get into that room and obtain possession of that gold. Do you think then that a man, firmly persuaded that there is a Reality behind all these appearances, that there is a God, that there is One who never dies, One who is infinite bliss, a bliss compared with which these pleasures of the senses are simply playthings, can rest contented without struggling to attain It? Can he cease his efforts for a moment?

No. He will become mad with longing.' This divine madness seized the boy. At that time he had no teacher, nobody to tell him anything, and everyone thought that he was out of his mind. This is the ordinary condition of things. If a man throws aside the vanities of the world, we hear him called mad. But such men are the salt of the earth. Out of such madness have come the powers that have moved this world of ours, and out of such madness alone will come the powers of the future that are going to move the world.

So days, weeks, months passed in continuous struggle of the soul to arrive at truth. The boy began to see visions, to see wonderful things; the secrets of his nature were beginning to open to him. Veil after veil was, as it were, being taken off. Mother Herself became the teacher and initiated the boy into the truths he sought. At this time there came to this place a woman of beautiful appearance, learned beyond compare. Later on, this saint used to say about her that she was not learned, but was the embodiment of learning; she was learning itself, in human form. There, too, you find the peculiarity of the Indian nation. In the midst of the ignorance in which the average Hindu woman lives, in the midst of what is called in Western countries her lack of freedom, there could arise a woman of supreme spirituality. She was a Sannyasini; for women also give up the world, throw away their property, do not marry, and devote themselves to the worship of the Lord. She came; and when she heard of this boy in the grove, she offered to go and see him; and hers was the first help he received. At once she recognized what his trouble was, and she said to him. 'My son blessed is the man upon whom such madness comes. The whole of this universe is mad—some for wealth, some for pleasure, some for fame, some for a hundred other things. They are mad for gold, or husbands, or wives, for little trifles, mad to tyrannize over somebody, mad to become rich, mad for every foolish thing except God. And they can understand only their own madness. When another man is mad after gold, they have fellow-feeling and sympathy for him, and they say he is the right man, as lunatics think that lunatics alone are sane. But if a man is mad after the Beloved, after the Lord, how can they understand? They think he has gone crazy; and they say, 'Have nothing to do with him.' That is why they call you mad; but yours is the right kind of madness. Blessed is the man who is mad after God. Such men are very few.' This woman remained near the boy for years, taught him the forms of the religions of India, initiated him into the different practises of Yoga, and, as it were, guided and brought into harmony this tremendous river of spirituality.

Later, there came to the same grove a Sannyasin, one of the begging friars of India, a learned man, a philosopher. He was a peculiar man, he was an idealist. He did not believe that this world existed in reality; and to demonstrate that, he would never go under a roof, he would always live out of doors, in storm and sunshine alike. This man began to teach the boy the philosophy of the Vedas; and he found very soon, to his astonishment, that the pupil was in some respects wiser than the master. He spent several months with the boy, after which he initiated him into the order of Sannyasins, and took his departure.

When as a temple priest his extraordinary worship made people think him deranged in his head, his relatives took him home and married him to a little girl, thinking that that would turn his thoughts and restore the balance of his mind. But he came back and, as we have seen, merged deeper in his madness. Sometimes, in our country, boys are married as children and have no voice in the matter; their parents marry them. Of course such a marriage is little more than a betrothal. When they are married they still continue to live with their parents, and the real marriage takes place when the wife grows older, Then it is customary for the husband to go and bring his bride to his own home. In this case, however, the husband had entirely forgotten that he had a wife. In her far off home the girl had heard that her husband had become a religious enthusiast, and that he was even considered insane by many. She resolved to learn the truth for herself, so she set out and walked to the place where her husband was. When at last she stood in her husband's presence, he at once admitted her right to his life, although in India any person, man or woman, who embraces a religious life, is thereby freed from all other obligations. The young man fell at the feet of his wife and said, 'As for me, the Mother has shown me that She resides in every woman, and so I have learnt to look upon every woman as Mother. That is the one idea I can have about you; but if you wish to drag me into the world, as I have been married to you, I am at your service.'

The maiden was a pure and noble soul and was able to understand her husband's aspirations and sympathize with them. She quickly told him that she had no wish to drag him down to a life of worldliness; but that all she desired was to remain near him, to serve him, and to learn of him. She became one of his most devoted disciples, always revering him as a divine being. Thus through his wife's consent the last barrier was removed, and he was free to lead the life he had chosen.

The next desire that seized upon the soul of this man as to know the truth about the various religions. Up to that time he had not known any religion but his own. He wanted to understand what other religions were like. So he sought teachers of other religions. By teachers you must always remember what we mean in India, not a bookworm, but a man of realization, one who knows truth a; first hand and not through an intermediary. He found a Mohammedan saint and placed himself under him; he underwent the disciplines prescribed by him, and to his astonishment found that when faithfully carried out, these devotional methods led him to the same goal he had already attained. He gathered similar experience from following the true religion of Jesus the Christ. He went to all the sects he could find, and whatever he took up he went into with his whole heart. He did exactly as he was told, and in every instance he arrived at the same result. Thus from actual experience, he came to know that the goal of every religion is the same, that each is trying to teach the same thing, the difference being largely in method and still more in language. At the core, all sects and all religions have the same aim; and they were only quarrelling for their own selfish purposes—they were not anxious about the truth, but about 'my name' and 'your name'. Two of them preached the same truth, but one of them said, 'That cannot be true, because I have not put upon it the seal of my name. Therefore do not listen to him.' And the other man said, 'Do not hear him, although he is preaching very much the same thing, yet it is not true because he does not preach it in my name.'

That is what my Master found, and he then set about to learn humility, because he had found that the one idea in all religions is, 'not me, but Thou', and he who says, 'not me', the Lord fills his

244 • THE DEFINITIVE VIVEKANANDA

heart. The less of this little 'I' the more of God there is in him. That he found to be the truth in every religion in the world, and he set himself to accomplish this. As I have told you, whenever he wanted to do anything he never confined himself to fine theories, but would enter into the practise immediately; We see many persons talking the most wonderfully fine things about charity and about equality and the rights of other people and all that, but it is only in theory. I was so fortunate as to find one who was able to carry theory into practise. He had the most wonderful faculty of carrying everything into practise which he thought was right.

Now, there was a family of Pariahs living near the place. The Pariahs number several millions in the whole of India and are a sect of people so low that some of our books say that if a Brahmin coming out from his house sees the face of a Pariah, he has to fast that day and recite certain prayers before he becomes holy again. In some Hindu cities when a Pariah enters, he has to put a crow's feather on his head as a sign that he is a Pariah, and he has to cry aloud, 'Save yourselves, the Pariah is passing through the street', and you will find people flying off from him as if by magic, because if they touch him by chance, they will have to change their clothes, bathe, and do other things. And the Pariah for thousands of years has believed that it is perfectly right; that his touch will make everybody unholy. Now my Master would go to a Pariah and ask to be allowed to clean his house. The business of the Pariah is to clean the streets of the cities and to keep houses clean. He cannot enter the house by the front door; by the back door he enters; and as soon as he has gone, the whole place over which he has passed is sprinkled with and made holy by a little Ganga water. By birth the Brahmin stands for holiness, and the Pariah for the very reverse. And this Brahmin asked to be allowed to do the menial services in the house of the Pariah. The Pariah of course could not allow that, for they all think that if they allow a Brahmin to do such menial work it will be an awful sin, and they will become extinct. The Pariah would not permit it; so in the dead of night, when all were sleeping, Ramakrishna would enter the house. He had long hair, and with his hair he would wipe the place, saying, 'Oh, my Mother, make me the servant of the Pariah, make me feel that I am even lower than the Pariah.' 'They worship Me best who worship My worshippers. These are all My children and your privilege is to serve them'—is the teaching of Hindu scriptures.

There were various other preparations which would take a long time to relate, and I want to give you just a sketch of his life. For years he thus educated himself. One of the Sadhanas was to root out the sex idea. Soul has no sex, it is neither male nor female. It is only in the body that sex exists, and the man who desires to reach the spirit cannot at the same time hold to sex distinctions. Having been born in a masculine body, this man wanted to bring the feminine idea into everything. He began to think that he was a woman, he dressed like a woman, spoke like a woman, gave up the occupations of men, and lived in the household among the women of a good family, until, after years of this discipline, his mind became changed, and he entirely forgot the idea of sex; thus the whole view of life became changed to him.

We hear in the West about worshipping woman, but this is usually for her youth and beauty. This man meant by worshipping woman, that to him every woman's face was that of the Blissful Mother, and nothing but that. I myself have seen this man standing before those women whom society would not touch, and falling at their feet bathed in tears, saying, 'Mother, in one form Thou art in the street, and in another form Thou art the universe. I salute Thee, Mother, I salute Thee.' Think of the blessedness of that life from which all carnality has vanished, which can look upon every woman with that love and reverence when every woman's face becomes transfigured, and only the face of the Divine Mother, the Blissful One, the Protectress of the human race, shines upon it! That is what we want. Do you mean to say that the divinity back of a woman can ever be cheated? It never was and never will be, It always asserts itself. Unfailingly it detects fraud, it detects hypocrisy, unerringly it feels the warmth of truth, the light of spirituality, the holiness of purity. Such purity is absolutely necessary if real spirituality is to be attained.

This rigorous, unsullied purity came into the life of that man. All the struggles which we have in our lives were past for him. His hard-earned jewels of spirituality, for which he had given three-quarters of his life, were now ready to be given to humanity, and then began his mission. His teaching and preaching were peculiar. In our country a teacher is a most highly venerated person, he is regarded as God Himself. We have not even the same respect for our father and mother. Father and mother give us our body, but the teacher shows us the way to salvation. We are his children, we are born in the spiritual line of the teacher. All Hindus come to pay respect to an extraordinary teacher, they crowd around him. And here was such a teacher, but the teacher had no thought whether he was to be respected or not, he had not the least idea that he was a great teacher, he thought that it was Mother who was doing everything and not he. He always said, 'If any good comes from my lips, it is the Mother who speaks; what have I to do with it?' That was his one idea about his work, and to the day of his death he never gave it up. This man sought no one. His principle was, first form character, first earn spirituality and results will come of themselves. His favourite illustration was, 'When the lotus opens, the bees come of their own accord to seek the honey; so let the lotus of your character be full-blown, and the results will follow.' This is a great lesson to learn.

My Master taught me this lesson hundreds of times, yet I often forget it. Few understand the power of thought. If a man goes into a cave, shuts himself in, and thinks one really great thought and dies, that thought will penetrate the walls of that cave, vibrate through space, and at last permeate the whole human race. Such is the power of thought; be in no hurry therefore to give your thoughts to others. First have something to give. He alone teaches who has something to give, for teaching is not talking, teaching is not imparting doctrines, it is communicating. Spirituality can be communicated just as really as I can give you a flower. This is true in the most literal sense. This idea is very old in India and finds illustration in the West in the 'theory, in the belief, of apostolic succession. Therefore first make character—that is the highest duty you can perform. Know Truth for yourself, and there will be many to whom you can teach it after wards; they will all come. This was the attitude of nay Master. He criticized no one. For years I lived with that man, but never did I hear those lips utter one word of condemnation for any sect. He had the same sympathy for all sects; he had found the harmony between them. A man may be intellectual, or devotional, or mystic, or active; the various religions represent one or the other of these types. Yet it is possible to combine all the four in one man, and this is what future humanity is going to do. That was his idea. He condemned no one, but saw the good in all.

People came by thousands to see and hear this wonderful man who spoke in a *patois* every word of which was forceful and instinct with light. For it is not what is spoken, much less the language in which it is spoken, but it is the personality of the speaker which dwells in everything he says that carries weight. Every one of us feels this at times. We hear most splendid orations, most wonderfully reasoned-out discourses, and we go home and forget them all. At other times we hear a few words in the simplest language, and they enter into our lives, become part and parcel of ourselves and produce lasting results. The words of a man who can put his personality into them take effect, but he must have tremendous personality. All teaching implies giving and taking, the teacher gives and the taught receives, but the one must have something to give, and the other must be open to receive.

This man came to live near Calcutta, the capital of India, the most important university town in our country which was sending out sceptics and materialists by the hundreds every year. Yet many of these university men—sceptics and agnostics—used to come and listen to him. I heard of this man, and I went to hear him. He looked just like an ordinary man, with nothing remarkable about him. He used the most simple language, and I thought 'Can this man be a great teacher?'—crept near to him and asked him the question which I had been asking others all my life: 'Do you believe in God, Sir?' 'Yes,' he replied. 'Can you prove it, Sir?' 'Yes.' 'How?' 'Because I see Him just as I see you here, only in a much intenser sense.' That impressed me at once. For the first time I found a man who dared to say that he saw God that religion was a reality to be felt, to be sensed in an infinitely more intense way than we can sense the world. I began to go to that man, day after day, and I actually saw that religion could be given. One touch, one glance, can change a whole life. I have read about Buddha and Christ and Mohammed, about all those different luminaries of ancient times, how they would stand up and say, 'Be thou whole', and the man became whole. I now found it to be true, and when I myself saw this man, all scepticism was brushed aside. It could be done; and my Master used to say, 'Religion can be given and taken more tangibly, more really than anything else in the world.' Be therefore spiritual first; have something to give and then stand before the world and give it. Religion is not talk, or doctrines, or theories; nor is it sectarianism. Religion cannot live in sects and societies. It is the relation between the soul and God; how can it be made into a society? It would then degenerate into business, and wherever there are business and business principles in religion, spirituality dies. Religion does not consist in erecting temples, or building churches, or attending public worship. It is not to be found in books, or in words, or in lectures, or in organizations. Religion consists in realization. As a fact, we all know that nothing will satisfy us until we know the truth for ourselves. However we may argue, however much we may hear, but one thing will satisfy us, and that is our own realization; and such an experience is possible for every one of us if we will only try. The first ideal of this attempt to realize religion is that of renunciation. As far as we can, we must give up. Darkness and light, enjoyment of the world and enjoyment of God will never go together. 'Ye cannot serve God and Mammon.' Let people try it if they will, and I have seen millions in every country who have tried; but after all, it comes to nothing. If one word remains true in the saying, it is, give up every thing for the sake of the Lord. This is a hard and long task, but you can begin it here and now. Bit by bit we must go towards it.

The second idea that I learnt from my Master, and which is perhaps the most vital, is the wonderful truth that the religions of the world are not contradictory or antagonistic. They are but various phases of one eternal religion. That one eternal religion is applied to different planes of existence, is applied to the opinions of various minds and various races. There never was my religion or yours, my national religion or your national religion; there never existed many religions, there is only the one. One infinite religion existed all through eternity and will ever exist, and this religion is expressing itself in various countries in various ways. Therefore we must respect all religions and we must try to accept them all as far as we can. Religions manifest themselves not only according to race and geographical position, but according to individual powers. In one man religion is manifesting itself as intense activity, as work. In another it is manifesting itself as intense devotion, in yet another, as mysticism, in others as philosophy, and so forth. It is wrong when we say to others, 'Your methods are not right.' Perhaps a man, whose nature is that of love, thinks that the man who does good to others is not on the right road to religion, because it is not his own way, and is therefore wrong. If the philosopher thinks, 'Oh, the poor ignorant people, what do they know about a God of Love, and loving Him? They do not know what they mean,' he is wrong, because they may be right and he also.

To learn this central secret that the truth may be one and yet many at the same time, that we may have different visions of the same truth from different standpoints, is exactly what must be done. Then, instead of antagonism to anyone, we shall have infinite sympathy with all. Knowing that as long as there are different natures born in this world, the same religious truth will require different adaptations, we shall understand that we are bound to have forbearance with each other. Just as nature is unity in variety—an infinite variation in the phenomenal—as in and through all these variations of the phenomenal runs the Infinite, the Unchangeable, the Absolute Unity, so it is with every man; the microcosm is but a miniature repetition of the macrocosm; in spite of all these variations, in and through them all runs this eternal harmony, and we have to recognize this. This idea, above all other ideas, I find to be the crying necessity of the day. Coming from a country which is a hotbed of religious sects—and to which, through its good fortune or ill fortune, everyone who has a religious idea wants to send an advance-guard—I have been acquainted from my childhood with the various sects of the world. Even the Mormons come to preach in India. Welcome them all! That is the soil on which to preach religion. There it takes root more than in any other country. If you come and teach politics to the Hindus, they do not understand; but if you come to preach religion, however curious it may be, you will have hundreds and thousands of followers in no time, and you have every chance of becoming a living God in your lifetime. I am glad it is so, it is the one thing we want in India.

The sects among the Hindus are various, a great many in number, and some of them apparently hopelessly contradictory. Yet they all tell you they are but different manifestations of religion. 'As different rivers, taking their start from different mountains, running crooked or straight, all come and mingle their waters in the ocean, so the different sects, with their different points of vied, at last all come unto Thee.' This is not a theory, it has to be recognized, but not in that patronising way which we see with some people: 'Oh yes, there are some very good things in it. These are what we call the ethnical religions. These ethnical religions have some good in them.' Some even have the most wonderfully liberal idea that other religions are all little bits of a prehistoric evolution, but 'ours is the fulfilment of things'. One man says, because his is the oldest religion, it is the best: another makes the same claim, because his is the latest.

We have to recognize that each one of them has the same saving power as the other. What you have heard about their difference, whether in the temple or in the church, is a mass of superstition. The same God answers all; and it is not you, or I, or any body of men that is responsible for the safety and salvation of the least little bit of the soul; the same Almighty God is responsible for all. I do not understand how people declare themselves to be believers in God, and at the same time think that God has handed over to a little body of men all truth, and that they are the guardians of the rest of humanity. How can you call that religion? Religion is realization; but mere talk— mere trying to believe, mere groping in darkness, mere parroting the words of ancestors and thinking it is religion, mere making a political something out of the truths of religion—is not religion at all. In every sect—even among the Mohammedans whom we always regard as the most exclusive—even among them we find that wherever there was a man trying to realize religion, from his lips have come the fiery words: 'Thou art the Lord of all, Thou art in the heart of all, Thou art the guide of all, Thou art the Teacher of all, and Thou caress infinitely more for the land of Thy children than we can ever do.' Do not try to disturb the faith of any man. If you can, give him something better; if you can, get hold of a man where he stands and give him a push upwards; do so, but do not destroy what he has. The only true teacher is he who can convert himself, as it were, into a thousand persons at a moment's notice. The only true teacher is he who can immediately come down to the level of the student, and transfer his soul to the student's soul and see through the student's eyes and hear through his ears and understand through his mind. Such a teacher can really teach and none else. All these negative, breaking-down, destructive teachers that are in the world can never do any good.

In the presence of my Master I found out that man could be perfect, even in this body. Those lips never cursed anyone, never even criticized anyone. Those eyes were beyond the possibility of seeing evil, that mind had lost the power of thinking evil. He saw nothing but good. That tremendous purity, that tremendous renunciation is the one secret of spirituality. 'Neither through wealth, nor through progeny, but through renunciation alone, is immortality to be reached', say the Vedas. 'Sell all that thou hast and give to the poor, and follow me', says the Christ. So all great saints and Prophets have expressed it, and have carried it out in their lives. How can great spirituality come without that renunciation? Renunciation is the background of all religious thought wherever it be, and you will always find that as this idea of renunciation lessens, the more will the senses creep into the field of religion, and spirituality will decrease in the same ratio.

That man was the embodiment of renunciation. In our country it is necessary for a man who becomes a Sannyasin to give up all worldly wealth and position, and this my Master carried out literally. There were many who would have felt themselves blest if he would only have accepted a present from their hands, who would gladly have given him thousands of rupees if he would have taken them, but these were the only men from whom he would turn away. He was a triumphant example, a living realization of the complete conquest of lust and of desire for money. He was beyond all ideas of either, and such men are necessary for this century. Such renunciation is necessary in these days when men have begun to think that they cannot live a month without what they call their 'necessities', and which they are increasing out of all proportion. It is necessary in a time like this that a man should arise to demonstrate to the sceptics of the world that there yet breathes a man who does not care a straw for all the gold or all the fame that is in the universe. Yet there are such men.

The other idea of his life was intense love for others. The first part of my Master's life was spent in acquiring spirituality, and the remaining years in distributing it. People in our country have not the same customs as you have in visiting a religious teacher or a Sannyasin. Somebody would come to ask him about something, some perhaps would come hundreds of miles, walking all the way, just to ask one question, to hear one word from him, 'Tell me one word for my salvation.' That is the way they come. They come in numbers, unceremoniously, to the place where he is mostly to be found; they may find him under a tree and question him; and before one set of people has gone, others have arrived. So if a man is greatly revered, he will sometimes have no rest day or night. He will have to talk constantly. For hours people will come pouring in, and this man will be teaching them.

So men came in crowds to hear him, and he would talk twenty hours in the twenty-four, and that not for one day, but for months and months until at last the body broke down under the pressure of this tremendous strain. His intense love for mankind would not let him refuse to help even the humblest of the thousands who sought his aid. Gradually, there developed a vital throat disorder and yet he could not be persuaded to refrain from these exertions. As soon as he heard that people were asking to see him, he would insist upon having them admitted and would answer all their questions. When expostulated with, he replied, 'I do not care. I will give up twenty thousand such bodies to help one man. It is glorious to help even one man.' There was no rest for him. Once a man asked him, 'Sir, you are a great Yogi. Why do you not put your mind a little on your body and cure your disease? 'At first he did not answer, but when the question had been repeated, he gently said, 'My friend, I thought you were a sage, but you talk like other men of the world. This mind has been given to the Lord. Do you mean to say that I should take it back and put it upon the body which is but a mere cage of the soul?'

So he went on preaching to the people, and the news spread that his body was about to pass away, and the people began to flock to him in greater crowds than ever. You cannot imagine the way they come to these great religious teachers in India, how they crowd round them and make gods of them while they are yet living. Thousands wait simply to touch the hem of their garments. It is through this appreciation of spirituality in others that spirituality is produced. Whatever man wants and appreciates, he will get; and it is the same with nations. If you go to India and deliver a political lecture, however grand it may be, you will scarcely find people to listen to you but just go and teach religion, live it, not merely talk it, and hundreds will crowd just to look at you, to touch your feet. When the people heard that this holy man was likely to go from them soon, they began to come round him more than ever, and my Master went on teaching them without the least regard for his health. We could not prevent this. Many of the people came from long distances, and he would not rest until he had answered their questions. 'While I can speak, I must teach them,' he would say, and he was as good as his word. One day, he told us that he would lay down the body that day, and repeating the most sacred word of the Vedas he entered into Samadhi and passed away.

His thoughts and his message were known to very few capable of giving them out. Among others, he left a few young boys who had renounced the world, and were ready to carry on his work. Attempts were made to crush them. But they stood firm, having the inspiration of that great life before them. Having had the contact of that blessed life for years, they stood their ground. These young men, living as Sannyasins, begged through the streets of the city where they were born, although some of them came from high families. At first they met with great antagonism, but they persevered and went on from day to day spreading all over India the message of that great man, until the whole country was filled with the ideas he had preached. This man, from a remote village of Bengal, without education, by the sheer force of his own determination, realized the truth and gave it to others, leaving only a few young boys to keep it alive.

Today the name of Shri Ramakrishna Paramahamsa is known all over India to its millions of people. Nay, the power of that man has spread beyond India; and if there has ever been a word of truth, a word of spirituality, that I have spoken anywhere in the world, I owe it to my Master; only the mistakes are mine.

This is the message of Shri Ramakrishna to the modern world: 'Do not care for doctrines, do not care for dogmas, or sects, or churches, or temples; they count for little compared with the essence of existence in each man which is spirituality; and the more this is developed in a man, the more powerful is he for good. Earn that first, acquire that, and criticize no one, for all doctrines and creeds have some good in them. Show by your lives that religion does not mean words, or names, or sects, but that it means spiritual realization. Only those can understand who have felt. Only those who have attained to spirituality can communicate it to others, can be great teachers of mankind. They alone are the powers of light.'

The more such men are produced in a country, the more that country will be raised; and that country where such men absolutely do not exist is simply doomed nothing can save it. Therefore, my Master's message to mankind is: 'Be spiritual and realize truth for Yourself.' He would have you give up for the sake of your fellow-beings. He would have you cease talking about love for your brother, and set to work to prove your words. The time has come for renunciation, for realization, and then you will see the harmony in all the religions of the world. You will know that there is no need of any quarrel. And then only will you be ready to help humanity. To proclaim and make clear the fundamental unity underlying all religions was the mission of my Master. Other teachers have taught special religions which bear their names, but this great teacher of the nineteenth century made no claim for himself. He left every religion undisturbed because he had realized that in reality they are all part and parcel of the one eternal religion.

29

THOUGHTS ON THE GITA

During his sojourn in Calcutta in 1897, Swami Vivekananda used to stay for the most part at the Math, the headquarters of the Ramakrisnna Mission, located then at Alambazar. During this time several young men, who had been preparing themselves for some time previously, gathered round him and took the vows of Brahmacharya and Sannyasa, and Swamiji began to train them for future work, by holding classes on the Gita and Vedanta, and initiating them into the practises of meditation. In one of these classes he talked eloquently in Bengali on the Gita. The following is the translation of the summary of the discourse as it was entered in the Math diary:

The book known as the Gita forms a part of the Mahabharata. To understand the Gita properly, several things are very important to know. First, whether it formed a part of the Mahabharata, i.e. whether the authorship attributed to Veda-Vyasa was true, or if it was merely interpolated within the great epic; secondly, whether there was any historical personality of the name of Krishna; thirdly, whether the great war of Kurukshetra as mentioned in the Gita actually took place; and fourthly, whether Arjuna and others were real historical persons.

Now in the first place, let us see what grounds there are for such inquiry. We know that there were many who went by the name of Veda-Vyasa; and among them who was the real author of the Gita— the Badarayana Vyasa or Dvaipayana Vyasa? 'Vyasa' was only a title. Anyone who composed a new Purana was known by the name of Vyasa, like the word Vikramaditya, which was also a general name. Another point is, the book, Gita, had not been much known to the generality of people before Shankaracharya made it famous by writing his great commentary on it. Long before that, there was current, according to many, the commentary on it by Bodhayana. If this could be proved, it would go a long way, no doubt, to establish the antiquity of the Gita and the authorship of Vyasa. But the Bodhayana Bhashya on the *Vedanta Sutras*—from which Ramanuja compiled his *Shri-Bhashya*, which Shankaracharya mentions and even quotes in part here and there in his own commentary, and which was so greatly discussed by the Swami Dayananda—not a copy even of that Bodhayana Bhashya could I find while travelling throughout India. It is said that even Ramanuja compiled his Bhashya from a worm-eaten manuscript which he happened to find. When even this great Bodhayana Bhashya on the *Vedanta-Sutras* is so much enshrouded in the darkness of uncertainty, it is simply useless to try to establish the existence of the Bodhayana Bhashya on the Gita. Some infer that Shankaracharya was the author of the Gita, and that it was he who foisted it into the body of the Mahabharata.

Then as to the second point in question, much doubt exists about the personality of Krishna. In one place in the Chhandogya Upanishad we find mention of Krishna, the son of Devaki, who received spiritual instructions from one Ghora, a Yogi. In the Mahabharata, Krishna is the king of Dwaraka; and in the *Vishnu Purana* we find a description of Krishna playing with the Gopis. Again, in the *Bhagavata*, the account of his Rasalila is detailed at length. In very ancient times in our country there was in vogue an Utsava called Madanotsava (celebration in honour of Cupid). That very thing was transformed into Dola and thrust upon the shoulders of Krishna. Who can be so bold as to assert that the Rasalila and other things connected with him were not similarly fastened upon him? In ancient times there was very little tendency in our country to find out truths by historical research. So any one could say what he thought best without substantiating it with proper facts and evidence. Another thing: in those ancient times there was very little hankering after name and fame in men. So it often happened that one man composed a book and made it pass current in the name of his Guru or of someone else. In such cases it is very hazardous for the investigator of historical facts to get at the truth. In ancient times they had no knowledge whatever of geography; imagination ran riot. And so we meet with such fantastic creations of the brain as sweet-ocean, milk-ocean, clarified-butter-ocean, curd-ocean, etc! In the Puranas, we find one living ten thousand years, another a hundred thousand years! But the Vedas say, शतायुर्वै पुरूष:—'Man lives a hundred years.' Whom shall we follow here? So, to reach a correct conclusion in the case of Krishna is well-nigh impossible.

It is human nature to build round the real character of a great man all sorts of imaginary superhuman attributes. As regards Krishna the same must have happened, but it seems quite probable that he was a king. Quite probable I say, because in ancient times in our country it was chiefly the kings who exerted themselves most in the preaching of Brahma-Jnana. Another point to be especially noted here is that whoever might have been the author of the Gita, we find its teachings the same as those in the whole of the Mahabharata. From this we can safely infer that in the age of the Mahabharata some great man arose and preached the Brahma-Jnana in this new garb to the then existing society. Another fact comes to the fore that in the olden days, as one sect after another arose, there also came into existence and use among them one new scripture or another. It happened, too, that in the lapse of time both the sect and its scripture died out, or the sect ceased to exist but its scripture remained. Similarly, it was quite probable that the Gita was the scripture of such a sect which had embodied its high and noble ideas in this sacred book.

Now to the third point, bearing on the subject of the Kurukshetra War, no special evidence in support of it can be adduced. But there is no doubt that there was a war fought between the Kurus and the Panchalas. Another thing: how could there be so much discussion about Jnana, Bhakti, and Yoga on the battle-field, where the huge army stood in battle array ready to fight, just waiting for the last signal? And was any shorthand writer present there to note down every word spoken between Krishna and Arjuna, in the din and turmoil of the battle-field? According to some, this Kurukshetra War is only an allegory. When we sum up its esoteric significance, it means the war which is constantly going on within man between the tendencies of good and evil. This meaning, too, may not be irrational.

About the fourth point, there is enough ground of doubt as regards the historicity of Arjuna and others, and it is this: Shatapatha Brahmana is a very ancient book. In it are mentioned somewhere all the names of those who were the performers of the Ashvamedha Yajna: but in those places there is not only no mention, but no hint even of the names of Arjuna and others, though it speaks of Janamejaya, the son of Parikshit who was a grandson of Arjuna. Yet in the Mahabharata and other books it is stated that Yudhishthira, Arjuna, and others celebrated the Ashvamedha sacrifice.

One thing should be especially remembered here, that there is no connection between these historical researches and our real aim, which is the knowledge that leads to the acquirement of Dharma. Even if the historicity of the whole thing is proved to be absolutely false today, it will not in the least be any loss to us. Then what is the use of so much historical research, you may ask. It has its use, because we have to get at the truth; it will not do for us to remain bound by wrong ideas born of ignorance. In this country people think very little of the importance of such inquiries. Many of the sects believe that in order to preach a good thing which may be beneficial to many, there is no harm in telling an untruth, if that helps such preaching, or in other words, the end justifies the means. Hence we find many of our Tantras beginning with, 'Mahadeva said to Parvati'. But our duty should be to convince ourselves of the truth, to believe in truth only. Such is the power of superstition, or faith in old traditions without inquiry into its truth, that it keeps men bound hand and foot, so much so, that even Jesus the Christ, Mohammed, and other great men believed in many such superstitions and could not shake them off. You have to keep your eye always fixed on truth only and shun all superstitions completely.

Now it is for us to see what there is in the Gita. If we study the Upanishads we notice, in wandering through the mazes of many irrelevant subjects, the sudden introduction of the discussion of a great truth, just as in the midst of a huge wilderness a traveller unexpectedly comes across here and there an exquisitely beautiful rose, with its leaves, thorns, roots, all entangled. Compared with that, the Gita is like these truths beautifully arranged together in their proper places—like a fine garland or a bouquet of the choicest flowers. The Upanishads deal elaborately with Shraddha in many places, but hardly mention Bhakti. In the Gita, on the other hand, the subject of Bhakti is not only again and again dealt with, but in it, the innate spirit of Bhakti has attained its culmination.

Now let us see some of the main points discussed in the Gita. Wherein lies the originality of the Gita which distinguishes it from all preceding scriptures? It is this: Though before its advent, Yoga, Jnana, Bhakti, etc. had each its strong adherents, they all quarrelled among themselves, each claiming superiority for his own chosen path; no one ever tried to seek for reconciliation among these different paths. It was the author of the Gita who for the first time tried to harmonize these. He took the best from what all the sects then existing had to offer and threaded them in the Gita. But even where Krishna failed to show a complete reconciliation (Samanvaya) among these warring sects, it was fully accomplished by Ramakrishna Paramahamsa in this nineteenth century.

The next is, Nishkama Karma, or work without desire or attachment. People nowadays understand what is meant by this in various ways. Some say what is implied by being unattached is to become purposeless. If that were its real meaning, then heartless brutes and the walls would be the best exponents of the performance of Nishkama Karma. Many others, again, give the example of Janaka, and wish themselves to be equally recognized as past masters in the practise of Nishkama Karma! Janaka (lit. father) did not acquire that distinction by bringing forth children, but these people all want to be Janakas, with the sole qualification of being the fathers of a brood of children! No! The true Nishkama Karmi (performer of work without desire) is neither to be like a brute, nor to be inert, nor heartless. He is not Tamasika but of pure Sattva. His heart is so full of love and sympathy that he can embrace the whole world with his love. The world at large cannot generally comprehend his all-embracing love and sympathy.

The reconciliation of the different paths of Dharma, and work without desire or attachment—these are the two special characteristics of the Gita.

Let us now read a little from the second chapter.

सञ्जय उवाच॥
तं तथा कृपयाविष्टश्रुपूर्णाकुलेक्षणम्।
विषीदन्तमिदं वाक्यमुवाच मधुसूदनः ॥1॥
श्रीभगवानुवाच॥
कुतस्त्वा कश्मलमिदं विषमे समुपस्थितम्।
अनार्यजुष्टमस्वर्ग्यमकीर्तिकरमर्जुन ॥2॥
क्लैब्यं मा स्म गमः पार्थ नैतत्त्वय्युपपद्यते।
क्षुद्रं हृदयदौर्बल्यं त्यक्त्वोत्तिष्ठ परंतप ॥3॥

'Sanjaya said:

To him who was thus overwhelmed with pity and sorrowing, and whose eyes were dimmed with tears, Madhusudana spoke these words.

The Blessed Lord said:

In such a strait, whence comes upon thee, O Arjuna, this dejection, un-Aryan-like, disgraceful, and contrary to the attainment of heaven?

Yield not to unmanliness, O son of Pritha! Ill doth it become thee. Cast off this mean faint-heartedness and arise, O scorcher of thine enemies!'

In the Shlokas beginning with तं तथा कृपयाविष्टं, how poetically, how beautifully, has Arjuna's real position been painted! Then Shri Krishna advises Arjuna; and in the words क्लैब्यं मा स्म गमः पार्थ नैतत्त्वय्युपपद्यते etc., why is he goading Arjuna to fight? Because it was not that the disinclination of Arjuna to fight arose out of the overwhelming predominance of pure Sattva Guna; it was all Tamas that brought on this unwillingness. The nature of a man of Sattva Guna is, that he is equally calm in all situations in life—whether it be prosperity or adversity. But Arjuna was afraid, he was overwhelmed with pity. That he had the instinct and the inclination to fight is proved by the simple fact that he came to the battle-field with no other purpose than that. Frequently in our lives also such things are seen to happen. Many people think they are Sattvika by nature, but they are really nothing but Tamasika. Many living in an uncleanly way regard themselves as Paramahamsas! Why? Because the Shastras say that Paramahamsas live like one inert, or mad, or like an unclean spirit. Paramahamsas are compared to children, but here it should be understood that the comparison is one-sided. The Paramahamsa and the child are not one and non-different. They only appear similar, being the two extreme poles, as it were. One has reached to a state beyond Jnana, and the other has not got even an inkling of Jnana. The quickest and the gentlest vibrations of light are both beyond the reach of our ordinary vision; but in the one it is intense heat, and in the other it may be said to be almost without any heat. So it is with the opposite qualities of Sattva and Tamas. They seem in some respects to be the same, no doubt, but there is a world of difference between them. The Tamoguna loves very much to array itself in the garb of the Sattva. Here, in Arjuna, the mighty warrior, it has come under the guise of Daya (pity).

In order to remove this delusion which had overtaken Arjuna, what did the Bhagavan say? As I always preach that you should not decry a man by calling him a sinner, but that you should draw his attention to the omnipotent power that is in him, in the same way does the Bhagavan speak to Arjuna. नैतत्त्वरूयुपपद्यते—'It doth not befit thee!' 'Thou art Atman imperishable, beyond all evil. Having forgotten thy real nature, thou hast, by thinking thyself a sinner, as one afflicted with bodily evils and mental grief, thou hast made thyself so—this doth not befit thee!'—so says the Bhagavan: क्लैब्यं मा स्म गम: पार्थ—Yield not to unmanliness, O son of Pritha. There is in the world neither sin nor misery, neither disease nor grief; if there is anything in the world which can be called sin, it is this—'fear'; know that any work which brings out the latent power in thee is Punya (virtue); and that which makes thy body and mind weak is, verily, sin. Shake off this weakness, this faintheartedness! क्लैब्यं मा स्म गम: पार्थ—Thou art a hero, a Vira; this is unbecoming of thee.'

If you, my sons, can proclaim this message to the world—क्लैब्यं मा स्म गम: पार्थ नैतत्त्वरूयुपपद्यते।—then all this disease, grief, sin, and sorrow will vanish from off the face of the earth in three days. All these ideas of weakness will be nowhere. Now it is everywhere—this current of the vibration of fear. Reverse the current: bring in the opposite vibration, and behold the magic transformation! Thou art omnipotent—go, go to the mouth of the cannon, fear not.

Hate not the most abject sinner, fool; not to his exterior. Turn thy gaze inward, where resides the Paramatman. Proclaim to the whole world with trumpet voice, 'There is no sin in thee, there is no misery in thee; thou art the reservoir of omnipotent power. Arise, awake, and manifest the Divinity within!'

If one reads this one Shloka—क्लैब्यं मा स्म गम: पार्थ नैतत्त्वय्युपपद्यते। क्षुद्रं हृदयदौर्बल्यं त्यक्त्वोत्तिष्ठ परंतप।।—one gets all the merits of reading the entire Gita; for in this one Shloka lies imbedded the whole Message of the Gita.

30

THE STORY OF JADA BHARATA
Delivered in California

There was a great monarch named Bharata. The land which is called India by foreigners is known to her children as Bharata Varsha. Now, it is enjoined on every Hindu when he becomes old, to give up all worldly pursuits—to leave the cares of the world, its wealth, happiness, and enjoyments to his son—and retire into the forest, there to meditate upon the Self which is the only reality in him, and thus break the bonds which bind him to life. King or priest, peasant or servant, man or woman, none is exempt from this duty: for all the duties of the householder—of the son, the brother, the husband, the father, the wife, the daughter, the mother, the sister—are but preparations towards that one stage, when all the bonds which bind the soul to matter are severed asunder for ever.

The great king Bharata in his old age gave over his throne to his son, and retired into the forest. He who had been ruler over millions and millions of subjects, who had lived in marble palaces, inlaid with gold and silver, who had drunk out of jewelled cups—this king built a little cottage with his own hands, made of reeds and grass, on the banks of a river in the Himalayan forests. There he lived on roots and wild herbs, collected by his own hands, and constantly meditated upon Him who is always present in the soul of man. Days, months, and years passed. One day, a deer came to drink water near by where the royal sage was meditating. At the same moment, a lion roared at a little distance off. The deer was so terrified that she, without satisfying her thirst, made a big jump to cross the river. The deer was with young, and this extreme exertion and sudden fright made her give birth to a little fawn, and immediately after she fell dead. The fawn fell into the water and was being carried rapidly away by the foaming stream, when it caught the eyes of the king. The king rose from his position of meditation and rescuing the fawn from the water, took it to his cottage, made a fire, and with care and attention fondled the little thing back to life. Then the kindly sage took the fawn under his protection, bringing it up on soft grass and fruits. The fawn thrived under the paternal care of the retired monarch, and grew into a beautiful deer. Then, he whose mind had been strong enough to break away from lifelong attachment to power, position, and family, became attached to the deer which he had saved from the stream. And as he became fonder and fonder of the deer, the less and less he could concentrate his mind upon the Lord. When the deer went out to graze in the forest, if it were late in returning, the mind of the royal sage would become anxious and worried. He would think, 'Perhaps my little one has been attacked by some tiger—or perhaps some other danger has befallen it; otherwise, why is it late?'

Some years passed in this way, but one day death came, and the royal sage laid himself down to die. But his mind, instead of being intent upon the Self, was thinking about the deer; and with his eyes fixed upon the sad looks of his beloved deer, his soul left the body. As the result of this, in the next birth he was born as a deer. But no Karma is lost, and all the great and good deeds done by him as a king and sage bore their fruit. This deer was a born Jatismara, and remembered his past birth, though he was bereft of speech and was living in an animal body. He always left his companions and was instinctively drawn to graze near hermitages where oblations were offered and the Upanishads were preached.

After the usual years of a deer's life had been spent, it died and was next born as the youngest son of a rich Brahmin. And in that life also, he remembered all his past, and even in his childhood was determined no more to get entangled in the good and evil of life. The child, as it grew up, was strong and healthy, but would not speak a word, and lived as one inert and insane, for fear of getting mixed up with worldly affairs. His thoughts were always on the Infinite, and he lived only to wear out his past Prarabdha Karma. In course of time the father died, and the sons divided the property among themselves; and thinking that the youngest was a dumb, good-for-nothing man, they seized his share. Their charity, however, extended only so far as to give him enough food to live upon. The wives of the brothers were often very harsh to him, putting him to do all the hard work; and if he was unable to do everything they wanted, they would treat him very unkindly. But he showed neither vexation nor fear, and neither did he speak a word. When they persecuted him very much, he would stroll out of the house and sit under a tree, by the hour, until their wrath was appeased, and then he would quietly go home again.

One day; when the wives of the brothers had treated him with more than usual unkindness, Bharata went out of the house, seated himself under the shadow of a tree and rested. Now it happened that the king of the country was passing by, carried in a palanquin on the shoulders of bearers. One of the bearers had unexpectedly fallen ill, and so his attendants were looking about for a man to replace him. They came upon Bharata seated under a tree; and seeing he was a strong young man, they asked him if he would take the place of the sick man in bearing the king's palanquin. But Bharata did not reply. Seeing that he was so able-bodied, the king's servants caught hold of him and placed the pole on his shoulders. Without speaking a word, Bharata went on. Very soon after this, the king remarked that the palanquin was not being evenly carried, and looking out of the palanquin addressed the new bearer, saying 'Fool, rest a while; if thy shoulders pain thee, rest a while.' Then Bharata laying the pole of the palanquin down, opened his lips for the first time in his life, and spoke, 'Whom dost thou, O King, call a fool? Whom dost thou ask to lay down the palanquin? Who dost thou say is weary? Whom dost thou address as 'thou'? If thou meanest, O King, by the word 'thee' this mass of flesh, it is composed of the same matter as thine; it is unconscious, and it knoweth no weariness, it knoweth no pain. If it is the mind, the mind is the same as thine; it is universal. But if the word 'thee' is applied to something beyond that, then it is the Self, the Reality in me, which is the same as in thee, and it is the One in the universe. Dost thou mean, O King, that the Self can ever be weary, that It can ever be tired, that It can ever be hurt? I did not want, O King—this body did not want—to trample upon the poor worms crawling on the road, and therefore, in trying to avoid them, the palanquin moved unevenly. But the Self was never tired; It was never weak; It never bore the pole of the palanquin: for It is omnipotent and omnipresent.' And so he dwelt eloquently on the nature of the soul, and on the highest knowledge, etc. The king, who was proud of his learning, knowledge, and philosophy, alighted from the palanquin, and fell at the feet of Bharata, saying, 'I ask thy pardon, O mighty one, I did not know that thou wast a sage, when I asked thee to carry me.' Bharata blessed him and departed. He then resumed the even tenor of his previous life. When Bharata left the body, he was freed for ever from the bondage of birth.

31

ON FANATICISM

There are fanatics of various kinds. Some people are wine fanatics and cigar fanatics. Some think that if men gave up smoking cigars, the world would arrive at the millennium. Women are generally amongst these fanatics. There was a young lady here one day, in this class. She was one of a number of ladies in Chicago who have built a house where they take in the working people and give them music and gymnastics. One day this young lady was talking about the evils of the world and said she knew the remedy. I asked, 'How do you know?' and she answered, 'Have you seen Hull House?' In her opinion, this Hull House is the one panacea for all the evils that flesh is heir to. This will grow upon her. I am sorry for her. There are some fanatics in India who think that if a woman could marry again when her husband died, it would cure all evil. This is fanaticism.

When I was a boy I thought that fanaticism was a great element in work, but now, as I grow older, I find out that it is not.

There may be a woman who would steal and make no objection to taking someone else's bag and going away with it. But perhaps that woman does not smoke. She becomes a smoke fanatic, and as soon as she finds a man smoking, she strongly disapproves of him, because he smokes a cigar. There may be a man who goes about cheating people; there is no trusting him; no woman is safe with him. But perhaps this scoundrel does not drink wine. If so, he sees nothing good in anyone who drinks wine. All these wicked things that he himself does are of no consideration. This is only natural human selfishness and one-sidedness.

You must also remember that the world has God to govern it, and He has not left it to our charity. The Lord God is its Governor and Maintainer, and in spite of these wine fanatics and cigar fanatics, and all sorts of marriage fanatics, it would go on. If all these persons were to die, it would go on none the worse.

Do you not remember in your own history how the 'Mayflower' people came out here, and began to call themselves Puritans? They were very pure and good as far as they went, until they began to persecute other people; and throughout the history of mankind it has been the same. Even those that run away from persecution indulge in persecuting others as soon as a favourable opportunity to do so occurs.

In ninety cases out of a hundred, fanatics must have bad livers, or they are dyspeptics, or are in some way diseased. By degrees even physicians will find out that fanaticism is a kind of disease. I have seen plenty of it. The Lord save me from it!

My experience comes to this, that it is rather wise to avoid all sorts of fanatical reforms. This world is slowly going on; let it go slowly. Why are you in a hurry? Sleep well and keep your nerves in good order; eat right food, and have sympathy with the world. Fanatics only make hatred. Do you mean to say that the temperance fanatic loves these poor people who become drunkards? A fanatic is a fanatic simply because he expects to get something for himself in return. As soon as the battle is over, he goes for the spoil. When you come out of the company of fanatics you may learn how really to love and sympathize. And the more you attain of love and sympathy, the less will be your power to condemn these poor creatures; rather you will sympathize with their faults. It will become possible for you to sympathize with the drunkard and to know that he is also a man like yourself. You will then try to understand the many circumstances that are dragging him down, and feel that if you had been in his place you would perhaps have committed suicide. I remember a woman whose husband was a great drunkard, and she complained to me of his becoming so. I replied, 'Madam, if there were twenty millions of wives like yourself, all husbands would become drunkards.' I am convinced that a large number of drunkards are manufactured by their wives. My business is to tell the truth and not to flatter anyone. These unruly women from whose minds the words *bear* and *forbear* are gone for ever, and whose false ideas of independence lead them to think that men should be at their feet, and who begin to howl as soon as men dare to say anything to them which they do not like—such women are becoming the bane of the world, and it is a wonder that they do not drive half the men in it to commit suicide. In this way things should not go on. Life is not so easy as they believe it to be; it is a more serious business!

A man must not only have faith but intellectual faith too. To make a man take up everything and believe it, would be to make him a lunatic. I once had a book sent me, which said I must believe everything told in it. It said there was no soul, but that there were gods and goddesses in heaven, and a thread of light going from each of our heads to heaven! How did the writer know all these things? She had been inspired, and wanted me to believe it too; and because I refused, she said, 'You must be a very bad man; there is no hope for you!' This is fanaticism.

32

WORK IS WORSHIP

The highest man *cannot* work, for there is no binding element, no attachment, no ignorance in him. A ship is said to have passed over a mountain of magnet ore, and all the bolts and bars were drawn out, and it went to pieces. It is in ignorance that struggle remains, because we are all really atheists. Real theists cannot work. We are atheists more or less. We do not see God or believe in Him. He is G-O-D to us, and nothing more. There are moments when we think He is near, but then we fall down again. When you see Him, who struggles for whom? Help the Lord! There is a proverb in our language, 'Shall we teach the Architect of the universe how to build?' So those are the highest of mankind who do not work. The next time you see these silly phrases about the world and how we must all help God and do this or that for Him, remember this. Do not think such thoughts; they are too selfish. All the work you do is subjective, is done for your own benefit. God has not fallen into a ditch for you and me to help Him out by building a hospital or something of that sort. He *allows* you to work. He allows you to exercise your muscles in this great gymnasium, not in order to help Him but that you may help yourself. Do you think even an ant will die for want of your help? Most arrant blasphemy! The world does not need you at all. The world goes on you are like a drop in the ocean. A leaf does not move, the wind does not blow without Him. Blessed are we that we are given the privilege of working for Him, not of helping Him. Cut out this word 'help' from your mind. You cannot help; it is blaspheming. You are here yourself at His pleasure. Do you mean to say, you help Him? You worship. When you give a morsel of food to the dog, you worship the dog as God. God is in that dog. He is the dog. He is all and in all. We are allowed to worship Him. Stand in that reverent attitude to the whole universe, and then will come perfect non-attachment. This should be your duty. This is the proper attitude of work. This is the secret taught by Karma-Yoga.

33

WORK WITHOUT MOTIVE

At the forty-second meeting of the Ramakrishna Mission held at the premises No. 57 Ramkanta Bose Street, Baghbazar, Calcutta, on the 20 March, 1898, Swami Vivekananda gave an address on 'Work without Motive', and spoke to the following effect:

When the Gita was first preached, there was then going on a great controversy between two sects. One party considered the Vedic Yajnas and animal sacrifices and such like Karmas to constitute the whole of religion. The other preached that the killing of numberless horses and cattle cannot be called religion. The people belonging to the latter party were mostly Sannyasins and followers of Jnana. They believed that the giving up of all work and the gaining of the knowledge of the Self was the only path to Moksha By the preaching of His great doctrine of work without motive, the Author of the Gita set at rest the disputes of these two antagonistic sects.

Many are of opinion that the Gita was not written at the time of the Mahabharata, but was subsequently added to it. This is not correct. The special teachings of the Gita are to be found in every part of the Mahabharata, and if the Gita is to be expunged, as forming no part of it, every other portion of it which embodies the same teachings should be similarly treated.

Now, what is the meaning of working without motive? Nowadays many understand it in the sense that one is to work in such a way that neither pleasure nor pain touches his mind. If this be its real meaning, then the animals might be said to work without motive. Some animals devour their own offspring, and they do not feel any pangs at all in doing so. Robbers ruin other people by robbing them of their possessions; but if they feel quite callous to pleasure or pain, then they also would be working without motive. If the meaning of it be such, then one who has a stony heart, the worst of criminals, might be considered to be working without motive. The walls have no feelings of pleasure or pain, neither has a stone, and it cannot be said that they are working without motive. In the above sense the doctrine is a potent instrument in the hands of the wicked. They would go on doing wicked deeds, and would pronounce themselves as working without a motive. If such be the significance of working without a motive, then a fearful doctrine has been put forth by the preaching of the Gita. Certainly this is not the meaning. Furthermore, if we look into the lives of those who were connected with the preaching of the Gita, we should find them living quite a different life. Arjuna killed Bhishma and Drona in battle, but withal, he sacrificed all his self-interest and desires and his lower self millions of times.

Gita teaches Karma-Yoga. We should work through Yoga (concentration). In such concentration in action (Karma-Yoga), there is no consciousness of the lower ego present. The consciousness that I am doing this and that is never present when one works through Yoga. The Western people do not understand this. They say that if there be no consciousness of ego, if this ego is gone, how then can a man work? But when one works with concentration, losing all consciousness of oneself the work that is done will be infinitely better, and this every one may have experienced in his own life. We perform many works subconsciously, such as the digestion of food etc., many others consciously, and others again by becoming immersed in Samadhi as it were, when there is no consciousness of the smaller ego. If the painter, losing the consciousness of his ego, becomes completely immersed in his painting, he will be able to produce masterpieces. The good cook concentrates his whole self on the food-material he handles; he loses all other consciousness for the time being. But they are only able to do perfectly a single work in this way, to which they are habituated. The Gita teaches that all works should be done thus. He who is one with the Lord through Yoga performs all his works by becoming immersed in concentration, and does not seek any personal benefit. Such a performance of work brings only good to the world, no evil can come out of it. Those who work thus never do anything for themselves.

The result of every work is mixed with good and evil. There is no good work that has not a touch of evil in it. Like smoke round the fire, some evil always clings to work. We should engage in such works as bring the largest amount of good and the smallest measure of evil. Arjuna killed Bhishma and Drona; if this had not been done Duryodhana could not have been conquered, the force of evil would have triumphed over the force of good, and thus a great calamity would have fallen on the country. The government of the country would have been usurped by a body of proud unrighteous kings, to the great misfortune of the people. Similarly, Shri Krishna killed Kamsa, Jarasandha, and others who were tyrants, but not a single one of his deeds was done for himself. Every one of them was for the good of others. We are reading the Gita by candle-light, but numbers of insects are being burnt to death. Thus it is seen that some evil clings to work. Those who work without any consciousness of their lower ego are not affected with evil, for they work for the good of the world. To work without motive, to work unattached, brings the highest bliss and freedom. This secret of Karma-Yoga is taught by the Lord Shri Krishna in the Gita.

34

SADHANAS OR PREPARATIONS
FOR HIGHER LIFE

If atavism gains, you go down; if evolution gains, you go on. Therefore, we must not allow atavism to take place. Here, in my own body, is the first work of the study. We are too busy trying to mend the ways of our neighbours, that is the difficulty. We must begin with our own bodies. The heart, the liver, etc., are all atavistic; bring them back into consciousness, control them, so that they will obey your commands and act up to your wishes. There was a time when we had control of the liver; we could shake the whole skin, as can the cow. I have seen many people bring the control back by sheer hard practise. Once an impress is made, it is there. Bring back all the submerged activities—the vast ocean of action. This is the first part of the great study, and it is absolutely necessary for our social well-being. On the other hand, only the consciousness need not be studied all the time.

Then there is the other part of study, not so necessary in our social life, which tends to liberation. Its direct action is to free the soul, to take the torch into the gloom, to clean out what is behind, to shake it up or even defy it, and to make us march onward piercing the gloom. That is the goal—the superconscious. Then when that state is reached, this very man becomes divine, becomes free. And to the mind thus trained to transcend all, gradually this universe will begin to give up its secrets; the book of nature will be read chapter after chapter, till the goal is attained, and we pass from this valley of life and death to that One, where death and life do not exist, and we know the Real and become the Real.

The first thing necessary is a quiet and peaceable life. If I have to go about the world the whole day to make a living, it is hard for me to attain to anything very high in this life. Perhaps in another life I shall be born under more propitious circumstances. But if I am earnest enough, these very circumstances will change even in this birth. Was there anything you did not get which you really wanted? It could not be. For it is the want that creates the body. It is the light that has bored the holes, as it were, in your head, called the eyes. If the light had not existed, you would have had no eyes. It is sound that had made the ears. The object of perception existed first, before you made the organ. In a few hundred thousand years or earlier, we may have other organs to perceive electricity and other things. There is no desire for a peaceful mind. Desire will not come unless there is something outside to fulfil it. The outside something just bores a hole in the body, as it were, and tries to get into the mind. So, when the desire will arise to have a peaceful, quiet life, that *shall come* where everything shall be propitious for the development of the mind—you may take that as my experience. It may come after thousands of lives, but it must come. Hold on to that, the desire. You cannot have the strong desire if its object was not outside for you already. Of course you must understand, there is a difference between desire and desire. The master said, 'My child, if you desire after God, God shall come to you.' The disciple did not understand his master fully. One day both went to bathe in a river, and the master said, 'Plunge in', and the boy did so. In a moment the master was upon him, holding him down. He would not let the boy come up. When the boy struggled and was exhausted, he let him go. 'Yes, my child, how did you feel there;' 'Oh, the desire for a breath of air!' 'Do you have that kind of desire for God?' 'No, sir.' 'Have that kind of desire for God and you shall have God.'

That, without which we cannot live, must come to us. If it did not come to us, life could not go on.

If you want to be a Yogi, you must be free and place yourself in circumstances where you are alone and free from all anxiety. He who desires for a comfortable and nice life and at the same time wants to realize the Self is like the fool who, wanting to cross the river, caught hold of a crocodile mistaking it for a log of wood. 'Seek ye first the Kingdom of God and His righteousness, and all these things shall be added unto you.' Unto him everything who does not care for anything. Fortune is like a flirt; she cares not for him who wants her, but she is at the feet of him who does not care for her. Money comes and showers itself upon one who does not care for it; so does fame come in abundance until it is a trouble and a burden. They always come to the Master. The slave never gets anything. The Master is he who can live in spite of them, whose life does not depend upon the little, foolish things of the world. Live for an ideal, and that one ideal alone. Let it be so great, so strong, that there may be nothing else left in the mind; no place for anything else, no time for anything else.

How some people give all their energies, time, brain, body, and everything, to become rich! They have no time for breakfast! Early in the morning they are out and at work! They die in the attempt—ninety per cent of them—and the rest when they make money, cannot enjoy it. That is grand! I do not say it is bad to try to be rich. It is marvellous, wonderful. Why, what does it show? It shows that one can have the same amount of energy and struggle for freedom as one has for money. We know we have to give up money and all other things when we die, and yet, see the amount of energy we can put forth for them. But we, the same human beings, should we not put forth a thousandfold more strength and energy to acquire that which never fades, but which remains to us for ever? For this is the one great friend, our own good deeds, our own spiritual excellence, that follows us beyond the grave. Everything else is left behind here with the body.

That is the one great first step—the real desire for the ideal. Everything comes easy after that. That the Indian mind found out; there, in India, men go to any length to find truth. But here, in the West, the difficulty is that everything is made so easy. It is not truth, but development, that is the great aim. The struggle is the great lesson. Mind you, the great benefit in this life is struggle. It is through that we pass. If there is any road to Heaven, it is through Hell. Through Hell to Heaven is always the way. When the soul has wrestled with circumstance and has met death, a thousand times death on the way, but nothing daunted has struggled forward again and again and yet again—then the soul comes out as a giant and laughs at the ideal he has been struggling for, because he finds how much greater is he than the ideal. I am the end, my own Self, and nothing else, for what is there to compare to me own Self? Can a bag of gold be the ideal of my Soul? Certainly not! My Soul is the highest ideal that I can have. Realizing my own real nature is the one goal of my life.

There is nothing that is absolutely evil. The devil has a place here as well as God, else he would not be here. Just as I told you, it is through Hell that we pass to Heaven. Our mistakes have places here. Go on! Do not look back if you think you have done something that is not right. Now, do you believe you could be what you are today, had you not made those mistakes before? Bless your mistakes, then. They have been angels unawares. Blessed be torture! Blessed be happiness! Do not care what be your lot. Hold on to the ideal. March on! Do not look back upon little mistakes and things. In this battlefield of ours, the dust of mistakes must be raised. Those who are so thin-skinned that they cannot bear the dust, let them get out of the ranks.

So, then, this tremendous determination to struggle a hundredfold more determination than that which you put forth to gain anything which belongs to this life, is the first great preparation.

And then along with it, there must be meditation Meditation is the one thing. Meditate! The greatest thing is meditation. It is the nearest approach to spiritual life—the mind meditating. It is the one moment in our daily life that we are not at all material—the Soul thinking of Itself, free from all matter—this marvellous touch of the Soul!

The body is our enemy, and yet is our friend. Which of you can bear the sight of misery? And which of you cannot do so when you see it only as a painting? Because it is unreal, we do not identify ourselves with it, eve know it is only a painting; it cannot bless us, it cannot hurt us. The most terrible misery painted upon a price of canvas, we may even enjoy; we praise the technique of the artist, we wonder at his marvellous genius, even though the scene he paints is most horrible. That is the secret; that non-attachment. Be the Witness.

No breathing, no physical training of Yoga, nothing is of any use until you reach to the idea, 'I am the Witness.' Say, when the tyrant hand is on your neck, 'I am the Witness! I am the Witness!' Say, 'I am the Spirit! Nothing external can touch me.' When evil thoughts arise, repeat that, give that sledge-hammer blow on their heads, 'I am the Spirit! I am the Witness, the Ever-Blessed! I have no reason to do, no reason to suffer, I have finished with everything, I am the Witness. I am in my picture gallery—this universe is my museum, I am looking at these successive paintings. They are all beautiful. Whether good or evil. I see the marvellous skill, but it is all one. Infinite flames of the Great Painter!' Really speaking, there is naught—neither volition, nor desire. He is all. He—She—the Mother, is playing, and we are like dolls, Her helpers in this play. Here, She puts one now in the garb of a beggar, another moment in the garb of a king, the next moment in the garb of a saint, and again in the garb of a devil. We are putting on different garbs to help the Mother Spirit in Her play.

When the baby is at play, she will not come even if called by her mother. But when she finishes her play, she will rush to her mother, and will have no play. So there come moments in our life, when we feel our play is finished, and we want to rush to the Mother. Then all our toil here will be of no value; men, women, and children—wealth, name, and fame, joys and glories of life—punishments and successes—will be no more, and the whole life will seem like a show. We shall see only the infinite rhythm going on, endless and purposeless, going we do not know where. Only this much shall we say; our play is done.

35

THE COSMOS AND THE SELF

Everything in nature rises from some fine seed-forms, becomes grosser and grosser, exists for a certain time, and again goes back to the original fine form. Our earth, for instance, has come out of a nebulous form which, becoming colder and colder, turned into this crystallized planet upon which we live, and in the future it will again go to pieces and return to its rudimentary nebulous form. This is happening in the universe, and has been through time immemorial. This is the whole history of man, the whole history of nature, the whole history of life.

Every evolution is preceded by an involution. The whole of the tree is present in the seed, its cause. The whole of the human being is present in that one protoplasm. The whole of this universe is present in the cosmic fine universe. Everything is present in its cause, in its fine form. This evolution, or gradual unfolding of grosser and grosser forms, is true, but each case has been preceded by an involution. The whole of this universe must have been involute before it came out, and has unfolded itself in all these various forms to be involved again once more. Take, for instance, the life of a little plant. We find two things that make the plant a unity by itself—its growth and development, its decay and death. These make one unity the plant life. So, taking that plant life as only one link in the chain of life, we may take the whole series as one life, beginning in the protoplasm and ending in the most perfect man. Man is one link, and the various beasts, the lower animals, and plants are other links. Now go back to the source, the finest particles from which they started, and take the whole series as but one life, and you will find that every evolution here is the evolution of something which existed previously.

Where it begins, there it ends. What is the end of this universe? Intelligence, is it not? The last to come in the order of creation, according to the evolutionists, was intelligence. That being so, it must be the cause, the beginning of creation also. At the beginning that intelligence remains involved, and in the end it gets evolved. The sum total of the intelligence displayed in the universe must therefore be the involved universal intelligence unfolding itself, and this universal intelligence is what we call God, from whom we come and to whom we return, as the scriptures say. Call it by any other name, you cannot deny that in the beginning there is that infinite cosmic intelligence.

What makes a compound? A compound is that in which the causes have combined and become the effect. So these compound things can be only within the circle of the law of causation; so far as the rules of cause and effect go, so far can we have compounds and combinations. Beyond that it is impossible to talk of combinations, because no law holds good therein. Law holds good only in that universe which we see, feel, hear, imagine, dream, and beyond that we cannot place any idea of law. That is our universe which we sense or imagine, and we sense what is within our direct perception, and we imagine what is in our mind. What is beyond the body is beyond the senses, and what is beyond the mind is beyond the imagination, and therefore is beyond our universe, and therefore beyond the law of causation. The Self of man being beyond the law of causation is not a compound, is not the effect of any cause, and therefore is ever free and is the ruler of everything that is within law. Not being a compound, it will never die, because death means going back to the component parts, destruction means going back to the cause. Because it cannot die, it cannot live; for both life and death are modes of manifestation of the same thing. So the Soul is beyond life and death. You were never born, and you will never die. Birth and death belong to the body only.

The doctrine of monism holds that this universe is all that exists; gross or fine, it is all here; the effect and the cause are both here; the explanation is here. What is known as the particular is simply repetition in a minute form of the universal. We get our idea of the universe from the study of our own Souls, and what is true there also holds good in the outside universe. The ideas of heaven and all these various places, even if they be true, are in the universe. They altogether make this Unity. The first idea, therefore, is that of a Whole, a Unit, composed of various minute particles, and each one of us is a part, as it were, of this Unit. As manifested beings we appear separate, but as a reality we are one. The more we think ourselves separate from this Whole, the more miserable we become. So, Advaita is the basis of ethics.

36

WHO IS A REAL GURU?

A real Guru is one who is born from time to time as a repository of spiritual force which he transmits to future generations through successive links of Guru and Shishya (disciple). The current of this spirit-force changes its course from time to time, just as a mighty stream of water opens up a new channel and leaves the old one for good. Thus, it is seen that old sects of religion grow lifeless in the course of time, and new sects arise with the fire of life in them. Men who are truly wise commit themselves to the mercy of that particular sect through which the current of life flows. Old forms of religion are like the skeletons of once mighty animals, preserved in museums. They should be regarded with the due honour. They cannot satisfy the true cravings of the soul for the Highest, just as a dead mango-tree cannot satisfy the cravings of a man for luscious mangoes.

The one thing necessary is to be stripped of our vanities—the sense that we possess any spiritual wisdom—and to surrender ourselves completely to the guidance of our Guru. The Guru only knows what will lead us towards perfection. We are quite blind to it. We do not know anything. This sort of humility will open the door of our heart for spiritual truths. Truth will never come into our minds so long as there will remain the faintest shadow of Ahamkara (egotism). All of you should try to root out this devil from your heart. Complete self-surrender is the only way to spiritual illumination.

37

ON ART

The secret of Greek Art is its imitation of nature even to the minutest details; whereas the secret of Indian Art is to represent the ideal. The energy of the Greek painter is spent in perhaps painting a piece of flesh, and he is so successful that a dog is deluded into taking it to be a real bit of meat and so goes to bite it. Now, what glory is there in merely imitating nature? Why not place an actual bit of flesh before the dog?

The Indian tendency, on the other hand, to represent the ideal, the supersensual, has become degraded into painting grotesque images. Now, true Art can be compared to a lily which springs from the ground, takes its nourishment from the ground, is in touch with the ground, and yet is quite high above it. So Art must be in touch with nature—and wherever that touch is gone, Art degenerates—yet it must be above nature.

Art is—representing the beautiful. There must be Art in everything.

The difference between architecture and building is that the former expresses an idea, while the latter is merely a structure built on economical principles. The value of matter depends solely on its capacities of expressing *ideas*.

The artistic faculty was highly developed in our Lord Shri Ramakrishna, and he used to say that without this faculty none can be truly spiritual.

38

ON LANGUAGE

Simplicity is the secret. My ideal of language is my Master's language, most colloquial and yet most expressive. It must express the thought which is intended to be conveyed.

The attempt to make the Bengali language perfect in so short a time will make it cut and dried. Properly speaking, it has no verbs. Michael Madhusudan Dutt attempted to remedy this in poetry. The greatest poet in Bengal was Kavikankana. The best prose in Sanskrit is Patanjali's *Mahabhashya*. There the language is vigorous. The language of *Hitopadesha* is not bad, but the language of *Kadambari* is an example of degradation.

The Bengali language must be modelled not after the Sanskrit, but rather after the Pali, which has a strong resemblance to it. In coining or translating technical terms in Bengali, one must, however, use all Sanskrit words for them, and an attempt should be made to coin new words. For this purpose, if a collection is made from a Sanskrit dictionary of all those technical terms, then it ill help greatly the constitution of the Bengali language.

39

THE SANNYASIN

In explanation of the term Sannyasin, the Swami in the course of one of his lectures in Boston said:

When a man has fulfilled the duties and obligations of that stage of life in which he is born, and his aspirations lead him to seek a spiritual life and to abandon altogether the worldly pursuits of possession, fame, or power, when, by the growth of insight into the nature of the world, he sees its impermanence, its strife, its misery, and the paltry nature of its prizes, and turns away from all these—then he seeks the True, the Eternal Love, the Refuge. He makes complete renunciation (Sannyasa) of all worldly position, property, and name, and wanders forth into the world to live a life of self-sacrifice and to persistently seek spiritual knowledge, striving to excel in love and compassion and to acquire lasting insight. Gaining these pearls of wisdom by years of meditation, discipline, and inquiry, he in his turn becomes a teacher and hands on to disciples, lay or professed, who may seek them from him, all that he can of wisdom and beneficence.

A Sannyasin cannot belong to any religion, for his is a life of independent thought, which draws from all religions; his is a life of realization, not merely of theory or belief, much less of dogma.

40

ON BHAKTI-YOGA

The dualist thinks you cannot be moral unless you have a God with a rod in His hand, ready to punish you. How is that? Suppose a horse had to give us a lecture on morality, one of those very wretched cab-horses who move only with the whip, to which he has become accustomed. He begins to speak about human beings and says that they must be very immoral. Why? 'Because I know they are not whipped regularly.' The fear of the whip only makes one more immoral.

You all say there is a God and that He is an omnipresent Being. Close your eyes and think what He is. What do you find? Either you are thinking, in bringing the idea of omnipresence in your mind, of the sea, or the blue sky, or an expanse of meadow, or such things as you have seen in your life. If that is so, you do not mean anything by omnipresent God; it has no meaning at all to you. So with every other attribute of God. What idea have we of omnipotence or omniscience? We have none. Religion is realising, and I shall call you a worshipper of God when you have become able to realize the Idea. Before that it is the spelling of words and no more. It is this power of realization that makes religion; no amount of doctrines or philosophies, or ethical books, that you may have stuffed into your brain, will matter much— only what you *are* and what you have *realized*.

The Personal God is the same Absolute looked at through the haze of Maya. When we approach Him with the five senses, we can see Him only as the Personal God. The idea is that the Self cannot be objectified. How can the Knower know Itself? But It can cast a shadow, as it were, if that can be called objectification. So the highest form of that shadow, that attempt at objectifying Itself, is the Personal God. The Self is the eternal subject, and we are struggling all the time to objectify that Self. And out of that struggle has come this phenomenal universe and what we call matter, and so on. But these are very weak attempts, and the highest objectification of the Self possible to us is the Personal God. This objectification is an attempt to reveal our own nature. According to the Sankhya, nature is showing all these experiences to the soul, and when it has got real experience it will know its own nature. According to the Advaita Vedantist, the soul is struggling to reveal itself. After long struggle, it finds that the subject must always remain the subject; and then begins non-attachment, and it becomes free.

When a man has reached that perfect state, he is of the same nature as the Personal God. 'I and my Father are one.' He knows that he is one with Brahman, the Absolute, and projects himself as the Personal God does. He plays—as even the mightiest of kings may sometimes play with dolls.

Some imaginations help to break the bondage of the rest. The whole universe is imagination, but one set of imaginations will cure another set. Those that tell us that there is sin and sorrow and death in the world are terrible. But the other set—thou art holy, there is God, there is no pain—these are good, and help to break the bondage of the others. The highest imagination that can break all the links of the chain is that of the Personal God.

To go and say, 'Lord, take care of this thing and give me that; Lord, I give you my little prayer and you give me this thing of daily necessity; Lord, cure my headache', and all that—these are not Bhakti. They are the lowest states of religion. They are the lowest form of Karma. If a man uses all his mental energy in seeking to satisfy his body and its wants, show me the difference between him and an animal. Bhakti is a higher thing higher than even desiring heaven. The idea of heaven is of a place of intensified enjoyment. How can that be God?

Only the fools rush after sense-enjoyments. It is easy to live in the senses. It is easier to run in the old groove, eating and drinking; but what these modern philosophers want to tell you is to take these comfortable ideas and put the stamp of religion on them. Such a doctrine is dangerous. Death lies in the senses. Life on the plane of the Spirit is the only life, life on any other plane is mere death; the whole of this life can be only described as a gymnasium. We must go beyond it to enjoy real life.

As long as *touch-me-not-ism* is your creed and the kitchen-pot your deity, you cannot rise spiritually. All the petty differences between religion and religion are mere word-struggles, nonsense. Everyone thinks, 'This is my original idea', and wants to have things his own way. That is how struggles come.

In criticising another, we always foolishly take one especially brilliant point as the whole of our life and compare that with the dark ones in the life of another. Thus we make mistakes in judging individuals.

Through fanaticism and bigotry a religion can be propagated very quickly, no doubt, but the preaching of that religion is firm-based on solid ground, which gives everyone liberty to his opinions and thus uplifts him to a higher path, though this process is slow

First deluge the land (India) with spiritual ideas, then other ideas will follow The gift of spirituality and spiritual knowledge is the highest, for it saves from many and many a birth; the next gift is secular knowledge, as it opens the eyes of human beings towards that spiritual knowledge; the next is the saving of life; and the fourth is the gift of food.

Even if the body goes in practising Sadhanas (austerities for realization), let it go; what of that? Realization will come in the fullness of time, by living constantly in the company of Sadhus (holy men). A time comes when one understands that to serve a man even by preparing a Chhilam (earthen pipe) of tobacco is far greater than millions of meditations. He who can properly prepare a Chhilam of tobacco can also properly meditate.

Gods are nothing but highly developed dead men. We can get help from them.

Anyone and everyone cannot be an Acharya (teacher of mankind); but many may become Mukta (liberated). The whole world seems like a dream to the liberated, but the Acharya has to take up his stand between the two states. He must have the knowledge that the world is true, or else why should he teach? Again, if he has not realized the world as a dream, then he is no better than an ordinary man, and what could he teach? The Guru has to bear the disciple's burden of sin; and that is the reason why diseases and other ailments appear even in the bodies of powerful Acharyas. But if he be imperfect, they attack his mind also, and he falls. So it is a difficult thing to be an Acharya.

It is easier to become a Jivanmukta (free in this very life) than to be an Acharya. For the former knows the world as a dream and has no concern with it; but an Acharya knows it as a dream and yet has to remain in it and work. It is not possible for everyone to be an Acharya. He is an Acharya through whom the divine power acts. The body in which one becomes an Acharya is very different from that of any other man. There is a science for keeping that body in a perfect state. His is the most delicate organism, very susceptible, capable of feeling intense joy and intense suffering. He is abnormal.

In every sphere of life we find that it is the person within that triumphs, and that personality is the secret of all success.

Nowhere is seen such sublime unfoldment of feeling as in Bhagavan Shri Krishna Chaitanya, the Prophet of Nadia.

Shri Ramakrishna is a force. You should not think that his doctrine is this or that. But he is a power, living even now in his disciples and working in the world. I saw him growing in his ideas. He is still growing. Shri Ramakrishna was both a Jivanmukta and an Acharya.

41

ISHVARA AND BRAHMAN

In reply to a question as to the exact position of Ishvara in Vedantic Philosophy, the Swami Vivekananda, while in Europe, gave the following definition:

'Ishvara is the sum total of individuals, yet He is an Individual, as the human body is a unit, of which each cell is an individual. Samashti or collected equals God; Vyashti or analysed equals the Jiva. The existence of Ishvara, therefore, depends on that of Jiva, as the body on the cell, and vice versa. Thus, Jiva and Ishvara are coexistent beings; when one exists, the other must. Also, because, except on our earth, in all the higher spheres, the amount of good being vastly in excess of the amount of evil, the sum total (Ishvara) may be said to be all-good. Omnipotence and omniscience are obvious qualities and need no argument to prove from the very fact of totality. Brahman is beyond both these and is not a conditioned state; it is the only Unit not composed of many units, the principle which runs through all from a cell to God, without which nothing can exist; and whatever is real is that principle, or Brahman. When I think I am Brahman, I alone exist; so with others. Therefore, each one is the whole of that principle.'

42

ON JNANA-YOGA

All souls are playing, some consciously, some unconsciously. Religion is learning to play consciously.

The same law which holds good in our worldly life also holds good in our religious life and in the life of the cosmos. It is one, it is universal. It is not that religion is guided by one law and the world by another. The flesh and the devil are but degrees of difference from God Himself.

Theologians, philosophers, and scientists in the West are ransacking everything to get a proof that they live afterwards! What a storm in a tea-cup! There are much higher things to think of. What silly superstition is this, that you ever die! It requires no priests or spirits or ghosts to tell us that we shall not die. It is the most self-evident of all truths. No man can imagine his own annihilation. The idea of immortality is inherent in man.

Wherever there is life, with it there is death. Life is the shadow of death, and death, the shadow of life. The line of demarcation is too fine to determine, too difficult to grasp, and most difficult to hold on to.

I do not believe in eternal progress, that we are growing on ever and ever in a straight line. It is too nonsensical to believe. There is no motion in a straight line. A straight line infinitely projected becomes a circle. The force sent out will complete the circle and return to its starting place.

There is no progress in a straight line. Every soul moves in a circle, as it were, and will have to complete it; and no soul can go so low but that there will come a time when it will have to go upwards. It may start straight down, but it has to take the upward curve to complete the circuit. We are all projected from a common centre, which is God, and will come back after completing the circuit to the centre from which we started.

Each soul is a circle. The centre is where the body is, and the activity is manifested there. You are omnipresent, though you have the consciousness of being concentrated in only one point. That point has taken up particles of matter and formed them into a machine to express itself. That through which it expresses itself is called the body. You are everywhere. When one body or machine fails you, the centre moves on and takes up other particles of matter, finer or grosser, and works through them. Here is man. And what is God? God is a circle with circumference nowhere and centre everywhere. Every point in that circle is living, conscious, active, and equally working. With our limited souls only one point is conscious, and that point moves forward and backward.

The soul is a circle whose circumference is nowhere (limitless), but whose centre is in some body. Death is but a change of centre. God is a circle whose circumference is nowhere, and whose centre is everywhere. When we can get out of the limited centre of body, we shall realize God, our true Self.

A tremendous stream is flowing towards the ocean, carrying little bits of paper and straw hither and thither on it. They may struggle to go back, but in the long run they; must flow down to the ocean. So you and I and all nature are like these little straws carried in mad currents towards that ocean of Life, Perfection, and God. We may struggle to go back, or float against the current and play all sorts of pranks, but in the long run we must go and join this great ocean of Life and Bliss.

Jnana (knowledge) is 'creedlessness'; but that does not mean that it despises creeds. It only means that a stage above and beyond creeds has been gained. The Jnani (true philosopher) strives to destroy nothing but to help all. All rivers roll their waters into the sea and become one. So all creeds should lead to Jnana and become one. Jnana teaches that the world should be renounced but not on that account abandoned. To live in the world and not to be of it is the true test of renunciation.

I cannot see how it can be otherwise than that all knowledge is stored up in us from the beginning. If you and I are little waves in the ocean, then that ocean is the background.

There is really no difference between matter, mind, and Spirit. They are only different phases of experiencing the One. This very world is seen by the five senses as matter, by the very wicked as hell, by the good as heaven, and by the perfect as God.

We cannot bring it to sense demonstration that Brahman is the only real thing; but we can point out that this is the only conclusion that one can come to. For instance, there must be this oneness in everything, even in common things. There is the human generalization, for example. We say that all the variety is created by name and form; yet when we want to grasp and separate it, it is nowhere. We can never see name or form or causes standing by themselves. So this phenomenon is Maya—something which depends on the noumenon and apart from it has no existence. Take a wave in the ocean. That wave exists so long as that quantity of water remains in a wave form; but as soon as it goes down and becomes the ocean, the wave ceases to exist. But the whole mass of water does not depend so much on its form. The ocean remains, while the wave form becomes absolute zero.

The real is one. It is the mind which makes it appear as many. When we perceive the diversity, the unity has gone; and as soon as we perceive the unity, the diversity has vanished. Just as in everyday life, when you perceive the unity, you do not perceive the diversity. At the beginning you start with unity. It is a curious fact that a Chinaman will not know the difference in appearance between one American and another; and you will not know the difference between different Chinamen.

It can be shown that it is the mind which makes things knowable. It is only things which have certain peculiarities that bring themselves within the range of the known and knowable. That which has no qualities is unknowable. For instance, there is some external world, X, unknown and unknowable. When I look at it, it is X plus mind. When I want to know the world, my mind contributes three quarters of it. The internal world is Y plus mind, and the external world X plus mind. All differentiation in either the external or internal world is created by the mind, and that which exists is unknown and unknowable. It is beyond the range of knowledge, and that which is beyond the range of knowledge can have no differentiation. Therefore, this X outside is the same as the Y inside, and therefore the real is one.

God does not reason. Why should you reason if you know? It is a sign of weakness that we have to go on crawling like worms to get a few facts, and then the whole thing tumbles down again. The Spirit is reflected in mind and in everything. It is the light of the Spirit that makes the mind sentient. Everything is an expression of the Spirit; the minds are so many mirrors. What you call love, fear, hatred, virtue, and vice are all reflections of the Spirit. When the reflector is base, the reflection is bad.

The real Existence is without manifestation. We cannot conceive It, because we should have to conceive through the mind, which is itself a manifestation. Its glory is that It is inconceivable. We must remember that in life the lowest and highest vibrations of light we do not see, but they are the opposite poles of existence. There are certain things which we do not know now, but which we can know. It is due to our ignorance that we do not know them. There are certain things which we can never know, because they are much higher than the highest vibrations of knowledge. But we are the Eternal all the time, although we cannot know it. Knowledge will be impossible there. The very fact of the limitations of the conception is the basis for its existence. For instance, there is nothing so certain in me as my Self; and yet I can only conceive of it as a body and mind, as happy or unhappy, as a man or a woman. At the same time, I try to conceive of it as it really is and find that there is no other way of doing it but by dragging it down; yet I am sure of that reality. 'No one, O beloved, loves the husband for the husband's sake, but because the Self is there. It is in and through the Self that she loves the husband. No one, O beloved, loves the wife for the wife's sake, but in and through the Self.' And that Reality is the only thing we know, because in and through It we know everything else; and yet we cannot conceive of It. How can we know the Knower? If we knew It, It would not be the knower, but the known; It would be objectified.

The man of highest realization exclaims, 'I am the King of kings; there is no king higher than I, I am the God of gods; there is no God higher than I! I alone exist, One without a second.' This monistic idea of the Vedanta seems to many, of course, very terrible, but that is on account of superstition.

We are the Self, eternally at rest and at peace. We must not weep; there is no weeping for the Soul. We in our imagination think that God is weeping on His throne out of sympathy. Such a God would not be worth attaining. Why should God weep at all? To weep is a sign of weakness, of bondage.

Seek the Highest, always the Highest, for in the Highest is eternal bliss. If I am to hunt, I will hunt the lion. If I am to rob, I will rob the treasury of the king. Seek the Highest.

Oh, One that cannot be confined or described! One that can be perceived in our heart of hearts! One beyond all compare, beyond limit, unchangeable like the blue sky! Oh, learn the All, holy one I Seek for nothing else!

Where changes of nature cannot reach, thought beyond all thought, Unchangeable, Immovable; whom all books declare, all sages worship; Oh, holy one, seek for nothing else!

Beyond compare, Infinite Oneness! No comparison is possible. Water above, water below, water on the right, water on the left; no wave on that water, no ripple, all silence; all eternal bliss. Such will come to thy heart. Seek for nothing else!

Why weepest thou, brother? There is neither death nor disease for thee. Why weepest thou, brother? There is neither misery nor misfortune for thee. Why weepest thou, brother? Neither change nor death was predicated of thee. Thou art Existence Absolute.

I know what God is—I cannot speak Him to you. I know not what God is—how can I speak Him to you? But seest thou not, my brother, that thou art He, thou art; He? Why go seeking God here and there? Seek not, and that is God. Be your own Self.

Thou art Our Father, our Mother, our dear Friend. Thou bearest the burden of the world. Help us to bear the burden of our lives. Thou art our Friend, our Lover, our Husband, Thou art ourselves!

43

THE CAUSE OF ILLUSION

The question—what is the cause of Maya (illusion)?—has been asked for the last three thousand years; and the only answer is: when the world is able to formulate a logical question, we shall answer it. The question is contradictory. Our position is that the Absolute has become this relative only apparently, that the Unconditioned has become the conditioned only in Maya. By the very admission of the Unconditioned, we admit that the Absolute cannot be acted upon by anything else. It is uncaused, which means that nothing outside Itself can act upon It. First of all, if It is unconditioned, It cannot have been acted upon by anything else. In the Unconditioned there cannot be time, space, or causation. That granted your question will be: 'What caused that which cannot be caused by anything to be changed into this?' Your question is only possible in the conditioned. But you take it out of the conditioned, and want to ask it in the Unconditioned. Only when the Unconditioned becomes conditioned, and space, time, and causation come in, can the question be asked. We can only say ignorance makes the illusion. The question is impossible. Nothing can have worked on the Absolute. There was no cause. Not that we do not know, or that we are ignorant; but It is above knowledge, and cannot be brought down to the plane of knowledge. We can use the words, 'I do not know' in two senses. In one way, they mean that we are lower than knowledge, and in the other way, that the thing is above knowledge. The X-rays have become known now. The very causes of these are disputed, but we are sure that we shall know them. Here we can say we do not know about the X-rays. But about the Absolute we cannot know. In the case of the X-rays we do not know, although they are within the range of knowledge; only we do not know them yet. But, in the other case, It is so much beyond knowledge that It ceases to be a matter of knowing. 'By what means can the Knower be known?' You are always yourself and cannot objectify yourself. This was one of the arguments used by our philosophers to prove immortality. If I try to think I am lying dead, what have I to imagine? That I am standing and looking down at myself, at some dead body. So that I cannot objectify myself.

44

EVOLUTION

In the matter of the projection of Akasha and Prana into manifested form and the return to fine state, there is a good deal of similarity between Indian thought and modern science. The moderns have their evolution, and so have the Yogis. But I think that the Yogis' explanation of evolution is the better one. 'The change of one species into another is attained by the infilling of nature.' The basic idea is that we are changing from one species to another, and that man is the highest species. Patanjali explains this 'infilling of nature' by the simile of peasants irrigating fields. Our education and progression simply mean taking away the obstacles, and by its own nature the divinity will manifest itself. This does away with all the struggle for existence. The miserable experiences of life are simply in the way, and can be eliminated entirely. They are not necessary for evolution. Even if they did not exist, we should progress. It is in the very nature of things to manifest themselves. The momentum is not from outside, but comes from inside. Each soul is the sum total of the universal experiences already coiled up there; and of all these experiences, only those will come out which find suitable circumstances.

So the external things can only give us the environments. These competitions and struggles and evils that we see are not the effect of the involution or the cause, but they are in the way. If they did not exist, still man would go on and evolve as God, because it is the very nature of that God to come out and manifest Himself. To my mind this seems very hopeful, instead of that horrible idea of competition. The more I study history, the more I find that idea to be wrong. Some say that if man did not fight with man, he would not progress. I also used to think so; but I find now that every war has thrown back human progress by fifty years instead of hurrying it forwards. The day will come when men will study history from a different light

300 • THE DEFINITIVE VIVEKANANDA

and find that competition is neither the cause nor the effect, simply a thing on the way, not necessary to evolution at all.

The theory of Patanjali is the only theory I think a rational man can accept. How much evil the modern system causes! Every wicked man has a licence to be wicked under it. I have seen in this country (America) physicists who say that all criminals ought to be exterminated and that that is the only way in which criminality can be eliminated from society. These environments can hinder, but they are not necessary to progress. The most horrible thing about competition is that one may conquer the environments, but that where one may conquer, thousands are crowded out. So it is evil at best. That cannot be good which helps only one and hinders the majority. Patanjali says that these struggles remain only through our ignorance, and are not necessary, and are not part of the evolution of man. It is just our impatience which creates them. We have not the patience to go and work our way out. For instance, there is a fire in a theatre, and only a few escape. The rest in trying to rush out crush one another down. That crush was not necessary for the salvation of the building nor of the two or three who escaped. If all had gone out slowly, not one would have been hurt. That is the case in life. The doors are open for us, and we can all get out without the competition and struggle; and yet we struggle. The struggle we create through our own ignorance, through impatience; we are in too great a hurry. The highest manifestation of strength is to keep ourselves calm and on our own feet.

45

BUDDHISM AND VEDANTA

The Vedanta philosophy is the foundation of Buddhism and everything else in India; but what we call the Advaita philosophy of the modern school has a great many conclusions of the Buddhists. Of course, the Hindus will not admit that—that is the orthodox Hindus, because to them the Buddhists are heretics. But there is a conscious attempt to stretch out the whole doctrine to include the heretics also.

The Vedanta has no quarrel with Buddhism. The idea of the Vedanta is to harmonize all. With the Northern Buddhists we have no quarrel at all. But the Burmese and Siamese and all the Southern Buddhists say that there is a phenomenal world, and ask what right we have to create a noumenal world behind this. The answer of the Vedanta is that this is a false statement. The Vedanta never contended that there was a noumenal and a phenomenal world. There is one. Seen through the senses it is phenomenal, but it is really the noumenal all the time. The man who sees the rope does not see the snake. It is either the rope or the snake, but never the two. So the Buddhistic statement of our position, that we believe there are two worlds, is entirely false. They have the right to say it is the phenomenal if they like, but no right to contend that other men have not the right to say it is the noumenal.

Buddhism does not want to have anything except phenomena. In phenomena alone is desire. It is desire that is creating all this. Modern Vedantists do not hold this at all. We say there is something which has become the will. Will is a manufactured something, a compound, not a 'simple'. There cannot be any will without an external object. We see that the very position that will created this universe is impossible. How could it? Have you ever known will without external stimulus? Desire cannot arise without stimulus, or in modern philosophic language, of nerve stimulus. Will is a sort of reaction of the brain, what the

Sankhya philosophers call Buddhi. This reaction must be preceded by action, and action presupposes an external universe. When there is no external universe, naturally there will be no will; and yet, according to your theory, it is will that created the universe. Who creates the will? Will is coexistent with the universe. Will is one phenomenon caused by the same impulse which created the universe. But philosophy must not stop there. Will is entirely personal; therefore we cannot go with Schopenhauer at all. Will is a compound—a mixture of the internal and the external. Suppose a man were born without any senses, he would have no will at all. Will requires something from outside, and the brain will get some energy from inside; therefore will is a compound, as much a compound as the wall or anything else. We do not agree with the will-theory of these German philosophers at all. Will itself is phenomenal and cannot be the Absolute. It is one of the many projections. There is something which is not will, but is manifesting itself as will. That I can understand. But that will is manifesting itself as everything else, I do not understand, seeing that we cannot have any conception of will, as separate from the universe. When that something which is freedom becomes will, it is caused by time, space, and causation. Take Kant's analysis. Will is within time, space, and causation. Then how can it be the Absolute? One cannot will without willing in time.

If we can stop all thought, then we know that we are beyond thought. We come to this by negation. When every phenomenon has been negatived, whatever remains, that is It. That cannot be expressed, cannot be manifested, because the manifestation will be, again, will.

46

ON THE VEDANTA PHILOSOPHY

The Vedantist says that a man is neither born nor dies nor goes to heaven, and that reincarnation is really a myth with regard to the soul. The example is given of a book being turned over. It is the book that evolves, not the man. Every soul is omnipresent, so where can it come or go? These births and deaths are changes in nature which we are mistaking for changes in us.

Reincarnation is the evolution of nature and the manifestation of the God within.

The Vedanta says that each life is built upon the past, and that when we can look back over the whole past we are free. The desire to be free will take the form of a religious disposition from childhood. A few years will, as it were, make all truth clear to one. After leaving this life, and while waiting for the next, a man is still in the phenomenal.

We would describe the soul in these words: This soul the sword cannot cut, nor the spear pierce; the fire cannot burn nor water melt it; indestructible, omnipresent is this soul. Therefore, weep not for it.

If it has been very bad, we believe that it will become good in the time to come. The fundamental principle is that there is eternal freedom for every one. Every one must come to it. We have to struggle, impelled by our desire to be free. Every other desire but that to be free is illusive. Every good action, the Vedantist says, is a manifestation of that freedom.

I do not believe that there will come a time when all the evil in the world will vanish. How could that be? This stream goes on. Masses of water go out at one end, but masses are coming in at the other end.

The Vedanta says that you are pure and perfect, and that there is a state beyond good and evil, and that is your own nature. It is higher even than good. Good is only a lesser differentiation than evil.

We have no theory of evil. We call it ignorance.

So far as it goes, all dealing with other people, all ethics, is in the phenomenal world. As a most complete statement of truth, we would not think of applying such things as ignorance to God. Of Him we say that He is Existence, Knowledge, and Bliss Absolute. Every effort of thought and speech will make the Absolute phenomenal and break Its character.

There is one thing to be remembered: that the assertion—I am God—cannot be made with regard to the sense-world. If you say in the sense-world that you are God, what is to prevent your doing wrong? So the affirmation of your divinity applies only to the noumenal. If I am God, I am beyond the tendencies of the senses and will not do evil. Morality of course is not the goal of man, but the means through which this freedom is attained. The Vedanta says that Yoga is one way that makes men realize this divinity. The Vedanta says this is done by the realization of the freedom within and that everything will give way to that. Morality and ethics will all range themselves in their proper places.

All the criticism against the Advaita philosophy can be summed up in this, that it does not conduce to sense-enjoyments; and we are glad to admit that.

The Vedanta system begins with tremendous pessimism, and ends with real optimism. We deny the sense-optimism but assert the real optimism of the Supersensuous. That real happiness is not in the senses but above the senses; and it is in every man. The sort of optimism which we see in the world is what will lead to ruin through the senses.

Abnegation has the greatest importance in our philosophy. Negation implies affirmation of the Real Self. The Vedanta is pessimistic so far as it negatives the world of the senses, but it is optimistic in its assertion of the real world.

The Vedanta recognizes the reasoning power of man a good deal, although it says there is something higher than intellect; but the road lies through intellect.

We need reason to drive out all the old superstitions; and what remains is Vedantism. There is a beautiful Sanskrit poem in which the sage says to himself: 'Why weepest thou, my friend? There is no fear nor death for thee. Why weepest thou? There is no misery for thee, for thou art like the infinite blue sky, unchangeable in thy nature. Clouds of all colours come before it, play for a moment, and pass away; it is the same sky. Thou hast only to drive away the clouds.'

We have to open the gates and clear the way. The water will rush in and fill in by its own nature, because it is there already.

Man is a good deal conscious, partly unconscious, and there is a possibility of getting beyond consciousness. It is only when we become *men* that we can go beyond all reason. The words *higher* or *lower* can be used only in the phenomenal world. To say them of the noumenal world is simply contradictory, because there is no differentiation there. Man-manifestation is the highest in the phenomenal world. The Vedantist says he is higher than the Devas. The gods will all have to die and will become men again, and in the man-body alone they will become perfect.

It is true that we create a system, but we have to admit that it is not perfect, because the reality must be beyond all systems. We are ready to compare it with other systems and are ready to show that this is the only rational system that can be; but it is not perfect, because reason is not perfect. It is, however, the only possible rational system that the human mind can conceive.

It is true to a certain extent that a system must disseminate itself to be strong. No system has disseminated itself so much as the Vedanta. It is the personal contact that teaches even now. A mass of reading does not make men; those who were real men were made so by personal contact. It is true that there are very few of these real men, but they will increase. Yet you cannot believe that there will come a day when we shall all be philosophers. We do not believe that there will come a time when there will be all happiness and no unhappiness.

Now and then we know a moment of supreme bliss, when we ask nothing, give nothing, know nothing but bliss. Then it passes, and we again see the panorama of the universe moving before us; and we know that it is but a mosaic work set upon God, who is the background of all things.

The Vedanta teaches that Nirvana can be attained here and now, that we do not have to wait for death to reach it. Nirvana is the realization of the Self; and after having once known that, if only for an instant, never again can one be deluded by the mirage of personality. Having eyes, we must see the apparent, but all the time we know what it is; we have found out its true nature. It is the screen that hides the Self, which is unchanging. The screen opens, and we find the Self behind it. All change is in the screen. In the saint the screen is thin, and the reality can almost shine through. In the sinner the screen is thick, and we are liable to lose sight of the truth that the Atman is there, as well as behind the saint's screen. When the screen is wholly removed, we find it really never existed—that we were the Atman and nothing else, even the screen is forgotten.

The two phases of this distinction in life are—first, that the man who knows the real Self, will not be affected by anything; secondly, that that man alone can do good to the world. That man alone will have seen the real motive of doing good to others, because there is only one, it cannot be called egoistic, because that would be differentiation. It is the only selflessness. It is the perception of the universal, not of the individual. Every case of love and sympathy is an assertion of this universal. 'Not I, but thou.' Help another because you are in him and he is in you, is the philosophical way of putting it. The real Vedantist alone will give up his life for a fellow-man without any compunction, because he knows he will not die. As long as there is one insect left in the world, he is living; as long as one mouth eats, he eats. So he goes on doing good to others; and is never hindered by the modern ideas of caring for the body. When a man reaches this point of abnegation, he goes beyond the moral struggle, beyond everything. He sees in the most learned priest, in the cow, in the dog, in the most miserable places, neither the learned man, nor the cow, nor the dog, nor the miserable place, but the same divinity manifesting itself in them all. He alone is the happy man; and the man who has acquired that sameness has, even in this life, conquered all existence. God is pure; therefore such a man is said to be living in God. Jesus says, 'Before Abraham was, I am.' That means that Jesus and others like him are free spirits; and Jesus of Nazareth took human form, not by the compulsion of his past actions, but just to do good to mankind. It is not that when a man becomes free, he will stop and become a dead lump; but he will be more active than any other being, because every other being acts only under compulsion, he alone through freedom.

If we are inseparable from God, have we no individuality? Oh, yes: that is God. Our individuality is God. This is not the individuality you have now; you are coming towards that. Individuality means what cannot be divided. How can you call this individuality? One hour you are thinking one way, and the next hour another way, and two hours after, another way. Individuality is that which changes not—is beyond all things, changeless. It would be tremendously dangerous for this state to remain in eternity, because then the thief would always remain a thief and the blackguard a blackguard. If a baby died, he would have to remain a baby. The real individuality is that which never changes and will never change; and that is the God within us.

Vedantism is an expansive ocean on the surface of which a man-of-war could be near a catamaran. So in the Vedantic ocean a real Yogi can be by the side of an idolater or even an atheist. What is more, in the Vedantic ocean, the Hindu, Mohammedan, Christian, and Parsee are all one, all children of the Almighty God.

47

LAW AND FREEDOM

The struggle never had meaning for the man who is free. But for us it has a meaning, because it is name-and-form that creates the world.

We have a place for struggle in the Vedanta, but not for fear. All fears will vanish when you begin to assert your own nature. If you think that you are bound, bound you will remain. If you think you are free, free you will be.

That sort of freedom which we can feel when we are yet in the phenomenal is a glimpse of the real but not yet the real.

I disagree with the idea that freedom is obedience to the laws of nature. I do not understand what it means. According to the history of human progress, it is disobedience to nature that has constituted that progress. It may be said that the conquest of lower laws was through the higher. But even there, the conquering mind was only trying to be free; and as soon as it found that the struggle was also through law, it wanted to conquer that also. So the ideal was freedom in every case. The trees never disobey law. I never saw a cow steal. An oyster never told a lie. Yet they are not greater than man. This life is a tremendous assertion of freedom; and this obedience to law, carried far enough, would make us simply matter—either in society, or in politics, or in religion. Too many laws are a sure sign of death. Wherever in any society there are too many laws, it is a sure sign that that society will soon die. If you study the characteristics of India, you will find that no nation possesses so many laws as the Hindus, and national death is the result. But the Hindus had one peculiar idea—they never made any doctrines or dogmas in religion; and the latter has had the greatest growth. Eternal law cannot be freedom, because to say that the eternal is inside law is to limit it.

There is no purpose in view with God, because if there were some purpose, He would be nothing better than a man. Why should He need any purpose? If He had any, He would be bound by it. There would be something besides Him which was greater. For instance, the carpet-weaver makes a piece of carpet. The idea was outside of him, something greater. Now where is the idea to which God would adjust Himself? Just as the greatest emperors sometimes play with dolls, so He is playing with this nature; and what we call law is this. We call it law, because we can see only little bits which run smoothly. All our ideas of law are within the little bit. It is nonsense to say that law is infinite, that throughout all time stones will fall. If all reason be based upon experience, who was there to see if stones fell five millions of years ago? So law is not constitutional in man. It is a scientific assertion as to man that where we begin, there we end. As a matter of fact, we get gradually outside of law, until we get out altogether, but with the added experience of a whole life. In God and freedom we began, and freedom and God will be the end. These laws are in the middle state through which we have to pass. Our Vedanta is the assertion of freedom always. The very idea of law will frighten the Vedantist; and eternal law is a very dreadful thing for him, because there would be no escape. If there is to be an eternal law binding him all the time, where is the difference between him and a blade of grass? We do not believe in that abstract idea of law.

We say that it is freedom that we are to seek, and that that freedom is God. It is the same happiness as in everything else; but when man seeks it in something which is finite, he gets only a spark of it. The thief when he steals gets the same happiness as the man who finds it in God; but the thief gets only a little spark with a mass of misery. The real happiness is God. Love is God, freedom is God; and everything that is bondage is not God.

Man has freedom already, but he will have to discover it. He has it, but every moment forgets it. That discovering, consciously or unconsciously, is the whole life of every one. But the difference between the sage and the ignorant man is that one does it consciously and the other unconsciously. Every one is struggling for freedom—from the atom to the star. The ignorant man is satisfied if he can get freedom within a certain limit—if he can get rid of the bondage of hunger or of being thirsty. But that sage feels that there is a stronger bondage which has to be thrown off. He would not consider the freedom of the Red Indian as freedom at all.

According to our philosophers, freedom is the goal. Knowledge cannot be the goal, because knowledge is a compound. It is a compound of power and freedom, and it is freedom alone that is desirable. That is what men struggle after. Simply the possession of power would not be knowledge. For instance, a scientist can send an electric shock to a distance of some miles; but nature can send it to an unlimited distance. Why do we not build statues to nature then? It is not law that we want but ability to break law. We want to be outlaws. If you are bound by laws, you will be a lump of clay. Whether you are beyond law or not is not the question; but the thought that we are beyond law—upon that is based the whole history of humanity. For instance, a man lives in a forest, and never has had any education or knowledge. He sees a stone falling down—a natural phenomenon happening—and he thinks it is freedom. He thinks it has a soul, and the central idea in that is freedom. But as soon as he knows that it must fall, he calls it nature—dead, mechanical action. I may or may not go into the street. In that is my glory as a man. If I am sure that I must go there, I give myself up and become a machine. Nature with its infinite power is only a machine; freedom alone constitutes sentient life.

The Vedanta says that the idea of the man in the forest is the right one; his glimpse is right, but the explanation is wrong. He holds to this nature as freedom and not as governed by law. Only after all this human experience we will come back to think the same, but in a more philosophical sense. For instance, I want to go out into the street. I get the impulse of my will, and then I stop; and in the time that intervenes between the will and going into the street, I am working uniformly. Uniformity of action is what we call law. This uniformity of my actions, I find, is broken into very short periods, and so I do not call my actions under law. I work through freedom. I walk for five minutes; but before those five minutes of walking, which are uniform, there was the action of the will, which gave the impulse to walk. Therefore, man says he is free, because all his actions can be cut up into small periods; and although there is sameness in the small periods, beyond the period there is not the same sameness. In this perception of non-uniformity is the idea of freedom. In nature we see only very large periods of uniformity; but the beginning and end must be free impulses. The impulse of freedom was given just at the beginning, and that has rolled on; but this, compared with our periods, is much longer. We find by analysis on philosophic grounds that we are not free. But there will remain this factor, this consciousness that I am free. What we have to explain is, how that comes. We will find that we have these two impulsions in us. Our reason tells us that all our actions are caused, and at the same time, with every impulse we are asserting our freedom. The solution of the Vedanta is that there is freedom inside—that the soul is really free—but that that soul's actions are percolating through body and mind, which are not free.

As soon as we react, we become slaves. A man blames me, and I immediately react in the form of anger. A little vibration which he created made me a slave. So we have to demonstrate our freedom. They alone are the sages who see in the highest, most learned man, or the lowest animal, or the worst and most wicked of mankind, neither a man nor a sage nor an animal, but the same God in all of them. Even in this life they have conquered relativity, and have taken a firm stand upon this equality. God is pure, the same to all. Therefore, such a sage would be a living God. This is the goal towards which we are going; and every form of worship, every action of mankind, is a method of attaining to it. The man who wants money is striving for freedom—to get rid of the bondage of poverty. Every action of man is worship, because the idea is to attain to freedom, and all action, directly or indirectly, tends to that. Only, those actions that deter are to be avoided. The whole universe is worshipping, consciously or unconsciously; only it does not know that even while it is cursing, it is in another form worshipping the same God it is cursing, because those who are cursing are also struggling for freedom. They never think that in reacting from a thing they are making themselves slaves to it. It is hard to kick against the pricks.

If we could get rid of the belief in our limitations, it would be possible for us to do everything just now. It is only a question of time.

If that is so, add power, and so diminish time. Remember the case of the professor who learnt the secret of the development of marble and who made marble in twelve years, while it took nature centuries.

LECTURES FROM COLOMBO TO ALMORA

48

THE RELIGION WE ARE BORN IN

At an open-air meeting convened at Dacca, on the 31 March 1901, the Swamiji spoke in English for two hours on the above subject before a vast audience. The following is a translation of the lecture from a Bengali report of a disciple:

In the remote past, our country made gigantic advances in spiritual ideas. Let us, today, bring before our mind's eye that ancient history. But the one great danger in meditating over long-past greatness is that we cease to exert ourselves for new things, and content ourselves with vegetating upon that by-gone ancestral glory and priding ourselves upon it. We should guard against that. In ancient times there were, no doubt, many Rishis and Maharshis who came face to face with Truth. But if this recalling of our ancient greatness is to be of real benefit, we too must become Rishis like them. Ay, not only that, but it is my firm conviction that we shall be even greater Rishis than any that our history presents to us. In the past, signal were our attainments—I glory in them, and I feel proud in thinking of them. I am not even in despair at seeing the present degradation, and I am full of hope in picturing to my mind what is to come in the future. Why? Because I know the seed undergoes a complete transformation, ay, the seed as seed is seemingly destroyed before it develops into a tree. In the same way, in the midst of our present degradation lies, only dormant for a time, the potentiality of the future greatness of our religion, ready to spring up again, perhaps more mighty and glorious than ever before.

Now let us consider what are the common grounds of agreement in the religion we are born in. At first sight we undeniably find various differences among our sects. Some are Advaitists, some are Vishishtadvaitists, and others are Dvaitists. Some believe in Incarnations of God, some in image-worship, while others are upholders of the doctrine of the Formless. Then as to customs also, various differences are known to exist. The Jats are not outcasted even if they marry among the Mohammedans and Christians. They can enter into any Hindu temple without hindrance. In many villages in the Punjab, one who does not eat swine will hardly be considered a Hindu. In Nepal, a Brahmin can marry in the four Varnas; while in Bengal, a Brahmin cannot marry even among the subdivisions of his own caste. So on and so forth. But in the midst of all these differences we note one point of unity among all Hindus, and it is this, that no Hindu eats beef. In the same way, there is a great common ground of unity underlying the various forms and sects of our religion.

First, in discussing the scriptures, one fact stands out prominently—that only those religions which had one or many scriptures of their own as their basis advanced by leaps and bounds and survive to the present day notwithstanding all the persecution and repression hurled against them. The Greek religion, with all its beauty, died out in the absence of any scripture to support it; but the religion of the Jews stands undiminished in its power, being based upon the authority of the Old Testament. The same is the case with the Hindu religion, with its scripture, the Vedas, the oldest in the world. The Vedas are divided into the Karma Kanda and the Jnana Kanda. Whether for good or for evil, the Karma Kanda has fallen into disuse in India, though there are some Brahmins in the Deccan who still perform Yajnas now and then with the sacrifice of goats; and also we find here and there, traces of the Vedic Kriya Kanda in the Mantras used in connection with our marriage and Shraddha ceremonies etc. But there is no chance of its being rehabilitated on its original footing. Kumarila Bhatta once tried to do so, but he was not successful in his attempt.

The Jnana Kanda of the Vedas comprises the Upanishads and is known by the name of Vedanta, the pinnacle of the Shrutis, as it is called. Wherever you find the Acharyas quoting a passage from the Shrutis, it is invariably from the Upanishads. The Vedanta is now the religion of the Hindus. If any sect in India wants to have its ideas established with a firm hold on the people it must base them on the authority of the Vedanta. They all have to do it, whether they are Dvaitists or Advaitists. Even the Vaishnavas have to go to Gopalatapini Upanishad to prove the truth of their own theories. If a new sect does not find anything in the Shrutis in confirmation of its ideas, it will go even to the length of manufacturing a new Upanishad, and making it pass current as one of the old original productions. There have been many such in the past.

Now as to the Vedas, the Hindus believe that they are not mere books composed by men in some remote age. They hold them to be an accumulated mass of endless divine wisdom, which is sometimes manifested and at other times remains unmanifested. Commentator Sayanacharya says somewhere in his works यो वेदेभ्योऽखिलं जगत् निर्ममे— 'Who created the whole universe out of the knowledge of the Vedas'. No one has ever seen the composer of the Vedas, and it is impossible to imagine one. The Rishis were only the discoverers of the Mantras or Eternal Laws; they merely came face to face with the Vedas, the infinite mine of knowledge, which has been there from time without beginning.

Who are these Rishis? Vatsyayana says, 'He who has attained through proper means the direct realization of Dharma, he alone can be a Rishi even if he is a Mlechchha by birth.' Thus it is that in ancient times, Vasishtha, born of an illegitimate union, Vyasa, the son of a fisherwoman, Narada, the son of a maidservant with uncertain parentage, and many others of like nature attained to Rishihood. Truly speaking, it comes to this then, that no distinction should be made with one who has realized the Truth. If the persons just named all became Rishis, then, O ye Kulin Brahmins of the present day, how much greater Rishis you can become! Strive after that Rishihood, stop not till you have attained the goal, and the whole world will of itself bow at your feet! Be a Rishi—that is the secret of power.

This Veda is our only authority, and everyone has the right to it.

यथेमां वाचं कल्याणीमावदानि जनेभ्य:।
ब्रह्मराजन्याभ्यां शूद्राय चार्याय च स्वाय चारणाय॥

—Thus says the Shukla Yajur Veda (XXVI. 2). Can you show any authority from this Veda of ours that everyone has not the right to it? The Puranas, no doubt, say that a certain caste has the right to such and such a recension of the Vedas, or a certain caste has no right to study them, or that this portion of the Vedas is for the Satya Yuga and that portion is for the Kali Yuga. But, mark you, the Veda does not say so; it is only your Puranas that do so. But can the servant dictate to the master? The Smritis, Puranas, Tantras—all these are acceptable only so far as they agree with the Vedas; and wherever they are contradictory, they are to be rejected as unreliable. But nowadays we have put the Puranas on even a higher pedestal than the Vedas! The study of the Vedas has almost disappeared from Bengal. How I wish that day will soon come when in every home the Veda will be worshipped together with Shalagrama, the household Deity, when the young, the old, and the women will inaugurate the worship of the Veda!

I have no faith in the theories advanced by Western savants with regard to the Vedas. They are today fixing the antiquity of the Vedas at a certain period, and again tomorrow upsetting it and bringing it one thousand years forward, and so on. However, about the Puranas, I have told you that they are authoritative only in so far as they agree with the Vedas, otherwise not. In the Puranas we find many things which do not agree with the Vedas. As for instance, it is written in the Puranas that some one lived ten thousand years, another twenty thousand years, but in the Vedas we find: शतायुर्वै पुरुष:—'Man lives indeed a hundred years.' Which are we to accept in this case? Certainly the Vedas. Notwithstanding statements like these, I do not depreciate the Puranas. They contain many beautiful and illuminating teachings and words of wisdom on Yoga, Bhakti, Jnana, and Karma; those, of course, we should accept. Then there are the Tantras. The real meaning of the word Tantra is Shastra, as for example, Kapila Tantra. But the word Tantra is generally used in a limited sense. Under the sway of kings who took up Buddhism and preached broadcast the doctrine of Ahimsa, the performances of the Vedic Yaga-Yajnas became a thing of the past, and no one could kill any animal in sacrifice for fear of the king. But subsequently amongst the Buddhists themselves—who were converts from Hinduism—the best parts of these Yaga-Yajnas were taken up, and practised in secret. From these sprang up the Tantras. Barring some of the abominable things in the Tantras, such as the Vamachara etc., the Tantras are not so bad as people are inclined to think. There are many high and sublime Vedantic thoughts in them. In fact, the Brahmana portions of the Vedas were modified a little and incorporated into the body of the Tantras. All the forms of our worship and the ceremonials of the present day, comprising the Karma Kanda, are observed in accordance with the Tantras.

Now let us discuss the principles of our religion a little. Notwithstanding the differences and controversies existing among our various sects, there are in them, too, several grounds of unity. First, almost all of them admit the existence of three things—three entities— Ishvara, Atman, and the Jagat. Ishvara is He who is eternally creating, preserving and destroying the whole universe. Excepting the Sankhyas, all the others believe in this. Then the doctrine of the Atman and the reincarnation of the soul; it maintains that innumerable individual souls, having taken body after body again and again, go round and round in the wheel of birth and death according to their respective Karmas; this is Samsaravada, or as it is commonly called the doctrine of rebirth. Then there is the Jagat or universe without beginning and without end. Though some hold these three as different phases of one only, and some others as three distinctly different entities, and others again in various other ways, yet they are all unanimous in believing in these three.

Here I should ask you to remember that Hindus, from time immemorial, knew the Atman as separate from Manas, mind. But the Occidentals could never soar beyond the mind. The West knows the universe to be full of happiness, and as such, it is to them a place where they can enjoy the most; but the East is born with the conviction that this Samsara, this ever-changing existence, is full of misery, and as such, it is nothing, nothing but unreal, not worth bartering the soul for its ephemeral joys and possessions. For this very reason, the West is ever especially adroit in organized action, and so also the East is ever bold in search of the mysteries of the internal world.

Let us, however, turn now to one or two other aspects of Hinduism. There is the doctrine of the Incarnations of God. In the Vedas we find mention of Matsya Avatara, the Fish Incarnation only. Whether all believe in this doctrine or not is not the point; the real meaning, however, of this Avataravada is the worship of Man—to see God in man is the real God-vision. The Hindu does not go through nature to nature's God—he goes to the God of man through Man.

Then there is image-worship. Except the five Devatas who are to be worshipped in every auspicious Karma as enjoined in our Shastras, all the other Devatas are merely the names of certain states held by them. But again, these five Devatas are nothing but the different names of the one God Only. This external worship of images has, however, been described in all our Shastras as the lowest of all the low forms of worship. But that does not mean that it is a wrong thing to do. Despite the many iniquities that have found entrance into the practises of image-worship as it is in vogue now, I do not condemn it. Ay, where would I have been if I had not been blessed with the dust of the holy feet of that orthodox, image-worshipping Brahmin!

Those reformers who preach against image-worship, or what they denounce as idolatry—to them I say 'Brothers, if you are fit to worship God-without-form discarding all external help, do so, but why do you condemn others who cannot do the same? A beautiful, large edifice, the glorious relic of a hoary antiquity has, out of neglect or disuse, fallen into a dilapidated condition; accumulations of dirt and dust may be lying everywhere within it, maybe, some portions are tumbling down to the ground. What will you do to it? Will you take in hand the necessary cleansing and repairs and thus restore the old, or will you pull the whole edifice down to the ground and seek to build another in its place, after a sordid modern plan whose permanence has yet to be established? We have to reform it, which truly means to make ready or perfect by necessary cleansing and repairs, not by demolishing the whole thing. There the function of reform ends. When the work of renovating the old is finished, what further necessity does it serve? Do that if you can, if not, hands off!' The band of reformers in our country want, on the contrary, to build up a separate sect of their own. They have, however, done good work; may the blessings of God be showered on their heads! But why should you, Hindus, want to separate yourselves from the great common fold? Why should you feel ashamed to take the name of Hindu, which is your greatest and most glorious possession? This national ship of ours, ye children of the Immortals, my countrymen, has been plying for ages, carrying civilization and enriching the whole world with its inestimable treasures. For scores of shining centuries this national ship of ours has been ferrying across the ocean of life, and has taken millions of souls to the other shore, beyond all misery. But today it may have sprung a leak and got damaged, through your own fault or whatever cause it matters not. What would you, who have placed yourselves in it, do now? Would you go about cursing it and quarrelling among yourselves! Would you not all unite together and put your best efforts to stop the holes? Let us all gladly give our hearts' blood to do this; and if we fail in the attempt, let us all sink and die together, with blessings and not curses on our lips.

And to the Brahmins I say, 'Vain is your pride of birth and ancestry. Shake it off. Brahminhood, according to your Shastras, you have no more now, because you have for so long lived under Mlechchha kings. If you at all believe in the words of your own ancestors, then go this very moment and make expiation by entering into the slow fire kindled by Tusha (husks), like that old Kumarila Bhatta, who with the purpose of ousting the Buddhists first became a disciple of the Buddhists and then defeating them in argument became the cause of death to many, and subsequently entered the Tushanala to expiate his sins. If you are not bold enough to do that, then admit your weakness and stretch forth a helping hand, and open the gates of knowledge to one and all, and give the downtrodden masses once more their just and legitimate rights and privileges.'

49

SANNYASA: ITS IDEAL AND PRACTICE

A parting Address was given to Swamiji by the junior Sannyasins of the Math (Belur), on the eve of his leaving for the West for the second time. The following is the substance of Swamiji's reply as entered in the Math Diary on 19th June 1899:

This is not the time for a long lecture. But I shall speak to you in brief about a few things which I should like you to carry into practice. First, we have to understand the ideal, and then the methods by which we can make it practical. Those of you who are Sannyasins must try to do good to others, for Sannyasa means that. There is no time to deliver a long discourse on 'Renunciation', but I shall very briefly characterize it as '*the love of death*'. Worldly people love life. The Sannyasin is to love death. Are we to commit suicide then? Far from it. For suicides are not lovers of death, as it is often seen that when a man trying to commit suicide fails, he never attempts it for a second time. What is the love of death then? We must die, that is certain; let us die then for a good cause. Let all our actions—eating, drinking, and everything that we do—tend towards the sacrifice of our self. You nourish your body by eating. What good is there in doing that if you do not hold it as a sacrifice to the well-being of others? You nourish your minds by reading books. There is no good in doing that unless you hold it also as a sacrifice to the whole world. For the whole world is one; you are rated a very insignificant part of it, and therefore it is right for you that you should serve your millions of brothers rather than aggrandize this little self.

सर्वतः पाणिपादं तत् सर्वतोऽक्षिशिरोमुखम्।
सर्वतः श्रुतिमल्लोके सर्वमावृत्य विष्टति॥

'With hands and feet everywhere, with eyes, heads, and mouths everywhere, with ears everywhere in the universe, That exists pervading all.' (Gita, XIII. 13)

Thus you must die a gradual death. In such a death is heaven, all good is stored therein—and in its opposite is all that is diabolical and evil.

Then as to the methods of carrying the ideals into practical life. First, we have to understand that we must not have any impossible ideal. An ideal which is too high makes a nation weak and degraded. This happened after the Buddhistic and the Jain reforms. On the other hand, too much practicality is also wrong. If you have not even a little imagination, if you have no ideal let guide you, you are simply a brute. So we must not lower our ideal, neither are we to lose sight of practicality. We must avoid the two extremes. In our country, the old idea is to sit in a cave and meditate and die. To go ahead of others in salvation is wrong. One must learn sooner or later that one cannot get salvation if one does not try to seek the salvation of his brothers. You must try to combine in your life immense idealism with immense practicality. You must be prepared to go into deep meditation now, and the next moment you must be ready to go and cultivate these fields (Swamiji said, pointing to the meadows of the Math). You must be prepared to explain the difficult intricacies of the Shastras now, and the next moment to go and sell the produce of the fields in the market. You must be prepared for all menial services, not only here, but elsewhere also.

The next thing to remember is that the aim of this institution is to make men. You must not merely learn what the Rishis taught. Those Rishis are gone, and their opinions are also gone with them. You must be Rishis yourselves. You are also men as much as the greatest men that were ever born—even our Incarnations. What can mere book-learning do? What can meditation do even? What can the Mantras and Tantras do? You must stand on your own feet. You must have this new method—the method of man-making. The true *man* is he who is strong as strength itself and yet possesses a woman's heart. You must feel for the millions of beings around you, and yet you must be strong and inflexible and you must also possess Obedience; though it may seem a little paradoxical—you must possess these apparently conflicting virtues. If your superior order you to throw yourself into a river and catch a crocodile, you must first obey and then reason with him. Even if the order be wrong, first obey and then contradict it. The bane of sects, especially in Bengal, is that if any one happens to have a different opinion, he immediately starts a new sect, he has no patience to wait. So you must have a deep regard for your Sangha. There is no place for disobedience here. Crush it out without mercy. No disobedient members here, you must turn them out. There must not be any traitors in the camp. You must be as free as the air, and as obedient as this plant and the dog.

50

THE SAGES OF INDIA

In speaking of the sages of India, my mind goes back to those periods of which history has no record, and tradition tries in vain to bring the secrets out of the gloom of the past. The sages of India have been almost innumerable, for what has the Hindu nation been doing for thousands of years except producing sages? I will take, therefore, the lives of a few of the most brilliant ones, the epoch-makers, and present them before you, that is to say, my study of them.

In the first place, we have to understand a little about our scriptures. Two ideals of truth are in our scriptures; the one is, what we call the eternal, and the other is not so authoritative, yet binding under particular circumstances, times, and places. The eternal relations which deal with the nature of the soul, and of God, and the relations between souls and God are embodied in what we call the Shrutis, the Vedas. The next set of truths is what we call the Smritis, as embodied in the words of Manu. Yajnavalkya, and other writers and also in the Puranas, down to the Tantras. The second class of books and teachings is subordinate to the Shrutis, inasmuch as whenever any one of these contradicts anything in the Shrutis, the Shrutis must prevail. This is the law. The idea is that the framework of the destiny and goal of man has been all delineated in the Vedas, the details have been left to be worked out in the Smritis and Puranas. As for general directions, the Shrutis are enough; for spiritual life, nothing more can be said, nothing more can be known. All that is necessary has been known, all the advice that is necessary to lead the soul to perfection has been completed in the Shrutis; the details alone were left out, and these the Smritis have supplied from time to time.

Another peculiarity is that these Shrutis have many sages as the recorders of the truths in them, mostly men, even some women. Very little is known of their personalities, the dates of their birth, and so forth, but their best thoughts, their best discoveries, I should say, are preserved there, embodied in the sacred literature of our country, the Vedas. In the Smritis, on the other hand, personalities are more in evidence. Startling, gigantic, impressive, world-moving persons stand before us, as it were, for the first time, sometimes of more magnitude even than their teachings.

This is a peculiarity which we have to understand—that our religion preaches an Impersonal Personal God. It preaches any amount of impersonal laws plus any amount of personality, but the very fountain-head of our religion is in the Shrutis, the Vedas, which are perfectly impersonal; the persons all come in the Smritis and Puranas—the great Avataras, Incarnations of God, Prophets, and so forth. And this ought also to be observed that except our religion every other religion in the world depends upon the life or lives of some personal founder or founders. Christianity is built upon the life of Jesus Christ, Mohammedanism upon Mohammed, Buddhism upon Buddha, Jainism upon the Jinas, and so on. It naturally follows that there must be in all these religions a good deal of fight about what they call the historical evidences of these great personalities. If at any time the historical evidences about the existence of these personages in ancient times become weak, the whole building of the religion tumbles down and is broken to pieces. We escaped this fate because our religion is not based upon persons but on principles. That you obey your religion is not because it came through the authority of a sage, no, not even of an Incarnation. Krishna is not the authority of the Vedas, but the Vedas are the authority of Krishna himself. His glory is that he is the greatest preacher of the Vedas that ever existed. So with the other Incarnations; so with all our sages. Our first principle is that all that is necessary for the perfection of man and for attaining unto freedom is there in the Vedas. You cannot find anything new. You cannot go beyond a perfect unity, which is the goal of all knowledge; this has been already reached there, and it is impossible to go beyond the unity. Religious knowledge became complete when Tat Twam Asi (Thou art That) was discovered, and that was in the Vedas. What remained was the guidance of people from time to time according to different times and places, according to different circumstances and environments; people had to be guided along the old, old path, and for this these great teachers came, these great sages. Nothing can bear out more clearly this position than the celebrated saying of Shri Krishna in the Gita: 'Whenever virtue subsides and irreligion prevails, I create Myself for the protection of the good; for the destruction of all immorality I am coming from time to time.' This is the idea in India.

What follows? That on the one hand, there are these eternal principles which stand upon their own foundations without depending on any reasoning even, much less on the authority of sages however great, of Incarnations however brilliant they may have been. We may remark that as this is the unique position in India, our claim is that the Vedanta only can be the universal religion, that it is already the existing universal religion in the world, because it teaches principles and not persons. No religion built upon a person can be taken up as a type by all the races of mankind. In our own country we find that there have been so many grand characters; in even a small city many persons are taken up as types by the different minds in that one city. How is it possible that one person as Mohammed or Buddha or Christ, can be taken up as the one type for the whole world, nay, that the whole of morality, ethics, spirituality, and religion can be true only from the sanction of that one person, and one person alone? Now, the Vedantic religion does not require any such personal authority. Its sanction is the eternal nature of man, its ethics are based upon the eternal spiritual solidarity of man, already existing, already attained and not to be attained. On the other hand, from the very earliest times, our sages have been feeling conscious of this fact that the vast majority of mankind require a personality. They must have a Personal God in some form or other. The very Buddha who declared against the existence of a Personal God had not died fifty years before his disciples manufactured a Personal God out of him. The Personal God is necessary, and at the same time we know that instead of and better than vain imaginations of a Personal God, which in ninety-nine cases out of a hundred are unworthy of human worship we have in this world, living and walking in our midst, living Gods, now and then. These are more worthy of worship than any imaginary God, any creation of our imagination, that is to say, any idea of God which we can form. Shri Krishna is much greater than any idea of God you or I can have. Buddha is a much higher idea, a more living and idolized idea, than the ideal you or I can conceive of in our minds; and therefore it is that they always command the worship of mankind even to the exclusion of all imaginary deities.

This our sages knew, and, therefore, left it open to all Indian people to worship such great Personages, such Incarnations. Nay, the greatest of these Incarnations goes further: 'Wherever an extraordinary spiritual power is manifested by external man, know that I am there, it is from Me that that manifestation comes.' That leaves the door open for the Hindu to worship the Incarnations of all the countries in the world. The Hindu can worship any sage and any saint from any country whatsoever, and as a fact we know that we go and worship many times in the churches of the Christians, and many, many times in the Mohammedan mosques, and that is good. Why not? Ours, as I have said, is the universal religion. It is inclusive enough, it is broad enough to include all the ideals. All the ideals of religion that already exist in the world can be immediately included, and we can patiently wait for all the ideals that are to come in the future to be taken in the same fashion, embraced in the infinite arms of the religion of the Vedanta.

This, more or less, is our position with regard to the great sages, the Incarnations of God. There are also secondary characters. We find the word Rishi again and again mentioned in the Vedas, and it has become a common word at the present time. The Rishi is the great authority. We have to understand that idea. The definition is that the Rishi is the Mantra-drashta, the seer of thought. What is the proof of religion?—this was asked in very ancient times. There is no proof in the senses was the declaration.

'There the eyes cannot reach, neither can speech, nor the mind'— that has been the declaration for ages and ages. Nature outside cannot give us any answer as to the existence of the soul, the existence of God, the eternal life, the goal of man, and all that. This mind is continually changing, always in a state of flux; it is finite, it is broken into pieces. How can nature tell of the Infinite, the Unchangeable, the

Unbroken, the Indivisible, the Eternal? It never can. And whenever mankind has striven to get an answer from dull dead matter, history shows how disastrous the results have been. How comes, then, the knowledge which the Vedas declare? It comes through being a Rishi. This knowledge is not in the senses; but are the senses the be-all and the end-all of the human being? Who dare say that the senses are the all-in-all of man? Even in our lives, in the life of every one of us here, there come moments of calmness, perhaps, when we see before us the death of one we loved, when some shock comes to us, or when extreme blessedness comes to us. Many other occasions there are when the mind, as it were, becomes calm, feels for the moment its real nature; and a glimpse of the Infinite beyond, where words cannot reach nor the mind go, is revealed to us. This happens in ordinary life, but it has to be heightened, practised, perfected. Men found out ages ago that the soul is not bound or limited by the senses, no, not even by consciousness. We have to understand that this consciousness is only the name of one link in the infinite chain. Being is not identical with consciousness, but consciousness is only one part of Being. Beyond consciousness is where the bold search lies. Consciousness is bound by the senses. Beyond that, beyond the senses, men must go in order to arrive at truths of the spiritual world, and there are even now persons who succeed in going beyond the bounds of the senses. These are called Rishis, because they come face to face with spiritual truths.

The proof, therefore, of the Vedas is just the same as the proof of this table before me, Pratyaksha, direct perception. This I see with the senses, and the truths of spirituality we also see in a superconscious state of the human soul. This Rishi-state is not limited by time or place, by sex or race. Vatsyayana boldly declares that this Rishihood is the common property of the descendants of the sage, of the Aryan, of the non-Aryan, of even the Mlechchha. This is the sageship of the Vedas, and constantly we ought to remember this ideal of religion in India, which I wish other nations of the world would also remember and learn, so that there may be less fight and less quarrel. Religion is not in books, nor in theories, nor in dogmas, nor in talking, not even in reasoning. It is being and becoming. Ay, my friends, until each one of you has become a Rishi and come face to face with spiritual facts,

330 • THE DEFINITIVE VIVEKANANDA

religious life has not begun for you. Until the superconscious opens for you, religion is mere talk, it is nothing but preparation. You are talking second-hand, third-hand, and here applies that beautiful saying of Buddha when he had a discussion with some Brahmins. They came discussing about the nature of Brahman, and the great sage asked, 'Have you seen Brahman?' 'No, said the Brahmin; 'Or your father?' 'No, neither has he'; 'Or your grandfather?' 'I don't think even he saw Him.' 'My friend, how can you discuss about a person whom your father and grandfather never saw, and try to put each other down?' That is what the whole world is doing. Let us say in the language of the Vedanta, 'This Atman is not to be reached by too much talk, no, not even by the highest intellect, no, not even by the study of the Vedas themselves.'

Let us speak to all the nations of the world in the language of the Vedas: Vain are your fights and your quarrels; have you seen God whom you want to preach? If you have not seen, vain is your preaching; you do not know what you say; and if you have seen God, you will not quarrel, your very face will shine. An ancient sage of the Upanishads sent his son out to learn about Brahman, and the child came back, and the father asked, 'what have you learnt?' The child replied he had learnt so many sciences. But the father said, 'That is nothing, go back.' And the son went back, and when he returned again the father asked the same question, and the same answer came from the child. Once more he had to go back. And the next time he came, his whole face was shining; and his father stood up and declared, 'Ay, today, my child, your face shines like a knower of Brahman.' When you have known God, your very face will be changed, your voice will be changed, your whole appearance will he changed. You will be a blessing to mankind; none will be able to resist the Rishi. This is the Rishihood, the ideal in our religion. The rest, all these talks and reasonings and philosophies and dualisms and monisms, and even the Vedas themselves are but preparations, secondary things. The other is primary. The Vedas, grammar, astronomy, etc., all these are secondary; that is supreme knowledge which makes us realize the Unchangeable One. Those who realized are the sages whom we find in the Vedas; and we understand how this Rishi is the name of a type, of a class, which every one of us, as true Hindus, is expected to become at some period of our life, and becoming which, to the Hindu, means salvation. Not belief in doctrines, not going to thousands of temples, nor bathing in all the rivers in the world, but becoming the Rishi, the Mantra-drashta—that is freedom, that is salvation.

Coming down to later times, there have been great world-moving sages, great Incarnations of whom there have been many; and according to the Bhagavata, they also are infinite in number, and those that are worshipped most in India are Rama and Krishna. Rama, the ancient idol of the heroic ages, the embodiment of truth, of morality, the ideal son, the ideal husband, the ideal father, and above all, the ideal king, this Rama has been presented before us by the great sage Valmiki. No language can be purer, none chaster, none more beautiful and at the same time simpler than the language in which the great poet has depicted the life of Rama. And what to speak of Sita? You may exhaust the literature of the world that is past, and I may assure you that you will have to exhaust the literature of the world of the future, before finding another Sita. Sita is unique; that character was depicted once and for all. There may have been several Ramas, perhaps, but never more than one Sita! She is the very type of the true Indian woman, for all the Indian ideals of a perfected woman have grown out of that one life of Sita; and here she stands these thousands of years, commanding the worship of every man, woman, and child throughout the length and breadth of the land of Aryavarta. There she will always be, this glorious Sita, purer than purity itself, all patience, and all suffering. She who suffered that life of suffering without a murmur, she the ever-chaste and ever-pure wife, she the ideal of the people, the ideal of the gods, the great Sita, our national God she must always remain. And every one of us knows her too well to require much delineation. All our mythology may vanish, even our Vedas may depart, and our Sanskrit language may vanish for ever, but so long as there will be five Hindus living here, even if only speaking the most vulgar patois, there will be the story of Sita present. Mark my words: Sita has gone into the very vitals of our race. She is there in the blood of every Hindu man and woman; we are all children of Sita. Any attempt to modernize our women, if it tries to take our women away from that ideal of Sita, is immediately a failure, as we see every day. The women of India must grow and develop in the footprints of Sita, and that is the only way.

The next is He who is worshipped in various forms, the favourite ideal of men as well as of women, the ideal of children, as well as of grown-up men. I mean He whom the writer of the Bhagavata was not content to call an Incarnation but says, 'The other Incarnations were but parts of the Lord. He, Krishna, was the Lord Himself.' And it is not strange that such adjectives are applied to him when we marvel at the many-sidedness of his character. He was the most wonderful Sannyasin, and the most wonderful householder in one; he had the most wonderful amount of Rajas, power, and was at the same time living in the midst of the most wonderful renunciation. Krishna can never he understood until you have studied the Gita, for he was the embodiment of his own teaching. Every one of these Incarnations came as a living illustration of what they came to preach. Krishna, the preacher of the Gita, was all his life the embodiment of that Song Celestial; he was the great illustration of non-attachment. He gives up his throne and never cares for it. He, the leader of India, at whose word kings come down from their thrones, never wants to be a king. He is the simple Krishna, ever the same Krishna who played with the Gopis. Ah, that most marvellous passage of his life, the most difficult to understand, and which none ought to attempt to understand until he has become perfectly chaste and pure, that most marvellous expansion of love, allegorized and expressed in that beautiful play at Vrindaban, which none can understand but he who has become mad with love, drunk deep of the cup of love! Who can understand the throes of the lore of the Gopis—the very ideal of love, love that wants nothing, love that even does not care for heaven, love that does not care for anything in this world or the world to come? And here, my friends, through this love of the Gopis has been found the only solution of the conflict between the Personal and the Impersonal God. We know how the Personal God is the highest point of human life; we know that it is philosophical to believe in an Impersonal God immanent in the universe, of whom everything is but a manifestation. At the same time our souls hanker after something concrete, something which we want to grasp, at whose feet we can pour out our soul, and so on. The Personal God is therefore the highest conception of human nature. Yet reason stands aghast at such an idea. It is the same old, old question which you find discussed in the Brahma-Sutras, which you find Draupadi discussing with Yudhishthira in the forest: If there is a Personal God, all-merciful, all-powerful, why is the hell of an earth here, why did He create this?—He must be a partial God. There was no solution, and the only solution that can be found is what you read about the love of the Gopis. They hated every adjective that was applied to Krishna; they did not care to know that he was the Lord of creation, they did not care to know that he was almighty, they did not care to know that he was omnipotent, and so forth. The only thing they understood was that he was infinite Love, that was all. The Gopis understood Krishna only as the Krishna of Vrindaban. He, the leader of the hosts, the King of kings, to them was the shepherd, and the shepherd for ever. 'I do not want wealth, nor many people, nor do I want learning; no, not even do I want to go to heaven. Let one be born again and again, but Lord, grant me this, that I may have love for Thee, and that for love's sake.' A great landmark in the history of religion is here, the ideal of love for love's sake, work for work's sake, duty for duty's sake, and it for the first time fell from the lips of the greatest of Incarnations, Krishna, and for the first time in the history of humanity, upon the soil of India. The religions of fear and of temptations were gone for ever, and in spite of the fear of hell and temptation of enjoyment in heaven, came the grandest of ideals, love for love's sake, duty for duty's sake, work for work's sake.

And what a love! I have told you just now that it is very difficult to understand the love of the Gopis. There are not wanting fools, even in the midst of us, who cannot understand the marvellous significance of that most marvellous of all episodes. There are, let me repeat, impure fools, even born of our blood, who try to shrink from that as if from something impure. To them I have only to say, first make yourselves pure; and you must remember that he who tells the history of the love of the Gopis is none else but Shuka Deva. The historian who records this marvellous love of the Gopis is one who was born pure, the eternally pure Shuka, the son of Vyasa. So long as there its selfishness in the heart, so long is love of God impossible; it is nothing but shopkeeping: 'I give you something; O Lord, you give me something in return'; and says the Lord, 'If you do not do this, I will take good care of you when you die. I will roast you all the rest of your lives. perhaps', and so on. So long as such ideas are in the brain, how can one understand the mad throes of the Gopis' love? 'O for one, one kiss of those lips! One who has been kissed by Thee, his thirst for Thee increases for ever, all sorrows vanish, and he forgets love for everything else but for Thee and Thee alone.' Ay, forget first the love for gold, and name and fame, and for this little trumpery world of ours. Then, only then, you will understand the love of the Gopis, too holy to be attempted without giving up everything, too sacred co be understood until the soul has become perfectly pure. People with ideas of sex, and of money, and of fame, bubbling up every minute in the heart, daring to criticize and understand the love of the Gopis! That is the very essence of the Krishna Incarnation. Even the Gita, the great philosophy itself, does not compare with that madness, for in the Gita the disciple is taught slowly how to walk towards the goal, but here is the madness of enjoyment, the drunkenness of love, where disciples and teachers and teachings and books and all these things have become one; even the ideas of fear, and God, and heaven—everything has been thrown away. What remains is the madness of love. It is forgetfulness of everything, and the lover sees nothing in the world except that Krishna and Krishna alone, when the face of every being becomes a Krishna, when his own face looks like Krishna, when his own soul has become tinged with the Krishna colour. That was the great Krishna!

Do not waste your time upon little details. Take up the framework, the essence of the life. There may be many historical discrepancies, there may be interpolations in the life of Krishna. All these things may be true; but, at the same time, there must have been a basis, a foundation for this new and tremendous departure. Taking the life of any other sage or prophet, we find that that prophet is only the evolution of what had gone before him, we find that that prophet is only preaching the ideas that had been scattered about his own country even in his own times. Great doubts may exist even as to whether that prophet existed or not. But here, I challenge any one to show whether these things, these ideals—work for work's sake, love for love's sake, duty for duty's sake, were not original ideas with Krishna, and as such, there must have been someone with whom these ideas originated. They could not have been borrowed from anybody else. They were not floating about in the atmosphere when Krishna was born. But the Lord Krishna was the first preacher of this; his disciple Vyasa took it up and preached it unto mankind. This is the highest idea to picture. The highest thing we can get out of him is Gopijanavallabha, the Beloved of the Gopis of Vrindaban. When that madness comes in your brain, when you understand the blessed Gopis, then you will understand what love is. When the whole world will vanish, when all other considerations will have died out, when you will become pure-hearted with no other aim, not even the search after truth, then and then alone will come to you the madness of that love, the strength and the power of that infinite love which the Gopis had, that love for love's sake. That is the goal. When you have got that, you have got everything.

To come down to the lower stratum—Krishna, the preacher of the Gita. Ay, there is an attempt in India now which is like putting the cart before the horse. Many of our people think that Krishna as the lover of the Gopis is something rather uncanny, and the Europeans do not like it much. Dr So-and-so does not like it. Certainly then, the Gopis have to go! Without the sanction of Europeans how can Krishna live? He cannot! In the Mahabharata there is no mention of the Gopis except in one or two places, and those not very remarkable places. In the prayer of Draupadi there is mention of a Vrindaban life, and in the speech of Shishupala there is again mention of this Vrindaban. All these are interpolations! What the Europeans do not want: must be thrown off. They are interpolations, the mention of the Gopis and of Krishna too! Well, with these men, steeped in commercialism, where even the ideal of religion has become commercial, they are all trying to go to heaven by doing something here; the bania wants compound interest, wants to lay by something here and enjoy it there. Certainly the Gopis have no place in such a system of thought. From that ideal lover we come down to the lower stratum of Krishna, the preacher of the Gita. Than the Gita no better commentary on the Vedas has been written or can be written. The essence of the Shrutis, or of the Upanishads, is hard to be understood, seeing that there are so many commentators, each one trying to interpret in his own way. Then the Lord Himself comes, He who is the inspirer of the Shrutis, to show us the meaning of them, as the preacher of the Gita, and today India wants nothing better, the world wants nothing better than that method of interpretation. It is a wonder that subsequent interpreters of the scriptures, even commenting upon the Gita, many times could not catch the meaning, many times could not catch the drift. For what do you find in the Gita, and what in modern commentators? One non-dualistic commentator takes up an Upanishad; there are so many dualistic passages, and he twists and tortures them into some meaning, and wants to bring them all into a meaning of his own. If a dualistic commentator comes, there are so many nondualistic texts which he begins to torture, to bring them all round to dualistic meaning. But you find in the Gita there is no attempt at torturing any one of them. They are all right, says the Lord; for slowly and gradually the human soul rises up and up, step after step, from the gross to the fine, from the fine to the finer, until it reaches the Absolute, the goal. That is what is in the Gita. Even the Karma Kanda is taken up, and it is shown that although it cannot give salvation direct; but only indirectly, yet that is also valid; images are valid indirectly; ceremonies, forms, everything is valid only with one condition, purity of the heart. For worship is valid and leads to the goal if the heart is pure and the heart is sincere; and all these various modes of worship are necessary, else why should they be there? Religions and sects are not the work of hypocrites and wicked people who invented all these to get a little money, as some of our modern men want to think. However reasonable that explanation may seem, it is not true, and they were not invented that way at all. They are the outcome of the necessity of the human soul. They are all here to satisfy the hankering and thirst of different classes of human minds, and you need not preach against them. The day when that necessity will cease, they will vanish along with the cessation of that necessity; and so long as that necessity remains, they must be there in spite of your preaching, in spite of your criticism. You may bring the sword or the gun into play, you may deluge the world with human blood, but so long as there is a necessity for idols, they must remain. These forms, and all the various steps in religion will remain, and we understand from the Lord Shri Krishna why they should.

A rather sadder chapter of India's history comes now. In the Gita we already hear the distant sound of the conflicts of sects, and the Lord comes in the middle to harmonize them all; He, the great preacher of harmony, the greatest teacher of harmony, Lord Shri Krishna. He says, 'In Me they are all strung like pearls upon a thread.' We already hear the distant sounds, the murmurs of the conflict, and possibly there was a period of harmony and calmness, when it broke out anew, not only on religious grounds, but roost possibly on caste grounds—the fight between the two powerful factors in our community, the kings and the priests. And from the topmost crest of the wave that deluged India for nearly a thousand years, we see another glorious figure, and that was our Gautama Shakyamuni. You all know about his teachings and preachings. We worship him as God incarnate, the greatest, the boldest preacher of morality that the world ever saw, the greatest Karma-Yogi; as disciple of himself, as it were, the same Krishna came to show how to make his theories practical. There came once again the same voice that in the Gita preached, 'Even the least bit done of this religion saves from great fear'. 'Women, or Vaishyas, or even Shudras, all reach the highest goal.' Breaking the bondages of all, the chains of all, declaring liberty to all to reach the highest goal, come the words of the Gita, rolls like thunder the mighty voice of Krishna: 'Even in this life they have conquered relativity, whose minds are firmly fixed upon the sameness, for God is pure and the same to all, therefore such are said to be living in God.' 'Thus seeing the same Lord equally present everywhere, the sage does not injure the Self by the self, and thus reaches the highest goal.' As it were to give a living example of this preaching, as it were to make at least one part of it practical, the preacher himself came in another form, and this was Shakyamuni, the preacher to the poor and the miserable, he who rejected even the language of the gods to speak in the language of the people, so that he might reach the hearts of the people, he who gave up a throne to live with beggars, and the poor, and the downcast, he who pressed the Pariah to his breast like a second Rama.

You all know about his great work, his grand character. But the work had one great defect, and for that we are suffering even today. No blame attaches to the Lord. He is pure and glorious, but unfortunately such high ideals could not be well assimilated by the different uncivilized and uncultured races of mankind who flocked within the fold of the Aryans. These races, with varieties of superstition and hideous worship, rushed within the fold of the Aryans and for a time appeared as if they had become civilized, but before a century had passed they brought out their snakes, their ghosts, and all the other things their ancestors used to worship, and thus the whole of India became one degraded mass of superstition. The earlier Buddhists in their rage against the killing of animals had denounced the sacrifices of the Vedas; and these sacrifices used to be held in every house. There was a fire burning, and that was all the paraphernalia of worship. These sacrifices were obliterated, and in their place came gorgeous temples, gorgeous ceremonies, and gorgeous priests, and all that you see in India in modern times. I smile when I read books written by some modern people who ought to have known better, that the Buddha was the destroyer of Brahminical idolatry. Little do they know that Buddhism created Brahminism and idolatry in India.

There was a book written a year or two ago by a Russian gentleman, who claimed to have found out a very curious life of Jesus Christ, and in one part of the book he says that Christ went to the temple of Jagannath to study with the Brahmins, but became disgusted with their exclusiveness and their idols, and so he went to the Lamas of Tibet instead, became perfect, and went home. To any man who knows anything about Indian history, that very statement proves that the whole thing was a fraud, because the temple of Jagannath is an old Buddhistic temple. We took this and others over and re-Hinduized them. We shall have to do many things like that yet. That is Jagannath, and there was not one Brahmin there then, and yet we are told that Jesus Christ came to study with the Brahmins there. So says our great Russian archaeologist.

Thus, in spite of the preaching of mercy to animals, in spite of the sublime ethical religion, in spite of the hairsplitting discussions about the existence or non-existence of a permanent soul, the whole building of Buddhism tumbled down piecemeal; and the ruin was simply hideous. I have neither the time nor the inclination to describe to you the hideousness that came in the wake of Buddhism. The most hideous ceremonies, the most horrible, the most obscene books that human hands ever wrote or the human brain ever conceived, the most bestial forms that ever passed under the name of religion, have all been the creation of degraded Buddhism.

But India has to live, and the spirit of the Lords descended again. He who declared, 'I will come whenever virtue subsides', came again, and this time the manifestation was in the South, and up rose that young Brahmin of whom it has been declared that at the age of sixteen he had completed all his writings; the marvellous boy Shankaracharya arose. The writings of this boy of sixteen are the wonders of the modern world, and so was the boy. He wanted to bring back the Indian world to its pristine purity, but think of the amount of the task before him. I have told you a few points about the state of things that existed in India. All these horrors that you are trying to reform are the outcome of that reign of degradation. The Tartars and the Baluchis and all the hideous races of mankind came to India and became Buddhists, and assimilated with us, and brought their national customs, and the whole of our national life became a huge page of the most horrible and the most bestial customs. That was the inheritance which that boy got from the Buddhists, and from that time to this, the whole work in India is a reconquest of this Buddhistic degradation by the Vedanta. It is still going on, it is not yet finished. Shankara came, a great philosopher, and showed that the real essence of Buddhism and that of the Vedanta are not very different, but that the disciples did not understand the Master and have degraded themselves, denied the existence of the soul and of God, and have become atheists. That was what Shankara showed, and all the Buddhists began to come back to the old religion. But then they had become accustomed to all these forms; what could be done?

Then came the brilliant Ramanuja. Shankara, with his great intellect, I am afraid, had not as great a heart. Ramanuja's heart was greater. He felt for the downtrodden, he sympathized with them. He took up the ceremonies, the accretions that had gathered, made them pure so far as they could be, and instituted new ceremonies, new methods of worship, for the people who absolutely required them. At the same time he opened the door to the highest; spiritual worship from the Brahmin to the Pariah. That was Ramanuja's work. That work rolled on, invaded the North, was taken up by some great leaders there; but that was much later, during the Mohammedan rule; and the brightest of these prophets of comparatively modern times in the North was Chaitanya.

You may mark one characteristic since the time of Ramanuja—the opening of the door of spirituality to every one. That has been the watchword of all prophets succeeding Ramanuja, as it had been the watchword of all the prophets before Shankara. I do not know why Shankara should be represented as rather exclusive; I do not find anything in his writings which is exclusive. As in the case of the declarations of the Lord Buddha, this exclusiveness that has been attributed to Shankara's teachings is most possibly not due to his teachings, but to the incapacity of his disciples. This one great Northern sage, Chaitanya, represented the mad love of the Gopis. Himself a Brahmin, born of one of the most rationalistic families of the day, himself a professor of logic fighting and gaining a word-victory—for, this he had learnt from his childhood as the highest ideal of life and yet through the mercy of some sage the whole life of that man became changed; he gave up his fight, his quarrels, his professorship of logic and became one of the greatest teachers of Bhakti the world has ever known—mad Chaitanya. His Bhakti rolled over the whole land of Bengal, bringing solace to every one. His love knew no bounds. The saint or the sinner, the Hindu or the Mohammedan, the pure or the impure, the prostitute, the streetwalker—all had a share in his love, all had a share in his mercy: and even to the present day, although greatly degenerated, as everything does become in time, his sect is the refuge of the poor, of the downtrodden, of the outcast, of the weak, of those who have been rejected by all society. But at the same time I must remark for truth's sake that we find this: In the philosophic sects we find wonderful liberalisms. There is not a man who follows Shankara who will say that all the different sects of India are really different. At the same time he was a tremendous upholder of exclusiveness as regards caste. But with every Vaishnavite preacher we find a wonderful liberalism as to the teaching of caste questions, but exclusiveness as regards religious questions.

The one had a great head, the other a large heart, and the time was ripe for one to be born, the embodiment of both this head and heart; the time was ripe for one to be born who in one body would have the brilliant intellect of Shankara and the wonderfully expansive, infinite heart of Chaitanya; one who would see in every sect the same spirit working, the same God; one who would see God in every being, one whose heart would weep for the poor, for the weak, for the outcast, for the downtrodden, for every one in this world, inside India or outside India; and at the same time whose grand brilliant intellect would conceive of such noble thoughts as would harmonize all conflicting sects, not only in India but outside of India, and bring a marvellous harmony, the universal religion of head and heart into existence. Such a man was born, and I had the good fortune to sit at his feet for years. The time was ripe, it was necessary that such a man should be born, and he came; and the most wonderful part of it was that his life's work was just near a city which was full of Western thought, a city which had run mad after these occidental ideas, a city which had become more Europeanized than any other city in India. There he lived, without any book-learning whatsoever; this great intellect never learnt even to write his own name,[6]* but the most graduates of our university found in him an intellectual giant. He was a strange man, this Shri Ramakrishna Paramahamsa. It is a long, long story, and I have no time to tell anything about him tonight. Let me now only mention the great Shri Ramakrishna, the fulfilment of the Indian sages, the sage for the time, one whose teaching is just now, in the present time, most beneficial. And mark the divine power working behind the man. The son of a poor priest, born in an out-of-the-way village, unknown and unthought of, today is worshipped literally by thousands in Europe and America, and tomorrow will be worshipped by thousands more. Who knows the plans of the Lord!

Now, my brothers, if you do not see the hand, the finger of Providence, it is because you are blind, born blind indeed. If time comes, and another opportunity, I will speak to you more fully about him. Only let me say now that if I have told you one word of truth, it was his and his alone, and if I have told you many things which were not true, which were not correct, which were not beneficial to the human race, they were all mine, and on me is the responsibility.

51

LECTURES FROM COLOMBO TO ALMORA

Away back, where no recorded history, nay, not even the dim light of tradition, can penetrate, has been steadily shining the light, sometimes dimmed by external circumstances, at others effulgent, but undying and steady, shedding its lustre not only over India, but permeating the whole thought-world with its power, silent, unperceived, gentle, yet omnipotent, like the dew that falls in the morning, unseen and unnoticed, yet bringing into bloom the fairest of roses: this has been the thought of the Upanishads, the philosophy of the Vedanta. Nobody knows when it first came to flourish on the soil of India. Guesswork has been vain. The guesses, especially of Western writers, have been so conflicting that no certain date can be ascribed to them. But we Hindus, from the spiritual standpoint, do not admit that they had any origin. This Vedanta, the philosophy of the Upanishads, I would make bold to state, has been the first as well as the final thought on the spiritual plane that has ever been vouchsafed to man.

From this ocean of the Vedanta, waves of light from time to time have been going Westward and Eastward. In the days of yore it travelled Westward and gave its impetus to the mind of the Greeks, either in Athens, or in Alexandria, or in Antioch. The Sankhya system must clearly have made its mark on the minds of the ancient Greeks; and the Sankhya and all other systems in India hail that one authority, the Upanishads, the Vedanta. In India, too, in spite of all these jarring sects that we see today and all those that have been in the past, the one authority, the basis of all these systems, has yet been the Upanishads, the Vedanta. Whether you are a dualist, or a qualified monist, an Advaitist, or a Vishishtadvaitist, a Shuddhadvaitist, or any other Advaitist, or Dvaitist, or whatever you may call yourself, there stand behind you as authority, your Shastras, your scriptures, the Upanishads. Whatever system in India does not obey the Upanishads cannot be called orthodox, and even the systems of the Jains and the Buddhists have been rejected from the soil of India only because they did not bear allegiance to the Upanishads. Thus the Vedanta, whether we know it or not, has penetrated all the sects in India, and what we call Hinduism, this mighty banyan with its immense, almost infinite ramifications, has been throughout interpenetrated by the influence of the Vedanta. Whether we are conscious of it or not, we think the Vedanta, we live in the Vedanta, we breathe the Vedanta, and we die in the Vedanta, and every Hindu does that. To preach Vedanta in the land of India, and before an Indian audience, seems, therefore, to be an anomaly. But it is the one thing that has to be preached, and it is the necessity of the age that it must be preached. For, as I have just told you, all the Indian sects must bear allegiance to the Upanishads; but among these sects there are many apparent contradictions. Many times the great sages of yore themselves could not understand the underlying harmony of the Upanishads. Many times, even sages quarrelled, so much so that it became a proverb that there are no sages who do not differ. But the time requires that a better interpretation should be given to this underlying harmony of the Upanishadic texts, whether they are dualistic, or non-dualistic, quasi-dualistic, or so forth. That has to be shown before the world at large, and this work is required as much in India as outside of India; and I, through the grace of God, had the great good fortune to sit at the feet of one whose whole life was such an interpretation, whose life, a thousandfold more than whose teaching, was a living commentary on the texts of the Upanishads, was in fact the spirit of the Upanishads living in a human form. Perhaps I have got a little of that harmony; I do not know whether I shall be able to express it or not. But this is my attempt, my mission in life, to show that the Vedantic schools are not contradictory, that they all necessitate each other, all fulfil each other, and one, as it were, is the stepping-stone to the other, until the goal, the Advaita, the Tat Tvam Asi, is reached. There was a time in India when the Karma Kanda had its sway. There are many grand ideals, no doubt, in that portion of the Vedas. Some of our present daily worship is still according to the precepts of the Karma Kanda. But with all that, the Karma Kanda of the Vedas has almost disappeared from India. Very little of our life today is bound and regulated by the orders of the Karma Kanda of the Vedas. In our ordinary lives we are mostly Pauranikas or Tantrikas, and, even where some Vedic texts are used by the Brahmins of India, the adjustment of the texts is mostly not according to the Vedas, but according to the Tantras or the Puranas. As such, to call ourselves Vaidikas in the sense of following the Karma Kanda of the Vedas, I do not think, would be proper. But the other fact stands that we are all of us Vedantists. The people who call themselves Hindus had better be called Vedantists, and, as I have shown you, under that one name Vaidantika come in all our various sects, whether dualists or non-dualists.

The sects that are at the present time in India come to be divided in general into the two great classes of dualists and monists. The little differences which some of these sects insist upon, and upon the authority of which want to take new names as pure Advaitists, or qualified Advaitists, and so forth, do not matter much. As a classification, either they are dualists or monists, and of the sects existing at the present time, some of them are very new, and others seem to be reproductions of very ancient sects. The one class I would present by the life and philosophy of Ramanuja, and the other by Shankaracharya.

Ramanuja is the leading dualistic philosopher of later India, whom all the other dualistic sects have followed, directly or indirectly, both in the substance of their teaching and in the organization of their sects even down to some of the most minute points of their organization. You will be astonished if you compare Ramanuja and his work with the other dualistic Vaishnava sects in India, to see how much they resemble each other in organization, teaching, and method. There is the great Southern preacher Madhva Muni, and following him, our great Chaitanya of Bengal who took up the philosophy of the Madhvas and preached it in Bengal. There are some other sects also in Southern India, as the qualified dualistic Shaivas. The Shaivas in most parts of India are Advaitists, except in some portions of Southern India and in Ceylon. But they also only substitute Shiva for Vishnu and are Ramanujists in every sense of the term except in the doctrine of the soul. The followers of Ramanuja hold that the soul is Anu, like a particle, very small, and the followers of Shankaracharya hold that it is Vibhu, omnipresent. There have been several non-dualistic sects. It seems that there have been sects in ancient times which Shankara's movement has entirely swallowed up and assimilated. You find sometimes a fling at Shankara himself in some of the commentaries, especially in that of Vijnana Bhikshu who, although an Advaitist, attempts to upset the Mayavzda of Shankara. It seems there were schools who did not believe in this Mayavada, and they went so far as to call Shankara a crypto-Buddhist, Prachchhanna Bauddha, and they thought this Mayavada was taken from the Buddhists and brought within the Vedantic fold. However that may be, in modern times the Advaitists have all ranged themselves under Shankaracharya; and Shankaracharya and his disciples have been the great preachers of Advaita both in Southern and in Northern India. The influence of Shankaracharya did not penetrate much into our country of Bengal and in Kashmir and the Punjab, but in Southern India the Smartas are all followers of Shankaracharya, and with Varanasi as the centre, his influence is simply immense even in many parts of Northern India.

Now both Shankara and Ramanuja laid aside all claim to originality. Ramanuja expressly tells us he is only following the great commentary of Bodhayana. भगवद् बोधायनकृतां विस्तीर्णां ब्रह्मसुत्रवृतिं पूर्वाचार्या: संचिक्षिपु: तन्मतानुसारेण सूत्राक्षराणि व्याख्यास्यन्ते—'Ancient teachers abridged that extensive commentary on the *Brahma-sutras* which was composed by the Bhagavan Bodhayana; in accordance with their opinion, the words of the Sutra are explained.' That is what Ramanuja says at the beginning of his commentary, the *Shri-Bhashya*. He takes it up and makes of it a Samkshepa, and that is what we have today. I myself never had an opportunity of seeing this commentary of Bodhayana. The late Swami Dayananda Saraswati wanted to reject every other commentary of the *Vyasa-Sutras* except that of Bodhayana; and although he never lost an opportunity of having a fling at Ramanuja, he himself could never produce the Bodhayana. I have sought for it all over India, and never yet have been able to see it. But Ramanuja is very plain on the point, and he tells us that he is taking the ideas, and sometimes the very passages out of Bodhayana, and condensing them into the present Ramanuja Bhashya. It seems that Shankaracharya was also doing the same. There are a few places in his Bhashya which mention older commentaries, and when we know that his Guru and his Guru's Guru had been Vedantists of the same school as he, sometimes corn more thorough-going, bolder even than Shankara himself on certain points, it seems pretty plain that he also was not preaching anything very original, and that even in his Bhashya he himself had been doing the same work that Ramanuja did with Bodhayana, but from what Bhashya, it cannot be discovered at the present time.

All these Darshanas that you have ever seen or heard of are based upon Upanishadic authority. Whenever they want to quote a Shruti, they mean the Upanishads. They are always quoting the Upanishads. Following the Upanishads there come other philosophies of India, but every one of them failed in getting that hold on India which the philosophy of Vyasa got, although the philosophy of Vyasa is a development out of an older one, the Sankhya, and every philosophy and every system in India—I mean throughout the world—owes much to Kapila, perhaps the greatest name in the history of India in psychological and philosophical lines. The influence of Kapila is everywhere seen throughout the world. Wherever there is a recognized system of thought, there you can trace his influence; even if it be thousands of years back, yet he stands there, the shining, glorious, wonderful Kapila. His psychology and a good deal of his philosophy have been accepted by all the sects of India with but very little differences. In our own country, our Naiyayika philosophers could not make much impression on the philosophical world of India. They were too busy with little things like species and genus, and so forth, and that most cumbersome terminology, which it is a life's work to study. As such, they were very busy with logic and left philosophy to the Vedantists, but every one of the Indian philosophic sects in modern times has adopted the logical terminology of the Naiyayikas of Bengal. Jagadisha, Gadadhara, and Shiromani are as well known at Nadia as in some of the cities in Malabar. But the philosophy of Vyasa, the *Vyasa-Sutras*, is firm-seated and has attained the permanence of that which it intended to present to men, the Brahman of the Vedantic side of philosophy. Reason was entirely subordinated to the Shrutis, and as Shankaracharya declares, Vyasa did not care to reason at all.

His idea in writing the Sutras was just to bring together, and with one thread to make a garland of the flowers of Vedantic texts. His Sutras are admitted so far as they are subordinate to the authority of the Upanishads, and no further.

And, as I have said, all the sects of India now hold these *Vyasa-Sutras* to be the great authority, and every new sect in India starts with a fresh commentary on the *Vyasa-Sutras* according to its light. The difference between some of these commentators is sometimes very great, sometimes the text-torturing is quite disgusting. The *Vyasa-Sutras* have got the place of authority, and no one can expect to found a sect in India until he can write a fresh commentary on the *Vyasa-Sutras*.

Next in authority is the celebrated Gita. The great glory of Shankaracharya was his preaching of the Gita. It is one of the greatest works that this great man did among the many noble works of his noble life—the preaching of the Gita and writing the most beautiful commentary upon it. And he has been followed by all founders of the orthodox sects in India, each of whom has written a commentary on the Gita.

The Upanishads are many, and said to be one hundred and eight, but some declare them to be still larger in number. Some of them are evidently of a much later date, as for instance, the Allopanishad in which Allah is praised and Mohammed is called the Rajasulla. I have been told that this was written during the reign of Akbar to bring the Hindus and Mohammedans together, and sometimes they got hold of some word, as Allah, or Illa in the Samhitas, and made an Upanishad on it. So in this Allopanishad, Mohammed is the Rajasulla, whatever that may mean. There are other sectarian Upanishads of the same species, which you find to be entirely modern, and it has been so easy to write them, seeing that this language of the Samhita portion of the Vedas is so archaic that there is no grammar to it. Years ago I had an idea of studying the grammar of the Vedas, and I began with all earnestness to study Panini and the *Mahabhashya*, but to my surprise I found that the best part of the Vedic grammar consists only of exceptions to rules. A rule is made, and after that comes a statement to the effect, 'This rule will be an exception'. So you see what an amount of liberty there is for anybody to write anything, the only safeguard being the dictionary of Yaska. Still, in this you will find, for the must part, but a large number of synonyms. Given all that, how easy it is to write any number of Upanishads you please. Just have a little knowledge of Sanskrit, enough to make words look like the old archaic words, and you have no fear of grammar. Then you bring in Rajasulla or any other Sulla you like. In that way many Upanishads have been manufactured, and I am told that that is being done even now. In some parts of India, I am perfectly certain, they are trying to manufacture such Upanishads among the different sects. But among the Upanishads are those, which, on the face of them, bear the evidence of genuineness, and these have been taken up by the great commentators and commented upon, especially by Shankara, followed by Ramanuja and all the rest.

There are one or two more ideas with regard to the Upanishads which I want to bring to your notice, for these are an ocean of knowledge, and to talk about the Upanishads, even for an incompetent person like myself, takes years and not one lecture only. I want, therefore, to bring to your notice one or two points in the study of the Upanishads. In the first place, they are the most wonderful poems in the world. If you read the Samhita portion of the Vedas, you now and then find passages of most marvellous beauty. For instance, the famous Shloka which describes Chaos—तम आसीत्तमसा गूढमगे etc.— 'When darkness was hidden in darkness', so on it goes. One reads and feels the wonderful sublimity of the poetry. Do you mark this that outside of India, and inside also, there have been attempts at painting the sublime. But outside, it has always been the infinite in the muscles the external world, the infinite of matter, or of space. When Milton or Dante, or any other great European poet, either ancient or modern, wants to paint a picture of the infinite, he tries to soar outside, to make you feel the infinite through the muscles. That attempt has been made here also. You find it in the Samhitas, the infinite of extension most marvellously painted and placed before the readers, such as has been done nowhere else. Mark that one sentence—तम आसीत् तमसा गूढम्,—and now mark the description of darkness by three poets. Take our own Kalidasa—'Darkness which can be penetrated with the point of a needle'; then Milton—'No light but rather darkness visible'; but come now to the Upanishad, 'Darkness was covering darkness', 'Darkness was hidden in darkness'. We who live in the tropics can understand it, the sudden outburst of the monsoon, when in a moment, the horizon becomes darkened and clouds become covered with more rolling black clouds. So on, the poem goes; but yet, in the Samhita portion, all these attempts are external. As everywhere else, the attempts at finding the solution of the great problems of life have been through the external world. Just as the Greek mind or the modern European mind wants to find the solution of life and of all the sacred problems of Being by searching into the external world. So also did our forefathers, and just as the Europeans failed, they failed also. But the Western people never made a move more, they remained there, they failed in the search for the solution of the great problems of life and death in the external world, and there they remained, stranded; our forefathers also found it impossible, but were bolder in declaring the utter helplessness of the senses to find the solution. Nowhere else was the answer better put than in the Upanishad: यतो वाचो निवर्तन्ते अप्राप्य मनसा सह।—'From whence words come back reflected, together with the mind'; न तत्रचक्षुर्गच्छति न वागच्छति।—'There the eye cannot go, nor can speech reach'. There are various sentences which declare the utter helplessness of the senses, but they did not stop there; they fell back upon the internal nature of man, they went to get the answer from their own soul, they became introspective; they gave up external nature as a failure, as nothing could be done there, as no hope, no answer could be found; they discovered that dull, dead matter would not give them truth, and they fell back upon the shining soul of man, and there the answer was found.

तमेवैकं जानथ आत्मनम् अन्या वाचो विमुञ्चथ।—'Know this Atman alone,' they declared, 'give up all other vain words, and hear no other.' In the Atman they found the solution—the greatest of all Atmans, the God, the Lord of this universe, His relation to the Atman of man, our duty to Him, and through that our relation to each other. And herein you find the most sublime poetry in the world. No more is the attempt made to paint this Atman in the language of matter. Nay, for it they have given up even all positive language. No more is there any attempt to come to the senses to give them the idea of the infinite, no more is there an external, dull, dead, material, spacious, sensuous infinite, but instead of that comes something which is as fine as even that mentioned in the saying—

न तत्र सूर्यो भाति न चन्द्रतारकं नेमा वेद्युतो भान्ति कुतोऽयमग्निः।
तमेव भान्तमनुभाति सर्वं तस्य भासा सर्वमिदं विभाति॥

What poetry in the world can be more sublime than this! 'There the sun cannot illumine, nor the moon, nor the stars, there this flash of lightning cannot illumine; what to speak of this mortal fire!' Such poetry you find nowhere else. Take that most marvellous Upanishad, the Katha. What a wonderful finish, what a most marvellous art displayed in that poem! How wonderfully it opens with that little boy to whom Shraddha came, who wanted to see Yama, and how that most marvellous of all teachers, Death himself, teaches him the great lessons of life and death! And what was his quest? To know the secret of death.

The second point that I want you to remember is the perfectly impersonal character of the Upanishads. Although we find many names, and many speakers, and many teachers in the Upanishads, not one of them stands as an authority of the Upanishads, not one verse is based upon the life of any one of them. These are simply figures like shadows moving in the background, unfelt, unseen, unrealized, but the real force is in the marvellous, the brilliant, the effulgent texts of the Upanishads, perfectly impersonal. If twenty Yajnavalkyas came and lived and died, it does not matter; the texts are there. And yet it is against no personality; it is broad and expansive enough to embrace all the personalities that the world has yet produced, and all that are yet to come. It has nothing to say against the worship of persons, or Avataras, or sages. On the other hand, it is always upholding it. At the same time, it is perfectly impersonal. It is a most marvellous idea, like the God it preaches, the impersonal idea of the Upanishads. For the sage, the thinker, the philosopher, for the rationalist, it is as much impersonal as any modern scientist can wish. And these are our scriptures. You must remember that what the Bible is to the Christians, what the Koran is to the Mohammedans, what the Tripitaka is to the

Buddhist, what the Zend Avesta is to the Parsees, these Upanishads are to us. These and nothing but these are our scriptures. The Puranas, the Tantras, and all the other books, even the Vyasa-Sutras, are of secondary, tertiary authority, but primary are the Vedas. Manu, and the Puranas, and all the other books are to be taken so far as they agree with the authority of the Upanishads, and when they disagree they are to be rejected without mercy. This we ought to remember always, but unfortunately for India, at the present time we have forgotten it. A petty village custom seems now the real authority and not the teaching of the Upanishads. A petty idea current in a wayside village in Bengal seems to have the authority of the Vedas, and even something better. And that word 'orthodox', how wonderful its influence! To the villager, the following of every little bit of the Karma Kanda is the very height of 'orthodoxy', and one who does not do it is told, 'Go away, you are no more a Hindu.' So there are, most unfortunately in my motherland, persons who will take up one of these Tantras and say, that the practise of this Tantra is to be obeyed; he who does not do so is no more orthodox in his views. Therefore it is better for us to remember that in the Upanishads is the primary authority, even the Grihya and Shrauta Sutras are subordinate to the authority of the Vedas. They are the words of the Rishis, our forefathers, and you have to believe them if you want to become a Hindu. You may even believe the most peculiar ideas about the Godhead, but if you deny the authority of the Vedas, you are a Nastika. Therein lies the difference between the scriptures of the Christians or the Buddhists and ours; theirs are all Puranas, and not scriptures, because they describe the history of the deluge, and the history of kings and reigning families, and record the lives of great men, and so on. This is the work of the Puranas, and so far as they agree with the Vedas, they are good. So far as the Bible and the scriptures of other nations agree with the Vedas, they are perfectly good, but when they do not agree, they are no more to be accepted. So with the Koran. There are many moral teachings in these, and so far as they agree with the Vedas they have the authority of the Puranas, but no more. The idea is that the Vedas were never written; the idea is, they never came into existence. I was told once by a Christian missionary that their scriptures have a historical character, and therefore are true, to which I replied, 'Mine have no historical character and *therefore* they are true; yours being historical, they were evidently made by some man the other day. Yours are man-made and mine are not; their non-historicity is in their favour.' Such is the relation of the Vedas with all the other scriptures at the present day.

We now come to the teachings of the Upanishads. Various texts are there. Some are perfectly dualistic, while others are monistic. But there are certain doctrines which are agreed to by all the different sects of India. First, there is the doctrine of Samsara or reincarnation of the soul. Secondly, they all agree in their psychology; first there is the body, behind that, what they call the Sukshma Sharira, the mind, and behind that even, is the Jiva. That is the great difference between Western and Indian psychology; in the Western psychology the mind is the soul, here it is not. The Antahkarana, the internal instrument, as the mind is called, is only an instrument in the hands of that Jiva, through which the Jiva works on the body or on the external world. Here they all agree, and they all also agree that this Jiva or Atman, Jivatman as it is called by various sects, is eternal, without beginning; and that it is going from birth to birth, until it gets a final release. They all agree in this, and they also all agree in one other most vital point, which alone marks characteristically, most prominently, most vitally, the difference between the Indian and the Western mind, and it is this, that everything is in the soul. There is no inspiration, but properly speaking, expiration. All powers and all purity and all greatness—everything is in the soul. The Yogi would tell you that the Siddhis-Anima, Laghima, and so on—that he wants to attain to are not to be attained, in the proper sense of the word, but are already there in the soul; the work is to make them manifest. Patanjali, for instance, would tell you that even in the lowest worm that crawls under your feet, all the eightfold Yogi's powers are already existing. The difference has been made by the body. As soon as it gets a better body, the powers will become manifest, but they are there.

निमित्तमप्रयोजकं पकृतीनां वरणभेदस्तु ततः क्षेत्रिकवत्—'Good and bad deeds are not the direct causes in the transformations of nature, but they act as breakers of obstacles to the evolutions of nature: as a farmer breaks the obstacles to the course of water, which then runs down by its own nature.' Here Patanjali gives the celebrated example of the cultivator bringing water into his field from a huge tank somewhere. The tank is already filled and the water would flood his land in a moment, only there is a mud-wall between the tank and his field. As soon as the barrier is broken, in rushes the water out of its own power and force. This mass of power and purity and perfection is in the soul already. The only difference is the Avarana—this veil—that has been cast over it. Once the veil is removed, the soul attains to purity, and its powers become manifest. This, you ought to remember, is the great difference between Eastern and Western thought. Hence you find people teaching such awful doctrines as that we are all born sinners, and because we do not believe in such awful doctrines we are all born wicked. They never stop to think that if we are by our very nature wicked, we can never be good—for how can nature change? If it changes, it contradicts itself; it is not nature. We ought to remember this. Here the dualist, and the Advaitist, and all others in India agree.

The next point, which all the sects in India believe in, is God. Of course their ideas of God will be different. The dualists believe in a Personal God, and a personal only. I want you to understand this word personal a little more. This word personal does not mean that God has a body, sits on a throne somewhere, and rules this world, but means Saguna, with qualities. There are many descriptions of the Personal God. This Personal God as the Ruler, the Creator, the Preserver, and the Destroyer of this universe is believed in by all the sects. The Advaitists believe something more. They believe in a still higher phase of this Personal God, which is personal-impersonal. No adjective can illustrate where there is no qualification, and the Advaitist would not give Him any qualities except the three—Sat-Chit-Ananda, Existence, Knowledge, and Bliss Absolute. This is what Shankara did. But in the Upanishads themselves you find they penetrate even further, and say, nothing can be predicated of it except Neti, Neti, 'Not this, Not this'.

Here all the different sects of India agree. But taking the dualistic side, as I have said, I will take Ramanuja as the typical dualist of India, the great modern representative of the dualistic system. It is a pity that our people in Bengal know so very little about the great religious leaders in India, who have been born in other parts of the country; and for the matter of that, during the whole of the Mohammedan period, with the exception of our Chaitanya, all the great religious leaders were born in Southern India, and it is the intellect of Southern India that is really governing India now; for even Chaitanya belonged to one of these sects, a sect of the Madhvas. According to Ramanuja, these three entities are eternal—God, and soul, and nature. The souls are eternal, and they will remain eternally existing, individualized through eternity, and will retain their individuality all through. Your soul will be different from my soul through all eternity, says Ramanuja, and so will this nature—which is an existing fact, as much a fact as the existence of soul or the existence of God—remain always different. And God is interpenetrating, the essence of the soul, He is the Antaryamin. In this sense Ramanuja sometimes thinks that God is one with the soul, the essence of the soul, and these souls—at the time of Pralaya, when the whole of nature becomes what he calls Sankuchita, contracted—become contracted and minute and remain so for a time. And at the beginning of the next cycle they all come out, according to their past Karma, and undergo the effect of that Karma. Every action that makes the natural inborn purity and perfection of the soul get contracted is a bad action, and every action that makes it come out and expand itself is a good action, says Ramanuja. Whatever helps to make the Vikasha of the soul is good, and whatever makes it Sankuchita is bad. And thus the soul is going on, expanding or contracting in its actions, till through the grace of God comes salvation. And that grace comes to all souls, says Ramanuja, that are pure and struggle for that grace.

There is a celebrated verse in the Shrutis, आहारशुध्दौ सत्त्वशुध्दि: सत्त्वशुध्दौ ध्रुवास्मृति: 'When the food is pure, then the Sattva becomes pure; when the Sattva is pure, then the Smriti'—the memory of the Lord, or the memory of our own perfection—if you are an Advaitist—'becomes truer, steadier, and absolute'. Here is a great discussion. First of all, what is this Sattva? We know that according to the Sankhya—and it has been admitted by all our sects of philosophy—the body is composed of three sorts of materials—not qualities. It is the general idea that Sattva, Rajas, and Tamas are qualities. Not at all, not qualities but the materials of this universe, and with Ahara-shuddhi, when the food is pure, the Sattva material becomes pure. The one theme of the

Vedanta is to get this Sattva. As I have told you, the soul is already pure and perfect, and it is, according to the Vedanta, covered up by Rajas and Tamas particles. The Sattva particles are the most luminous, and the effulgence of the soul penetrates through them as easily as light through glass. So if the Rajas and Tamas particles go, and leave the Sattva particles, in this state the power and purity of the soul will appear, and leave the soul more manifest.

Therefore it is necessary to have this Sattva. And the text says, 'When Ahara becomes pure'. Ramanuja takes this word Ahara to mean food, and he has made it one of the turning points of his philosophy. Not only so, it has affected the whole of India, and all the different sects. Therefore it is necessary for us to understand what it means, for that, according to Ramanuja, is one of the principal factors in our life, Ahara-shuddhi. What makes food impure? asks Ramanuja. Three sorts of defects make food impure—first, Jati-dosha, the defect in the very nature of the class to which the food belongs, as the smell in onions, garlic, and suchlike. The next is Ashraya-dosha, the defect in the person from whom the food comes; food coming from a wicked person will make you impure. I myself have seen many great sages in India following strictly that advice all their lives. Of course they had the power to know who brought the food, and even who had touched the food, and I have seen it in my own life, not once, but hundreds of times. Then Nimitta-dosha, the defect of impure things or influences coming in contact with food is another. We had better attend to that a little more now. It has become too prevalent in India to take food with dirt and dust and bits of hair in it. If food is taken from which these three defects have been removed, that makes Sattva-shuddhi, purifies the Sattva. Religion seems to be a very easy task then. Then every one can have religion if it comes by eating pure food only. There is none so weak or incompetent in this world, that I know, who cannot save himself from these defects. Then comes Shankaracharya, who says this word Ahara means thought collected in the mind; when that becomes pure, the Sattva becomes pure, and not before that. You may eat what you like. If food alone would purify the Sattva, then feed the monkey with milk and rice all its life; would it become a great Yogi? Then the cows and the deer would be great Yogis. As has been said, 'If it is by bathing much that heaven is reached, the fishes will get to heaven first. If by eating vegetables a man gets to heaven, the cows and the deer will get to heaven first.'

But what is the solution? Both are necessary. Of course the idea that Shankaracharya gives us of Ahara is the primary idea. But pure food, no doubt, helps pure thought; it has an intimate connection; both ought to be there. But the defect is that in modern India we have forgotten the advice of Shankaracharya and taken only the 'pure food' meaning. That is why people get mad with me when I say, religion has got into the kitchen; and if you had been in Madras with me, you would have agreed with me. The Bengalis are better than that. In Madras, they throw away food if anybody looks at it. And with all this, I do not see that the people are any the better there. If only eating this and that sort of food and saving it from the looks of this person and that person would give them perfection, you would expect them all to be perfect men, which they are not.

Thus, although these are to be combined and linked together to make a perfect whole, do not put the cart before the horse. There is a cry nowadays about this and that food and about Varnashrama, and the Bengalis are the most vociferous in these cries. I would ask every one of you, what do you know about this Varnashrama? Where are the four castes today in this country? Answer me; I do not see the four castes. Just as our Bengali proverb has it, 'A headache without a head', so you want to make this Varnashrama here. There are not four castes here. I see only the Brahmin and the Shudra. If there are the Kshatriyas and the Vaishyas, where are they and why do not you Brahmins order them to take the Yajnopavita and study the Vedas, as every Hindu ought to do? And if the Vaishyas and the Kshatriyas do not exist, but only the Brahmins and the Shudras, the Shastras say that the Brahmin must not live in a country where there are only Shudras; so depart bag and baggage! Do you know what the Shastras say about people who have been eating Mlechchha food and living under a government of the Mlechchhas, as you have for the past thousand years? Do you know the penance for that? The penance would be burning oneself with one's own hands. Do you want to pass as teachers and walk like hypocrisies? If you believe in your Shastras, burn yourselves first like the one great Brahmin did who went with Alexander the Great and burnt himself because he thought he had eaten the food of a Mlechchha. Do like that, and you will see that the whole nation will be at your feet. You do not believe in your own Shastras and yet want to make others believe in them. If you think you are not able to do that in this age, admit your weakness and excuse the weakness of others, take the other castes up, give them a helping hand, let them study the Vedas and become just as good Aryans as any other Aryans in the world, and be you likewise Aryans, you Brahmins of Bengal.

Give up this filthy Vamachara that is killing your country. You have not seen the other parts of India. When I see how much the Vamachara has entered our society, I find it a most disgraceful place with all its boast of culture. These Vamachara sects are honeycombing our society in Bengal. Those who come out in the daytime and preach most loudly about Achara, it is they who carry on the horrible debauchery at night and are backed by the most dreadful books. They are ordered by the books to do these things. You who are of Bengal know it. The Bengali Shastras are the Vamachara Tantras. They are published by the cart-load, and you poison the minds of your children with them instead of teaching them your Shrutis. Fathers of Calcutta, do you not feel ashamed that such horrible stuff as these Vamachara Tantras, with translations too, should be put into the hands of your boys and girls, and their minds poisoned, and that they should be brought up with the idea that these are the Shastras of the Hindus? If you are ashamed, take them away from your children, and let them read the true Shastras, the Vedas, the Gita, the Upanishads.

According to the dualistic sects of India, the individual souls remain as individuals throughout, and God creates the universe out of pre-existing material only as the efficient cause. According to the Advaitists, on the other hand, God is both the material and the efficient cause of the universe. He is not only the Creator of the universe, but He creates it out of Himself. That is the Advaitist position. There are crude dualistic sects who believe that this world has been created by God out of Himself, and at the same time God is eternally separate from the universe, and everything is eternally subordinate to the Ruler of the universe. There are sects too who also believe that out of Himself God has evolved this universe, and individuals in the long run attain to Nirvana to give up the finite and become the Infinite. But these sects have disappeared. The one sect of Advaitists that you see in modern India is composed of the followers of Shankara. According to Shankara, God is both the material and the efficient cause through Maya, but not in reality. God has not become this universe; but the universe is not, and God is. This is one of the highest points to understand of Advaita Vedanta, this idea of Maya. I am afraid I have no time to discuss this one most difficult point in our philosophy. Those of you who are acquainted with Western philosophy will find something very similar in Kant. But I must warn you, those of you who have studied Professor Max Müller's writings on Kant, that there is one idea most misleading. It was Shankara who first found out the idea of the identity of time, space, and causation with Maya, and I had the good fortune to find one or two passages in Shankara's commentaries and send them to my friend the Professor. So even that idea was here in India. Now this is a peculiar theory—this Maya theory of the Advaita Vedantists. The Brahman is all that exists, but differentiation has been caused by this Maya. Unity, the one Brahman, is the ultimate, the goal, and herein is an eternal dissension again between Indian and Western thought. India has thrown this challenge to the world for thousands of years, and the challenge has been taken up by different nations, and the result is that they all succumbed and you live. This is the challenge that this world is a delusion, that it is all Maya, that whether you eat off the ground with your fingers or dine off golden plates, whether you live in palaces and are one of the mightiest monarchs or are the poorest of beggars, death is the one result; it is all the same, all Maya. That is the old Indian theme, and again and again nations are springing up trying to unsay it, to disprove it; becoming great, with enjoyment as their watchword, power in their hands, they use that power to the utmost, enjoy to the utmost, and the next moment they die. We stand for ever because we see that everything is Maya. The children of Maya live for ever, but the children of enjoyment die.

Here again is another great difference. Just as you find the attempts of Hegel and Schopenhauer in German philosophy, so you will find the very same ideas brought forward in ancient India. Fortunately for us, Hegelianism was nipped in the bud and not allowed to sprout and cast its baneful shoots over this motherland of ours. Hegel's one idea is that the one, the absolute, is only chaos, and that the individualized form is the greater. The world is greater than the non-world, Samsara is greater than salvation. That is the one idea, and the more you plunge into this Samsara the more your soul is covered with the workings of life, the better you are. They say, do you not see how we build houses, cleanse the streets, enjoy the senses? Ay, behind that they may hide rancour, misery, horror—behind every bit of that enjoyment.

On the other hand, our philosophers have from the very first declared that every manifestation, what you call evolution, is vain, a vain attempt of the unmanifested to manifest itself. Ay, you the mighty cause of this universe, trying to reflect yourself in little mud puddles! But after making the attempt for a time you find out it was all in vain and beat a retreat to the place from whence you came. This is Vairagya, or renunciation, and the very beginning of religion. How can religion or morality begin without renunciation itself ? The Alpha and Omega is renunciation. 'Give up,' says the Veda, 'give up.' That is the one way, 'Give up'. न प्रजया धनेन त्यागेनैकेऽमृतत्वमानशुः—'Neither through wealth, nor through progeny, but by giving up alone that immortality is to be reached.' That is the dictate of the Indian books. Of course, there have been great givers-up of the world, even sitting on thrones. But even (King) Janaka himself had to renounce; who was a greater renouncer than he? But in modern times we all want to be called Janakas! They are all Janakas (lit. fathers) of children—unclad, ill-fed, miserable children. The word Janaka can be applied to them in that sense only; they have none of the shining, Godlike thoughts as the old Janaka had. These are our modern Janakas! A little less of this Janakism now, and come straight to the mark! If you can give up, you will have religion. If you cannot, you may read all the books that are in the world, from East to West, swallow all the libraries, and become the greatest of Pandits, but if you have Karma Kanda only, you are nothing; there is no spirituality. Through renunciation alone this immortality is to be reached. It is the power, the great power, that cares not even for the universe; then it is that ब्रह्माण्डम् गोष्पदायजे।

'The whole universe becomes like a hollow made by a cow's foot.'

Renunciation, that is the flag, the banner of India, floating over the world, the one undying thought which India sends again and again as a warning to dying races, as a warning to all tyranny, as a warning to wickedness in the world. Ay, Hindus, let not your hold of that banner go. Hold it aloft. Even if you are weak and cannot renounce, do not lower the ideal. Say, 'I am weak and cannot renounce the world', but do not try to be hypocrites, torturing texts, and making specious arguments, and trying to throw dust in the eyes of people who are ignorant. Do not do that, but own you are weak. For the idea is great, that of renunciation. What matters it if millions fail in the attempt, if ten soldiers or even two return victorious! Blessed be the millions dead! Their blood has bought the victory. This renunciation is the one ideal throughout the different Vedic sects except one, and that is the Vallabhacharya sect in Bombay Presidency, and most of you are aware what comes where renunciation does not exist. We want orthodoxy—even the hideously orthodox, even those who smother themselves with ashes, even those who stand with their hands uplifted. Ay, we want them, unnatural though they be, for standing for that idea of giving up, and acting as a warning to the race against succumbing to the effeminate luxuries that are creeping into India, eating into our very vitals, and tending to make the whole race a race of hypocrites. We want to have a little of asceticism. Renunciation conquered India in days of yore, it has still to conquer India. Still it stands as the greatest and highest of Indian ideals—this renunciation. The land of Buddha, the land of Ramanuja, of Ramakrishna Paramahamsa, the land of renunciation, the land where, from the days of yore, Karma Kanda was preached against, and even today there are hundreds who have given up everything, and become Jivanmuktas—ay, will that land give up its ideals? Certainly not. There may be people whose brains have become turned by the Western luxurious ideals; there may be thousands and hundreds of thousands who have drunk deep of enjoyment, this curse of the West—the senses—the curse of the world; yet for all that, there will be other thousands in this motherland of mine to whom religion will ever be a reality, and who will be ever ready to give up without counting the cost, if need be.

Another ideal very common in all our sects, I want to place before you; it is also a vast subject. This unique idea that religion is to be realized is in India alone...नायमात्मा प्रवचनेन लभ्यो न मेधाया न बहुना श्रुतेन—'This Atman is not to be reached by too much talking, nor is it to be reached by the power of intellect, nor by much study of the scriptures.' Nay, ours is the only scripture in the world that declares, not even by the study of the scriptures can the Atman be realized—not talks, not lecturing, none of that, but It is to be realized. It comes from the teacher to the disciple. When this insight comes to the disciple, everything is cleared up and realization follows.

One more idea. There is a peculiar custom in Bengal, which they call Kula-Guru, or hereditary Guruship. 'My father was your Guru, now I shall be your Guru. My father was the Guru of your father, so shall I be yours.' What is a Guru? Let us go back to the Shrutis—'He who knows the secret of the Vedas', not bookworms, not grammarians, not Pandits in general, but he who knows the meaning. यथा खरश्चन्दनभारवाही भारस्य वेत्ता न तु चन्दनस्य।—'An ass laden with a load of sandalwood knows only the weight of the wood, but not its precious qualities'; so are these Pandits. We do not want such. What can they teach if they have no realization? When I was a boy here, in this city of Calcutta, I used to go from place to place in search of religion, and everywhere I asked the lecturer after hearing very big lectures, 'Have you seen God?' The man was taken aback at the idea of seeing God; and the only man who told me, 'I have', was Ramakrishna Paramahamsa, and not only so, but he said, 'I will put you in the way of seeing Him too'. The Guru is not a man who twists and tortures texts. वाग्वैखरी शब्दझरी शास्त्रव्याख्यानकौशलं वैदुष्यं विदुषां तद्वद् भुद्रये न तु मुद्रये। —'Different ways of throwing out words, different ways of explaining texts of the scriptures, these are for the enjoyment of the learned, not for freedom.' Shrotriya, he who knows the secret of the Shrutis, Avrijina, the sinless, and Akamahata, unpierced by desire—he who does not want to make money by teaching you—he is the Shanta, the Sadhu, who comes as the spring which brings the leaves and blossoms to various plants but does not ask anything from the plant, for its very nature is to do good. It does good and there it is. Such is the Guru, तीर्णा: स्वयं भीमभवार्णवं जनानहेतुनान्यानपि तारयन्त:—'Who has himself crossed this terrible ocean of life, and without any idea of gain to himself, helps others also to cross the ocean.' This is the Guru, and mark that none else can be a Guru, for अविद्यायामन्तरे वर्तमाना: स्वयं धीरा: पण्डितम्मन्यमाना:। दन्द्रम्यमाणा: परियन्ति मूढा: अन्धेनैव नीयमाना यथान्धा:—'Themselves steeped in darkness, but in the pride of their hearts, thinking they know everything, the fools want to help others, and they go round and round in many crooked ways, staggering to and fro, and thus like the blind leading the blind, both fall into the ditch.' Thus say the Vedas. Compare that and your present custom. You are Vedantists, you are very orthodox, are you not? You are great Hindus and very orthodox. Ay, what I want to do is to make you more orthodox. The more orthodox you are, the more sensible; and the more you think of modern orthodoxy, the more foolish you are. Go back to your old orthodoxy, for in those days every sound that came from these books, every pulsation, was out of a strong, steady, and sincere heart; every note was true. After that came degradation in art, in science, in religion, in everything, national degradation. We have no time to discuss the causes, but all the books written about that period breathe of the pestilence—the national decay; instead of vigour, only wails and cries. Go back, go back to the old days when there was strength and vitality. Be strong once more, drink deep of this fountain of yore, and that is the only condition of life in India.

According to the Advaitist, this individuality which we have today is a delusion. This has been a hard nut to crack all over the world. Forthwith you tell a man he is not an individual, he is so much afraid that his individuality, whatever that may be, will be lost! But the Advaitist says there never has been an individuality, you have been changing every moment of your life. You were a child and thought in one way, now you are a man and think another way, again you will be an old man and think differently. Everybody is changing. If so, where is your individuality? Certainly not in the body, or in the mind, or in thought. And beyond that is your Atman, and, says the Advaitist, this Atman is the Brahman Itself. There cannot be two infinites. There is only one individual and it is infinite. In plain words, we are rational beings, and we want to reason. And what is reason? More or less of classification, until you cannot go on any further. And the finite can only find its ultimate rest when it is classified into the infinite. Take up a finite thing and go on analysing it, but you will find rest nowhere until you reach the ultimate or infinite, and that infinite, says the Advaitist, is what alone exists. Everything else is Maya, nothing else has real existence; whatever is of existence in any material thing is this Brahman; we are this Brahman, and the shape and everything else is Maya. Take away the form and shape, and you and I are all one. But we have to guard against the word, 'I'. Generally people say, 'If I am the Brahman, why cannot I do this and that?' But this is using the word in a different sense. As soon as you think you are bound, no more you are Brahman, the Self, who wants nothing, whose light is inside. All His pleasures and bliss are inside; perfectly satisfied with Himself, He wants nothing, expects nothing, perfectly fearless, perfectly free. That is Brahman. In That we are all one.

Now this seems, therefore, to be the great point of difference between the dualist and the Advaitist. You find even great commentators like Shankaracharya making meanings of texts, which, to my mind, sometimes do not seem to be justified. Sometimes you find Ramanuja dealing with texts in a way that is not very clear. The idea has been even among our Pandits that only one of these sects can be true and the rest must be false, although they have the idea in the Shrutis, the most wonderful idea that India has yet to give to the world: एकं सद्विप्रा बहुधा वदन्ति।—'That which exists is One; sages call It by various names.' That has been the theme, and the working out of the whole of this life-problem of the nation is the working out of that theme—एकं सद्विप्रा बहुधा वदन्ति। Yea, except a very few learned men, I mean, barring a very few spiritual men, in India, we always forget this. We forget this great idea, and you will find that there are persons among Pandits—I should think ninety-eight per cent—who are of opinion that either the Advaitist will be true, or the Vishishtadvaitist will be true, or the Dvaitist will be true; and if you go to Varanasi, and sit for five minutes in one of the Ghats there, you will have demonstration of what I say. You will see a regular bull-fight going on about these various sects and things.

Thus it remains. Then came one whose life was the explanation, whose life was the working out of the harmony that is the background of all the different sects of India, I mean Ramakrishna Paramahamsa. It is his life that explains that both of these are necessary, that they are like the geocentric and the heliocentric theories in astronomy. When a child is taught astronomy, he is taught the geocentric first, and works out similar ideas of astronomy to the geocentric. But when he comes to finer points of astronomy, the heliocentric will be necessary, and he will understand it better. Dualism is the natural idea of the senses; as long as we are bound by the senses we are bound to see a God who is only Personal, and nothing but Personal, we are bound to see the world as it is. Says Ramanuja, 'So long as you think you are a body, and you think you are a mind, and you think you are a Jiva, every act of perception will give you the three—Soul, and nature, and something as causing both.' But yet, at the same time, even the idea of the body disappears where the mind itself becomes finer and finer, till it has almost disappeared, when all the different things that make us fear, make us weak, and bind us down to this body-life have disappeared. Then and then alone one finds out the truth of that grand old teaching. What is the teaching?

इहैव तैर्जित: सर्गो येषां साम्ये स्थितं मन:।
निर्दोषं हि समं ब्रह्म तस्माद् ब्रह्मणि ते स्थिता:॥

'Even in this life they have conquered the round of birth and death whose minds are firm-fixed on the sameness of everything, for God is pure and the same to all, and therefore such are said to be living in God.'

समं पश्यन् हि सर्वत्र समवस्थितमीश्वरम्।
न हिनस्त्यात्मनात्मानं ततो याति परां गतिम्॥

'Thus seeing the Lord the same everywhere, he, the sage, does not hurt the Self by the self, and so goes to the highest goal.'

52

THE FUTURE OF INDIA

This is the ancient land where wisdom made its home before it went into any other country, the same India whose influx of spirituality is represented, as it were, on the material plane, by rolling rivers like oceans, where the eternal Himalayas, rising tier above tier with their snowcaps, look as it were into the very mysteries of heaven. Here is the same India whose soil has been trodden by the feet of the greatest sages that ever lived. Here first sprang up inquiries into the nature of man and into the internal world. Here first arose the doctrines of the immortality of the soul, the existence of a supervising God, an immanent God in nature and in man, and here the highest ideals of religion and philosophy have attained their culminating points. This is the land from whence, like the tidal waves, spirituality and philosophy have again and again rushed out and deluged the world, and this is the land from whence once more such tides must proceed in order to bring life and vigour into the decaying races of mankind. It is the same India which has withstood the shocks of centuries, of hundreds of foreign invasions of hundreds of upheavals of manners and customs. It is the same land which stands firmer than any rock in the world, with its undying vigour, indestructible life. Its life is of the same nature as the soul, without beginning and without end, immortal; and we are the children of such a country.

Children of India, I am here to speak to you today about some practical things, and my object in reminding you about the glories of the past is simply this. Many times have I been told that looking into the past only degenerates and leads to nothing, and that we should look to the future. That is true. But out of the past is built the future. Look back, therefore, as far as you can, drink deep of the eternal fountains that are behind, and after that, look forward, march forward and make India brighter, greater, much higher than she ever was. Our ancestors were great. We must first recall that. We must learn the elements of our being, the blood that courses in our veins; we must have faith in that blood and what it did in the past; and out of that faith and consciousness of past greatness, we must build an India yet greater than what she has been. There have been periods of decay and degradation. I do not attach much importance to them; we all know that. Such periods have been necessary. A mighty tree produces a beautiful ripe fruit. That fruit falls on the ground, it decays and rots, and out of that decay springs the root and the future tree, perhaps mightier than the first one. This period of decay through which we have passed was all the more necessary. Out of this decay is coming the India of the future; it is sprouting, its first leaves are already out; and a mighty, gigantic tree, the Urdhvamula, is here, already beginning to appear; and it is about that that I am going to speak to you.

The problems in India are more complicated, more momentous, than the problems in any other country. Race, religion, language, government—all these together make a nation The elements which compose the nations of the world are indeed very few, taking race after race, compared to this country. Here have been the Aryan, the Dravidian, the Tartar, the Turk, the Mogul, the European—all the nations of the world, as it were, pouring their blood into this land. Of languages the most wonderful conglomeration is here; of manners and customs there is more difference between two Indian races than between the European and the Eastern races.

The one common ground that we have is our sacred tradition, our religion. That is the only common ground, and upon that we shall have to build. In Europe, political ideas form the national unity. In Asia, religious ideals form the national unity. The unity in religion, therefore, is absolutely necessary as the first condition of the future of India. There must be the recognition of one religion throughout the length and breadth of this land. What do I mean by one religion? Not in the sense of one religion as held among the Christians, or the Mohammedans, of the Buddhists. We know that our religion has certain common grounds, common to all our sects, however varying their conclusions may be, however different their claims may be. So there are certain common grounds; and within their limitation this religion of ours admits of a marvellous variation, an infinite amount of liberty to think and live our own lives. We all know that, at least those of us who have thought; and what we want is to bring out these lifegiving common principles of our religion, and let every man, woman, and child, throughout the length and breadth of this country, understand them, know them, and try to bring them out in their lives. This is the first step; and, therefore, it has to be taken.

We see how in Asia, and especially in India, race difficulties, linguistic difficulties, social difficulties, national difficulties, all melt away before this unifying power of religion. We know that to the Indian mind there is nothing higher than religious ideals, that this is the keynote of Indian life, and we can only work in the line of least resistance. It is not only true that the ideal of religion is the highest ideal; in the case of India it is the only possible means of work; work in any other line, without first strengthening this, would be disastrous. Therefore, the first plank in the making of a future India, the first step that is to be hewn out of that rock of ages, is this unification of religion. All of us have to be taught that we Hindus—dualists, qualified monists, or monists, Shaivas, Vaishnavas, or Pashupatas—to whatever denomination we may belong, have certain common ideas behind us, and that the time has come when for the well-being of ourselves, for the well-being of our race, we must give up all our little quarrels and differences. Be sure, these quarrels are entirely wrong; they are condemned by our scriptures, forbidden by our forefathers; and those great men from whom we claim our descent, whose blood is in our veins, look down with contempt on their children quarrelling about minute differences.

With the giving up of quarrels all other improvements will come. When the life-blood is strong and pure, no disease germ can live in that body. Our life-blood is spirituality. If it flows clear, if it flows strong and pure and vigorous, everything is right; political, social, any other material defects, even the poverty of the land, will all be cured if that blood is pure. For if the disease germ be thrown out, nothing will be able to enter into the blood. To take a simile from modern medicine, we know that there must be two causes to produce a disease, some poison germ outside, and the state of the body. Until the body is in a state to admit the germs, until the body is degraded to a lower vitality so that the germs may enter and thrive and multiply, there is no power in any germ in the world to produce a disease in the body. In fact, millions of germs are continually passing through everyone's body; but so long as it is vigorous, it never is conscious of them. It is only when the body is weak that these germs take possession of it and produce disease. Just so with the national life. It is when the national body is weak that all sorts of disease germs, in the political state of the race or in its social state, in its educational or intellectual state, crowd into the system and produce disease. To remedy it, therefore, we must go to the root of this disease and cleanse the blood of all impurities. The one tendency will be to strengthen the man, to make the blood pure, the body vigorous, so that it will be able to resist and throw off all external poisons.

We have seen that our vigour, our strength, nay, our national life is in our religion. I am not going to discuss now whether it is right or not, whether it is correct or not, whether it is beneficial or not in the long run, to have this vitality in religion, but for good or evil it is there; you cannot get out of it, you have it now and for ever, and you have to stand by it, even if you have not the same faith that I have in our religion. You are bound by it, and if you give it up, you are smashed to pieces. That is the life of our race and that must be strengthened. You have withstood the shocks of centuries simply because you took great care of it, you sacrificed everything else for it. Your forefathers underwent everything boldly, even death itself, but preserved their religion. Temple alter temple was broken down by the foreign conqueror, but no sooner had the wave passed than the spire of the temple rose up again. Some of these old temples of Southern India and those like Somnath of Gujarat will teach you volumes of wisdom, will give you a keener insight into the history of the race than any amount of books. Mark how these temples bear the marks of a hundred attacks and a hundred regenerations, continually destroyed and continually springing up out of the ruins, rejuvenated and strong as ever! That is the national mind, that is the national life-current. Follow it and it leads to glory. Give it up and you die;

death will be the only result, annihilation the only effect, the moment you step beyond that life-current. I do not mean to say that other things are not necessary. I do not mean to say that political or social improvements are not necessary, but what I mean is this, and I want you to bear it in mind, that they are secondary here and that religion is primary. The Indian mind is first religious, then anything else. So this is to be strengthened, and how to do it? I will lay before you my ideas. They have been in my mind for a long time, even years before I left the shores of Madras for America, and that I went to America and England was simply for propagating those ideas. I did not care at all for the Parliament of Religions or anything else; it was simply an opportunity; for it was really those ideas of mine that took me all over the world.

My idea is first of all to bring out the gems of spirituality that are stored up in our books and in the possession of a few only, hidden, as it were, in monasteries and in forests—to bring them out; to bring the knowledge out of them, not only from the hands where it is hidden, but from the still more inaccessible chest, the language in which it is preserved, the incrustation of centuries of Sanskrit words. In one word, I want to make them popular. I want to bring out these ideas and let them be the common property of all, of every man in India, whether he knows the Sanskrit language or not. The great difficulty in the way is the Sanskrit language—the glorious language of ours; and this difficulty cannot be removed until—if it is possible—the whole of our nation are good Sanskrit scholars. You will understand the difficulty when I tell you that I have been studying this language all my life, and yet every new book is new to me. How much more difficult would it then be for people who never had time to study the language thoroughly! Therefore the ideas must be taught in the language of the people; at the same time, Sanskrit education must go on along with it, because the very sound of Sanskrit words gives a prestige and a power and a strength to the race. The attempts of the great Ramanuja and of Chaitanya and of Kabir to raise the lower classes of India show that marvellous results were attained during the lifetime of those great prophets; yet the later failures have to be explained, and cause shown why the effect of their teachings stopped almost within a century of the passing away of these great Masters. The secret is here. They raised the lower classes; they had all the wish that these should come up, but they did not apply their energies to the spreading of the Sanskrit language among the masses. Even the great Buddha made one false step when he stopped the Sanskrit language from being studied by the masses. He wanted rapid and immediate results, and translated and preached in the language of the day, Pali. That was grand; he spoke in the language of the people, and the people understood him. That was great; it spread the ideas quickly and made them reach far and wide. But along with that, Sanskrit ought to have spread. Knowledge came, but the prestige was not there, culture was not there. It is culture that withstands shocks, not a simple mass of knowledge. You can put a mass of knowledge into the world, but that will not do it much good. There must come culture into the blood. We all know in modern times of nations which have masses of knowledge, but what of them? They are like tigers, they are like savages, because culture is not there. Knowledge is only skin-deep, as civilization is, and a little scratch brings out the old savage. Such things happen; this is the danger. Teach the masses in the vernaculars, give them ideas; they will get information, but something more is necessary; give them culture. Until you give them that, there can be no permanence in the raised condition of the masses. There will be another caste created, having the advantage of the Sanskrit language, which will quickly get above the rest and rule them all the same. The only safety, I tell you men who belong to the lower castes, the only way to raise your condition is to study Sanskrit, and this fighting and writing and frothing against the higher castes is in vain, it does no good, and it creates fight and quarrel, and this race, unfortunately already divided, is going to be divided more and more. The only way to bring about the levelling of caste is to appropriate the culture, the education which is the strength of the higher castes. That done, you have what you want

In connection with this I want to discuss one question which it has a particular bearing with regard to Madras. There is a theory that there was a race of mankind in Southern India called Dravidians, entirely differing from another race in Northern India called the Aryans, and that the Southern India Brahmins are the only Aryans that came from the North, the other men of Southern India belong to an entirely different caste and race to those of Southern India Brahmins. Now I beg your pardon, Mr Philologist, this is entirely unfounded. The only proof of it is that there is a difference of language between the North and the South. I do not see any other difference. We are so many Northern men here, and I ask my European friends to pick out the Northern and Southern men from this assembly. Where is the difference? A little difference of language. But the Brahmins are a race that came here speaking the Sanskrit language! Well then, they took up the Dravidian language and forgot their Sanskrit. Why should not the other castes have done the same? Why should not all the other castes have come one after the other from Northern India, taken up the Dravidian language, and so forgotten their own? That is an argument working both ways. Do not believe in such silly things. There may have been a Dravidian people who vanished from here, and the few who remained lived in forests and other places. It is quite possible that the language may have been taken up, but all these are Aryans who came from the North. The whole of India is Aryan, nothing else.

Then there is the other idea that the Shudra caste are surely the aborigines. What are they? They are slaves. They say history repeats itself. The Americans, English, Dutch, and the Portuguese got hold of the poor Africans and made them work hard while they lived, and their children of mixed birth were born in slavery and kept in that condition for a long period. From that wonderful example, the mind jumps back several thousand years and fancies that the same thing happened here, and our archaeologist dreams of India being full of dark-eyed aborigines, and the bright Aryan came from—the Lord knows where. According to some, they came from Central Tibet, others will have it that they came from Central Asia. There are patriotic Englishmen who think that the Aryans were all red-haired. Others, according to their idea, think that they were all black-haired. If the writer happens to be a black-haired man, the Aryans were all black-haired. Of late, there was an attempt made to prove that the Aryans lived on the Swiss lakes. I should not be sorry if they had been all drowned there, theory and all. Some say now that they lived at the North Pole. Lord bless the Aryans and their habitations! As for the truth of these theories, there is not one word in our scriptures, not one, to prove that the Aryan ever came from anywhere outside of India, and in ancient India was included Afghanistan. There it ends. And the theory that the Shudra caste were all non-Aryans and they were a multitude, is equally illogical and equally irrational. It could not have been possible in those days that a few Aryans settled and lived there with a hundred thousand slaves at their command. These slaves would have eaten them up, made 'chutney' of them in five minutes. The only explanation is to be found in the Mahabharata, which says that in the beginning of the Satya Yuga there was one caste, the Brahmins, and then by difference of occupations they went on dividing themselves into different castes, and that is the only true and rational explanation that has been given. And in the coming Satya Yuga all the other castes will have to go back to the same condition.

The solution of the caste problem in India, therefore, assumes this form, not to degrade the higher castes, not to crush out the Brahmin. The Brahminhood is the ideal of humanity in India, as wonderfully put forward by Shankaracharya at the beginning of his commentary on the Gita, where he speaks about the reason for Krishna's coming as a preacher for the preservation of Brahminhood, of Brahminness. That was the great end. This Brahmin, the man of God, he who has known Brahman, the ideal man, the perfect man, must remain; he must not go. And with all the defects of the caste now, we know that we must all be ready to give to the Brahmins this credit, that from them have come more men with real Brahminness in them than from all the other castes. That is true. That is the credit due to them from all the other castes. We must be bold enough, must be brave enough to speak of their defects, but at the same time we must give the credit that is due to them. Remember the old English proverb, 'Give every man his due'. Therefore, my friends, it is no use fighting among the castes. What good will it do? It will divide us all the more, weaken us all the more, degrade us all the more. The days of exclusive privileges and exclusive claims are gone, gone for ever from the soil of India, and it is one of the great blessings of the British Rule in India. Even to the Mohammedan Rule we owe that great blessing, the destruction of exclusive privilege. That Rule was, after all, not all bad nothing is all bad, and nothing is all good. The Mohammedan conquest of India came as a salvation to the downtrodden, to the poor. That is why one-fifth of our people have become Mohammedans. It was not the sword that did it all. It would be the height of madness to think it was all the work of sword and fire. And one-fifth—one-half—of your Madras people will become Christians if you do not take care. Was there ever a sillier thing before in the world than what I saw in Malabar country? The poor Pariah is not allowed to pass through the same street as the high-caste man, but if he changes his name to a hodge-podge English name, it is all right; or to a Mohammedan name, it is all right. What inference would you draw except that these Malabaris are all lunatics, their homes so many lunatic asylums, and that they are to be treated with derision by every race in India until they mend their manners and know better. Shame upon them that such wicked and diabolical customs are allowed; their own children are allowed to die of starvation, but as soon as they take up some other religion they are well fed. There ought to be no more fight between the castes.

The solution is not by bringing down the higher, but by raising the lower up to the level of the higher. And that is the line of work that is found in all our books, in spite of what you may hear from some people whose knowledge of their own scriptures and whose capacity to understand the mighty plans of the ancients are only zero. They do not understand, but those do that have brains, that have the intellect to grasp the whole scope of the work. They stand aside and follow the wonderful procession of national life through the ages. They can trace it step by step through all the books, ancient and modern. What is the plan? The ideal at one end is the Brahmin and the ideal at the other end is the Chandala, and the whole work is to raise the Chandala up to the Brahmin. Slowly and slowly you find more and more privileges granted to them. There are books where you read such fierce words as these: 'If the Shudra hears the Vedas, fill his ears with molten lead, and if he remembers a line, cut his tongue out. If he says to the Brahmin, "You Brahmin", cut his tongue out'. This is diabolical old barbarism no doubt; that goes without saying; but do not blame the law-givers, who simply record the customs of some section of the community. Such devils sometimes arose among the ancients. There have been devils everywhere more or less in all ages. Accordingly, you will find that later on, this tone is modified a little, as for instance, 'Do not disturb the Shudras, but do not teach them higher things'. Then gradually we find in other Smritis, especially in those that have full power now, that if the Shudras imitate the manners and customs of the Brahmins they do well, they ought to be encouraged. Thus it is going on. I have no time to place before you all these workings, nor how they can be traced in detail; but coming to plain facts, we find that all the castes are to rise slowly and slowly. There are thousands of castes, and some are even getting admission into Brahminhood, for what prevents any caste from declaring they are Brahmins? Thus caste, with all its rigour, has been created in that manner. Let us suppose that there are castes here with ten thousand people in each. If these put their heads together and say, we will call ourselves Brahmins, nothing can stop them; I have seen it in my own life. Some castes become strong, and as soon as they all agree, who is to say nay? Because whatever it was, each caste was exclusive of the other. It did not meddle with others' affairs; even the several divisions of one caste did not meddle with the other divisions, and those powerful epoch-makers, Shankaracharya and others, were the great caste-makers. I cannot tell you all the wonderful things they fabricated, and some of you may resent what I have to say. But in my travels and experiences I have traced them out, and have arrived at most wonderful results. They would sometimes get hordes of Baluchis and at once make them Kshatriyas, also get hold of hordes of fishermen and make them Brahmins forthwith. They were all Rishis and sages, and we have to bow down to their memory. So, be you all Rishis and sages; that is the secret. More or less we shall all be Rishis. What is meant by a Rishi? The pure one. Be pure first, and you will have power. Simply saying, 'I am a Rishi', will not do; but when you are a Rishi you will find that others obey you instinctively. Something mysterious emanates from you, which makes them follow you, makes them hear you, makes them unconsciously, even against their will, carry out your plans. That is Rishihood.

Now as to the details, they of course have to be worked out through generations. But this is merely a suggestion in order to show you that these quarrels should cease. Especially do I regret that in Moslem times there should be so much dissension between the castes. This must stop. It is useless on both sides, especially on the side of the higher caste, the Brahmin, because the day for these privileges and exclusive claims is gone. The duty of every aristocracy is to dig its own grave, and the sooner it does so, the better. The more it delays, the more it will fester and the worse death it will die. It is the duty of the Brahmin, therefore, to work for the salvation of the rest of mankind in India. If he does that, and so long as he does that, he is a Brahmin, but he is no Brahmin when he goes about making money. You on the other hand should give help only to the real Brahmin who deserves it; that leads to heaven. But sometimes a gift to another person who does not deserve it leads to the other place, says our scripture. You must be on your guard about that. He only is the Brahmin who has no secular employment. Secular employment is not for the Brahmin but for the other castes. To the Brahmins I appeal, that they must work hard to raise the Indian people by teaching them what they know, by giving out the culture that they have accumulated for centuries. It is clearly the duty of the Brahmins of India to remember what real Brahminhood is. As Manu says, all these privileges and honours are given to the Brahmin, because 'with him is the treasury of virtue'. He must open that treasury and distribute its valuables to the world. It is true that he was the earliest preacher to the Indian races, he was the first to renounce everything in order to attain to the higher realization of life before others could reach to the idea. It was not his fault that he marched ahead of the other caste. Why did not the other castes so understand and do as he did? Why did they sit down and be lazy, and let the Brahmins win the race?

But it is one thing to gain an advantage, and another thing to preserve it for evil use. Whenever power is used for evil, it becomes diabolical; it must be used for good only. So this accumulated culture of ages of which the Brahmin has been the trustee, he must now give to the people at large, and it was because he did not give it to the people that the Mohammedan invasion was possible. It was because he did not open this treasury to the people from the beginning, that for a thousand years we have been trodden under the heels of every one who chose to come to India. It was through that we have become degraded, and the first task must be to break open the cells that hide the wonderful treasures which our common ancestors accumulated; bring them out and give them to everybody and the Brahmin must be the first to do it. There is an old superstition in Bengal that if the cobra that bites, sucks out his own poison from the patient, the man must survive. Well then, the Brahmin must suck out his own poison. To the non-Brahmin castes I say, wait, be not in a hurry. Do not seize every opportunity of fighting the Brahmin, because, as I have shown, you are suffering from your own fault. Who told you to neglect spirituality and Sanskrit learning? What have you been doing all this time? Why have you been indifferent? Why do you now fret and fume because somebody else had more brains, more energy, more pluck and go, than you? Instead of wasting your energies in vain discussions and quarrels in the newspapers, instead of fighting and quarrelling in your own homes—which is sinful—use all your energies in acquiring the culture which the Brahmin has, and the thing is done. Why do you not become Sanskrit scholars? Why do you not spend millions to bring Sanskrit education to all the castes of India? That is the question. The moment you do these things, you are equal to the Brahmin. That is the secret of power in India.

Sanskrit and prestige go together in India. As soon as you have that, none dares say anything against you. That is the one secret; take that up. The whole universe, to use the ancient Advaitist's simile, is in a state of self-hypnotism. It is will that is the power. It is the man of strong will that throws, as it were, a halo round him and brings all other people to the same state of vibration as he has in his own mind. Such gigantic men do appear. And what is the idea? When a powerful individual appears, his personality infuses his thoughts into us, and many of us come to have the same thoughts, and thus we become powerful. Why is it that organizations are so powerful? Do not say organization is material. Why is it, to take a case in point, that forty millions of Englishmen rule three hundred millions of people here? What is the psychological explanation? These forty millions put their wills together and that means infinite power, and you three hundred millions have a will each separate from the other. Therefore to make a great future India, the whole secret lies in organization, accumulation of power, co-ordination of wills.

Already before my mind rises one of the marvellous verses of the Rig-Veda Samhita which says, 'Be thou all of one mind, be thou all of one thought, for in the days of yore, the gods being of one mind were enabled to receive oblations.' That the gods can be worshipped by men is because they are of one mind. Being of one mind is the secret of society. And the more you go on fighting and quarrelling about all trivialities such as 'Dravidian' and 'Aryan', and the question of Brahmins and non-Brahmins and all that, the further you are off from that accumulation of energy and power which is going to make the future India. For mark you, the future India depends entirely upon that. That is the secret—accumulation of will-power, co-ordination, bringing them all, as it here, into one focus. Each Chinaman thinks in his own way, and a handful of Japanese all think in the same way, and you know the result. That is how it goes throughout the history of the world. You find in every case, compact little nations always governing and ruling huge unwieldy nations, and this is natural, because it is easier for the little compact nations to bring their ideas into the same focus, and thus they become developed. And the bigger the nation, the more unwieldy it is. Born, as it were, a disorganized mob, they cannot combine. All these dissensions must stop.

There is yet another defect in us. Ladies, excuse me, but through centuries of slavery, we have become like a nation of women. You scarcely can get three women together for five minutes in this country or any other country, but they quarrel. Women make big societies in European countries, and make tremendous declarations of women's power and so on; then they quarrel, and some man comes and rules them all. All over the world they still require some man to rule them. We are like them. Women we are. If a woman comes to lead women, they all begin immediately to criticize her, tear her to pieces, and make her sit down. If a man comes and gives them a little harsh treatment, scolds them now and then, it is all right, they have been used to that sort of mesmerism. The whole world is full of such mesmerists and hypnotists. In the same way, if one of our countrymen stands up and tries to become great, we all try to hold him down, but if a foreigner comes and tries to kick us, it is all right. We have been used to it, have we not? And slaves must become great masters! So give up being a slave. For the next fifty years this alone shall be our keynote—this, our great Mother India. Let all other vain gods disappear for the time from our minds. This is the only god that is awake, our own race—'everywhere his hands, everywhere his feet, everywhere his ears, he covers everything.' All other gods are sleeping. What vain gods shall we go after and yet cannot worship the god that we see all round us, the Virat? When we have worshipped this, we shall be able to worship all other gods. Before we can crawl half a mile, we want to cross the ocean like Hanuman! It cannot be. Everyone going to be a Yogi, everyone going to meditate! It cannot be. The whole day mixing with the world with Karma Kanda, and in the evening sitting down and blowing through your nose! Is it so easy? Should Rishis come flying through the air, because you have blown three times through the nose? Is it a joke? It is all nonsense. What is needed is Chittashuddhi, purification of the heart. And how does that come? The first of all worship is the worship of the Virat—of those all around us. Worship It. Worship is the exact equivalent of the Sanskrit word, and no other English word will do. These are all our gods—men and animals; and the first gods we have to worship are our countrymen. These we have to worship, instead of being jealous of each other and fighting each other. It is the most terrible Karma for which we are suffering, and yet it does not open our eyes!

Well, the subject is so great that I do not know where to stop, and I must bring my lecture to a close by placing before you in a few words the plans I want to carry out in Madras. We must have a hold on the spiritual and secular education of the nation. Do you understand that? You must dream it, you must talk it, you must think its and you must work it out. Till then there is no salvation for the race. The education that you are getting now has some good points, but it has a tremendous disadvantage which is so great that the good things are all weighed down. In the first place it is not a man-making education, it is merely and entirely a negative education. A negative education or any training that is based on negation, is worse than death. The child is taken to school, and the first thing he learns is that his father is a fool, the second thing that his grandfather is a lunatic, the third thing that all his teachers are hypocrites, the fourth that all the sacred books are lies! By the time he is sixteen he is a mass of negation, lifeless and boneless. And the result is that fifty years of such education has not produced one original man in the three Presidencies. Every man of originality that has been produced has been educated elsewhere, and not in this country, or they have gone to the old universities once more to cleanse themselves of superstitions. Education is not the amount of information that is put into your brain and runs riot there, undigested, all your life. We must have life-building, man-making, character-making assimilation of ideas. If you have assimilated five ideas and made them your life and character, you have more education than any man who has got by heart a whole library यथा खरश्चन्दनभारवाही भारस्य वेत्ता न तु चन्दनस्य।—'The ass carrying its load of sandalwood knows only the weight and not the value of the sandalwood.' If education is identical with information, the libraries are the greatest sages in the world, and encyclopaedias are the Rishis. The ideal, therefore, is that we must have the whole education of our country, spiritual and secular, in our own hands, and it must be on national lines, through national methods as far as practical.

Of course this is a very big scheme, a very big plan. I do not know whether it will ever work out. But we must begin the work. But how? Take Madras, for instance. We must have a temple, for with Hindus religion must come first. Then, you may say, all sects will quarrel about it. But we will make it a non-sectarian temple, having only 'Om' as the symbol, the greatest symbol of any sect. If there is any sect here which believes that 'Om' ought not to be the symbol, it has no right to call itself Hindu. All will have the right to interpret Hinduism, each one according to his own sect ideas, but we must have a common temple. You can have your own images and symbols in other places, but do not quarrel here with those who differ from you. Here should be taught the common grounds of our different sects, and at the same time the different sects should have perfect liberty to come and teach their doctrines, with only one restriction, that is, not to quarrel with other sects. Say what you have to say, the world wants it; but the world has no time to hear what you think about other people; you can keep that to yourselves.

Secondly, in connection with this temple there should be an institution to train teachers who must go about preaching religion and giving secular education to our people; they must carry both. As we have been already carrying religion from door to door, let us along with it carry secular education also. That can be easily done. Then the work will extend through these bands of teachers and preachers, and gradually we shall have similar temples in other places, until we have covered the whole of India. That is my plan. It may appear gigantic, but it is much needed. You may ask, where is the money. Money is not needed. Money is nothing. For the last twelve years of my life, I did not know where the next meal would come from; but money and everything else I want must come, because they are my slaves, and not I theirs; money and everything else must come. Must—that is the word. Where are the men? That is the question. Young men of Madras, my hope is in you. Will you respond to the call of your nation? Each one of you has a glorious future if you dare believe me. Have a tremendous faith in yourselves, like the faith I had when I was a child, and which I am working out now. Have that faith, each one of you, in yourself—that eternal power is lodged in every soul— and you will revive the whole of India. Ay, we will then go to every country under the sun, and our ideas will before long be a component of the many forces that are working to make up every nation in the world. We must enter into the life of every race in India and abroad; shall have to *work* to bring this about. Now for that, I want young men. 'It is the young, the strong, and healthy, of sharp intellect that will reach the Lord', say the Vedas. This is the time to decide your future—while you possess the energy of youth, not when you are worn out and jaded, but in the freshness and vigour of youth. Work—this is the time; for the freshest, the untouched, and unsmelled flowers alone are to be laid at the feet of the Lord, and such He receives. Rouse yourselves, therefore, or life is short. There are greater works to be done than aspiring to become lawyers and picking quarrels and such things. A far greater work is this sacrifice of yourselves for the benefit of your race, for the welfare of humanity. What is in this life? You are

Hindus, and there is the instinctive belief in you that life is eternal. Sometimes I have young men come and talk to me about atheism; I do not believe a Hindu can become an atheist. He may read European books, and persuade himself he is a materialist, but it is only for a time. It is not in your blood. You cannot believe what is not in your constitution; it would be a hopeless task for you. Do not attempt that sort of thing. I once attempted it when I was a boy, but it could not be. Life is short, but the soul is immortal and eternal, and one thing being certain, death, let us therefore take up a great ideal and give up our whole life to it. Let this be our determination, and may He, the Lord, who 'comes again and again for the salvation of His own people', to quote from our scriptures—may the great Krishna bless us and lead us all to the fulfilment of our aims!

53

WHAT HAVE I LEARNT?

Delivered at Dacca

(30 March 1901)

At Dacca, Swámiji delivered two lectures in English. The first was on 'What have I learnt?' and the second one was 'The Religion We are Born in'. The following is translated from a report in Bengali by a disciple, and it contains the substance of the first lecture:

First of all, I must express my pleasure at the opportunity afforded me of coming to Eastern Bengal to acquire an intimate knowledge of this part of the country, which I hitherto lacked in spite of my wanderings through many civilized countries of the West, as well as my gratification at the sight of majestic rivers, wide fertile plains, and picturesque villages in this, my own country of Bengal, which I had not the good fortune of seeing for myself before. I did not know that there was everywhere in my country of Bengal—on land and water—so much beauty and charm. But this much has been my gain that after seeing the various countries of the world I can now much more appreciate the beauties of my own land.

In the same way also, in search of religion, I had travelled among various sects—sects which had taken up the ideals of foreign nations as their own, and I had begged at the door of others, not knowing then that in the religion of my country, in our national religion, there was so much beauty and grandeur. It is now many years since I found Hinduism to be the most perfectly satisfying religion in the world. Hence I feel sad at heart when I see existing among my own countrymen, professing a peerless faith, such a widespread indifference to our religion—though I am very well aware of the unfavourable materialistic conditions in which they pass their lives—owing to the diffusion of European modes of thought in this, our great motherland.

There are among us at the present day certain reformers who want to reform our religion or rather turn it topsyturvy with a view to the regeneration of the Hindu nation. There are, no doubt, some thoughtful people among them, but there are also many who follow others blindly and act most foolishly, not knowing what they are about. This class of reformers are very enthusiastic in introducing foreign ideas into our religion. They have taken hold of the word 'idolatry', and aver that Hinduism is not true, because it is idolatrous. They never seek to find out what this so-called 'idolatry' is, whether it is good or bad; only taking their cue from others, they are bold enough to shout down Hinduism as untrue. There is another class of men among us who are intent upon giving some slippery scientific explanations for any and every Hindu custom, rite, etc., and who are always talking of electricity, magnetism, air vibration, and all that sort of thing. Who knows but they will perhaps some day define God Himself as nothing but a mass of electric vibrations! However, Mother bless them all! She it is who is having Her work done in various ways through multifarious natures and tendencies.

In contradistinction to these, there is that ancient class who say, 'I do not know, I do not care to know or understand all these your hair-splitting ratiocinations; I want God, I want the Atman, I want to go to that Beyond, where there is no universe, where there is no pleasure or pain, where dwells the Bliss Supreme'; who say, 'I believe in salvation by bathing in the holy Ganga with faith'; who say, 'whomsoever you may worship with singleness of faith and devotion as the one God of the universe, in whatsoever form as Shiva, Rama, Vishnu, etc., you will get Moksha'; to that sturdy ancient class I am proud to belong.

Then there is a sect who advise us to follow God and the world together. They are not sincere, they do not express what they feel in their hearts. What is the teaching of the Great Ones?—'Where there is Rama, there is no Kama; where there is Kama, there Rama is not. Night and day can never exist together.' The voice of the ancient sages proclaim to us, 'If you desire to attain God, you will have to renounce Kama-Kanchana (lust and possession). The Samsara is unreal, hollow, void of substance. Unless you give it up, you can never reach God, try however you may. If you cannot do that, own that you are weak, but by no means lower the Ideal. Do not cover the corrupting corpse with leaves of gold!' So according to them, if you want to gain spirituality, to attain God, the first thing that you have to do is to give up this playing 'hide-and-seek with your ideas', this dishonesty, this 'theft within the chamber of thought'.

What have I learnt? What have I learnt from this ancient sect? I have learnt:

दुर्लभं त्रयमेवैतत् देवानुग्रहहेतुकम्।
मनुष्यत्वं मुमुक्षुत्वं महापुरुषसंश्रयः॥

—'Verily, these three are rare to obtain and come only through the grace of God—human birth, desire to obtain Moksha, and the company of the great-souled ones.' The first thing needed is Manushyatva, human birth, because it only is favourable to the attainment of Mukti. The next is Mumukshutva. Though our means of realization vary according to the difference in sects and individuals—though different individuals can lay claim to their special rights and means to gain knowledge, which vary according to their different stations in life—yet it can be said in general without fear of contradiction that without this Mumukshuta, realization of God is impossible. What is Mumukshutva? It is the strong desire for Moksha—earnest yearning to get out of the sphere of pain and pleasure—utter disgust for the world. When that intense burning desire to see God comes, then you should know that you are entitled to the realization of the Supreme.

Then another thing is necessary, and that is the coming in direct contact with the Mahapurushas, and thus molding our lives in accordance with those of the great-souled ones who have reached the Goal. Even disgust for the world and a burning desire for God are not sufficient. Initiation by the Guru is necessary. Why? Because it is the bringing of yourself into connection with that great source of power which has been handed down through generations from one Guru to another, in uninterrupted succession. The devotee must seek and accept the Guru or spiritual preceptor as his counsellor, philosopher, friend, and guide. In short, the Guru is the *sine qua non* of progress in the path of spirituality. Whom then shall I accept as my Guru?

श्रित्रियोऽवृजिनोऽकामहतो यो ब्रह्मवित्तम:

—'He who is versed in the Vedas, without taint, unhurt by desire, he who is the best of the knowers of Brahman.' Shrotriya—he who is not only learned in the Shastras, but who knows their subtle secrets, who has realized their true import in his life. 'Reading merely the various scriptures, they have become only parrots, and not Pandits. He indeed has become a Pandit who has gained Prema (Divine Love) by reading even one word of the Shastras.' Mere book-learned Pandits are of no avail. Nowadays, everyone wants to be a Guru; even a poor beggar wants to make a gift of a lakh of rupees! Then the Guru must be without a touch of taint, and he must be Akamahata—unhurt by any desire—he should have no other motive except that of purely doing good to others, he should be an ocean of mercy-without-reason and not impart religious teaching with a view to gaining name or fame, or anything pertaining to selfish interest. And he must be the intense knower of Brahman, that is, one who has realized Brahman even as tangibly as an Amalaka-fruit in the palm of the hand. Such is the Guru, says the Shruti. When spiritual union is established with such a Guru, then comes realization of God—then god-vision becomes easy of attainment.

After initiation there should be in the aspirant after Truth, Abhyasa or earnest and repeated attempt at practical application of the Truth by prescribed means of constant meditation upon the Chosen Ideal. Even if you have a burning thirst for God, or have gained the Guru, unless you have along with it the Abhyasa, unless you practise what you have been taught, you cannot get realization. When all these are firmly established in you, then you will reach the Goal.

Therefore, I say unto you, as Hindus, as descendants of the glorious Aryans, do not forget the great ideal of our religion, that great ideal of the Hindus, which is, to go beyond this Samsara—not only to renounce the world, but to give up heaven too; ay, not only to give up evil, but to give up good too; and thus to go beyond all, beyond this phenomenal existence, and ultimately realize the Sat-Chit-Ananda Brahman—the Absolute Existence-Knowledge-Bliss, which is Brahman.

FROM THE RAJA-YOGA

54

THE FIRST STEPS

Raja-Yoga is divided into eight steps. The first is Yama—non-killing, truthfulness, non-stealing, continence, and non-receiving of any gifts. Next is Niyama—cleanliness, contentment, austerity, study, and self-surrender to God. Then comes Asana, or posture; Pranayama, or control of Prana; Pratyahara, or restraint of the senses from their objects; Dharana, or fixing the mind on a spot; Dhyana, or meditation; and Samadhi, or superconsciousness. The Yama and Niyama, as we see, are moral trainings; without these as the basis no practise of Yoga will succeed. As these two become established, the Yogi will begin to realize the fruits of his practise; without these it will never bear fruit. A Yogi must not think of injuring anyone, by thought, word, or deed. Mercy shall not be for men alone, but shall go beyond, and embrace the whole world.

The next step is Asana, posture. A series of exercises, physical and mental, is to be gone through every day, until certain higher states are reached. Therefore it is quite necessary that we should find a posture in which we can remain long. That posture which is the easiest for one should be the one chosen. For thinking, a certain posture may be very easy for one man, while to another it may be very difficult. We will find later on that during the study of these psychological matters a good deal of activity goes on in the body. Nerve currents will have to be displaced and given a new channel. New sorts of vibrations will begin, the whole constitution will be remodelled as it were. But the main part of the activity will lie along the spinal column, so that the one thing necessary for the posture is to hold the spinal column free, sitting erect, holding the three parts—the chest, neck, and head—in a straight line. Let the whole weight of the body be supported by the ribs, and then you have an easy natural postures with the spine straight. You will easily see that you cannot think very high thoughts with the chest in. This portion of the Yoga is a little similar to the Hatha-Yoga which deals entirely with the physical body, its aim being to make the physical body very strong. We have nothing to do with it here, because its practises are very difficult, and cannot be learned in a day, and, after all, do not lead to much spiritual growth. Many of these practises you will find in Delsarte and other teachers, such as placing the body in different postures, but the object in these is physical, not psychological. There is not one muscle in the body over which a man cannot establish a perfect control. The heart can be made to stop or go on at his bidding, and each part of the organism can be similarly controlled.

The result of this branch of Yoga is to make men live long; health is the chief idea, the one goal of the Hatha-Yogi. He is determined not to fall sick, and he never does. He lives long; a hundred years is nothing to him; he is quite young and fresh when he is 150, without one hair turned grey. But that is all. A banyan tree lives sometimes 5000 years, but it is a banyan tree and nothing more. So, if a man lives long, he is only a healthy animal. One or two ordinary lessons of the Hatha-Yogis are very useful. For instance, some of you will find it a good thing for headaches to drink cold water through the nose as soon as you get up in the morning; the whole day your brain will be nice and cool, and you will never catch cold. It is very easy to do; put your nose into the water, draw it up through the nostrils and make a pump action in the throat.

After one has learned to have a firm erect seat, one has to perform, according to certain schools, a practise called the purifying of the nerves. This part has been rejected by some as not belonging to Raja-Yoga, but as so great an authority as the commentator Shankaracharya advises it, I think fit that it should be mentioned, and I will quote his own directions from his commentary on the Shvetashvatara Upanishad: 'The mind whose dross has been cleared away by Pranayama, becomes fixed in Brahman; therefore, Pranayama is declared. First the nerves are to be purified, then comes the power to practise Pranayama. Stopping the right nostril with the thumb, through the left nostril fill in air, according to capacity; then, without any interval, throw the air out through the right nostril, closing the left one. Again inhaling through the right nostril eject through the left, according to capacity; practising this three or five times at four hours of the day, before dawn, during midday, in the evening, and at midnight, in fifteen days or a month purity of the nerves is attained; then begins Pranayama.'

Practise is absolutely necessary. You may sit down and listen to me by the hour every day, but if you do not practise, you will not get one step further. It all depends on practise. We never understand these things until we experience them. We will have to see and feel them for ourselves. Simply listening to explanations and theories will not do. There are several obstructions to practise. The first obstruction is an unhealthy body: if the body is not in a fit state, the practise will be obstructed. Therefore we have to keep the body in good health; we have to take care of what we eat and drink, and what we do. Always use a mental effort, what is usually called 'Christian Science,' to keep the body strong. That is all—nothing further of the body. We must not forget that health is only a means to an end. If health were the end, we would be like animals; animals rarely become unhealthy.

The second obstruction is doubt; we always feel doubtful about things we do not see. Man cannot live upon words, however he may try. So, doubt comes to us as to whether there is any truth in these things or not; even the best of us will doubt sometimes: With practise, within a few days, a little glimpse will come, enough to give one encouragement and hope. As a certain commentator on Yoga philosophy says, 'When one proof is obtained, however little that may be, it will give us faith in the whole teaching of Yoga.' For instance, after the first few months of practise, you will begin to find you can read another's thoughts; they will come to you in picture form. Perhaps you will hear something happening at a long distance, when you concentrate your mind with a wish to hear. These glimpses will come, by little bits at first, but enough to give you faith, and strength, and hope. For instance, if you concentrate your thoughts on the tip of your nose, in a few days you will begin to smell most beautiful fragrance, which will be enough to show you that there are certain mental perceptions that can be made obvious without the contact of physical objects. But we must always remember that these are only the means; the aim, the end, the goal, of all this training is liberation of the soul. Absolute control of nature, and nothing short of it, must be the goal. We must be the masters, and not the slaves of nature; neither body nor mind must be our master, nor must we forget that the body is mine, and not I the body's.

A god and a demon went to learn about the Self from a great sage. They studied with him for a long time. At last the sage told them, 'You yourselves are the Being you are seeking.' Both of them thought that their bodies were the Self. They went back to their people quite satisfied and said, 'We have learned everything that was to be learned; eat, drink, and be merry; we are the Self; there is nothing beyond us.' The nature of the demon was ignorant, clouded; so he never inquired any further, but was perfectly contented with the idea that he was God, that by the Self was meant the body. The god had a purer nature. He at first committed the mistake of thinking: I, this body, am Brahman: so keep it strong and in health, and well dressed, and give it all sorts of enjoyments. But, in a few days, he found out that that could not be the meaning of the sage, their master; there must be something higher. So he came back and said, 'Sir, did you teach me that this body was the Self? If so, I see all bodies die; the Self cannot die.' The sage said, 'Find it out; thou art That.' Then the god thought that the vital forces which work the body were what the sage meant. But. after a time, he found that if he ate, these vital forces remained strong, but, if he starved, they became weak. The god then went back to the sage and said, 'Sir, do you mean that the vital forces are the Self ?' The sage said, 'Find out for yourself; thou art That.' The god returned home once more, thinking that it was the mind, perhaps, that was the Self. But in a short while he saw that thoughts were so various, now good, again bad; the mind was too changeable to be the Self. He went back to the sage and said, 'Sir, I do not think that the mind is the Self; did you mean that?' 'No,' replied the sage, 'thou art That; find out for yourself.' The god went home, and at last found that he was the Self, beyond all thought, one without birth or death, whom the sword cannot pierce or the fire burn, whom the air cannot dry or the water melt, the beginningless and endless, the immovable, the intangible, the omniscient, the omnipotent Being; that It was neither the body nor the mind, but beyond them all. So he was satisfied; but the poor demon did not get the truth, owing to his fondness for the body.

This world has a good many of these demoniac natures, but there are some gods too. If one proposes to teach any science to increase the power of sense-enjoyment, one finds multitudes ready for it. If one undertakes to show the supreme goal, one finds few to listen to him. Very few have the power to grasp the higher, fewer still the patience to attain to it. But there are a few also who know that even if the body can be made to live for a thousand years, the result in the end will be the same. When the forces that hold it together go away, the body must fall. No man was ever born who could stop his body one moment from changing. Body is the name of a series of changes. 'As in a river the masses of water are changing before you every moment, and new masses are coming, yet taking similar form, so is it with this body.' Yet the body must be kept strong and healthy. It is the best instrument we have.

This human body is the greatest body in the universe, and a human being the greatest being. Man is higher than all animals, than all angels; none is greater than man. Even the Devas (gods) will have to come down again and attain to salvation through a human body. Man alone attains to perfection, not even the Devas. According to the Jews and Mohammedans, God created man after creating the angels and everything else, and after creating man He asked the angels to come and salute him, and all did so except Iblis; so God cursed him and he became Satan. Behind this allegory is the great truth that this human birth is the greatest birth we can have. The lower creation, the animal, is dull, and manufactured mostly out of Tamas. Animals cannot have any high thoughts; nor can the angels, or Devas, attain to direct freedom without human birth. In human society, in the same way, too much wealth or too much poverty is a great impediment to the higher development of the soul. It is from the middle classes that the great ones of the world come. Here the forces are very equally adjusted and balanced.

Returning to our subject, we come next to Pranayarna, controlling the breathing. What has that to do with concentrating the powers of the mind? Breath is like the fly-wheel of this machine, the body. In a big engine you find the fly-wheel first moving, and that motion is conveyed to finer and finer machinery until the most delicate and finest mechanism in the machine is in motion. The breath is that fly-wheel, supplying and regulating the motive power to everything in this body.

There was once a minister to a great king. He fell into disgrace. The king, as a punishment, ordered him to be shut up in the top of a very high tower. This was done, and the minister was left there to perish. He had a faithful wife, however, who came to the tower at night and called to her husband at the top to know what she could do to help him. He told her to return to the tower the following night and bring with her a long rope, some stout twine, pack thread, silken thread, a beetle, and a little honey. Wondering much, the good wife obeyed her husband, and brought him the desired articles. The husband directed her to attach the silken thread firmly to the beetle, then to smear its horns with a drop of honey, and to set it free on the wall of the tower, with its head pointing upwards. She obeyed all these instructions, and the beetle started on its long journey. Smelling the honey ahead it slowly crept onwards, in the hope of reaching the honey, until at last it reached the top of the tower, when the minister grasped the beetle, and got possession of the silken thread. He told his wife to tie the other end to the pack thread, and after he had drawn up the pack thread, he repeated the process with the stout twine, and lastly with the rope. Then the rest was easy. The minister descended from the tower by means of the rope, and made his escape. In this body of ours the breath motion is the 'silken thread'; by laying hold of and learning to control it we grasp the pack thread of the nerve currents, and from these the stout twine of our thoughts, and lastly the rope of Prana, controlling which we reach freedom.

We do not know anything about our own bodies; we cannot know. At best we can take a dead body, and cut it in pieces, and there are some who can take a live animal and cut it in pieces in order to see what is inside the body. Still, that has nothing to do with our own bodies. We know very little about them. Why do we not? Because our attention is not discriminating enough to catch the very fine movements that are going on within. We can know of them only when the mind becomes more subtle and enters, as it were, deeper into the body. To get the subtle perception we have to begin with the grosser perceptions. We have to get hold of that which is setting the whole engine in motion. That is the Prana, the most obvious manifestation of which is the breath. Then, along with the breath, we shall slowly enter the body, which will enable us to find out about the subtle forces, the nerve currents that are moving all over the body. As soon as we perceive and learn to feel them, we shall begin to get control over them, and over the body. The mind is also set in motion by these different nerve currents, so at last we shall reach the state of perfect control over the body and the mind, making both our servants. Knowledge is power. We have to get this power. So we must begin at the beginning, with Pranayama, restraining the Prana. This Pranayama is a long subject, and will take several lessons to illustrate it thoroughly. We shall take it part by part.

We shall gradually see the reasons for each exercise and what forces in the body are set in motion. All these things will come to us, but it requires constant practise, and the proof will come by practise. No amount of reasoning which I can give you will be proof to you, until you have demonstrated it for yourselves. As soon as you begin to feel these currents in motion all over you, doubts will vanish, but it requires hard practise every day. You must practise at least twice every day, and the best times are towards the morning and the evening. When night passes into day, and day into night, a state of relative calmness ensues. The early morning and the early evening are the two periods of calmness. Your body will have a like tendency to become calm at those times. We should take advantage of that natural condition and begin then to practise. Make it a rule not to eat until you have practised; if you do this, the sheer force of hunger will break your laziness. In India they teach children never to eat until they have practised or worshipped, and it becomes natural to them after a time; a boy will not feel hungry until he has bathed and practised.

Those of you who can afford it will do better to have a room for this practise alone. Do not sleep in that room, it must be kept holy. You must not enter the room until you have bathed, and are perfectly

clean in body and mind. Place flowers in that room always; they are
the best surroundings for a Yogi; also pictures that are pleasing. Burn
incense morning and evening. Have no quarrelling, nor anger, nor
unholy thought in that room. Only allow those persons to enter it
who are of the same thought as you. Then gradually there will be an
atmosphere of holiness in the room, so that when you are miserable,
sorrowful, doubtful, or your mind is disturbed, the very fact of entering
that room will make you calm. This was the idea of the temple and
the church, and in some temples and churches you will find it even
now, but in the majority of them the very idea has been lost. The
idea is that by keeping holy vibrations there the place becomes and
remains illumined. Those who cannot afford to have a room set apart
can practise anywhere they like. Sit in a straight posture, and the
first thing to do is to send a current of holy thought to all creation.
Mentally repeat, 'Let all beings be happy; let all beings be peaceful;
let all beings be blissful.' So do to the east, south, north and west.
The more you do that the better you will feel yourself. You will find
at last that the easiest way to make ourselves healthy is to see that
others are healthy, and the easiest way to make ourselves happy is to
see that others are happy. After doing that, those who believe in God
should pray—not for money, not for health, nor for heaven; pray
for knowledge and light; every other prayer is selfish. Then the next
thing to do is to think of your own body, and see that it is strong
and healthy; it is the best instrument you have. Think of it as being
as strong as adamant, and that with the help of this body you will
cross the ocean of life. Freedom is never to be reached by the weak.
Throw away all weakness. Tell your body that it is strong, tell your
mind that it is strong, and have unbounded faith and hope in yourself.

55

PRANA

Pranayama is not, as many think, something about breath; breath indeed has very little to do with it, if anything. Breathing is only one of the many exercises through which we get to the real Pranayama. Pranayama means the control of Prana. According to the philosophers of India, the whole universe is composed of two materials, one of which they call Akasha. It is the omnipresent, all-penetrating existence. Everything that has form, everything that is the result of combination, is evolved out of this Akasha. It is the Akasha that becomes the air, that becomes the liquids, that becomes the solids; it is the Akasha that becomes the sun, the earth, the moon, the stars, the comets; it is the Akasha that becomes the human body, the animal body, the plants, every form that we see, everything that can be sensed, everything that exists. It cannot be perceived; it is so subtle that it is beyond all ordinary perception; it can only be seen when it has become gross, has taken form. At the beginning of creation there is only this Akasha. At the end of the cycle the solids, the liquids, and the gases all melt into the Akasha again, and the next creation similarly proceeds out of this Akasha.

By what power is this Akasha manufactured into this universe? By the power of Prana. Just as Akasha is the infinite, omnipresent material of this universe, so is this Prana the infinite, omnipresent manifesting power of this universe. At the beginning and at the end of a cycle everything becomes Akasha, and all the forces that are in the universe resolve back into the Prana; in the next cycle, out of this Prana is evolved everything that we call energy, everything that we call force. It is the Prana that is manifesting as motion; it is the Prana that is manifesting as gravitation, as magnetism. It is the Prana that is manifesting as the actions of the body, as the nerve currents, as thought force. From thought down to the lowest force, everything is but the manifestation of Prana. The sum total of all forces in the universe, mental or physical, when resolved back to their original state, is called Prana. 'When there was neither aught nor naught, when darkness was covering darkness, what existed then? That Akasha existed without motion.' The physical motion of the Prana was stopped, but it existed all the same.

At the end of a cycle the energies now displayed in the universe quiet down and become potential. At the beginning of the next cycle they start up, strike upon the Akasha, and out of the Akasha evolve these various forms, and as the Akasha changes, this Prana changes also into all these manifestations of energy. The knowledge and control of this Prana is really what is meant by Pranayama.

This opens to us the door to almost unlimited power. Suppose, for instance, a man understood the Prana perfectly, and could control it, what power on earth would not be his? He would be able to move the sun and stars out of their places, to control everything in the universe, from the atoms to the biggest suns, because he would control the Prana. This is the end and aim of Pranayama. When the Yogi becomes perfect, there will be nothing in nature not under his control. If he orders the gods or the souls of the departed to come, they will come at his bidding. All the forces of nature will obey him as slaves. When the ignorant see these powers of the Yogi, they call them the miracles. One peculiarity of the Hindu mind is that it always inquires for the last possible generalization, leaving the details to be worked out afterwards. The question is raised in the Vedas, 'What is that, knowing which, we shall know everything?' Thus, all books, and all philosophies that have been written, have been only to prove that by knowing which everything is known. If a man wants to know this universe bit by bit he must know every individual grain of sand, which means infinite time; he cannot know all of them. Then how can knowledge be? How is it possible for a man to be all-knowing through particulars? The Yogis say that behind this particular manifestation there is a generalization. Behind all particular ideas stands a generalized, an abstract principle; grasp it, and you have grasped everything. Just as this whole universe has been generalized in the Vedas into that One Absolute Existence, and he who has grasped that Existence has grasped the whole universe, so all forces have been generalized into this Prana, and he who has grasped the Prana has grasped all the forces of the universe, mental or physical. He who has controlled the Prana has controlled his own mind, and all the minds that exist. He who has controlled the Prana has controlled his body, and all the bodies that exist, because the Prana is the generalized manifestation of force.

How to control the Prana is the one idea of Pranayama. All the trainings and exercises in this regard are for that one end. Each man must begin where he stands, must learn how to control the things that are nearest to him. This body is very near to us, nearer than anything in the external universe, and this mind is the nearest of all. The Prana which is working this mind and body is the nearest to us of all the Prana in this universe. This little wave of the Prana which represents our own energies, mental and physical, is the nearest to us of all the waves of the infinite ocean of Prana. If we can succeed in controlling that little wave, then alone we can hope to control the whole of Prana. The Yogi who has done this gains perfection; no longer is he under any power. He becomes almost almighty, almost all-knowing. We see sects in every country who have attempted this control of Prana. In this country there are Mind-healers, Faith-healers, Spiritualists, Christian Scientists, Hypnotists, etc., and if we examine these different bodies, we shall find at the back of each this control of the Prana, whether they know it or not. If you boil all their theories down, the residuum will be that. It is the one and the same force they are manipulating, only unknowingly. They have stumbled on the discovery of a force and are using it unconsciously without knowing its nature, but it is the same as the Yogi uses, and which comes from Prana.

The Prana is the vital force in every being. Thought is the finest and highest action of Prana. Thought, again, as we see, is not all. There is also what we call instinct or unconscious thought, the lowest plane of action. If a mosquito stings us, our hand will strike it automatically, instinctively. This is one expression of thought. All reflex actions of the body belong to this plane of thought. There is again the other plane of thought, the conscious. I reason, I judge, I think, I see the pros and cons of certain things, yet that is not all. We know that reason is limited. Reason can go only to a certain extent, beyond that it cannot reach. The circle within which it runs is very very limited indeed. Yet at the same time, we find facts rush into this circle. Like the coming of comets certain things come into this circle; it is certain they come from outside the limit, although our reason cannot go beyond. The causes of the phenomena intruding themselves in this small limit are outside of this limit. The mind can exist on a still higher plane, the superconscious. When the mind has attained to that state, which is called Samadhi—perfect concentration, superconsciousness—it goes beyond the limits of reason, and comes face to face with facts which no instinct or reason can ever know. All manipulations of the subtle forces of the body, the different manifestations of Prana, if trained, give a push to the mind, help it to go up higher, and become superconscious, from where it acts.

In this universe there is one continuous substance on every plane of existence. Physically this universe is one: there is no difference between the sun and you. The scientist will tell you it is only a fiction to say the contrary. There is no real difference between the table and me; the table is one point in the mass of matter, and I another point. Each form represents, as it were, one whirlpool in the infinite ocean of matter, of which not one is constant. Just as in a rushing stream there may be millions of whirlpools, the water in each of which is different every moment, turning round and round for a few seconds, and then passing out, replaced by a fresh quantity, so the whole universe is one constantly changing mass of matter, in which all forms of existence are so many whirlpools. A mass of matter enters into one whirlpool, say a human body, stays there for a period, becomes changed, and goes out into another, say an animal body this time, from which again after a few years, it enters into another whirlpool, called a lump of mineral. It is a constant change. Not one body is constant. There is no such thing as my body, or your body, except in words. Of the one huge mass of matter, one point is called a moon, another a sun, another a man, another the earth, another a plant, another a mineral. Not one is constant, but everything is changing, matter eternally concreting and disintegrating. So it is with the mind. Matter is represented by the ether; when the action of Prana is most subtle, this very ether, in the finer state of vibration, will represent the mind and there it will be still one unbroken mass. If you can simply get to that subtle vibration, you will see and feel that the whole universe is composed of subtle vibrations. Sometimes certain drugs have the power to take us, while as yet in the senses, to that condition. Many of you may remember the celebrated experiment of Sir Humphrey Davy, when the laughing gas overpowered him—how, during the lecture, he remained motionless, stupefied and after that, he said that the whole universe was made up of ideas. For, the time being, as it were, the gross vibrations had ceased, and only the subtle vibrations which he called ideas, were present to him. He could only see the subtle vibrations round him; everything had become thought; the whole universe was an ocean of thought, he and everyone else had become little thought whirlpools.

Thus, even in the universe of thought we find unity, and at last, when we get to the Self, we know that that Self can only be One. Beyond the vibrations of matter in its gross and subtle aspects, beyond motion there is but One. Even in manifested motion there is only unity. These facts can no more be denied. Modern physics also has demonstrated that the sum total of the energies in the universe is the same throughout. It has also been proved that this sum total of energy exists in two forms. It becomes potential, toned down, and calmed, and next it comes out manifested as all these various forces; again it goes back to the quiet state, and again it manifests. Thus it goes on evolving and involving through eternity. The control of this Prana, as before stated, is what is called Pranayama.

The most obvious manifestation of this Prana in the human body is the motion of the lungs. If that stops, as a rule all the other manifestations of force in the body will immediately stop. But there are persons who can train themselves in such a manner that the body will live on, even when this motion has stopped. There are some persons who can bury themselves for days, and yet live without breathing. To reach the subtle we must take the help of the grosser, and so, slowly travel towards the most subtle until we gain our point. Pranayama really means controlling this motion of the lungs and this motion is associated with the breath. Not that breath is producing it; on the contrary it is producing breath. This motion draws in the air by pump action. The Prana is moving the lungs, the movement of the lungs draws in the air. So Pranayama is not breathing, but controlling that muscular power which moves the lungs. That muscular power which goes out through the nerves to the muscles and from them to the lungs, making them move in a certain manner, is the Prana, which we have to control in the practise of Pranayama. When the Prana has become controlled, then we shall immediately find that all the other actions of the Prana in the body will slowly come under control. I myself have seen men who have controlled almost every muscle of the body; and why not? If I have control over certain muscles, why not over every muscle and nerve of the body? What impossibility is there? At present the control is lost, and the motion has become automatic. We cannot move our ears at will, but we know that animals can. We have not that power because we do not exercise it. This is what is called atavism.

Again, we know that motion which has become latent can be brought back to manifestation. By hard work and practise certain motions of the body which are most dormant can be brought back under perfect control. Reasoning thus we find there is no impossibility, but, on the other hand. every probability that each part of the body can be brought under perfect control. This the Yogi does through Pranayama. Perhaps some of you have read that in Pranayama, when drawing in the breath, you must fill your whole body with Prana. In the English translations Prana is given as breath, and you are inclined to ask how that is to be done. The fault is with the translator. Every part of the body can be filled with Prana, this vital force, and when you are able to do that, you can control the whole body. All the sickness and misery felt in the body will be perfectly controlled; not only so, you will be able to control another's body. Everything is infectious in this world, good or bad. If your body be in a certain state of tension, it will have a tendency to produce the same tension in others. If you are strong and healthy, those that live near you will also have the tendency to become strong and healthy, but if you are sick and weak, those around you will have the tendency to become the same. In the case of one man trying to heal another, the first idea is simply transferring his own health to the other. This is the primitive sort of healing. Consciously or unconsciously, health can be transmitted. A very strong man, living with a weak man, will make him a little stronger, whether he knows it or not. When consciously done, it becomes quicker and better in its action. Next come those cases in which a man may not be very healthy himself, yet we know that he can bring health to another. The first man, in such a case, has a little more control over the Prana, and can rouse, for the time being, his Prana, as it were, to a certain state of vibration, and transmit it to another person.

There have been cases where this process has been carried on at a distance, but in reality there is no distance in the sense of a break. Where is the distance that has a break? Is there any break between you and the sun? It is a continuous mass of matter, the sun being one part, and you another. Is there a break between one part of a river and another? Then why cannot any force travel? There is no reason against it. Cases of healing from a distance are perfectly true. The Prana can be transmitted to a very great distance; but to one genuine case, there are hundreds of frauds. This process of healing is not so easy as it is thought to be. In the most ordinary cases of such healing you will find that the healers simply take advantage of the naturally healthy state of the human body. An allopath comes and treats cholera patients, and gives them his medicines. The homoeopath comes and gives his medicines, and cures perhaps more than the allopath does, because the homoeopath does not disturb his patients, but allows nature to deal with them. The Faith-healer cures more still, because he brings the strength of his mind to bear, and rouses, through faith, the dormant Prana of the patient.

There is a mistake constantly made by Faith-healers: they think that faith directly heals a man. But faith alone does not cover all the ground. There are diseases where the worst symptoms are that the patient never thinks that he has that disease. That tremendous faith of the patient is itself one symptom of the disease, and usually indicates that he will die quickly. In such cases the principle that faith cures does not apply. If it were faith alone that cured, these patients also would be cured. It is by the Prana that real curing comes. The pure man, who has controlled the Prana, has the power of bringing it into a certain state of vibration, which can be conveyed to others, arousing in them a similar vibration. You see that in everyday actions. I am talking to you. What am I trying to do? I am, so to say, bringing my mind to a certain state of vibration, and the more I succeed in bringing it to that state, the more you will be affected by what I say. All of you know that the day I am more enthusiastic, the more you enjoy the lecture; and when I am less enthusiastic, you feel lack of interest.

The gigantic will-powers of the world, the world-movers, can bring their Prana into a high state of vibration, and it is so great and powerful that it catches others in a moment, and thousands are drawn towards them, and half the world think as they do. Great prophets of the world had the most wonderful control of the Prana, which gave them tremendous will-power; they had brought their Prana to the highest state of motion, and this is what gave them power to sway the world. All manifestations of power arise from this control. Men may not know the secret, but this is the one explanation. Sometimes in your own body the supply of Prana gravitates more or less to one part; the balance is disturbed, and when the balance of Prana is disturbed, what we call disease is produced. To take away the superfluous Prana, or to supply the Prana that is wanting, will be curing the disease. That again is Pranayama—to learn when there is more or less Prana in one part of the body than there should be. The feelings will become so subtle that the mind will feel that there is less Prana in the toe or the finger than there should be, and will possess the power to supply it. These are among the various functions of Pranayama. They have to be learned slowly and gradually, and as you see, the whole scope of Raja-Yoga is really to teach the control and direction in different planes of the Prana. When a man has concentrated his energies, he masters the Prana that is in his body. When a man is meditating, he is also concentrating the Prana.

In an ocean there are huge waves, like mountains, then smaller waves, and still smaller, down to little bubbles, but back of all these is the infinite ocean. The bubble is connected with the infinite ocean at one end, and the huge wave at the other end. So, one may be a gigantic man, and another a little bubble, but each is connected with that infinite ocean of energy, which is the common birthright of every animal that exists. Wherever there is life, the storehouse of infinite energy is behind it. Starting as some fungus, some very minute, microscopic bubble, and all the time drawing from that infinite storehouse of energy, a form is changed slowly and steadily until in course of time it becomes a plant, then an animal, then man, ultimately God. This is attained through millions of aeons, but what is time? An increase of speed, an increase of struggle, is able to bridge the gulf of time. That which naturally takes a long time to accomplish can be shortened by the intensity of the action, says the Yogi. A man may go on slowly drawing in this energy from the infinite mass that exists in the universe, and, perhaps, he will require a hundred thousand years to become a Deva, and then, perhaps, five hundred thousand years to become still higher, and, perhaps, five millions of years to become perfect. Given rapid growth, the time will be lessened. Why is it not possible, with sufficient effort, to reach this very perfection in six months or six years? There is no limit. Reason shows that. If an engine, with a certain amount of coal, runs two miles an hour, it will run the distance in less time with a greater supply of coal. Similarly, why shall not the soul, by intensifying its action, attain perfection in this very life? All beings will at last attain to that goal, we know. But who cares to wait all these millions of aeons? Why not reach it immediately, in this body even, in this human form? Why shall I not get that infinite knowledge, infinite power, now?

The ideal of the Yogi, the whole science of Yoga, is directed to the end of teaching men how, by intensifying the power of assimilation, to shorten the time for reaching perfection, instead of slowly advancing from point to point and waiting until the whole human race has become perfect. All the great prophets, saints, and seers of the world—what did they do? In one span of life they lived the whole life of humanity, traversed the whole length of time that it takes ordinary humanity to come to perfection. In one life they perfect themselves; they have no thought for anything else, never live a moment for any other idea, and thus the way is shortened for them. This is what is meant by concentration, intensifying the power of assimilation, thus shortening the time. Raja-Yoga is the science which teaches us how to gain the power of concentration.

What has Pranayama to do with spiritualism? Spiritualism is also a manifestation of Pranayama. If it be true that the departed spirits exist, only we cannot see them, it is quite probable that there may be hundreds and millions of them about us we can neither see, feel, nor touch. We may be continually passing and repassing through their bodies, and they do not see or feel us. It is a circle within a circle, universe within universe. We have five senses, and we represent Prana in a certain state of vibration. All beings in the same state of vibration will see one another, but if there are beings who represent Prana in a higher state of vibration, they will not be seen. We may increase the intensity of a light until we cannot see it at all, but there may be beings with eyes so powerful that they can see such light. Again, if its vibrations are very low, we do not see a light, but there are animals that may see it, as cats and owls. Our range of vision is only one plane of the vibrations of this Prana. Take this atmosphere, for instance; it is piled up layer on layer, but the layers nearer to the earth are denser than those above, and as you go higher the atmosphere becomes finer and finer. Or take the case of the ocean; as you go deeper and deeper the pressure of the water increases, and animals which live at the bottom of the sea can never come up, or they will be broken into pieces.

Think of the universe as an ocean of ether, consisting of layer after layer of varying degrees of vibration under the action of Prana; away from the centre the vibrations are less, nearer to it they become quicker and quicker; one order of vibration makes one plane. Then suppose these ranges of vibrations are cut into planes, so many millions of miles one set of vibration, and then so many millions of miles another still higher set of vibration, and so on. It is, therefore, probable, that those who live on the plane of a certain state of vibration will have the power of recognising one another, but will not recognize those above them. Yet, just as by the telescope and the microscope we can increase the scope of our vision, similarly we can by Yoga bring ourselves to the state of vibration of another plane, and thus enable ourselves to see what is going on there. Suppose this room is full of beings whom we do not see. They represent Prana in a certain state of vibration while we represent another. Suppose they represent a quick one, and we the opposite. Prana is the material of which the: are composed, as well as we. All are parts of the same ocean of Prana, they differ only in their rate of vibration. If I can bring myself to the quick vibration, this plane will immediately change for me: I shall not see you any more; you vanish and they appear. Some of you, perhaps, know this to be true. All this bringing of the mind into a higher state of vibration is included in one word in Yoga—Samadhi. All these states of higher vibration, superconscious vibrations of the mind, are grouped in that one word, Samadhi, and the lower states of Samadhi give us visions of these beings. The highest grade of Samadhi is when we see the real thing, when we see the material out of which the whole of these grades of beings are composed, and that one lump of clay being known, we know all the clay in the universe.

Thus we see that Pranayama includes all that is true of spiritualism even. Similarly, you will find that wherever any sect or body of people is trying to search out anything occult and mystical, or hidden, what they are doing is really this Yoga, this attempt to control the Prana. You will find that wherever there is any extraordinary display of power, it is the manifestation of this Prana. Even the physical sciences can be included in Pranayama. What moves the steam engine? Prana, acting through the steam. What are all these phenomena of electricity and so forth but Prana? What is physical science? The science of Pranayama, by external means. Prana, manifesting itself as mental power, can only be controlled by mental means. That part of Pranayama which attempts to control the physical manifestations of the Prana by physical means is called physical science, and that part which tries to control the manifestations of the Prana as mental force by mental means is called Raja-Yoga.

56

THE PSYCHIC PRANA

According to the Yogis, there are two nerve currents in the spinal column, called Pingala and Ida, and a hollow canal called Sushumna running through the spinal cord. At the lower end of the hollow canal is what the Yogis call the 'Lotus of the Kundalini'. They describe it as triangular in form in which, in the symbolical language of the Yogis, there is a power called the Kundalini, coiled up. When that Kundalini awakes, it tries to force a passage through this hollow canal, and as it rises step by step, as it were, layer after layer of the mind becomes open and all the different visions and wonderful powers come to the Yogi. When it reaches the brain, the Yogi is perfectly detached from the body and mind; the soul finds itself free. We know that the spinal cord is composed in a peculiar manner. If we take the figure eight horizontally (∞) there are two parts which are connected in the middle. Suppose you add eight after eight, piled one on top of the other, that will represent the spinal cord. The left is the Ida, the right Pingala, and that hollow canal which runs through the centre of the spinal cord is the Sushumna. Where the spinal cord ends in some of the lumbar vertebrae, a fine fibre issues downwards, and the canal runs up even within that fibre, only much finer. The canal is closed at the lower end, which is situated near what is called the sacral plexus, which, according to modern physiology, is triangular in form. The different plexuses that have their centres in the spinal canal can very well stand for the different 'lotuses' of the Yogi.

The Yogi conceives of several centres, beginning with the Muladhara, the basic, and ending with the Sahasrara, the thousand-petalled Lotus in the brain. So, if we take these different plexuses as representing these lotuses, the idea of the Yogi can be understood very easily in the language of modern physiology. We know there are two sorts of actions in these nerve currents, one afferent, the other efferent; one sensory and the other motor; one centripetal, and the other centrifugal. One carries the sensations to the brain, and the other from the brain to the outer body. These vibrations are all connected with the brain in the long run. Several other facts we have to remember, in order to clear the way for the explanation which is to come. This spinal cord, at the brain, ends in a sort of bulb, in the medulla, which is not attached to the brain, but floats in a fluid in the brain, so that if there be a blow on the head the force of that blow will be dissipated in the fluid, and will not hurt the bulb. This is an important fact to remember. Secondly, we have also to know that, of all the centres, we have particularly to remember three, the Muladhara (the basic), the Sahasrara (the thousand-petalled lotus of the brain) and the Manipura (the lotus of the navel).

Next we shall take one fact from physics. We all hear of electricity and various other forces connected with it. What electricity is no one knows, but so far as it is known, it is a sort of motion. There are various other motions in the universe; what is the difference between them and electricity? Suppose this table moves—that the molecules which compose this table are moving in different directions; if they are all made to move in the same direction, it will be through electricity. Electric motion makes the molecules of a body move in the same direction. If all the air molecules in a room are made to move in the same direction, it will make a gigantic battery of electricity of the room. Another point from physiology we must remember, that the centre which regulates the respiratory system, the breathing system, has a sort of controlling action over the system of nerve currents.

Now we shall see why breathing is practised. In the first place, from rhythmical breathing comes a tendency of all the molecules in the body to move in the same direction. When mind changes into will, the nerve currents change into a motion similar to electricity, because the nerves have been proved to show polarity under the action of electric currents. This shows that when the will is transformed into the nerve currents, it is changed into something like electricity. When all the motions of the body have become perfectly rhythmical, the body has, as it were, become a gigantic battery of will. This tremendous will is exactly what the Yogi wants. This is, therefore, a physiological explanation of the breathing exercise. It tends to bring a rhythmic action in the body, and helps us, through the respiratory centre, to control the other centres. The aim of Pranayama here is to rouse the coiled-up power in the Muladhara, called the Kundalini.

Everything that we see, or imagine, or dream, we have to perceive in space. This is the ordinary space, called the Mahakasha, or elemental space. When a Yogi reads the thoughts of other men, or perceives supersensuous objects he sees them in another sort of space called the Chittakasha, the mental space. When perception has become objectless, and the soul shines in its own nature, it is called the Chidakasha, or knowledge space. When the Kundalini is aroused, and enters the canal of the Sushumna, all the perceptions are in the mental space. When it has reached that end of the canal which opens out into the brain, the objectless perception is in the knowledge space. Taking the analogy of electricity, we find that man can send a current only along a wire,[1] but nature requires no wires to send her tremendous currents. This proves that the wire is not really necessary, but that only our inability to dispense with it compels us to use it.

Similarly, all the sensations and motions of the body are being sent into the brain, and sent out of it, through these wires of nerve fibres. The columns of sensory and motor fibres in the spinal cord are the Ida and Pingala of the Yogis. They are the main channels through which the afferent and efferent currents travel. But why should not the mind send news without any wire, or react without any wire? We see this is done in nature. The Yogi says, if you can do that, you have got rid of the bondage of matter. How to do it? If you can make the current pass through the Sushumna, the canal in the middle of the spinal column, you have solved the problem. The mind has made this network of the nervous system, and has to break it, so that no wires will be required to work through. Then alone will all knowledge come to us—no more bondage of body; that is why it is so important that we should get control of that Sushumna. If we can send the mental current through the hollow canal without any nerve fibres to act as wires, the Yogi says, the problem is solved, and he also says it can be done.

This Sushumna is in ordinary persons closed up at the lower

extremity; no action comes through it. The Yogi proposes a practise by which it can be opened, and the nerve currents made to travel through. When a sensation is carried to a centre, the centre reacts. This reaction, in the case of automatic centres, is followed by motion; in the case of conscious centres it is followed first by perception, and secondly by motion. All perception is the reaction to action from outside. How, then, do perceptions in dreams arise? There is then no action from outside. The sensory motions, therefore, are coiled up somewhere. For instance, I see a city; the perception of that city is from the reaction to the sensations brought from outside objects comprising that city. That is to say, a certain motion in the brain molecules has been set up by the motion in the incarrying nerves, which again are set in motion by external objects in the city. Now, even after a long time I can remember the city. This memory is exactly the same phenomenon, only it is in a milder form. But whence is the action that sets up even the milder form of similar vibrations in the brain? Not certainly from the primary sensations. Therefore it must be that the sensations are coiled up somewhere, and they, by their acting, bring out the mild reaction which we call dream perception.

Now the centre where all these residual sensations are, as it were, stored up, is called the Muladhara, the root receptacle, and the coiled-up energy of action is Kundalini, 'the coiled up'. It is very probable that the residual motor energy is also stored up in the same centre, as, after deep study or meditation on external objects, the part of the body where the Muladhara centre is situated (probably the sacral plexus) gets heated. Now, if this coiled-up energy be roused and made active, and then consciously made to travel up the Sushumna canal, as it acts upon centre after centre, a tremendous reaction will set in. When a minute portion of energy travels along a nerve fibre and causes reaction from centres, the perception is either dream or imagination. But when by the power of long internal meditation the vast mass of energy stored up travels along the Sushumna, and strikes the centres, the reaction is tremendous, immensely superior to the reaction of dream or imagination, immensely more intense than the reaction of sense-perception. It is super-sensuous perception. And when it reaches the metropolis of all sensations, the brain, the whole brain, as it were, reacts, and the result is the full blaze of illumination, the perception of the Self. As this Kundalini force travels from centre to centre, layer after layer of the mind, as it were, opens up, and this universe is perceived by the Yogi in its fine, or causal form. Then alone the causes of this universe, both as sensation and reaction, are known as they are, and hence comes all knowledge. The causes being known, the knowledge of the effects is sure to follow.

Thus the rousing of the Kundalini is the one and only way to attaining Divine Wisdom, superconscious perception, realization of the spirit. The rousing may come in various ways, through love for God, through the mercy of perfected sages, or through the power of the analytic will of the philosopher. Wherever there was any manifestation of what is ordinarily called supernatural power or wisdom, there a little current of Kundalini must have found its way into the Sushumna. Only, in the vast majority of such cases, people had ignorantly stumbled on some practise which set free a minute portion of the coiled-up Kundalini. All worship, consciously or unconsciously, leads to this end. The man who thinks that he is receiving response to his prayers does not know that the fulfilment comes from his own nature, that he has succeeded by the mental attitude of prayer in waking up a bit of this infinite power which is coiled up within himself. What, thus, men ignorantly worship under various names, through fear and tribulation, the Yogi declares to the world to be the real power coiled up in every being, the mother of eternal happiness, if we but know how to approach her. And Raja-Yoga is the science of religion, the rationale of all worship, all prayers, forms, ceremonies, and miracles.

THE CONTROL OF PSYCHIC PRANA

We have now to deal with the exercises in Pranayama. We have seen that the first step, according to the Yogis, is to control the motion of the lungs. What we want to do is to feel the finer motions that are going on in the body. Our minds have become externalized, and have lost sight of the fine motions inside. If we can begin to feel them, we can begin to control them. These nerve currents go on all over the body, bringing life and vitality to every muscle, but we do not feel them. The Yogi says we can learn to do so. How? By taking up and controlling the motion of the lungs; when we have done that for a sufficient length of time, we shall be able to control the finer motions.

We now come to the exercises in Pranayama. Sit upright; the body must be kept straight. The spinal cord, although not attached to the vertebral column, is yet inside of it. If you sit crookedly you disturb this spinal cord, so let it be free. Any time that you sit crookedly and try to meditate you do yourself an injury. The three parts of the body, the chest, the neck, and the head, must be always held straight in one line. You will find that by a little practise this will come to you as easy as breathing. The second thing is to get control of the nerves. We have said that the nerve centre that controls the respiratory organs has a sort of controlling effect on the other nerves, and rhythmical breathing is, therefore, necessary. The breathing that we generally use should not be called breathing at all. It is very irregular. Then there are some natural differences of breathing between men and women.

The first lesson is just to breathe in a measured way, in and out. That will harmonize the system. When you have practised this for some time, you will do well to join to it the repetition of some word as 'Om,' or any other sacred word. In India, we use certain symbolical words instead of counting one, two, three, four. That is why I advise you to join the mental repetition of the 'Om,' or some other sacred word to the Pranayama. Let the word flow in and out with the breath, rhythmically, harmoniously, and you will find the whole body is becoming rhythmical. Then you will learn what rest is. Compared with it, sleep is not rest. Once this rest comes the most tired nerves will be calmed down, and you will find that you have never before really rested.

The first effect of this practise is perceived in the change of expression of one's face; harsh lines disappear; with calm thought calmness comes over the face. Next comes beautiful voice. I never saw a Yogi with a croaking voice. These signs come after a few months' practise. After practising the above mentioned breathing for a few days, you should take up a higher one. Slowly fill the lungs with breath through the Ida, the left nostril, and at the same time concentrate the mind on the nerve current. You are, as it were, sending the nerve current down the spinal column, and striking violently on the last plexus, the basic lotus which is triangular in form, the seat of the Kundalini. Then hold the current there for some time. Imagine that you are slowly drawing that nerve current with the breath through the other side, the Pingala, then slowly throw it out through the right nostril. This you will find a little difficult to practise. The easiest way is to stop the right nostril with the thumb, and then slowly draw in the breath through the left; then close both nostrils with thumb and forefinger, and imagine that you are sending that current down, and striking the base of the Sushumna; then take the thumb off, and let the breath out through the right nostril. Next inhale slowly through that nostril, keeping the other closed by the forefinger, then close both, as before. The way the Hindus practise this would be very difficult for this country, because they do it from their childhood, and their lungs are prepared for it. Here it is well to begin with four seconds, and slowly increase. Draw in four seconds, hold in sixteen seconds, then throw out in eight seconds. This makes one Pranayama. At the same time think of the basic lotus, triangular in form; concentrate the mind on that centre. The imagination can help you a great deal. The next breathing is slowly drawing the breath in, and then immediately throwing it out slowly, and then stopping the breath out, using the same numbers. The only difference is that in the first case the breath was held in, and in the second, held out. This last is the easier one. The breathing in which you hold the breath in the lungs must not be practised too much. Do it only four times in the morning, and four times in the evening. Then you can slowly increase the time and number. You will find that you have the power to do so, and that you take pleasure in it. So very carefully and cautiously increase as you feel that you have the power, to six instead of four. It may injure you if you practise it irregularly.

Of the three processes for the purification of the nerves, described above, the first and the last are neither difficult nor dangerous. The more you practise the first one the calmer you will be. Just think of 'Om,' and you can practise even while you are sitting at your work. You will be all the better for it. Some day, if you practise hard, the Kundalini will be aroused. For those who practise once or twice a day, just a little calmness of the body and mind will come, and beautiful voice; only for those who can go on further with it will Kundalini be aroused, and the whole of nature will begin to change, and the book of knowledge will open. No more will you need to go to books for knowledge; your own mind will have become your book, containing infinite knowledge. I have already spoken of the Ida and Pingala currents, flowing through either side of the spinal column, and also of the Sushumna, the passage through the centre of the spinal cord. These three are present in every animal; whatever being has a spinal column has these three lines of action. But the Yogis claim that in an ordinary man the Sushumna is closed; its action is not evident while that of the other two is carrying power to different parts of the body.

The Yogi alone has the Sushumna open. When this Sushumna current opens, and begins to rise, we get beyond the sense, our minds become supersensuous, superconscious—we get beyond even the intellect, where reasoning cannot reach. To open that Sushumna is the prime object of the Yogi. According to him, along this Sushumna are ranged these centres, or, in more figurative language, these lotuses, as they are called. The lowest one is at the lower end of the spinal cord, and is called Muladhara, the next higher is called Svadhishthana, the third Manipura, the fourth Anahata, the fifth Vishuddha, the sixth Ajna and the last, which is in the brain, is the Sahasrara, or 'the thousand-petalled'. Of these we have to take cognition just now of two centres only, the lowest, the Muladhara, and the highest, the Sahasrara. All energy has to be taken up from its seat in the Muladhara and brought to the Sahasrara. The Yogis claim that of all the energies that are in the human body the highest is what they call 'Ojas'. Now this Ojas is stored up in the brain, and the more Ojas is in a man's head, the more powerful he is, the more intellectual, the more spiritually strong. One man may speak beautiful language and beautiful thoughts, but they, do not impress people; another man speaks neither beautiful language nor beautiful thoughts, yet his words charm. Every movement of his is powerful. That is the power of Ojas.

Now in every man there is more or less of this Ojas stored up. All the forces that are working in the body in their highest become Ojas. You must remember that it is only a question of transformation. The same force which is working outside as electricity or magnetism will become changed into inner force; the same forces that are working as muscular energy will be changed into Ojas. The Yogis say that that part of the human energy which is expressed as sex energy, in sexual thought, when checked and controlled, easily becomes changed into Ojas, and as the Muladhara guides these, the Yogi pays particular attention to that centre. He tries to take up all his sexual energy and convert it into Ojas. It is only the chaste man or woman who can make the Ojas rise and store it in the brain; that is why chastity has always been considered the highest virtue. A man feels that if he is unchaste, spirituality goes away, he loses mental vigour and moral stamina. That is why in all the religious orders in the world which have produced spiritual giants you will always find absolute chastity insisted upon. That is why the monks came into existence, giving up marriage. There must be perfect chastity in thought, word, and deed; without it the practise of Raja-Yoga is dangerous, and may lead to insanity. If people practise Raja-Yoga and at the same time lead an impure life, how can they expect to become Yogis?

58

PRATYAHARA AND DHARANA

The next step is called Pratyahara. What is this? You know how perceptions come. First of all there are the external instruments, then the internal organs acting in the body through the brain centres, and there is the mind. When these come together and attach themselves to some external object, then we perceive it. At the same time it is a very difficult thing to concentrate the mind and attach it to one organ only; the mind is a slave.

We hear 'Be good,' and 'Be good,' and 'Be good,' taught all over the world. There is hardly a child, born in any country in the world, who has not been told, 'Do not steal,' 'Do not tell a lie,' but nobody tells the child how he can help doing them. Talking will not help him. Why should he not become a thief? We do not teach him how not to steal; we simply tell him, 'Do not steal.' Only when we teach him to control his mind do we really help him. All actions, internal and external, occur when the mind joins itself to certain centres, called the organs. Willingly or unwillingly it is drawn to join itself to the centres, and that is why people do foolish deeds and feel miserable, which, if the mind were under control, they would not do. What would be the result of controlling the mind? It then would not join itself to the centres of perception, and, naturally, feeling and willing would be under control. It is clear so far. Is it possible? It is perfectly possible. You see it in modern times; the faith-healers teach people to deny misery and pain and evil. Their philosophy is rather roundabout, but it is a part of Yoga upon which they have somehow stumbled. Where they succeed in making a person throw off suffering by denying it, they really use a part of Pratyahara, as they make the mind of the person strong enough to ignore the senses. The hypnotists in a similar manner, by their suggestion, excite in the patient a sort of morbid Pratyahara for the time being. The so-called hypnotic suggestion can only act upon a weak mind. And until the operator, by means of fixed gaze or otherwise, has succeeded in putting the mind of the subject in a sort of passive, morbid condition, his suggestions never work.

Now the control of the centres which is established in a hypnotic patient or the patient of faith-healing, by the operator, for a time, is reprehensible, because it leads to ultimate ruin. It is not really controlling the brain centres by the power of one's own will, but is, as it were, stunning the patient's mind for a time by sudden blows which another's will delivers to it. It is not checking by means of reins and muscular strength the mad career of a fiery team, but rather by asking another to deliver heavy blows on the heads of the horses, to stun them for a time into gentleness. At each one of these processes the man operated upon loses a part of his mental energies, till at last, the mind, instead of gaining the power of perfect control, becomes a shapeless, powerless mass, and the only goal of the patient is the lunatic asylum.

Every attempt at control which is not voluntary, not with the controller's own mind, is not only disastrous, but it defeats the end. The goal of each soul is freedom, mastery—freedom from the slavery of matter and thought, mastery of external and internal nature. Instead of leading towards that, every will-current from another, in whatever form it comes, either as direct control of organs, or as forcing to control them while under a morbid condition, only rivets one link more to the already existing heavy chain of bondage of past thoughts, past superstitions. Therefore, beware how you allow yourselves to be acted upon by others. Beware how you unknowingly bring another to ruin. True, some succeed in doing good to many for a time, by giving a new trend to their propensities, but at the same time, they bring ruin to millions by the unconscious suggestions they throw around, rousing in men and women that morbid, passive, hypnotic condition which makes them almost soulless at last. Whosoever, therefore, asks any one to believe blindly, or drags people behind him by the controlling power of his superior will, does an injury to humanity, though he may not intend it.

Therefore, use your own minds, control body and mind yourselves, remember that until you are a diseased person, no extraneous will can work upon you; avoid everyone, however great and good he may be, who asks you to believe blindly. All over the world there have been dancing and jumping and howling sects, who spread like infection when they begin to sing and dance and preach; they also are a sort of hypnotists. They exercise a singular control for the time being over sensitive persons, alas! often, in the long run, to degenerate whole races. Ay, it is healthier for the individual or the race to remain wicked than be made apparently good by such morbid extraneous control. One's heart sinks to think of the amount of injury done to humanity by such irresponsible yet well-meaning religious fanatics. They little know that the minds which attain to sudden spiritual upheaval under their suggestions, with music and prayers, are simply making themselves passive, morbid, and powerless, and opening themselves to any other suggestion, be it ever so evil. Little do these ignorant, deluded persons dream that whilst they are congratulating themselves upon their miraculous power to transform human hearts, which power they think was poured upon them by some Being above the clouds, they are sowing the seeds of future decay, of crime, of lunacy, and of death. Therefore, beware of everything that takes away your freedom. Know that it is dangerous, and avoid it by all the means in your power.

He who has succeeded in attaching or detaching his mind to or from the centres at will has succeeded in Pratyahara, which means, 'gathering towards,' checking the outgoing powers of the mind, freeing it from the thraldom of the senses. When we can do this, we shall really possess character; then alone we shall have taken a long step towards freedom; before that we are mere machines.

How hard it is to control the mind! Well has it been compared to the maddened monkey. There was a monkey, restless by his own nature, as all monkeys are. As if that were not enough some one made him drink freely of wine, so that he became still more restless. Then a scorpion stung him. When a man is stung by a scorpion, he jumps about for a whole day; so the poor monkey found his condition worse than ever. To complete his misery a demon entered into him. What language can describe the uncontrollable restlessness of that monkey? The human mind is like that monkey, incessantly active by its own nature; then it becomes drunk with the wine of desire, thus increasing its turbulence. After desire takes possession comes the sting of the scorpion of jealousy at the success of others, and last of all the demon of pride enters the mind, making it think itself of all importance. How hard to control such a mind!

The first lesson, then, is to sit for some time and let the mind run on. The mind is bubbling up all the time. It is like that monkey jumping about. Let the monkey jump as much as he can; you simply wait and watch. Knowledge is power, says the proverb, and that is true. Until you know what the mind is doing you cannot control it. Give it the rein; many hideous thoughts may come into it; you will be astonished that it was possible for you to think such thoughts. But you will find that each day the mind's vagaries are becoming less and less violent, that each day it is becoming calmer. In the first few months you will find that the mind will have a great many thoughts, later you will find that they have somewhat decreased, and in a few more months they will be fewer and fewer, until at last the mind will be under perfect control; but we must patiently practise every day. As soon as the steam is turned on, the engine must run; as soon as things are before us we must perceive; so a man, to prove that he is not a machine, must demonstrate that he is under the control of nothing. This controlling of the mind, and not allowing it to join itself to the centres, is Pratyahara. How is this practised? It is a tremendous work, not to be done in a day. Only after a patient, continuous struggle for years can we succeed.

After you have practised Pratyahara for a time, take the next step, the Dharana, holding the mind to certain points. What is meant by holding the mind to certain points? Forcing the mind to feel certain parts of the body to the exclusion of others. For instance, try to feel only the hand, to the exclusion of other parts of the body. When the Chitta, or mind-stuff, is confined and limited to a certain place it is Dharana. This Dharana is of various sorts, and along with it, it is better to have a little play of the imagination. For instance, the mind should be made to think of one point in the heart. That is very difficult; an easier way is to imagine a lotus there. That lotus is full of light, effulgent light. Put the mind there. Or think of the lotus in the brain as full of light, or of the different centres in the Sushumna mentioned before.

The Yogi must always practise. He should try to live alone; the companionship of different sorts of people distracts the mind; he should not speak much, because to speak distracts the mind; not work much, because too much work distracts the mind; the mind cannot be controlled after a whole day's hard work. One observing the above rules becomes a Yogi. Such is the power of Yoga that even the least of it will bring a great amount of benefit. It will not hurt anyone, but will benefit everyone. First of all, it will tone down nervous excitement, bring calmness, enable us to see things more clearly. The temperament will be better, and the health will be better. Sound health will be one of the first signs, and a beautiful voice. Defects in the voice will be changed. This will be among the first of the many effects that will come. Those who practise hard will get many other signs. Sometimes there will be sounds, as a peal of bells heard at a distance, commingling, and falling on the ear as one continuous sound. Sometimes things will be seen, little specks of light floating and becoming bigger and bigger; and when these things come, know that you are progressing fast.

Those who want to be Yogis, and practise hard, must take care of their diet at first. But for those who want only a little practise for everyday business sort of life, let them not eat too much; otherwise they may eat whatever they please. For those who want to make rapid progress, and to practise hard, a strict diet is absolutely necessary. They will find it advantageous to live only on milk and cereals for some months. As the organization becomes finer and finer, it will be found in the beginning that the least irregularity throws one out of balance. One bit of food more or less will disturb the whole system, until one gets perfect control, and then one will be able to eat whatever one likes.

When one begins to concentrate, the dropping of a pin will seem like a thunderbolt going through the brain. As the organs get finer, the perceptions get finer. These are the stages through which we have to pass, and all those who persevere will succeed. Give up all argumentation and other distractions. Is there anything in dry intellectual jargon? It only throws the mind off its balance and disturbs it. Things of subtler planes have to be realized. Will talking do that? So give up all vain talk. Read only those books which have been written by persons who have had realization.

Be like the pearl oyster. There is a pretty Indian fable to the effect that if it rains when the star Svati is in the ascendant, and a drop of rain falls into an oyster, that drop becomes a pearl. The oysters know this, so they come to the surface when that star shines, and wait to catch the precious raindrop. When a drop falls into them, quickly the oysters close their shells and dive down to the bottom of the sea, there to patiently develop the drop into the pearl. We should be like that. First hear, then understand, and then, leaving all distractions, shut your minds to outside influences, and devote yourselves to developing the truth within you. There is the danger of frittering away your energies by taking up an idea only for its novelty, and then giving it up for another that is newer. Take one thing up and do it, and see the end of it, and before you have seen the end, do not give it up. He who can become mad with an idea, he alone sees light. Those that only take a nibble here and a nibble there will never attain anything. They may titillate their nerves for a moment, but there it will end. They will be slaves in the hands of nature, and will never get beyond the senses.

Those who really want to be Yogis must give up, once for all, this nibbling at things. Take up one idea. Make that one idea your life—think of it, dream of it, live on that idea. Let the brain, muscles, nerves, every part of your body, be full of that idea, and just leave every other idea alone. This is the way to success, and this is the way great spiritual giants are produced. Others are mere talking machines. If we really want to be blessed, and make others blessed, we must go deeper. The first step is not to disturb the mind, not to associate with persons whose ideas are disturbing. All of you know that certain persons, certain places, certain foods, repel you. Avoid them; and those who want to go to the highest, must avoid all company, good or bad. Practise hard; whether you live or die does not matter. You have to plunge in and work, without thinking of the result. If you are brave enough, in six months you will be a perfect Yogi. But those who take up just a bit of it and a little of everything else make no progress. It is of no use simply to take a course of lessons. To those who are full of Tamas, ignorant and dull—those whose minds never get fixed on any idea, who only crave for something to amuse them—religion and philosophy are simply objects of entertainment. These are the unpersevering. They hear a talk, think it very nice, and then go home and forget all about it. To succeed, you must have tremendous perseverance, tremendous will. 'I will drink the ocean,' says the persevering soul, 'at my will mountains will crumble up.' Have that sort of energy, that sort of will, work hard, and you will reach the goal.

59

DHYANA AND SAMADHI

We have taken a cursory view of the different steps in Raja-Yoga, except the finer ones, the training in concentration, which is the goal to which Raja-Yoga will lead us. We see, as human beings, that all our knowledge which is called rational is referred to consciousness. My consciousness of this table, and of your presence, makes me know that the table and you are here. At the same time, there is a very great part of my existence of which I am not conscious. All the different organs inside the body, the different parts of the brain—nobody is conscious of these.

When I eat food, I do it consciously; when I assimilate it, I do it unconsciously. When the food is manufactured into blood, it is done unconsciously. When out of the blood all the different parts of my body are strengthened, it is done unconsciously. And yet it is I who am doing all this; there cannot be twenty people in this one body. How do I know that I do it, and nobody else? It may be urged that my business is only in eating and assimilating the food, and that strengthening the body by the food is done for me by somebody else. That cannot be, because it can be demonstrated that almost every action of which we are now unconscious can be brought up to the plane of consciousness. The heart is beating apparently without our control. None of us here can control the heart; it goes on its own way. But by practise men can bring even the heart under control, until it will just beat at will, slowly, or quickly, or almost stop. Nearly every part of the body can be brought under control. What does this show? That the functions which are beneath consciousness are also performed by us, only we are doing it unconsciously. We have, then, two planes in which the human mind works. First is the conscious plane, in which all work is always accompanied with the feeling of egoism. Next comes the unconscious plane, where all work is unaccompanied by the feeling of egoism.

That part of mind-work which is unaccompanied with the feeling of egoism is unconscious work, and that part which is accompanied with the feeling of egoism is conscious work. In the lower animals this unconscious work is called instinct. In higher animals, and in the highest of all animals, man, what is called conscious work prevails.

But it does not end here. There is a still higher plane upon which the mind can work. It can go beyond consciousness. Just as unconscious work is beneath consciousness, so there is another work which is above consciousness, and which also is not accompanied with the feeling of egoism. The feeling of egoism is only on the middle plane. When the mind is above or below that line, there is no feeling of 'I', and yet the mind works. When the mind goes beyond this line of self-consciousness, it is called Samadhi or superconsciousness. How, for instance, do we know that a man in Samadhi has not gone below consciousness, has not degenerated instead of going higher? In both cases the works are unaccompanied with egoism. The answer is, by the effects, by the results of the work, we know that which is below, and that which is above. When a man goes into deep sleep, he enters a plane beneath consciousness. He works the body all the time, he breathes, he moves the body, perhaps, in his sleep, without any accompanying feeling of ego; he is unconscious, and when he returns from his sleep, he is the same man who went into it. The sum total of the knowledge which he had before he went into the sleep remains the same; it does not increase at all. No enlightenment comes. But when a man goes into Samadhi, if he goes into it a fool, he comes out a sage.

What makes the difference? From one state a man comes out the very same man that he went in, and from another state the man comes out enlightened, a sage, a prophet, a saint, his whole character changed, his life changed, illumined. These are the two effects. Now the effects being different, the causes must be different. As this illumination with which a man comes back from Samadhi is much higher than can be got from unconsciousness, or much higher than can be got by reasoning in a conscious state, it must, therefore, be superconsciousness, and Samadhi is called the superconscious state.

This, in short, is the idea of Samadhi. What is its application? The application is here. The field of reason, or of the conscious workings of the mind, is narrow and limited. There is a little circle within which human reason must move. It cannot go beyond. Every attempt to go beyond is impossible, yet it is beyond this circle of reason that there lies all that humanity holds most dear. All these questions, whether there is an immortal soul, whether there is a God, whether there is any supreme intelligence guiding this universe or not, are beyond the field of reason. Reason can never answer these questions. What does reason say? It says, 'I am agnostic; I do not know either yea or nay.' Yet these questions are so important to us. Without a proper answer to them, human life will be purposeless. All our ethical theories, all our moral attitudes, all that is good and great in human nature, have been moulded upon answers that have come from beyond the circle. It is very important, therefore, that we should have answers to these questions. If life is only a short play, if the universe is only a 'fortuitous combination of atoms,' then why should I do good to another? Why should there be mercy, justice, or fellow-feeling? The best thing for this world would be to make hay while the sun shines, each man for himself. If there is no hope, why should I love my brother, and not cut his throat? If there is nothing beyond, if there is no freedom, but only rigorous dead laws, I should only try to make myself happy here. You will find people saying nowadays that they have utilitarian grounds as the basis of morality. What is this basis? Procuring the greatest amount of happiness to the greatest number. Why should I do this? Why should I not produce the greatest unhappiness to the greatest number, if that serves my purpose? How will utilitarians answer this question? How do you know what is right, or what is wrong? I am impelled by my desire for happiness, and I fulfil it, and it is in my nature; I know nothing beyond. I have these desires, and must fulfil them; why should you complain? Whence come all these truths about human life, about morality, about the immortal soul, about God, about love and sympathy, about being good, and, above all, about being unselfish?

All ethics, all human action and all human thought, hang upon this one idea of unselfishness. The whole idea of human life can be put into that one word, unselfishness. Why should we be unselfish? Where is the necessity, the force, the power, of my being unselfish?

You call yourself a rational man, a utilitarian; but if you do not show me a reason for utility, I say you are irrational. Show me the reason why I should not be selfish. To ask one to be unselfish may be good as poetry, but poetry is not reason. Show me a reason. Why shall I be unselfish, and why be good? Because Mr and Mrs So-and-so say so does not weigh with me. Where is the utility of my being unselfish? My utility is to be selfish if utility means the greatest amount of happiness. What is the answer? The utilitarian can never give it. The answer is that this world is only one drop in an infinite ocean, one link in an infinite chain. Where did those that preached unselfishness, and taught it to the human race, get this idea? We know it is not instinctive; the animals, which have instinct, do not know it. Neither is it reason; reason does not know anything about these ideas. Whence then did they come?

We find, in studying history, one fact held in common by all the great teachers of religion the world ever had. They all claim to have got their truths from beyond, only many of them did not know where they got them from. For instance, one would say that an angel came down in the form of a human being, with wings, and said to him, 'Hear, O man, this is the message.' Another says that a Deva, a bright being, appeared to him. A third says he dreamed that his ancestor came and told him certain things. He did not know anything beyond that. But this is common that all claim that this knowledge has come to them from beyond, not through their reasoning power. What does the science of Yoga teach? It teaches that they were right in claiming that all this knowledge came to them from beyond reasoning, but that it came from within themselves.

The Yogi teaches that the mind itself has a higher state of existence, beyond reason, a superconscious state, and when the mind gets to that higher state, then this knowledge, beyond reasoning, comes to man. Metaphysical and transcendental knowledge comes to that man. This state of going beyond reason, transcending ordinary human nature, may sometimes come by chance to a man who does not understand its science; he, as it were, stumbles upon it. When he stumbles upon it, he generally interprets it as coming from outside. So this explains why an inspiration, or transcendental knowledge, may be the same in different countries, but in one country it will seem to come through an angel, and in another through a Deva, and in a third through God. What does it mean? It means that the mind brought the knowledge by its own nature, and that the finding of the knowledge was interpreted according to the belief and education of the person through whom it came. The real fact is that these various men, as it were, stumbled upon this superconscious state.

The Yogi says there is a great danger in stumbling upon this state. In a good many cases there is the danger of the brain being deranged, and, as a rule, you will find that all those men, however great they were, who had stumbled upon this superconscious state without understanding it, groped in the dark, and generally had, along with their knowledge, some quaint superstition. They opened themselves to hallucinations. Mohammed claimed that the Angel Gabriel came to him in a cave one day and took him on the heavenly horse, Harak, and he visited the heavens. But with all that, Mohammed spoke some wonderful truths. If you read the Koran, you find the most wonderful truths mixed with superstitions. How will you explain it? That man was inspired, no doubt, but that inspiration was, as it were, stumbled upon. He was not a trained Yogi, and did not know the reason of what he was doing. Think of the good Mohammed did to the world, and think of the great evil that has been done through his fanaticism! Think of the millions massacred through his teachings, mothers bereft of their children, children made orphans, whole countries destroyed, millions upon millions of people killed!

So we see this danger by studying the lives of great teachers like Mohammed and others. Yet we find, at the same time, that they were all inspired. Whenever a prophet got into the superconscious state by heightening his emotional nature, he brought away from it not only some truths, but some fanaticism also, some superstition which injured the world as much as the greatness of the teaching helped. To get any reason out of the mass of incongruity we call human life, we have to transcend our reason, but we must do it scientifically, slowly, by regular practise, and we must cast off all superstition. We must take up the study of the superconscious state just as any other science. On reason we must have to lay our foundation, we must follow reason as far as it leads, and when reason fails, reason itself will show us the way to the highest plane. When you hear a man say, 'I am inspired,' and then talk irrationally, reject it. Why? Because these three states—instinct, reason, and superconsciousness, or the unconscious, conscious, and superconscious states—belong to one and the same mind. There are not three minds in one man, but one state of it develops into the others. Instinct develops into reason, and reason into the transcendental consciousness; therefore, not one of the states contradicts the others. Real inspiration never contradicts reason, but fulfils it. Just as you find the great prophets saying, 'I come not to destroy but to fulfil,' so inspiration always comes to fulfil reason, and is in harmony with it.

All the different steps in Yoga are intended to bring us scientifically to the superconscious state, or Samadhi. Furthermore, this is a most vital point to understand, that inspiration is as much in every man's nature as it was in that of the ancient prophets. These prophets were not unique; they were men as you or I. They were great Yogis. They had gained this superconsciousness, and you and I can get the same. They were not peculiar people. The very fact that one man ever reached that state, proves that it is possible for every man to do so. Not only is it possible, but every man must, eventually, get to that state, and that is religion. Experience is the only teacher we have. We may talk and reason all our lives, but we shall not understand a word of truth, until we experience it ourselves. You cannot hope to make a man a surgeon by simply giving him a few books. You cannot satisfy my curiosity to see a country by showing me a map; I must have actual experience. Maps can only create curiosity in us to get more perfect knowledge. Beyond that, they have no value whatever. Clinging to books only degenerates the human mind. Was there ever a more horrible blasphemy than the statement that all the knowledge of God is confined to this or that book? How dare men call God infinite, and yet try to compress Him within the covers of a little book! Millions of people have been killed because they did not believe what the books said, because they would not see all the knowledge of God within the covers of a book. Of course this killing and murdering has gone by, but the world is still tremendously bound up in a belief in books.

In order to reach the superconscious state in a scientific manner it is necessary to pass through the various steps of Raja-Yoga I have been teaching. After Pratyahara and Dharana, we come to Dhyana, meditation. When the mind has been trained to remain fixed on a certain internal or external location, there comes to it the power of flowing in an unbroken current, as it were, towards that point. This state is called Dhyana. When one has so intensified the power of Dhyana as to be able to reject the external part of perception and remain meditating only on the internal part, the meaning, that state is called Samadhi. The three—Dharana, Dhyana, and Samadhi—together, are called Samyama. That is, if the mind can first concentrate upon an object, and then is able to continue in that concentration for a length of time, and then, by continued concentration, to dwell only on the internal part of the perception of which the object was the effect, everything comes under the control of such a mind.

This meditative state is the highest state of existence. So long as there is desire, no real happiness can come. It is only the contemplative, witness-like study of objects that brings to us real enjoyment and happiness. The animal has its happiness in the senses, the man in his intellect, and the god in spiritual contemplation. It is only to the soul that has attained to this contemplative state that the world really becomes beautiful. To him who desires nothing, and does not mix himself up with them, the manifold changes of nature are one panorama of beauty and sublimity.

These ideas have to be understood in Dhyana, or meditation. We hear a sound. First, there is the external vibration; second, the nerve motion that carries it to the mind; third, the reaction from the mind, along with which flashes the knowledge of the object which was the external cause of these different changes from the ethereal vibrations to the mental reactions. These three are called in Yoga, Shabda (sound), Artha (meaning), and Jnana (knowledge). In the language of physics and physiology they are called the ethereal vibration, the motion in the nerve and brain, and the mental reaction. Now these, though distinct processes, have become mixed up in such a fashion as to become quite indistinct. In fact, we cannot now perceive any of these, we only perceive their combined effect, what we call the external object. Every act of perception includes these three, and there is no reason why we should not be able to distinguish them.

When, by the previous preparations, it becomes strong and controlled, and has the power of finer perception, the mind should be employed in meditation. This meditation must begin with gross objects and slowly rise to finer and finer, until it becomes objectless. The mind should first be employed in perceiving the external causes of sensations, then the internal motions, and then its own reaction. When it has succeeded in perceiving the external causes of sensations by themselves, the mind will acquire the power of perceiving all fine material existences, all fine bodies and forms. When it can succeed in perceiving the motions inside by themselves, it will gain the control of all mental waves, in itself or in others, even before they have translated themselves into physical energy; and when he will be able to perceive the mental reaction by itself, the Yogi will acquire the knowledge of everything, as every sensible object, and every thought is the result of this reaction. Then will he have seen the very foundations of his mind, and it will be under his perfect control. Different powers will come to the Yogi, and if he yields to the temptations of any one of these, the road to his further progress will be barred. Such is the evil of running after enjoyments. But if he is strong enough to reject even these miraculous powers, he will attain to the goal of Yoga, the complete suppression of the waves in the ocean of the mind. Then the glory of the soul, undisturbed by the distractions of the mind, or motions of the body, will shine in its full effulgence; and the Yogi will find himself as he is and as he always was, the essence of knowledge, the immortal, the all-pervading.

Samadhi is the property of every human being—nay, every animal. From the lowest animal to the highest angel, some time or other, each one will have to come to that state, and then, and then alone, will real religion begin for him. Until then we only struggle towards that stage. There is no difference now between us and those who have no religion, because we have no experience. What is concentration good for, save to bring us to this experience? Each one of the steps to attain Samadhi has been reasoned out, properly adjusted, scientifically organized, and, when faithfully practised, will surely lead us to the desired end. Then will all sorrows cease, all miseries vanish; the seeds for actions will be burnt, and the soul will be free for ever.

60

RAJA-YOGA IN BRIEF

The following is a summary of Raja-Yoga freely translated from the Kurma-Purana.

The fire of Yoga burns the cage of sin that is around a man. Knowledge becomes purified and Nirvana is directly obtained. From Yoga comes knowledge; knowledge again helps the Yogi. He who combines in himself both Yoga and knowledge, with him the Lord is pleased. Those that practise Mahayoga, either once a day, or twice a day, or thrice, or always, know them to be gods. Yoga is divided into two parts. One is called Abhava, and the other, Mahayoga. Where one's self is meditated upon as zero, and bereft of quality, that is called Abhava. That in which one sees the self as full of bliss and bereft of all impurities, and one with God, is called Mahayoga. The Yogi, by each one, realizes his Self. The other Yogas that we read and hear of, do not deserve to be ranked with the excellent Mahayoga in which the Yogi finds himself and the whole universe as God. This is the highest of all Yogas.

Yama, Niyama, Asana, Pranayama, Pratyahara, Dharana, Dhyana, and Samadhi are the steps in Raja-Yoga, of which non-injury, truthfulness, non-covetousness, chastity, not receiving anything from another are called Yama. This purifies the mind, the Chitta. Never producing pain by thought, word, and deed, in any living being, is what is called Ahimsa, non-injury. There is no virtue higher than non-injury. There is no happiness higher than what a man obtains by this attitude of non-offensiveness, to all creation. By truth we attain fruits of work. Through truth everything is attained. In truth everything is established. Relating facts as they are—this is truth. Not taking others' goods by stealth or by force, is called Asteya, non-covetousness. Chastity in thought, word, and deed, always, and in all conditions, is what is called Brahmacharya. Not receiving any present from anybody, even when one is suffering terribly, is what is called Aparigraha. The idea is, when a man receives a gift from another, his heart becomes impure, he becomes low, he loses his independence, he becomes bound and attached.

The following are helps to success in Yoga and are called Niyama or regular habits and observances; Tapas, austerity; Svadhyaya, study; Santosha, contentment; Shaucha, purity; Ishvara-pranidhana, worshipping God. Fasting, or in other ways controlling the body, is called physical Tapas. Repeating the Vedas and other Mantras, by which the Sattva material in the body is purified, is called study, Svadhyaya. There are three sorts of repetitions of these Mantras. One is called the verbal, another semi-verbal, and the third mental. The verbal or audible is the lowest, and the inaudible is the highest of all. The repetition which is loud is the verbal; the next one is where only the lips move, but no sound is heard. The inaudible repetition of the Mantra, accompanied with the thinking of its meaning, is called the 'mental repetition,' and is the highest. The sages have said that there are two sorts of purification, external and internal. The purification of the body by water, earth, or other materials is the external purification, as bathing etc. Purification of the mind by truth, and by all the other virtues, is what is called internal purification. Both are necessary. It is not sufficient that a man should be internally pure and externally dirty. When both are not attainable the internal purity is the better, but no one will be a Yogi until he has both. Worship of God is by praise, by thought, by devotion.

We have spoken about Yama and Niyama. The next is Asana (posture). The only thing to understand about it is leaving the body free, holding the chest, shoulders, and head straight. Then comes Pranayama. Prana means the vital forces in one's own body, Ayama means controlling them. There are three sorts of Pranayama, the very simple, the middle, and the very high. Pranayama is divided into three parts: filling, restraining, and emptying. When you begin with twelve seconds it is the lowest Pranayama; when you begin with twenty-four seconds it is the middle Pranayama; that Pranayama is the best which begins with thirty-six seconds. In the lowest kind of Pranayama there is perspiration, in the medium kind, quivering of the body, and in the highest Pranayama levitation of the body and influx of great bliss. There is a Mantra called the Gayatri. It is a very holy verse of the Vedas. 'We meditate on the glory of that Being who has produced this universe; may He enlighten our minds.' Om is joined to it at the beginning and the end. In one Pranayama repeat three Gayatris. In all books they speak of Pranayama being divided into Rechaka (rejecting or exhaling), Puraka (inhaling), and Kurnbhaka (restraining, stationary). The Indriyas, the organs of the senses, are acting outwards and coming in contact with external objects. Bringing them under the control of the will is what is called Pratyahara or gathering towards oneself. Fixing the mind on the lotus of the heart, or on the centre of the head, is what is called Dharana. Limited to one spot, making that spot the base, a particular kind of mental waves rises; these are not swallowed up by other kinds of waves, but by degrees become prominent, while all the others recede and finally disappear. Next the multiplicity of these waves gives place to unity and one wave only is left in the mind. This is Dhyana, meditation. When no basis is necessary, when the whole of the mind has become one wave, one-formedness, it is called Samadhi. Bereft of all help from places and centres, only the meaning of the thought is present. If the mind can be fixed on the centre for twelve seconds it will be a Dharana, twelve such Dharanas will be a Dhyana, and twelve such Dhyanas will be a Samadhi.

Where there is fire, or in water or on ground which is strewn with dry leaves, where there are many ant-hills, where there are wild animals, or danger, where four streets meet, where there is too much noise, where there are many wicked persons, Yoga must not be practised. This applies more particularly to India. Do not practise when the body feels very lazy or ill, or when the mind is very miserable and sorrowful. Go to a place which is well hidden, and where people do not come to disturb you. Do not choose dirty places. Rather choose beautiful scenery, or a room in your own house which is beautiful. When you practise, first salute all the ancient Yogis, and your own Guru, and God, and then begin.

Dhyana is spoken of, and a few examples are given of what to meditate upon. Sit straight, and look at the tip of your nose. Later on, we shall come to know how that concentrates the mind, how by controlling the two optic nerves one advances a long way towards the control of the arc of reaction, and so to the control of the will. Here are a few specimens of meditation. Imagine a lotus upon the top of the head, several inches up, with virtue as its centre, and knowledge as its stalk. The eight petals of the lotus are the eight powers of the Yogi. Inside, the stamens and pistils are renunciation. If the Yogi refuses the external powers he will come to salvation. So the eight petals of the lotus are the eight powers, but the internal stamens and pistils are extreme renunciation, the renunciation of all these powers. Inside of that lotus think of the Golden One, the Almighty, the Intangible, He whose name is Om, the Inexpressible, surrounded with effulgent light. Meditate on that. Another meditation is given. Think of a space in your heart, and in the midst of that space think that a flame is burning. Think of that flame as your own soul and inside the flame is another effulgent light, and that is the Soul of your soul, God. Meditate upon that in the heart. Chastity, non-injury, forgiving even the greatest enemy, truth, faith in the Lord, these are all different Vrittis. Be not afraid if you are not perfect in all of these; work, they will come. He who has given up all attachment, all fear, and all anger, he whose whole soul has gone unto the Lord, he who has taken refuge in the Lord, whose heart has become purified, with whatsoever desire he comes to the Lord, He will grant that to him. Therefore, worship Him through knowledge, love, or renunciation.

'He who hates none, who is the friend of all, who is merciful to all, who has nothing of his own, who is free from egoism, who is even-minded in pain and pleasure, who is forbearing, who is always satisfied, who works always in Yoga, whose self has become controlled, whose will is firm, whose mind and intellect are given up unto Me, such a one is My beloved Bhakta. From whom comes no disturbance, who cannot be disturbed by others, who is free from joy, anger, fear, and anxiety, such a one is My beloved. He who does not depend on anything, who is pure and active, who does not care whether good comes or evil, and never becomes miserable, who has given up all efforts for himself; who is the same in praise or in blame, with a silent, thoughtful mind, blessed with what little comes in his way, homeless, for the whole world is his home, and who is steady in his ideas, such a one is My beloved Bhakta.' Such alone become Yogis.

◆

There was a great god-sage called Narada. Just as there are sages among mankind, great Yogis, so there are great Yogis among the gods. Narada was a good Yogi, and very great. He travelled everywhere. One day he was passing through a forest, and saw a man who had been meditating until the white ants had built a huge mound round his body—so long had he been sitting in that position. He said to Narada, 'Where are you going?' Narada replied, 'I am going to heaven.' 'Then ask God when He will be merciful to me; when I shall attain freedom.' Further on Narada saw another man. He was jumping about, singing, dancing, and said, 'Oh, Narada, where are you going?' His voice and his gestures were wild. Narada said, 'I am going to heaven.' 'Then, ask when I shall be free.' Narada went on. In the course of time he came again by the same road, and there was the man who had been meditating with the ant-hill round him. He said, 'Oh, Narada, did you ask the Lord about me?' 'Oh, yes.' 'What did He say?' 'The Lord told me that you would attain freedom in four more births.' Then the man began to weep and wail, and said, 'I have meditated until an ant-hill has grown around me, and I have four more births yet!' Narada went to the other man. 'Did you ask my question?' 'Oh, yes. Do you see this tamarind tree? I have to tell you that as many leaves as there are on that tree, so many times, you shall be born, and then you shall attain freedom.' The man began to dance for joy, and said, 'I shall have freedom after such a short time!' A voice came, 'My child, you will have freedom this minute.' That was the reward for his perseverance. He was ready to work through all those births, nothing discouraged him. But the first man felt that even four more births were too long. Only perseverance, like that of the man who was willing to wait aeons brings about the highest result.

THOUGHTS OF SWAMI VIVEKANANDA

THOUGHTS OF SWAMI VIVEKANANDA

AHIMSA
There is no virtue higher than non-injury.

ASPIRATION
Seek only after one thing, and that, God!

Anything that brings spiritual, mental, or physical
weakness touch it not with the toes of your feet.

BHAKTI
To obtain Bhakti, seek the company of holy men who have Bhakti,
and read books like the Gita and the *Imitation of Christ*; always
think of the attributes of God.

Bhakti is a higher thing higher than even desiring heaven.
The idea of heaven is of a place of intensified enjoyment.
How can that be God?

Bhakti-Yoga is the path of systematized devotion for the attainment
of union with the Absolute. It is the easiest and surest path to
religion or realization.

When love to God is revealed and is all,
this world appears like a drop.

BOOKS
Books are infinite in number and time is short
The secret of knowledge is to take what is essential
Take that and try to live up to it

Even he who has seen only a spook is more spiritual
than book-learned pundits.

BRAHMIN

The Brahmin has done great things for India ; he is doing great
things for India, and he is destined to do still greater things for
India in the future.

BUDDHA AND BUDDHISM

Surely he was the greatest man who ever lived. He never
drew a breath for himself. Above all, he never claimed worship.
He said, 'Buddha is not a man, but a state. I have found the door.
Enter, all of you!'

Go thou and follow Him, who was born and gave His life for
others *five hundred times* before
He attained the vision of the Buddha!

Buddha's Sermon on the Mount was,
'As thou thinkest, so art thou.'

A religion invented by the Kshattriyas as a crushing
rejoinder to Brahminism!

I am the servant of the servants of the servants of Buddha. Who
was there ever like Him—the Lord—who never performed one
action for Himself—with a heart that embraced the whole world!

COMPETITION

The day will come when men will study history from a different
light and find that competition is neither the cause nor the effect,
simply a thing on the way, not necessary to evolution at all.

CHASTITY

Brahmacharya should burn like the fire of God within the veins.

No force can be created; it can only be directed. Therefore, we must learn to control the grand powers that are already in our hands, and by will power make them spiritual, instead of merely animal. Thus, it is clearly seen that chastity is the cornerstone of all morality and of all religion.

Chastity is the basis of all religions.

Chastity is the life of a nation.

CONCENTRATION

The mind has to be made malleable like clay. Just as clay sticks wherever you throw it, so the mind must be made to dwell upon whatever object you concentrate it.

Concentration is the essence of all knowledge,
nothing can be done without it.

CONTENTMENT

From contentment comes superlative happiness.

COURAGE

The brave alone can afford to be sincere.
Compare the lion and the fox.

DARJEELING

It is the most picturesque city in the world.

DECISION-MAKING

When once you consider an action, do not let anything dissuade you. Consult your heart, not others, and then follow its dictates.

DEVOTION

The devotion to God as seen in every religion is divided into two parts: the devotion which works through forms and ceremonies and through words, and that which works through love.

EAST AND WEST

Social life in the West is like a peal of laughter; but underneath, it is a wail. It ends in a sob. Really it is full of tragic intensity. Now here, it is sad and gloomy on the outside, but underneath are carelessness and merriment.

EDUCATION

The ideal of all education, all training, should be this, man-making. But, instead of that, we are always trying to polish up the outside.

The end and aim of all training is to make the man grow. The man who influences, who throws his magic, as it were, upon his fellow-beings, is a dynamo of power.

We want that education by which character is formed, strength of mind is increased, the intellect is expanded, and by which one can stand on one's own feet.

Education is the manifestation of the perfection already in man.

ETHICS

Renunciation is the very basis upon which ethics stands. There never was an ethical code preached which had not renunciation for its basis.

Ethics always says, 'Not I, but thou.' Its motto is, 'Not self, but non-self.'

The vain ideas of individualism, to which man clings when he is trying to find that Infinite Power or that Infinite Pleasure through the senses, have to be given up—say the laws of ethics.

You have to put yourself last, and others before you. The senses say, 'Myself first.' Ethics says, 'I must hold myself last.'

THOUGHTS OF SWAMI VIVEKANANDA • 443

All codes of ethics are based upon renunciation; destruction, not construction, of the individual on the material plane.

FAITH IN ONESELF

The old religions said that he was an atheist who did not believe in God. The new religion says that he is the atheist who does not believe in himself.

FANATICS AND FANATICISM

In ninety cases out of a hundred, fanatics must have bad livers, or they are dyspeptics, or are in some way diseased. By degrees even physicians will find out that fanaticism is a kind of disease.

FLESH

The flesh and the devil are but degrees of difference from God Himself.

FAITH IN ONESELF

The old religions said that he was an atheist who did not believe in God. The new religion says that he is the atheist who does not believe in himself.

FREEDOM

All our struggle is for freedom. We seek neither misery nor happiness, but freedom, freedom alone.

The constitutional belief in freedom is the basis of all reasoning.

FRIENDSHIP

Friendship with many is good at a distance.

GITA

This is the one central idea in the Gita: work incessantly, but be not attached to it.

That wonderful poem, without one note in it,
of weakness or unmanliness.

GOD

The Impersonal God seen through the mists of sense is personal.

Some imaginations help to break the bondage of the rest. The whole universe is imagination, but one set of imaginations will cure another set.

Those that tell us that there is sin and sorrow and death in the world are terrible. But the other set—thou art holy, there is God, there is no pain—these are good, and help to break the bondage of the others.

The highest imagination that can break all the links of the chain is that of the Personal God.

Can you see your own eyes? God is like that. He is as close as your own eyes. He is your own, even though you can't see Him.

GODS AND GODDESSES

These gods are not merely symbols! They are the forms that the Bhaktas have seen!

GOOD AND EVIL

Who can say that God does not manifest Himself as Evil as well as Good? But only the Hindu dares to worship Him in the evil.

GREATNESS

Great occasions rouse even the lowest of human beings to some kind of greatness, but he alone is the really great man whose character is great always, the same wherever he be.

HEROES

Have you never thought of the hearts of the heroes? How they
were great, great, great—and soft as butter?'

HINDUISM

My religion is one of which Christianity is an offshoot and
Buddhism a rebel child.

There is no new religious idea preached anywhere which is not
found in the Vedas.

The three essentials of Hinduism are belief in God, in the Vedas as
revelation, in the doctrine of Karma and transmigration.

The Vedas contain not only the means how to obtain Bhakti
but also the means for obtaining any earthly good or evil. Take
whatever you want

HOUSEHOLDERS

Never forget, to say to yourself, and to teach to your children, as
the difference between a firefly and the blazing sun, between the
infinite ocean and a little pond, between a mustard-seed and the
mountain of Meru, such is the difference between the householder
and the Sannyasin.

ITALY

Greatest of the countries of Europe, land of religion and of art;
alike of imperial organization and of Mazzini—mother of ideas, of
culture, and of freedom!

INDIVIDUALITY

The real individuality is that which never changes and will never
change; and that is the God within us.

JAPAN

Their country is their religion. The national cry is *Dai Nippon, Banzai!* Live long, great Japan! The country before and above everything else.

JESUS

Had I lived in Palestine, in the days of Jesus of Nazareth, I would have washed his feet, not with my tears, but with my heart's blood!

JNANA (True Knowledge)

Jnana (knowledge) is 'creedlessness'; but that does not mean that it despises creeds. It only means that a stage above and beyond creeds has been gained.

KARMA

No one can get anything unless he earns it.
This is an eternal law.

KARMA YOGA

I want sappers and miners in the army of religion. So, boys, set yourselves to the task of training your muscles.

KRISHNA

This was the great work of Krishna: To clear our eyes and make us look with broader vision upon humanity in its march upward and onward.

Krishna talks of himself as God, as Christ does. He sees the Deity in himself. And he says, 'None can go a day out of my path. All have to come to me. Whosoever wants to worship in whatsoever form, I give him faith in that form, and through that I meet him...'(Gita, IV. 12.)

Shri Krishna is the God of the poor, the beggar, the the sinner, the son, the father, the wife, and of everyone.

He enters intimately into all our human relations and makes everything holy and in the end brings us to salvation.

He is the God who hides himself from the philosopher and the learned and reveals himself to the ignorant and the children.

He is the God of faith and love and not of learning. With the Gopis, love and God were the same thing—they knew Him to be love incarnate.

LEADERSHIP

I am persuaded that a leader is not made in one life.
He has to be born for it.

The test, the real test, of the leader, lies in holding widely different people together along the line of their common sympathies. And this can only be done unconsciously, never by trying.
The giver of the head is alone the leader.

LIBERTY

To care only for spiritual liberty and not for social liberty is a defect, but the opposite is a still greater defect. Liberty of both soul and body is to be striven for.

This life is a tremendous assertion of freedom; and this obedience to law, carried far enough, would make us simply matter—either in society, or in politics, or in religion.

Too many laws are a sure sign of death.

LIFE

Life is but a dream of death.

Always free on the spiritual plane; never free on the mental and physical—hence the struggle.

LOVE

Pure love has no motive. It has nothing to gain.

MANHOOD

When the soul wants to depend upon nothing, not even upon life, that is the height of philosophy, the height of manhood.

You are also as much a man as the greatest of men-even an Incarnation.

MARRIAGE

Though the love of a mother is in some ways greater, yet the whole world takes the love of man and woman as the type. No other has such tremendous idealising power. The beloved actually becomes what he is imagined to be.

MAYA

He who knows the Real sees in Maya not illusion, but reality. He who knows not the Real sees in Maya illusion and thinks it real.
We learn as we grow. Alas! we cannot use our knowledge here. The moment we seem to learn, we are hurried off the stage. And this is Maya!

MEDITATION

The greatest thing is meditation. It is the nearest approach to spiritual life—the mind meditating.

It is the one moment in our daily life that we are not at all material—the Soul thinking of Itself, free from all matter—this marvellous touch of the Soul!

MERCY

Mercy is heaven itself; to be good, we have all to be merciful. Even justice and right should stand on mercy.

Mercy shall not be for men alone, but shall go beyond, and embrace the whole world.

MIND

The universe is like a cobweb and minds are the spiders; for mind is one as well as many.

MISERY

Unborn and uncreated, without beginning and without end, deathless, birthless and omnipresent—that is what I am; and all misery comes just because I think this little lump of clay is myself.

I am identifying myself with matter and taking all the consequences.

Misery is caused by sin, and by no other cause.

MISTAKES

Our mistakes have places here. Go on! Do not look back if you think you have done something that is not right.

Now, do you believe you could be what you are today, had you not made those mistakes before? Bless your mistakes, then.

In this battlefield of ours, the dust of mistakes must be raized. Those who are so thin-skinned that they cannot bear the dust, let them get out of the ranks.

MONEY AND FAME

Fortune is like a flirt; she cares not for him who wants her, but she is at the feet of him who does not care for her.

Money comes and showers itself upon one who does not care for it.

MOTHERHOOD

The highest of all feminine types in India is mother,
higher than wife.

Mother represents colorless love that knows no barter,
love that never dies.

NATIONHOOD

National prosperity is another name for death and degradation to
millions of other races.

NATURE

The more you fly from nature, the more she follows you; and if
you do not care for her at all, she becomes your slave.

He who has conquered the internal nature controls the whole
universe; it becomes his servant.

ORDINARY MANKIND

Ordinary mankind cannot understand anything that is subtle.

PERSONAL GOD

The totality of all souls, not the human alone,
is the Personal God.

That which is bound is nature, not the soul.

PHILOSOPHERS

The true philosopher strives to destroy nothing, but to help all.

POLITICS

In order to become a nation, it appears that *we need a common hate*
as well as a common love.

PROGRESS

Things do not grow better. They remain as they are; and we grow better by the changes we make in them.

RACE AND RACISM

If I am grateful to my white-skinned Aryan ancestor, I am far more so to my yellow-skinned Mongolian ancestor, and most so of all, to the black-skinned Negritoid!

The Tartar is the wine of the race! He gives energy and power to every blood!

REALIZATION

Do not accept anything because I have said so; but test everything for yourself.

It is not in assent or dissent that the goal is to be attained, but in actual and concrete realization.

When a man has reached that perfect state, he is of the same nature as the Personal God. 'I and my Father are one.'

REFORM

If you want to reform John Doe, go and live with him; don't try to reform him. If you have any of the Divine Fire, he will catch it.

RELIGION

The ultimate goal of all mankind, the aim and end of all religions, is but one—re-union with God.

When men have come to the real, universal, spiritual concept, then, and then alone, religion will become real and living.

No man is born to any religion; he has a
religion in his own soul.

Religion is the manifestation of the Divinity already in man.

It is good and very grand to conquer external nature, but grander
still to conquer the internal nature of man.

As soon as you make a sect, you protest against
universal brotherhood.

RENUNCIATION

Renunciation is the very basis upon which ethics stands.
Everything is fraught with fear: Renunciation alone is fearless.

This hideous world is Maya. Renounce and be happy.

Give up the idea of sex and possessions. There is no other bond.
Marriage and sex and money are the only living devils.

All earthly love proceeds from the body. No sex, no possessions; as
these fall off, the eyes open to spiritual vision.

SALVATION

Each individual has to work out his own salvation; there is no
other way, and so also with nations.

SAMADHI

Samadhi is perfect absorption of thought into the Supreme Spirit,
when one realizes. 'I and my Father are one.'

SANYASINS

Never forget that the Sannyasin takes two vows: one to realize the
truth and one to help the world.

Let us never, never, forget our Ideal.

Blessed be even the fraudulent *sadhus,* and those who
have failed to carry out their vows, in as much as they also
have witnessed to the ideal, and so are in some degree the
cause of the success of others!

THE SELF

If we can find in our self-something that is not acted on by any
cause, then we have known the Self.

STRENGTH

The highest manifestation of strength is to keep ourselves calm and
on our own feet.

Whatever you think, that you will be. If you think yourselves weak,
weak you will be; if you think yourselves strong, strong you will be.

The only test of good things is that they make us strong.

Strength is the medicine which the poor must have
when tyrannized over by the rich. Strength is the medicine
that the ignorant must have when oppressed by the learned;
and it is the medicine that sinners must have when tyrannized
over by other sinners.

Make your nerves strong. What we want is muscles of iron and
nerves of steel. We have wept long enough. No more weeping, but
stand on your feet and be men.

POWER

All power is within you; you can do anything and everything.
Believe in that; do not believe that you are weak;

What makes you weep, my friend? In you is all power. Summon up your all-powerful nature, O mighty one, and this whole universe will lie at your feet.

TRUTH

Stand firm like a rock. Truth always triumphs.

It is the Self alone that predominates, and not matter.

Truth is strengthening. Truth is purity, truth is all-knowledge; truth must be strengthening, must be enlightening, must be invigorating.

REVENGE

I have never spoken of revenge. I have always spoken of strength. Do we dream of revenging ourselves on this drop of sea spray? But is a great thing to a mosquito!

SENSE CONTROL

There is but one way to control the senses—to see Him who is the Reality in the universe. Then and only then can we really conquer our senses.

THE SOUL

The soul lives and forever expands. Worlds must come into the soul. Worlds must disappear in the soul like drops in the ocean.

Evolution is in nature, not in the soul—evolution of nature, manifestation of the soul.

SUCCESS

Purity, patience, and perseverance are the three essentials to success, and above all, love.

TEACHER

There is no other teacher but your own soul.

UNSELFISHNESS

The degree of unselfishness marks the degree
of success everywhere.

WEAKNESS

Strength, strength it is that we want so much in this life, for what
we call sin and sorrow have all one cause, and that is our weakness.
With weakness comes ignorance, and with ignorance comes misery.

The weak have no place here, in this life or in any other life

Weakness leads to slavery. Weakness leads to all kinds of misery,
physical and mental. Weakness is death.

Know that all sins and all evils can be summed up in
that one word, weakness. It is weakness that is the
motive power in all evil doing.

WILL

You must have an iron will if you would cross the ocean. You must
be strong enough to pierce mountains.

WORK

It is always good to give a few strong strokes and rest on your oars.

He who in good action sees that there is something evil in it,
and in the midst of evil sees that there is something good in it
somewhere, has known the secret of work.

To work! In full speed, and with undaunted zeal.

WOMANHOOD

O India! Forget not that the ideal of thy womanhood is Sita, Savitri, Damayanti.

The women of India must grow and develop in the footprints of Sita, and that is the only way.

Sita is the name in India for everything that is good, pure, and holy; everything that in women we call woman.

WORLDLY WISDOM

Please everyone without becoming a hypocrite or a coward.

WORSHIP

This is the gist of all worship—to be pure and to do good to others.

Various sorts of worship we see in this world. The sick man is very worshipful to God... There is the man who loses his fortune; he also prays very much—to get money.

The highest worship is that of the man who loves God for God's sake.

The only worship is love.

WORK

The best work is only done by alternate repose and work.

THE YOGI

A mongoose is generally kept in a glass-case with a long chain attached to it, so that it may go about freely. When it scents danger as it wanders about, with one jump it goes into the glass-case. So is a Yogi in this world.

The strong, the well-knit, the young, the healthy, the daring alone
are fit to be Yogis.

To the Yogi everything is bliss.